Diaspora and Identity

DIASPORA AND IDENTITY

Japanese Brazilians in Brazil and Japan

Mieko Nishida

University of Hawai'i Press
Honolulu

Library of Congress Cataloging-in-Publication Data

Names: Nishida, Mieko, author.
Title: Diaspora and identity : Japanese Brazilians in Brazil and Japan /
Mieko Nishida.
Description: Honolulu : University of Hawai'i Press, [2017] | Includes
bibliographical references and index. |
Identifiers: LCCN 2017025979 (print) | LCCN 2017029402 (ebook) | ISBN
9780824874285 (e-book) | ISBN 9780824867935 | ISBN
9780824867935 q(cloth qalk. paper)
Subjects: LCSH: Japanese—Brazil—Ethnic identity. | Return migrants—Japan.
| Japan—Emigration and immigration. | Brazil—Emigration and immigration.
Classification: LCC F2659.J3 (ebook) | LCC F2659.J3 N58 2017 (print) | DDC
981/.004956—dc23

ISBN 978-0-8248-6792-8 (pbk.)

LC record available at https://lccn.loc.gov/2017025979University of Hawai'i Press books
are printed on acid-free
paper and meet the guidelines for permanence and durability
of the Council on Library Resources.

Cultural identity . . . is a matter of "becoming" as well as "being." It belongs to the future as much as to the past. It is not something which already exists, transcending place, history and culture. Cultural identities come from somewhere, have histories. But, like everything which is historical, they undergo constant transformation.

—Stuart Hall, *"Cultural Identity and Diaspora"*

Contents

Acknowledgments

This book examines the historical formation and transformation of the Japanese diaspora in São Paulo, Brazil, and the Brazilian diaspora in Japan. Much has been published on Japanese immigration to Brazil, Japanese descendants in Brazil, and their "return" labor migration to Japan (*dekassegui*). My work differs from all previous studies for its extensive use of life history as a major methodology, careful treatment of gendered norms and gender relations, and examination of *dekassegui*'s historical impact on Japanese Brazilian experiences and identities. Throughout my research, I found it difficult fitting any of my informants into the simplistic representations of identity made in preceding studies. In short, this book illustrates the nuances and complexities of identity formation over time and space, in relation to nation, ethnicity, gender, class, and race.

I owe great debts to many individuals and institutions. My deep gratitude goes to the people who agreed to be interviewed; this book would never have been written without their stories. In São Paulo, I owe thanks to the Museu Histórico da Imigração Japonesa no Brasil, especially Yasumi Nakayama; the Museu da Imigração do Estado de São Paulo, especially Midory Kimura Figuchi; the Arquivo Público do Estado de São Paulo; and the Arquivo Municipal de São Paulo. In Japan, my thanks are due to the Modern Japanese Political History Materials Room of the National Diet Library; the Japanese Overseas Migration Museum; the Diplomatic Archives of the Ministry of Foreign Affairs of Japan; the Nippon Rikkokai Foundation; the Hamamatsu Foundation for International Communication and Exchange; and the Comunidade Brasileira de Kansai.

I remain most thankful to the National Humanities Center for the award of its residential National Endowment for the Humanities Fellowship, which enabled me to finish the first draft of this book. I embarked on this project on a postdoctoral fellowship in History and Latin American Studies at the University of Maryland at College Park. I am indebted to

Acknowledgments

the American Historical Association for an Albert J. Beveridge Grant, as well as to the University of Chicago and University of Illinois at Urbana–Champaign Joint Center for Latin American Studies and the David Rockefeller Center for Latin American Studies of Harvard University for the award of their summer library research grants. I acknowledge the institutional support from Hartwick College through the award of faculty research grants and the positions of Winifred D. Wandersee Scholar-in-Residence and Dewar Professor of History.

I would like to express my profound gratitude to Professors William B. Taylor and Franklin W. Knight for their tremendous help, unfailing support, and warm friendship all these years. They and Professor Howard B. Johnson generously took time to critique my entire manuscript. I am thankful to Professor Joseph L. Love, Professor Mary C. Karasch, Dr. Georgette Dorn, Professor Saúl Sosnowski, Professor Iraci del Nero da Costa, James Sidbury, Ronald M. Brzenk, David C. Cody, Peter Rieseler, Kathleen Bentley, Frank Werdann, Dawn Baker, Carla J. Kinser, Fumiko Saito Shinohara, Yukiko Watanabe, Koei Ogasawara, Jun Okamura, Masao Daigo, Dr. Fausto Haruki Hironaka, Professor Daphne Patai, Professor Chandra de Silva, and Professor Barton St. Armand for their help, support, and encouragement. At the University of Hawai'i Press, I had the good fortune to work with Masako Ikeda, Debra Tang, and Grace Wen. I owe thanks to Kerrie Maynes for her meticulous copyediting, and to Bill Nelson for his fine maps. I would like to acknowledge permission to reprint small portions of several chapters in different forms: *Japanese Brazilian Women and Their Ambiguous Identities: Gender, Ethnicity, and Class in São Paulo*, Latin American Studies Working Paper Series, No. 5, Latin American Studies Center, University of Maryland at College Park, 2000; and "'Why Does a Nikkei Want to Talk to Other Nikkeis?': Japanese Brazilians and Their Identities in São Paulo," *Critique of Anthropology* 29, no. 4 (2009): 423–445.

This book is dedicated to Taketoshi Nishida, my late father. Despite having endured historical tragedies in Hiroshima and several serious illnesses, he never failed to say how happy he was just to be alive. Lastly but not least importantly, my thanks go to Michael D. Woost, who tirelessly listened to me and critiqued my writings. This book would not have been completed without his friendship over the years.

Note on Personal Names and Currency

Many of my informants' names in the text have been changed at their request and/or in order to protect their privacy. Throughout the text, the currency (such as Brazilian conto, Japanese yen, and US dollars) reflects the nominal value of the period. No currency has been converted into its value for the present day.

Abbreviations

APESP	Arquivo Público do Estado de São Paulo (Public Archives of the State of São Paulo)
BRATAC	Burajiru Takushoku Kumiai / Sociedade Colonizadora do Brazil Limitada (Brazil Colonization Society)
Bunkyo	Burajiru Nihon Bunka Kyokai / Sociedade Brasileira de Cultura Japonesa (Brazilian Society of Japanese Culture)
CBK	Comunidade Brasileira de Kansai (Brazilian Community of Kansai)
CIATE	Centro de Informação e Apoio ao Trabalhador no Exterior (Center of Information and Help for Emigrant Workers)
ESPM	Escola Superior de Propaganda e Marketing (Superior School of Propaganda and Marketing)
FATEC	Faculdade de Tecnologia de São Paulo (São Paulo College of Technology)
FAU	Faculdade de Arquitetura e Urbanismo do USP (USP School of Architecture)
FGV	Fundação Getúlio Vargas (Getúlio Vargas Foundation)
GV	Escola Técnica Estudal "Getúlio Vargas" (São Paulo State Technical School "Getúlio Vargas")
HICE	Hamamatsu Foundation for International Communication and Exchange
ITA	Instituto Tecnológico de Aeronáutica (Technological Institute of Aeronautics)
JAMIC	Imigração e Colonização Ltda. (Colonization and Immigration Ltd.)
JEMIS	Kaigai Ijū Jigyodan / Japan Emigration Service
JICA	Kokusai Kyōryoku Kikō / Japanese International Cooperation Agency

JOMM	Japanese Overseas Migration Museum
Kaikyoren	Nihon Kaigai Kyokai Rengōkai (Federation of Japan Overseas Associations)
Kenren	Burajiru Todōfukenjinkai Rengōkai / Federação das Associações de Províncias do Japão no Brasil (Federation of the Prefectural Associations of Japan in Brazil)
KKKK	Kaigai Kōgyo Kabushiki Kaisha (Overseas Development Company)
MAM	Museu de Arte Moderna de São Paulo (São Paulo Museum of Modern Art)
MHIJB	Museu Histórico da Imigração Japonesa no Brasil (Historical Museum of Japanese Immigration to Brazil)
NHK	Nippon Hōsō Kyokai / Japan Broadcasting Corporation
Poli	Escola Politécnica de USP (USP School of Engineering)
PUC	Pontifícia Universidade Católica de São Paulo (Catholic University of São Paulo)
Rōkuren	Burajiru Nikkei Rōjin Kurabu Rengōkai / Associação dos Clubes de Anciões do Brasil (Association of the Brazilian Nikkei Clubs for the Elderly, or Rōkuren)
UNESP	Universidade Estadual Paulista (State University of São Paulo)
UNICAMP	Universidade Estadual de Campinas (State University of Campinas)
USP	Universidade de São Paulo (University of São Paulo)

States of Brazil

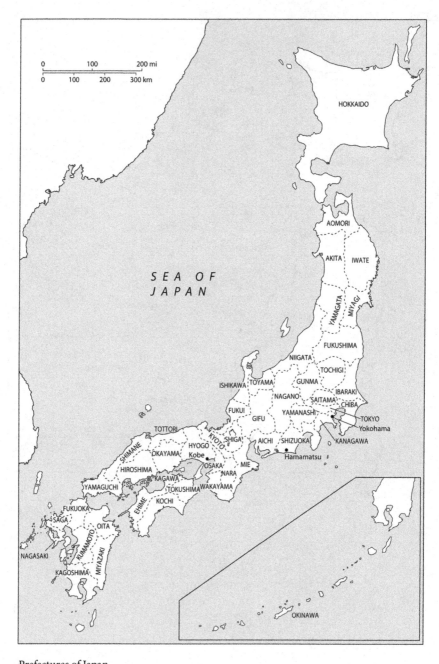

Prefectures of Japan

INTRODUCTION

In 1980, Tizuka Yamasaki, the first Japanese Brazilian woman to direct cinema, made a sensational international debut with a bilingual movie about Japanese immigration to Brazil, *Gaijin: Os caminhos da liberdade* (Gaijin: The Pathways to Liberty). The film's release was perfectly timed; Brazil had celebrated the seventieth anniversary of Japanese immigration to Brazil two years earlier, in 1978, in which the "Japanese" in Brazil were remembered in glorious, nationwide festivities attended by President Ernest Geisel of Brazil, a retired general, as well as Crown Prince Akihito and Princess Michiko (now emperor and empress) of Japan. This was the largest-scale celebration of Japanese immigration to Brazil to date, and is known among Japanese Brazilians as the last one led by Japanese immigrants, during which the Museu Histórico do Imigração Japonesa no Brasil (Historical Museum of Japanese Immigration to Brazil, hereafter MHIJB) in São Paulo City was inaugurated, with Hiroshi Saito (1919–1983) as its first director.[1] Brazil had been ruled by a military government since 1964, but under Geisel's presidency (1974–1979), the country began its gradual democratization.

Gaijin starts with several busy scenes of São Paulo City, including Avenida Paulista, the city's Fifth Avenue; the Companhia de Entrepostos e Armazéns Gerais de São Paulo (Company of General Warehouses of São Paulo), dominated by Japanese immigrants and their descendants; and the *bairro oriental* (Oriental neighborhood) of Liberdade, with its metro station of the same name. The protagonist and narrator of *Gaijin* is Titoe Yamada, a young married Japanese immigrant woman, who, at age sixteen, arrives in Brazil on June 18, 1908, on the first Japanese immigrant ship, the *Kasato*

1

Maru. The film vividly captures various aspects of prewar Japanese immigration to Brazil, including the hardships endured by *colonos* (contract coffee plantation workers),[2] marriage and family life, illness and death in plantation life, and immigrants' flight from the plantation to São Paulo City. At the end of the movie, Titoe, a single working mother, goes to see an Italian immigrant, Tonho, who has left his position as a plantation overseer and works as a labor organizer for immigrant workers in the city.

Gaijin is a Japanese word that originally referred to Caucasian foreigners in Japan, but in Brazil, Japanese immigrants began to call all Brazilians *gaijin*, and it has been commonly used until today by Japanese Brazilians to refer to Brazilians of non-Japanese ancestry. Yamasaki says of the title's double meaning: "It is indeed the Japanese who have been *gaijin* in Brazil. They had been abandoned by their native country, and have been alienated in a new land."[3] The movie's subtitle, *Os caminhos da liberdade*, also has a double meaning. For one, it suggests the protagonist's self-liberation: the choice of the term "liberty" is clearly a reference to women's liberation. *Liberdade* also refers to São Paulo City's Japanese neighborhood, where Titoe and her daughter, Sinobu, eventually settle. In that regard, the movie follows the protagonist's physical "pathways," from Japan to Brazil, and then from the coffee plantation to the city. By going to see Tonho, who is fighting with and for immigrant workers, Titoe demonstrates her sense of national belonging to Brazil. Thus, *Gaijin* is indeed "a story of how a foreign-born woman becomes a 'Brazilian,'" as Japanese musicologist Shuhei Hosokawa puts it.[4] Hosokawa maintains that while Yamasaki portrays Titoe as a pioneering figure, in reality, back in the 1910s and 1920s there were few "Titoes" who managed to break from the rigid gender norms among Japanese immigrants and "liberate" themselves.[5] In this historical context, Titoe is definitely Yamasaki's creation, based on her own struggle to become an independent Brazilian woman through women's liberation and resistance against Brazil's military government.

Tizuka Yamasaki was born in 1949 in Porto Alegre, Rio Grande do Sul state to Toshio and Sumino Yamasaki, who married in 1948. Toshio Yamasaki was an Issei (first-generation Japanese Brazilian) from Chiba prefecture; he arrived in Brazil in May 1941 on the Japanese immigrant ship *Arabia Maru*. Tizuka's mother, Sumiko (Rosa) Akiyoshi Yamasaki, was a Nisei (second-generation Japanese Brazilian) born in 1924 in the town of Mairiporã, São Paulo state. Soon after her birth, Tizuka and her parents moved from Porto Alegre to Atibaia, São Paulo state, where her mother's immigrant parents, Shimeichi and Titoe Nishi, owned the Nishi Farm. Yamasaki's younger sister, Yurika, who was to become an art director for

Yamasaki's movies, was born in Atibaia in 1952. Their father passed away in 1954, and the Yamasaki sisters grew up with their Nisei mother and her Issei parents on the Nishi Farm; their mother worked as a sewing teacher in Atibaia for the next thirty years or so.[6] Yamasaki has stated that *Gaijin* is loosely based on the true story of her maternal grandmother, Titoe Nishi, who immigrated to Brazil in 1917. Yamasaki grew up hearing her grandmother's stories at home.

"With strong desire to escape from the Nikkei (Japanese descendant) community in São Paulo," Yamasaki chose to attend college in Brasília.[7] She completed an undergraduate degree in architecture and then studied filmmaking at the Fluminense Federal University in Rio de Janeiro. Yamasaki chose to become a single mother: "He [my American boyfriend] does not want to leave New York, and I would hate to be out of Brazil. Plus, movie directorship does not go with homemaking. . . . Yes, I always avoided dating Nikkei men, but I also say 'no thanks' to Brazilian men, many of whom are sexists."[8] After having distanced herself from her Japanese roots geographically and culturally for years, Yamasaki made *Gaijin,* of which she says, "I feel like I faced 'my inner Japan' for the first time by making this movie."[9] Jamaican-born British cultural theorist Stuart Hall elucidates this idea: "As a process, as a narrative, as a discourse, it [identity] is always told from the position of the Other. It is always within representation. Identity is not something which is formed outside and then we tell stories about it. It is that which is narrated in one's own self."[10]

In June 1985, Yamasaki visited Tokyo to participate in an international film festival and was interviewed by journalists. Yamasaki revealed that she is not fluent in Japanese, a fact she attributes to her rigorous resistance to her parents, who wanted her to be "Japanese." According to Yamasaki, when she was young, while "behaving as if she were Japanese with her family, she would identify herself as Brazilian outside her household."[11] Yamasaki, a Sansei (third-generation) on her mother's side, stated, "The Issei did struggle greatly with the terrible hardships of life, but we the Sansei have surely continued to suffer from the ambiguity of our identity."[12]

The predominantly male and Japanese-speaking Japanese Brazilian enterprises, organizations, and associations in São Paulo City did not support Yamasaki's film project financially, and the so-called Japanese Brazilian intellectuals were also indifferent or even hostile to the prize-winning movie and director.[13] Not many Japanese immigrants or Japanese Brazilians I met in São Paulo City have watched or even heard of *Gaijin.* In São Paulo City, I heard older generations of Japanese Brazilians, both women and men, comment on *Gaijin* with such remarks as "I have not seen it. And

I will never watch it, either. Why should I? I have been there and have done it all" and "Details of the movie are not accurate. We did not live like that when we were children back in the countryside. That is not the way the Japanese bathed in the countryside."[14] These voices usually expressed intense irritation and frustration with my own enthusiasm for this particular movie. Yet these same people refused to share their own versions of rural immigrant life, aside from remarks such as that of a female prewar child immigrant, who commented, "It was awful. Somebody like you can never imagine. There is nothing I can be proud of in my life."[15] What prompted such statements?

Shuhei Hosokawa's study of *Gaijin* not only corroborates my interactions with Japanese Brazilians but also answers my questions. Hosokawa has carefully examined what was written about *Gaijin* in Japanese-language newspapers in São Paulo City just after the release of the movie. Naturally, both the journalists and the majority of the newspapers' readers were Japanese immigrants who were native speakers of Japanese. Some of them reacted positively to the movie, finding it valuable as a tool for passing historical knowledge on to the younger generation of Japanese Brazilians, while others identified themselves with the Japanese immigrant characters in the movie.[16] But, according to Hosokawa, Japanese Brazilians' public reactions to the movie were overwhelmingly negative. The first of the negative reactions were in reply to Yamasaki's critiques of Japanese Brazilian associations and organizations for their lack of support that were published in a Portuguese-language Japanese Brazilian newspaper. The Japanese-language newspapers in São Paulo City characterized Yamasaki as "arrogant" and stated that "she should not have assumed that she would be supported by the Nikkei community just because she is a Nikkei, on the ground that she was not an accomplished movie director."[17] This harsh public judgment was followed by milder criticism by some Isseis that it was "natural for the Nikkei community not to support Yamasaki," but that now, recognizing the value of the movie, they could celebrate her success after the fact. Many other Issei readers criticized Yamasaki for not knowing their "real" immigrant lives in enough detail (and for telling many "lies" in the movie, as one reader wrote).[18] Hosokawa presents a most insightful observation: "The Issei got panicked because this was the first time for Brazilian society and the Nikkei community to get connected through a single movie, so that their internal situation has come to be known to Brazilians."[19] One may wonder what part of their immigrant past Japanese Brazilians, under the leadership of prominent immigrant men, wished to keep to themselves. What part of the movie betrayed their Japanese pride? What would be an ideal "Japanese" in the Japanese Brazilian mind? *Gaijin* has a female protagonist who narrates her own story from an "ordinary" immigrant woman's perspective. And in her story, men openly reveal their weaknesses, shortcomings, sexism, and abusiveness, while women have to work much more, not only as contract plantation workers but also as homemakers, and to endure many more hardships under patriarchy than their male counterparts. In short, this is far beyond the normative discourse on the ideal Japanese immigrant in Brazil, a strong patriarch who protects his wife and children and thrives as a member of the Japanese immigrant community. The female version of this ideal could have been a loyal and obedient wife and self-sacrificing mother, but not an urban factory worker or a single mother who proclaims independence from patriarchal rule among Japanese Brazilians and is willing to live in Brazil as the mother of a Brazilian.

Hosokawa, himself an elite Japanese man, in his analyses of Japanese Brazilians' largely negative reception of Yamasaki and her movie, fails to take into consideration gender and gender relations in the male-dominant diaspora. Hosokawa even says he understands one possible reason why Yamasaki was denied any financial support for her filmmaking: "They could have thought: 'There is a way to ask a favor.' Yamasaki possibly does not know how to do so with proper Japanese manners, as she has distanced herself from Japanese Brazilian organizations and associations for many years. That could possibly have created a 'ditch' in their communication."[20] That is, Hosokawa blames the victim. But wouldn't Yamasaki have been treated differently simply if she were a man? Furthermore, Yamasaki is not only a woman but a single professional woman who chose to live as a Brazilian, detached from any Japanese Brazilian organizations or associations, while bearing a child out of wedlock by an American man of no Japanese ancestry. In other words, Yamasaki never relied on the patronage of any prominent Japanese or Japanese Brazilian man. At least at the beginning of the 1980s, Yamasaki could have been perceived as the opposite of what a "good Japanese woman" was expected to be, and to make it worse, she spoke out, as a Brazilian woman, against Japanese Brazilian men. Furthermore, she revealed to a wide Brazilian and international audience the "hidden" gender inequality embedded deeply among Japanese Brazilians. No wonder Yamasaki came to be ignored, criticized, and even attacked for shaming the Japanese in Brazil; her *Gaijin* turned out to be a huge slap in the face for elite Japanese Brazilians, who represented "a fixed masculinist identity," to borrow Lisa Lowe's wording in her critical study of Asian American literature.[21]

Yamasaki and her *Gaijin* suggest that there could be many other diverse "voices" among Japanese Brazilians that have not been heard in public. The MHIJB, which is known for its extensive collection of primary sources on Japanese immigration to Brazil, houses numerous self-published autobiographies and memoirs by Japanese Brazilian men, as well as many biographies of successful immigrant men, all glorifying Japanese male *seikōshas* (winners). But there are no writings on "ordinary" men, who did not make money or a name for themselves and therefore have been buried in the past as *shippaishas* (losers). Thus teachers and intellectuals have tended to be despised for lacking financial power. Furthermore, one can find only a few documents written by or about women of Japanese descent in Brazil. That itself is a good indicator of one structure of gender inequality confronted by Japanese Brazilian women. In order to understand the complexities of Japanese Brazilians' historical experiences and self-perceptions, I concluded it is imperative to "hear" them narrate their stories in their own words.

In order to hear the voice of the "voiceless," I turned to life history as exemplified by the works of scholars such as Sidney W. Mintz, Daphne Patai, Daniel James, and, most recently, Mathew Gutmann and Catherine Lutz.[22] From December 1997 to June 2013, I conducted in-depth life history interviews in São Paulo City, with ninety-six Japanese immigrants and their descendants. These ranged in age from nineteen to ninety-five at the time of the interviews, and are of several generations and of diverse regional, educational, and socioeconomic backgrounds. I also conducted interviews with a postwar Taiwanese immigrant woman and two nonimmigrant Japanese men in São Paulo City, and with ten Japanese Brazilians and eight Japanese in Japan. These interviews have demonstrated some distinctive generational and historical patterns in collective behaviors. Much more surprisingly, they have revealed great diversity in individual experiences and self-perceptions, which cannot possibly confirm the dominant historical narrative of Japanese immigrants and descendants in Brazil.

I do not mean to present my informants as an exact statistical representation of Japanese Brazilians in São Paulo; such a quantitative sampling is impossible for this kind of qualitative research. At the same time, I wanted to document a variety of individual experiences in order to examine how identifies were formed, individually or collectively, and/or transformed in diverse situations, rather than presenting an essentialized "Japanese" subject in Brazil. To achieve this goal, I actively sought "diversity" among my informants by fully using my professional connections and the personal networks I had established since the late 1980s. As Steve J. Stern did for his study of how Chileans had remembered Pinochet's Chile, I conducted "semistructured yet open-ended interviews" rather than following a set of questionnaires.[23] I had my informants narrate their life stories in their own words, and examined their accounts as carefully as possible in relation and/ or in contrast to written primary and secondary documents; oral histories can be "read against written ones" and serve "as counterpoints of clarification, suggesting alternative meanings."[24] I read and analyzed all of the interviews in combination with, or in contrast to, all of the invaluable primary sources in Japanese and Portuguese and a variety of secondary sources in Portuguese, Japanese, and English I collected at archives and libraries in Brazil, the United States, and Japan. Such primary sources include Japanese Brazilian newspapers, journals, and periodicals, and various Japanese Brazilian associations' newsletters and other publications, many of which I was able to use in this book, particularly for chapters 2, 3, and 4.

Before starting to interview, I asked each informant what language s/he wanted to speak. Not only was it important for each one to feel most comfortable in expressing him/herself, but also one's identity is embodied deeply and expressed carefully in the language or languages one chooses to use. I never told them what language I would prefer to use for my own convenience. However, immigrants—both prewar and postwar, men and women—generally chose to speak Japanese to me. In fact, some of them, especially prewar immigrant women, agreed to be interviewed simply because they wanted to talk about themselves to a native speaker of Japanese. However, in some cases their spoken Japanese was a regional dialect, and in most cases it had been creolized over the years with many Portuguese terms and Brazilianized Japanese words, so that it would not have been easy to understand what they were talking about without knowing Portuguese at all. At the same time, some prewar child immigrants had taught themselves and attained a superb level of Japanese language proficiency not only in speaking but also in reading and writing. Older generations of Niseis, who grew up among the Japanese, are often bilingual in Portuguese and Japanese, but even among bilingual Niseis there are not many who know how to read and write Japanese well. Some older Niseis and many younger Niseis are monolingual in Portuguese, although the degree of their language skills varies with educational background. Sanseis and Yonseis (fourth generation) usually chose to speak in Portuguese, but some preferred Japanese or English over Portuguese for personal reasons. The choice of language often reflected the informant's politics of position, based on his/her perception of the person who was to interview him/her. Accordingly, some chose specific places for their interviews. For instance, a young college-educated Sansei man chose to be interviewed in Liberdade, at a popular Japanese restaurant where only Japanese is spoken. And he insisted we should communicate in English, saying that he found it interesting for the Japanese to speak another language. While we were talking, one of his young Sansei women acquaintances, a college-educated professional, happened to come by to have a Japanese dinner after having taken an evening Japanese language class at a nearby Japanese Brazilian association. Because of her unexpected presence, he began to reveal more of himself in English and then a little bit in Japanese.

I greatly benefitted from Daphne Patai's articulation of her experiences as a foreign woman researcher with her Brazilian women informants:

> Certain things that I had worried about turned out to be assets: I was a foreigner and would not be sticking around, tempted to let other people on the block know what I had been told; my fluent-but-not-native Portuguese, my occasional groping for words and having to ask for elaboration of simple things, not only led to interesting and unpredictable explanation but seemed to help restore a needed balance between the researcher and the researched, especially in the case of poor and uneducated women. I also found that I was implicitly cast into different roles during these interviews: I became older woman, younger woman, friend, authority figure, peer, White woman, exotic visitor, professional woman, Jewish woman, political ally, childless woman, privileged woman—depending on the particular contrasts and similarities that the person I was interviewing perceived (often in response to her own questions) between herself and me.[25]

Many of my informants opened up to me with their personal stories (or confided in me their "secrets"), knowing I was a foreigner who was "not sticking around." This is exemplified by a postwar child immigrant woman's statement: "I am telling you all because you do not live here and you would never say to me that I said this and that before."[26] Like Patai, I was cast in different roles in relation to each informant I was interviewing. But my situation turned out to be much more complicated than Patai's, as I am not simply a foreign researcher to my Japanese Brazilian informants, due to our "naturally shared" Japaneseness. In fact, my experiences with Japanese Brazilians in Brazil are similar to those of Michael George Hanchard, who conducted three years of fieldwork on Brazil's Movimento Negro (Black Movement) in Rio de Janeiro and São Paulo during the late 1980s:

> As a U.S. African-American male, I occupied several positions simultaneously. Depending on the observer, I could be an interloper or intimate friend; an "American" first and a black second; a male researcher to be viewed with

gendered suspicion, or a black male who could serve as a platonic friend; a political progressive or sometimes (through rarely) an automatic embodiment of U.S. imperialism; a black scholar with much to learn, but also with something to offer the black activist community in the form of "outside knowledge."[27]

Hanchard notes that his "presence evoked a variety of reactions in activist and intellectual circles, family and familiar gatherings, as well as my neighborhoods of residence." His blackness gave him "structures of feeling," which enabled him "to grasp what was being offered as sources of information in the stories people would tell about themselves and the world they found themselves in."[28]

Unlike Hanchard, an African American who was born in the United States to Jamaican immigrant parents, I am not only a Japanese descendant but also Japanese-born. I may mean many things to Japanese Brazilians, depending on who and what they are in each context, and sometimes I appear to have provoked strong reactions from some of them, especially older men. Some took me as an insider; others were more negatively focused on my outsiderness and/or otherness. In most cases, my gender mattered a great deal. For instance, elderly prewar immigrant members of Esperança Fujinkai (Women's Association Esperança), a Japanese Brazilian women's voluntary association established in 1949,[29] always commented on my "beautiful Japanese with no accent" and were willing to talk with me whenever I visited with them. Without asking a single question, they instantly identified me as an Issei, as they themselves were. By contrast, younger Nisei members who are bilingual and college-educated asked me if I was a Japanese woman from Japan (*japonesa mesma*), and if I was doing my graduate studies in Brazil as an international student. They always chose to be interviewed in Portuguese. However, some of the less-educated Niseis (typically with four-year primary educations) who were born in the 1930s and 1940s were very critical of my Portuguese. Having grown up among the Japanese in rural Brazil, they are often fluent in Japanese (albeit occasionally with a strong regional accent and/or class-defined vocabulary), even though they did not know how to read or write basic Japanese. As it turns out, their immigrant parents were very hard on them for their poor language skills in Japanese when they were growing up as Niseis. By contrast, many of my younger Sansei informants in their twenties chose to converse with me in English, while expressing their surprise at my speaking Portuguese or even Japanese. Besides the question of the language, my ostensible Japaneseness turned out to be a critical issue for many of my informants, as I am neither a Japanese directly from Japan nor a Japanese Brazilian. In their view, I could possibly have been "one of them," but at the same time, I was beyond their imagination. That confused some of them, who attempted to understand what I was only within their own frame of reference. Furthermore, my single womanhood annoyed or even offended some of my elderly prewar immigrant informants, both women and men, especially those who seem to have lived rather comfortably under patriarchal rule. One extreme case was a prewar child immigrant man in his eighties, a very successful businessman. I met with him in his office in June 2008, and after I answered his questions on my marital status, he suddenly raised his voice: "You have done the worst thing to your parents. You know what it is? You have never got married. Well, in fact, no woman can get married unless a man wants her."[30] His statement reveals his "traditional" belief that Japanese women, including educated, professional ones, have no agency because of their gender. Most of my informants were not even slightly interested in finding out who and what I really was, beyond being "Japanese." In a way, what I represented to them provoked strong emotional reactions from some of my informants, shaking their self-perceptions, and, as a result, they ended up revealing to me the ambiguities and complexities of their identities. Such is the case of my very first informant: Haruko Fujitani, a prewar female child immigrant, whom I had met in July 1989 through a mutual acquaintance, another prewar female child immigrant. Fujitani has an impeccable command of spoken Japanese, and also reads and writes Japanese very well.

In the hot afternoon of December 31, 1997, Fujitani and I were sitting together in her living room as she waited for her extended family members to arrive for her New Year's Eve dinner. Her house is located in the working-class Pirituba district, where she is known as Dona Maria among her "Brazilian" neighbors, with whom she generously shares herbs she grows in her garden. Facing a *favela* (shantytown) across the street, Fujitani said to me, "Those who live [in the *favela*] on the other side of the street are different from us. They do not say hello to us, who live on this side." Pointing out a white clock hanging in her living room, Fujitani proudly said, "That is a gift from one of my nieces. She went to Japan for *dekassegui* [Japanese Brazilians' "return" labor migration to Japan] and is now married to a Japanese man. She will not be coming back to Brazil," adding, "Those who are gone to Japan for *dekassegui* complain of their hard life in Japan, but what they are going through is nothing in comparison with our hardships as immigrants here in Brazil." Fujitani then made a quick comment on the clock, when it announced the hour in Japanese: "Anything made in Japan speaks Japanese only." In the midst of her interview, she suddenly turned to me and asked, "You are no longer Japanese. You are not an American. You will never become a Brazilian. What are you then?"[31] She did not seem to expect me to reply to her, as she quickly moved back to her own story, but she repeated the same words every time I visited with her for the next several weeks.

Fujitani was born in Okayama prefecture in 1934 and moved to Brazil in 1936, with her parents, paternal grandmother, and maternal grandparents. She has never been back to Japan: "Why would I want to go to Japan? I don't know anything there." Fujitani grew up in rural São Paulo as the oldest and the only Japanese-born child, with five younger siblings (one sister and four brothers), all born in Brazil. While she and her family constantly moved around rural São Paulo in search of better economic opportunities, Fujitani was raised as a "good Japanese woman" by her maternal grandmother, who claimed to be "a daughter of a samurai" and did not allow her granddaughter to speak Portuguese at home. Having been expected to take care of her younger siblings at home while her parents were at work, Fujitani received no formal education except for three months as a teenager, when she was able to attend a night school to learn Portuguese while working at a ceramics factory. In 1958, Fujitani married Tadayoshi (b. 1927), a prewar child immigrant from Kumamoto prefecture who worked as a truck driver, and together they moved to Pirituba, where their only child, Mariana Kazumi, was born. Tadayoshi, who goes by his Portuguese name, Joaquim, became a mechanic and the owner of a car repair shop. In 1964, Fujitani's parents, with their younger sons, moved to be close to her and her family in Pirituba. Sitting next to Fujitani in the living room, her eighty-five-year old mother, Masae Okada, said to me, "We have always depended on her. Poor Haruko. She has really suffered."[32] As a widow, Okada lived in her own small house, with a young Afro-Brazilian woman from Ceará state, whom Fujitani hired as Okada's live-in maid and caregiver. She had become a devout believer in the brown-faced Nossa Senhora da Apparecida, Brazil's principal patroness.

At the end of her second interview, on January 10, 1998, Fujitani asked, "When will you go back to Japan? You have to go home to take care of your parents. How does your mother think of you as a daughter?" She seemed to find no contradiction in positioning me as both a non-Japanese and a Japanese woman at the same time: while refusing to recognize me as Japanese, she expected me to fulfill such "daughterly duties" as she had been taught in her Japanese family. Her only child, Mariana, is a single professional woman who still lives at home; she purchased an apartment but has been renting it out without ever moving in. With my departure date approaching, Fujitani called me at my hotel and insisted that she and her husband give me a ride to the airport: "No worries. We have been to the airport so many times to see our nephews and nieces off to Japan for their *dekassegui*." It was the evening of January 25, 1998. I quickly checked in for my night flight but noted a very long line of Japanese Brazilian *dekassegui* workers and their families, moving slowly, with many heavy bags on carts, waiting to check in to travel to Japan as a group escorted by a few *dekassegui* travel agents. Many of them looked mixed racially. Fujitani, Tadayoshi, and I stood there in silence for a little while until she spoke to me, "You are also Japanese, but they've treated you differently from those Japanese who are going to Japan. You've just checked in as a real customer and a human being for the airlines." Fujitani finally identified me as "Japanese"—as Japanese as these Japanese Brazilians could be. That is when I realized that my own identity did not matter to Fujitani, who seemed to be reevaluating herself as a "Japanese" woman by identifying me in her own terms. As Fujitani's case demonstrates, what I represented to each of my informants inevitably provoked in him/her some self-reflections as a Japanese descendant, which were clearly expressed in their narratives. Thus their life history interviews became the most indispensable primary sources for my discussions on identity.

Brazilians in general call any Japanese descendant or any person who looks Japanese to them (including Korean and Chinese descendants) *japonês* (Japanese), regardless of generation or degree of racial mixture. Some have called them *o Japão* to make fun of and insult them. The pejorative term *japa*, derived from the English "Jap," is also in common use. So is its diminutive, *japinha*.

Japanese Brazilians refer to any Brazilian of non-Japanese descent as *brasileiro* (Brazilian) or *gaijin* even to this day. Regarding race and class among Brazilians, prewar Japanese immigrants and older generations of Niseis use the Japanese term *kokujin* (black person), which is relatively neutral, but also such pejorative Japanese terms as *kuronbo* (nigger) and *kuro-chan* (little nigger). Prewar Japanese immigrants also coined a "Japanese" term, *hanguro* (half-black), to refer to lighter-skinned Afro-Brazilians, who are called *pardo/parda* or *moreno/morena* in Portuguese.

By now Japanese descendants in Brazil have extended to the sixth generation. Immigrants are Issei, followed by Nisei, Sansei, Yonsei, Gosei (fifth generation), and Rokusei (sixth generation). Nikkei (*nikkei* in Portuguese), originally a Japanese term, refers to any Japanese descendant who lives outside Japan, and is often used as an umbrella term to refer to all those of Japanese descent, including Japanese immigrants.

The term *nihonji* (Japanese) is used by Japanese Brazilians as interchangeable with Issei to refer to Japanese from Japan, or when they need to distinguish themselves among themselves by place of birth (Japanese-born vs. Brazilian-born). Immigrants and some of the older generation of less-educated Niseis (see chapter 3) identify themselves as such. They also use such Portuguese words as *japonês japonês / japonesa japonesa* (Japanese Japanese) and *japonês mesmo / japonesa mesma* (real Japanese) to refer to *nihonjin*/Issei in Japanese. I have heard them apply the same usage to non-Japanese Brazilians, calling an Italian immigrant *italiano italiano*. *Filho/filha dos japoneses* (son/daughter of the Japanese) has been in common usage among the Niseis for self-identification or for the Sanseis to refer to their Nisei parents, emphasizing the person's pure Japanese ancestry. Japanese Brazilians distinguish unmixed Japanese Brazilians as *japonês puro / japonesa pura* ("pure Japanese") from mixed ones as *mestiço/mestiça,* a term that originally referred to racial mixture with non-Asian Brazilians but has recently come to include those mixed with Korean and Chinese descendants, as interethnic marriage among Asian descendants in Brazil has begun to increase.

The Portuguese term *colônia* (colony) has frequently been used by Japanese descendants in Brazil from the beginning of their immigration until the present day. Originally *colônia* referred to each agricultural settlement, which was also called a *shokuminchi* in Japanese. By the beginning of the 1920s, Japanese immigrants in São Paulo had come to see themselves forming a *hōjin shakai* (Japanese society) and/or *colônia japonesa* (Japanese colony) among themselves. At this point, *colônia* began to imply community, on the assumption any Japanese was a member of the community, due to their Japanese citizenship. After the war, *hōjin shakai* and *colônia japonesa* shifted to *nikkei shakai* (Nikkei society) and *nikkei colônia* (Nikkei colony), inclusive of the Brazilian-born population of Japanese descent. Japanese Brazilians often omitted "Nikkei" and referred to their Japanese-speaking ethnic Japanese community simply as the *colônia.* Accordingly, during the 1960s and 1970s prewar immigrants who were involved in ethnic Japanese organizations and associations identified themselves as *colônia-jin* (people of the colony). Until the present day, many immigrants, as well as São Paulo's Japanese-language newspapers, have continued to use the term *colônia* to refer to a collective of Japanese-speaking Japanese Brazilian organizations and associations, while others have insisted since the 1980s that *colônia* is an inappropriate and outdated term and that it should to be replaced by *comunidade nikkei* (Nikkei community) or *segmento nikkei* (Nikkei segment). There has been no clear definition of what the "(Nikkei) community" (*colônia/comunidade nikkei*) is by and/or among Japanese Brazilians. Many Japanese Brazilians I met over the years "naturally" assumed or imagined such a definite "community" when they talked about those who were involved in major Japanese Brazilian institutions, organizations, and associations, whether they identified themselves as Japanese descendants or not. Oftentimes they simply imagined the presence of such an ethnic community and defined their positions in relation to it, as insiders or outsiders, for their shared Japanese ancestry, which itself no longer defined its membership exclusively or guaranteed any sort of group solidarity.

Nipo (or *nippo*) and *niponica*, adjectives that were coined by Brazilians after Nippon (Japan), have been used mainly by non-Japanese Brazilians, in formations such as *nipo-brasileiro* (Japanese Brazilian) or *comunidade niponica* (Japanese community). Exceptions include the Centro de Estudos Nipo-Brasileiro (Center for Japanese Brazilian Studies), a private Japanese Brazilian research institute in São Paulo City, which also has a Japanese name: São Paulo Jinmon Kagaku Kenkyusho (São Paulo Humanities Research Center); and *Jornal Nippo-Brasil*, a Japanese Brazilian weekly newspaper in Portuguese, founded in 1992, mainly for present and prospective Brazilian *dekassegui* workers in Japan.

This book includes Okinawan Brazilians but does not discuss them separately from other Japanese descendants. Instead, it allows each informant of Okinawan descent to narrate his/her own story in a specific context. In Brazil, many Japanese immigrants of non-Okinawan ancestry have been biased against Okinawan immigrants (who were or are, of course, Japanese nationals) and their descendants. That is the reflection of the historically marginalized position of Okinawa and Okinawans in modern Japanese history; the Kingdom of Ryuku was annexed to Japan in 1872 and became Okinawa prefecture in 1879. Furthermore, following the US military invasion in 1945, postwar Okinawa was occupied by the United States for the next twenty-two years. Okinawan Brazilian identity has its own complexity, which requires another book-length study.

In this book, I use the concept of diaspora as a demographic category that denotes the shared ancestral origins of groups of people living beyond the borders of that shared origin. Following Max Weber, I aim to avoid attributing any sort of natural collective agency to this concept. As Weber wrote, we should never allow ourselves to think that because people can be said to belong to the same conceptual category they also uniformly share a sense of community, the same cultural values, the same social experience, or anything else. Cultural belonging and/or collective agency comes in many forms because it is created in experience. Collective belonging or agency is never simply a necessary outcome of being a member of a certain social category. In Weber's discussion, the problematic category in question was class. He stated that it was impossible to assume that all members of a class shared the same basic interests, motivations, or experience, that is, that they naturally formed a community; this was because the members of any class could also be seen as members of competing social categories that brought them into conflict with other members of their class category.[33] The same should be said of the concept of "diaspora." It really doesn't reveal anything more than the existence of a group of people who share a common origin. While "diaspora" denotes a group of people who share a departure or distance from a common ancestral space or origin, that part of their identity, to the extent that it matters to them, is still mediated by other structural forces having to do with class, gender, nation, generation, and so on. For this reason it is impossible to reduce the lived experience of "diaspora" to any essential set of characteristics shared by all who fall into that category; in many cases the only thing they may share is common ancestral origin, and nothing more. In short, my goal is to avoid using the notion of diaspora in a way that allows for the erasure of such difference. Categories don't think or have agency or have feelings. Therefore, no diaspora can possibly be characterized as "discontented" or anything else.[34]

This book is divided into eight chapters. Chapter 1 provides a historical context for the entire book, from the beginning of Japanese immigration to Brazil (1908) to 2014, and includes prewar Japanese immigration; immigrant life in the countryside; the "Japanese" under Brazilian nationalism in the time of President Getúlio Vargas, World War II, and the end of prewar Japanese immigration (1942); migration and urbanization; postwar Japanese immigration starting in 1953; *dekassegui* and its impact on Japanese Brazilians; and the centenary of Japanese immigration to Brazil and the effect of global recessions on Japanese Brazilians.

Chapter 2 examines the construction of Japanese identity by prewar child immigrants and older generations of Niseis, who grew up among the Japanese in the Brazilian countryside. It discusses the formation of immigrant families in Japan, gender subordination among the Japanese in Brazil, and the formation of ethnic Japanese communities in rural São Paulo and in the city, where women's sexual honor was defined in relation to family honor, as well as in the broader context of mediated national identity.

Chapter 3 examines the experiences and identities of Niseis born in the 1930s and 1940s. During the 1950s and 1960s, the Niseis in the city established Nisei clubs, which were divided by class, and practiced ethnic-class endogamy. Many college-educated Niseis tend to position themselves as Brazilians/Westerners in contrast to the Japanese and other Asians. This chapter also touches on some elite Nisei men's eventual "return" to major ethnic associations and their claim of Nikkei identity, which started around the beginning of the twenty-first century.

Chapter 4 focuses on postwar Japanese immigrants, who came from much more diverse backgrounds than their prewar counterparts and brought new values and ideas from postwar Japan, ideas that not only created conflicts with prewar immigrants but also challenged and/or confirmed patriarchy among Japanese Brazilians. Many postwar immigrant men arrived as single agricultural and industrial workers in the 1950s and 1960s. Many married Nisei and Brazilian women, but others preferred to look for women back in Japan to marry. Thus their new wives arrived in Brazil as "bride immigrants," whose main role was to support their husbands in Brazil.

Chapter 5 examines how Niseis and Sanseis, born in the 1950s and 1960s, have attempted to define themselves in their own terms, through the choice of careers, choice of marriage partners, and adoption of certain political ideologies. While some educated Niseis, especially men, rigorously resisted what was expected of them as "Japanese," many educated Nisei and Sansei women chose to remain single to become their parents' caretakers and/or chose to work in Japan as *dekasseguis* to serve the financial needs of their families. This chapter also examines the significant impact *dekassegui* has made on gender relations among educated Niseis and Sanseis.

Chapter 6 demonstrates how upper-middle-class Sanseis and Yonseis in their twenties and thirties have continued to struggle to find their positions under the fluid racial hegemony in Brazil, despite their educated parents' individual "whitening." Some choose to affirm their Japaneseness collectively as self-identified Nikkeis and practice ethnic-class endogamy, whereas many others continue to intermarry with white Brazilians in order to "whiten" themselves.

Chapter 7 focuses on Japanese Brazilians in Japan and examines their identities after the global recession prompted unemployed Brazilians and their families to return to Brazil. In Japan, gender subordination had often come to be reproduced and even strengthened among Japanese Brazilians. Many of the Japanese Brazilians remaining in Japan for various reasons had settled there permanently with their Japanese-born Brazilian children. At the same time, they became increasingly nationalistic as Brazilians. This chapter also examines Japanese Brazilians' individual politics of position among themselves, as well as in relation to the local Japanese.

The concluding chapter summarizes my arguments on gender, race, and national identity in the Japanese diaspora in Brazil, as well as in the Brazilian diaspora in Japan. I use historical events surrounding the Japanese immigrants monument in the port city of Santo, São Paulo, as an example that illustrates that Japanese Brazilians are not completely in control of how their identity is constructed and represented under hegemonic power. This book demonstrates that the histories of the "Japanese" in Brazil needs ultimately to be rethought and rewritten with closer attention to the multiple, and historically changing, determinations of Japanese Brazilian identity in Brazil and Japan over the years.

Chapter One

IMMIGRATION AND DIASPORA

Brazilians say São Paulo is "full of the Japanese." In fact, São Paulo also holds the largest concentration of Japanese descendants outside Japan. The Japanese Brazilian population is estimated at approximately 1.6 million, and most of them live in the southeast of Brazil, especially in São Paulo and Paraná states, with the densest population in metropolitan São Paulo. In 1987, when the last official censuses on Japanese immigrants and their descendants in Brazil were conducted with funding from the Japanese government, the "Japanese" constituted 0.868 percent of the entire Brazilian population. But 72.23 percent of them lived in the state of São Paulo, including 26.55 percent in São Paulo City.[1] There is no way of knowing the exact number of Japanese Brazilians from Brazilian census data, in which one is required to identify oneself by "color," not by ancestry. In 1940, the color category of *amarelo* (yellow) was added to *branco* (white), *preto* (black), and *pardo* (brown), and it referred to Japanese immigrants and their descendants only until other Asian immigrants began to arrive in Brazil on a large scale in the 1960s. According to Brazilian censuses, the percentage of those who identified themselves as "yellow" in the entire Brazilian population remained less than 1 percent over the years, and even went down to 0.4 percent (1991).[2] Of course, not all Asian descendants identify themselves as "yellow," and some non-Asian descendants do. After all, in Brazil, one's subjective "color" does not have to reflect any of his/her exact ancestries.

How do Japanese Brazilians perceive themselves in relation to color and race in Brazil? Suely Harumi Satow, a Nisei psychologist (chapter 5), maintains, "Japanese Brazilians classify their color as 'yellow' in censuses but, in reality, they usually think that they are whites and they act accordingly." Edna Roland, an Afro-Brazilian woman activist, states that Japanese Brazilians are perceived generally as whites, and that they are "stereotyped positively as excellent workers, very studious and very productive," in contrast to black Brazilians, whose stereotypes are "all negative." But Roland also notes that these "positive" Japanese Brazilian stereotypes apply to men only, and Japanese Brazilian women are known "negatively as submissive."[3]

In Brazil, the "Japanese" have been identified in public not for their color but for their "slanted eyes" (*olhos puxados*). Certainly, "slanted eyes" keep appearing in the Brazilian mass media referring to "things Japanese," including "products made by the Japanese," exemplified by Semp-Toshiba's TV commercials.[4] During my numerous periods of fieldwork in São Paulo, I was surprised to find that such designations of racial difference as "slanted eyes" did not seem offensive to many Japanese Brazilians whom I interviewed and lived among. For instance, on Sunday, July 1, 2001, the major São Paulo newspaper *Folha de São Paulo*, on the front page of its cultural events section, published two articles on special Japanese movie series to be held at the Museu de Arte Moderna de São Paulo (São Paulo Museum of Modern Art, MAM) and the Pontifícia Universidade Católica de São Paulo (Catholic University of São Paulo, or PUC), under the headline *Cinema de Olhos Puxados* (Cinema of Slanted Eyes).[5] The announcement featured a large black-and-white photo of actress Kinuyo Tanaka from a scene of Kenji Mizoguchi's *Sanshō Dayū* (Sansho the Bailiff, 1954). The headline, in white letters on a red background, reversing the color scheme of the Japanese flag, suggested that the general Brazilian readership clearly understands the phrase "slanted eyes" to mean Japaneseness. When I asked him what he thought of this headline, Katsunori Wakisaka of the Centro de Estudos Nipo-Brasileiros replied, "This is not racism at all. They just describe our eyes. You do not understand this because you come from North America."[6] Thus it appears that, within public Japanese Brazilian discourse, "slanted eyes" is supposed to be taken as "an amusing comment" or "ethnic humor," and does not imply racial prejudice.[7] In fact, Japanese Brazilians themselves often attribute their Japaneseness to their "face," especially their "slanted eyes," not to their Japanese cultural heritage.

What does it mean to be "Japanese" for Japanese Brazilians? How do they identify themselves? How are they perceived? And how do Japanese Brazilians position themselves in Brazil and Japan? To answer these questions, one needs to historicize the subject.

Japanese overseas migration started in 1868 with Hawai'i, and quickly extended to the mainland United States, Mexico, Peru, and Canada, among other countries, and eventually made it to Brazil. Brazil and Japan concluded the Treaty of Friendship, Commerce, and Navigation in 1895, but Japanese mass migration to Brazil did not begin until 1908, at which point it represented a compromise solution for urgent problems each nation was facing. Brazil, especially São Paulo state, was in desperate need of cheap labor for its coffee cultivation to replace the European (especially Italian) immigrants who had virtually stopped arriving in Brazil by the beginning of the twentieth century. Representing the interests of its wealthy coffee planters, São Paulo's state government decided to subsidize Japanese immigration to replace European *colonos*. In doing so, it overrode the federal government's decision against Asian immigration and was therefore severely criticized by the Brazilian elites, who had aimed at creating a modern and civilized Brazil by "whitening" the nation through allowing entry to European immigrants only. The same elites had campaigned against the introduction of Chinese coolies for fear of "mongolizing" the country. Chinese laborers had already been introduced in small numbers to Brazil in 1810 and 1812 for tea cultivation in Rio de Janeiro, but the experiment was regarded as a failure and did not continue.[8]

In the 1830s coffee replaced sugar as Brazil's principal export commodity as Paraiba Valley of Rio de Janeiro quickly developed Brazil's first major coffee-producing region with the use of slave labor. Around the time the transatlantic slave trade was terminated (1851), coffee production began to spread to western São Paulo, which began to flourish a few decades later as the center of Brazil's coffee industry with the free *colono* labor. As of the beginning of the 1870s, São Paulo's provincial government turned to European immigration for coffee production, and in 1886, São Paulo's prominent coffee planters established its civil agency, the Sociedade Promotora de Imigração de São Paulo (Immigration Promotion Society of São Paulo), for the recruitment of European immigrants, especially from southern Europe. From 1886 to the early 1930s, the total of roughly 2,750,000 immigrants entered São Paulo, and some 46 percent of them were Italians. Furthermore, of all incoming Italian immigrants for 1882–1930, 74 percent arrived before 1903; from 1887 to 1900, Italians constituted 73 percent of incoming immigrants, and they were primarily from the area north of Rome.[9]

Coffee constituted more than half of all Brazilian exports during the huge coffee boom around 1870, and accounted for 67 percent of Brazil's exports for 1889–1897. However, the price of Brazilian coffee hit bottom in 1897, owing to excessive production, and the Brazilian currency lost much of its value in the world market. That was the beginning of a serious economic depression in Brazil, and many plantation workers received no wages. Upon receiving reports of these problems, the Italian government severely restricted subsidized emigration to Brazil for 1889–1890, and prohibited it in 1902. Not only did the number of incoming immigrants drop drastically, but many also left the plantations for São Paulo City, returned to their homeland, or moved to Argentina or the United States in search of better economic opportunities. In 1907, outgoing immigrants (44,000) outnumbered incoming ones (40,000).[10] Thus São Paulo's coffee planters suffered from an acute shortage of plantation labor.

Meanwhile, Japan faced ongoing overpopulation with significant internal migration and economic depression. But the Japanese perceived Brazil as the least desirable destination for emigration—"five times farther, with five times less wages than in Hawai'i," with travel expenses that were easily five times more.[11] Owing to Brazil's troubled coffee economy, the Japanese government had refused to approve emigration to Brazil for years, despite repeated requests from Japan's private emigration companies (*imingaisha*), which thrived on the business of emigration to Hawai'i.[12] But after Japan's victory in the Russo-Japanese War (1904–1905), the Japanese economy sank back into a serious depression, and upon the United States' enactment of the Gentlemen's Agreement (1907), which effectively eliminated new Japanese immigration, the Japanese government finally approved Japanese emigration to Brazil, but the subsidy given by the state of São Paulo covered barely half of the expenses for each emigrant.[13] Kōkoku Imin Kaisha (the Royal Emigration Company), an emigration company newly established by Ryu Mizuno, was allowed by the São Paulo state government to transport 1,000 Japanese immigrants to Brazil on three-year contracts. Mizuno's company targeted Okinawans as the most desirable immigrants to Brazil for their familiarity with a semitropical climate, and 325 of the 791 *Kasato Maru* immigrants were from Okinawa. Only 781 people, out of the permitted 1,000 immigrants, agreed to emigrate to Brazil as *colonos*, as well as 10 others who paid their passages on their own. Kōkoku Imin Kaisha could barely pay the mandatory fee to the Japanese government and went broke after the *Kasato Maru* passage, as it was not allowed to carry on with a second voyage to Brazil.[14]

In 1914, the São Paulo state government suspended subsidizing Japanese immigration, as more Europeans had become available as *colono* immigrants. This political action also reflected anti-Japanese laws in the United States. Luckily for Japan, with the outbreak of World War I, European immigration to Brazil virtually stopped, and in 1917 the state government of São Paulo resumed subsidized Japanese immigration.[15] In the same year, the Japanese government established the Kaigai Kōgyo Kabushiki

Kaisha (Overseas Development Company, KKKK), through the merger of private emigration companies. In 1920, KKKK bought the very last independent emigrant company, Morioka Imingaisha, and thenceforth it dominated the entire prewar emigration business in Japan. In 1921, the state government of São Paulo stopped subsidizing Japanese immigration, while continuing to subsidize European immigrants.[16]

In 1924, the United States enacted the Immigration Act, which prohibited the entry of the Japanese. In the same year, the Japanese government fully subsidized emigration to Brazil for victims of the 1923 Great Kanto Earthquake. In 1925, to solve its continuing problem of overpopulation with an annual increase of seven million, Japan officially began its policy of state-sponsored immigration to Brazil; the Japanese government paid full passage (200 yen) for all emigrants to Brazil and also covered the fee (35 yen) that each emigrant paid to KKKK. This policy subsidized all emigrants to Brazil, including young children and the elderly. Furthermore, in 1928, the Japanese government increased the subsidy by 50 yen to cover each emigrant's personal expenses for preparing to emigrate, including travel expenses from home to the port of Kobe. State-sponsored Japanese immigration to the Brazilian Amazon also started in 1925, with the establishment of the Nanbei Takushoku Kabushiki Kaisha (South American Colonization and Immigration Co. Ltd.) and its Brazilian agency, Amazon Kōgyo Kabushiki Gaisha (Amazonian Development Co. Ltd.). In 1928, the Japanese government also established the National Asylum of Emigrants in Kobe, which was to house emigrants for a week before departure, free of charge, during which time they would be trained to prepare for immigrant life in Brazil, including basic language skills in Portuguese. As a result, the total number of Japanese in Brazil rose to 100,000 by the beginning of the 1930s. Japanese immigration peaked in 1933, with the entry of 24,494.[17]

As a private agency of emigration, Nippon Rikkokai played a unique role in Japanese immigration to Brazil. It had been established in 1897 by Pastor Hyodayu Shimanuki as Tokyo Rōdōkai (Tokyo Labor Association) and was renamed Rikkokai in 1900. Rikkokai started out with the purpose of helping financially struggling young students but evolved into an agency to facilitate young adult Japanese men's emigration to the United States, under the slogan "Spiritual and physical salvation of the Japanese." After the enactment of the Gentleman's Agreement in the United States, Rikkokai shifted its geographical focus of emigration from "the racist United States" to "friendly Brazil." Shigeshi Nagata (1881–1973), originally from Nagano prefecture, who became Rikkokai's second president in 1914, traveled to Brazil in 1920 and became acquainted with Shunkoro Wako (1890–1965), an elite immigrant, also from Nagano.[18] Upon returning to Japan Nagata and Wako asked the governor of Nagano prefecture to establish a prefectural agency for emigration to Brazil, Sinano Kaigaki Kyokai (Shinano [Nagano] Overseas Cooperative, 1922). Nagata also established the Rikkokai Overseas School, a special school for the training of prospective Rikkokai immigrants to Brazil (1922). Rikkokai immigration to Brazil began in 1925, and a total of 506 prewar Rikkokai immigrants arrived in Brazil. Many Rikkokai immigrant men emerged as intellectual leaders among Japanese immigrants in Brazil, including Isamu Yuba (1906–1976), who founded Yuba Farm, a "Japanese" Christian commune, in Mirandópolis, São Paulo.[19]

In the late 1920s, cooperative immigration started officially in order to promote immigration to Brazil by Japanese independent farmers. Members of such cooperatives emigrated without labor contracts as *colonos*, yet with all expenses for their emigration paid fully by the Japanese government. Cooperative immigrants constituted only 9.5 percent of prewar Japanese immigrants to Brazil.[20] Several Japanese independent farmers' settlements had already been constructed with public and private funding since the 1910s: Colônia Iguape (1912) by Tokyo Syndicate, Colônia Katsura (1913) and Colônia Registro (1917) by Burajiru Takushoku Gaisha (Brazil Colonization Company), and Colônia Aliança (1924) by Shinano Kaigaki Kyokai. Those were followed by other prefectural overseas associations: Colônia Aliança II (Tottori, 1926), Colônia Aliança III (Toyama, 1927), and Vila Nova (Kumamoto, 1926). In March 1927, the Japanese government enacted the Law of Cooperative Overseas Emigration, which enabled each prefecture's overseas emigration cooperative to purchase land in Brazil in order to construct its own *ijūchi* (independent farmers' settlement), where members of the cooperative received loans for the purchase of land to start as independent farmers. With the enactment of the law, Okayama, Yamaguchi, Hiroshima, and Mie founded their prefectural overseas cooperatives in July 1927, and on August 1, 1927, Kaigai Ijū Kumiai Rengōkai (Federation of the Cooperatives of Overseas Emigration) was established. A total of thirteen prefectural cooperatives had come to function by 1928, when the federation established four new colonies: Bastos, Nova Aliança, and Tietê (present-day Pereira Barreto) in São Paulo state; and Três Barras (Assaí) in Paraná state. But the federation's policy that each prefecture should form its own "colony" in Brazil was eventually opposed by the Japanese government for fear it would be perceived as Japanese antiassimilationism. Therefore, in 1929 the federation founded its Brazilian agency, Burajiru Takushoku Kumiai / Sociedade Colonizadora do Brazil Limitada (Brazil Colonization Society, or BRATAC), which dealt not only with the purchase of land and its distribution to Japanese immigrants but also with the construction of roads, bridges, schools, and factories to process agricultural products for the Japanese. It also made loans of living expenses to Japanese immigrants for their general well-being.[21]

By the mid-1930s, the political situation in Brazil had begun to change for the Japanese government and for prospective Japanese emigrants to Brazil. In 1933–1934, anti-Japanese sentiment reached its height among the Brazilian elite, and in 1934 the Brazilian government enacted a law limiting the number of incoming immigrants of each nationality to 2 percent of the total number of immigrants of that nationality arriving in Brazil for the last fifty years. The law clearly targeted the Japanese, as it did not affect the entry of Europeans, who had constituted the great majority of immigrants in Brazil since the late nineteenth century.[22] The number of incoming Japanese immigrants dropped drastically, from 9,611 (1935) to 1,548 (1941). Japan turned to Manchuria as its new destination for emigration; state-sponsored pioneering immigration to Manchuria started in 1935, with 225,585 migrants in total by May 1945.[23] After the outbreak of the Second Sino-Japanese War in 1937, Japan aggressively expanded its empire to construct the Greater East Asia Co-Prosperity Sphere (1940), comprising Japan, Manchuko, China, and parts of Southeast Asia.

Prewar Japanese immigration to Brazil took on several very specific characteristics that determined the historical course of the "Japanese" in Brazil. First, the majority of prewar Japanese immigrants settled in rural areas as agricultural laborers; 94.3 percent started their lives in agriculture, and 77.5 percent were *colonos*.[24] Second, most arrived in the 1920s and 1930s, with those entering Brazil from 1925 to 1934 constituting 67.9 percent of all prewar Japanese immigrants.[25] Third, the Japanese were required to immigrate in family units. São Paulo's plantation owners had learned from experience with European immigrants that isolated single male workers would not stay on the plantations, contract or no contract. In accordance with the newly established Brazilian immigration laws, prospective emigrants in Japan had to form appropriate immigrant families, each made of three to ten members, headed by a married patriarch, including three "economically active" members aged twelve to forty-five. Some hurriedly got married for the sake of immigration. Others, following the traditional Japanese custom of adoption called *yōshi*, adopted young adults, usually nephews and nieces or the children of friends or neighbors, to create suitable families, sometimes just on paper. Such additional family members were called *kōsei-kazoku* (incorporated family members) or *tsure-kazoku* (companions to the family).[26] In the case of young married couples, there was a strong tendency for a wife's younger brother to be chosen as a *tsure-kazoku*. Japanese anthropologist Takashi Maeyama maintains that the youth chosen were usually over twelve but under fifteen, as Japan's local emigrant runners advocated, knowing how difficult it was for the family head to control those over fifteen.[27]

The majority of prewar Japanese immigrants in Brazil planned to return home as soon as possible after making a sizable fortune. "We will return within five, if not, ten years," my prewar child immigrant informants remember their fathers would say. But it was difficult to make money in Brazil by accumulating an agricultural worker's wages. Also, most of the immigrants were not single young men without family members to support; each immigrant family had to accumulate enough money for the passages of all of the family members. Furthermore, most of the Japanese immigrants arrived after Brazil's coffee economy had begun to decline critically because of bad harvests, excessive production, and the Great Depression. Good virgin land had been planned for future coffee cultivation in the opening area of the Noroeste zone, and although it lacked the Mogiana zone's fertile *terra roxa* (purple land), land became available for purchase in small plots (five or ten *alqueires*; one *alqueire* equals 242 acres in the case of São Paulo state) at a lower price.[28] That enabled former *colonos* to purchase or rent sufficient land for the long-term cultivation of cotton, rice, coffee beans, and so on.[29] Thus, despite their strong determination to return to Japan, Japanese immigrants ended up settling in rural Brazil as independent farmers and landowners. To make enough money to return to the homeland, they had to invest their limited capital in land to make the most of it. Consequently, most Japanese immigrants eventually stayed in Brazil permanently.[30]

Already in the 1910s, upon completing their *colono* contracts, Japanese immigrants were becoming independent farmers, as leaseholders, sharecroppers, and small landowners. They formed ethnic agricultural settlements (*shokuminchi/colônias*) and called themselves *shokumin* (colonists) now that they were no longer *colonos*. In these settlements, they built Japanese language schools for their children and formed various ethnic mutual-aid associations, such as *nihonjinkai* (Japanese association), *kenjinkai* (association for those from the same prefecture), *seinenkai* (young men's association), *shojokai* (young women's association), and *fujinkai* (married women's association).[31] In fact, the first *kenjinkai* had been established already by immigrants from Kagoshima in 1913, followed by immigrants from Fukushima in 1917, for the sake of matchmaking among immigrants from the same prefecture.[32] During the 1930s, the Japanese came to be reputed in

Brazil as "unwilling to assimilate themselves" and "as insoluble as sulfur," forming "racial cysts" (*quistos raciais*), without learning the Portuguese language or mixing with the local Brazilian population.[33] The analogy of sulfur is worth noting; sulfur stinks but burns. Naturally, middle-class white Brazilians refused to marry Japanese descendants. In a survey conducted at 220 public schools in the state of São Paulo (1941), only 5.12 percent of 1,960 students responded that they would approve of having Japanese descendants as family members. The same survey demonstrates that middle-class Brazilians were even more strongly prejudiced against Jews, mulattoes, and blacks than against Japanese descendants.[34]

Prewar Japanese immigrants in Brazil perceived themselves and their children, both Japanese- and Brazilian-born, as *zairyumin* (overseas Japanese) or *zeihaku hōjin* (overseas Japanese in Brazil).[35] The Japanese called one another *dōhō* (compatriot) and formed a *dōhō shakai* (compatriots' society) that was connected to the Japanese government directly though the imperial consulate general of Japan in São Paulo, KKKK, and BRATAC.[36] As of 1927, the consulate general of Japan got directly involved in the education of Japanese children in Brazil with the establishment of Zaihaku Nihonjin Kyoikukai (Association of Education for the Overseas Japanese in Brazil). With funding from the Japanese government, *nihonjin shōgakko* (elementary schools for the Japanese), commonly known as *nihon gakko* (Japanese schools) were built and teachers were recruited directly from Japan through the Japanese government.[37] Modeled after the Japanese education system, each Japanese elementary school program was composed of six grades; some built in the major Japanese settlements even had two additional upper-level grades (*kōtō shōgakko* or *kōtōka*).[38]

Thus in rural Brazil "Japanese" children were educated at Japanese elementary schools, which functioned as the center of emperor worship for the Japanese in rural Brazil.[39] Inevitably imperial Japan's ultranationalism and militarism became the backbone of mediated Japanese national identity in Brazil. In such schools, all young students were forced to recite the Imperial Rescript on Education by the Meiji emperor (1890). The Japanese identified themselves as imperial subjects under the rule of the emperor and were proud of Japanese militaristic expansion to Asia and the Pacific. In the late 1920s and early 1930s, the Japanese in Brazil felt as if "Brazil had existed within the world of Japan," as a Japanese newspaper reporter recalled in 1941.[40] At the beginning of the 1930s, according to the consulate general of Japan in São Paulo, the population of overseas Japanese in Brazil was around 120,000, of whom 90 percent were engaged in agriculture while the rest were living in urban areas, and, among those who were farmers, one-third were *colonos*, while another third were independent farmers, and the rest leaseholders and sharecroppers.[41]

Meanwhile, some Japanese parents became concerned about their children's formal education. In São Paulo City, Taisho Shoggako / Escola Primária Taisho, the first private Japanese primary school, had been founded as early as 1915, and was followed by Seishu Gijuku (1925), San Francisco Gakuen (1928), and Myojō Gakuen (1932). The three major Japanese women's schools for bridal training opened in the early 1930s: Santa Cecilia Kappō Gakko (Santa Cecilia Cooking School, 1931); Nippaku Saihō Jogakko (Japan-Brazil Women's Sewing School, 1932), later renamed Nippaku Jikka Jogakko (Japan-Brazil Women's School for Practical Training in São Paulo); and São Paulo Saihō Joshi Gakuin (Young Women's School for Sewing in São Paulo, 1933), later renamed Akama Jogakuen (Akama Women's School). All of these schools were equipped with dormitories for their students, who would arrive on their own from the countryside.

In the 1930s and 1940s, Japanese immigrants and their descendants in Brazil were faced with two drastic changes. One was President Getúlio Vargas' nationalistic policies; the other, Japan's involvement in World War II. During Vargas' fascist regime, called the Estado Novo (New State; 1937–1945), under a new constitution, immigration laws and the assimilation policy were strictly enforced. First, as of 1938, it was no longer allowed to teach children under the age of fourteen any foreign language. Education led by foreigners and taught in foreign languages was suppressed in 1939, and foreigners were not allowed to operate any schools in rural areas. Japanese schools in Brazil, which had developed with the great financial aid and strong leadership of the imperial Japanese government and numbered 476 in 1938, including 294 elementary schools, suddenly ceased operations.[42] Upon Japan's military occupation of Hainan Island of China in February 1939, a number of Japanese immigrants in Brazil began to return to Japan permanently with the intention of remigrating to Asia under Japan's Greater East Asia Co-Prosperity Sphere. According to a survey conducted by Shunkoro Wako in 1939 of Japanese living within the jurisdiction of the consul of Japan in Bauru, located in northeastern São Paulo state, 85 percent of the 12,000 who replied intended to return to Japan permanently. Those included not only "failures" but also "the successful," plus Niseis who had never been to Japan. However, those who intended to live in Brazil permanently were largely recent arrivals from Japan, and most of them were *colonos* and tenants who had not achieved financial independence.[43] In fact, for the same year of 1939, outgoing Japanese returning to Japan (2,011) outnumbered incoming ones from Japan (1,546). The number of such returnees to Japan peaked in August 1941 with a total of 487 emigrants departing Santos for Kobe and Yokohama (330 Isseis and 157 Niseis).[44]

Under Vargas, beginning in 1940, newspapers in foreign languages were subjected to censorship. Furthermore, after Pearl Harbor (December 7, 1941), Japanese immigrants were no longer permitted to publish newspapers even in Portuguese; with the termination of Japanese-language newspapers, the estimated two hundred thousand Japanese, most of whom did not read Portuguese, lost their only means of staying connected with the news on and from Japan. Brazil severed its diplomatic relations with Japan on January 29, 1942, and Japanese immigration was not resumed until a decade later. All Japanese leaders—diplomats; executives of KKKK, BRATAC, and other enterprises; and journalists and bankers—left Brazil with their families for Japan on July 4, 1942, on the Swedish ship *Gripsholm*, which had already been boarded by Japanese diplomats to the United States.[45] The abrupt departure of all of the Japanese leaders naturally made Japanese immigrants and their descendants feel deserted and more abandoned by their homeland. Furthermore, the Japanese in Brazil not only lost all freedom to travel within the country, as they had to carry officially issued *salvo-condutos* (travel passes), but were imprisoned if they were caught by the police speaking in public a single word in Japanese. Japanese descendants in Brazil came to be suspected widely as fifth columnists. Since because of their race the Japanese stood out among Brazilians, unlike Germans and Italians, many Japanese and their descendants were constantly harassed, arrested, and imprisoned. In February and September of 1942 Japanese living on and around Rua Conde de Sarzedas of Liberdade, known as the "Conde neighborhood," were notified by the police that they must move immediately. This resulted in the sudden demise of Brazil's oldest "Japan Town." In 1943, the Japanese were evacuated from Santos. The Brazilian government also froze assets owned by all enemy aliens, including Senich Hachiya, who owned the largest Japanese import business in São Paulo.[46]

Internal conflicts began to emerge among Japanese immigrants during World War II. Such Japanese secret societies as Tenchu-gumi (Company for Heaven's Punishment) and Seinen Aikoku Undo (Association for Patriotic Youth) conducted terrorist actions against other Japanese farmers engaged in sericulture and peppermint cultivation for Brazil's thriving war economy. The situation worsened at the end of the war, when the Japanese in Brazil were divided into two groups over the defeat of Japan: *kachigumi* (the victory group), also known as *kyōkōha* (the sect for force), who believed in Japan's victory; and *makegumi* (the defeat group), also known as *ninshi-kiha* (the sect for recognition), who accepted Japan's defeat.[47] Like Yasumi

Nakayama (b. 1927), a prewar child immigrant, who states that he was "a *kachigumi* on an emotional level," whether they took any collective action or not, more than 90 percent of the Japanese in Brazil identified themselves as *kachigumi*, because of their faith in imperial Japan.[48] Those who identified themselves as *makegumi* were a small number of Japanese immigrant intellectuals, also known as "assimilationists," who spread the news of the defeat of Japan among the Japanese in São Paulo. Shindō Renmei (The League of the Way of the Subjects), the largest and best-known *kachigumi* association, was established officially in September 1945 as a federation of the Japanese secret societies formed during the war. Within a few months Shindō Renmei's membership extended to some twenty thousand Japanese families comprising one hundred thousand persons. Some Shindō Renmei young male members who identified themselves as Tokkotai (Special Attack Corps) resorted to violence against prominent *makegumi* members, such as retired colonel Jinsaku Wakisaka and Ikuta Mizobe of the Bastos Agricultural Cooperative, and this group's terrorism resulted in twenty-three dead (including one *kachigumi* member) and eighty-six injured. The escalated terrorism terrified Brazilians, and anti-Japanese sentiment peaked in 1946, when the Brazilian Congress almost voted to permanently ban Japanese immigration to Brazil.[49] Shindō Reimei was dissolved in 1947 after the Brazilian police had arrested a few thousand *kachigumi* members and imprisoned 180 of them.[50] Meanwhile, a new *kachigumi* group, Sakuragumi Teishintai (Cherry Group of Volunteer Corps), was formed in Londrina, Paraná, in 1953; opened new headquarters in the town of Santo Andre, São Paulo, in 1955; held a general meeting that attracted 150 people in São Paulo City; and paraded repeatedly in public to advocate the return of all Japanese to Japan. Another extremist *kachigumi* group, Hōkoku Doshikai (Patriotic Association of Kindred Spirits), was formed in Pedro de Toledo of São Paulo. On November 17, 1973, its remaining three families, all Okinawan descendants (fourteen members in total) living in poverty, returned to Japan permanently, with their passages paid by the Japanese government.[51]

By the end of the war, the majority of the Japanese immigrants had finally given up their hope of returning to Japan; instead they decided to remain in Brazil permanently with and for their Brazilian-born children. In the late 1940s, the Japanese and their families began to move on a large scale from the countryside to major cities, especially São Paulo City. As a result, 44.9 percent of Japanese descendants in Brazil were already living in urban areas by 1958.[52]

With little capital to invest, Japanese Brazilian migrant families in São Paulo City employed themselves in small family businesses, such as laundry and dyeing services (*tintureiros*), open-air marketing (*feira*), vegetable stands/stores (*quitandas*), mechanic shops, grocery stores, beauty salons, and craft shops.[53] Photo studios also became a predominantly Japanese business in the city, while many other men worked as *viajantes* (traveling salesmen). Japanese immigrants' small entrepreneurship relied heavily on the unpaid labor of family members, particularly Nisei children. Thus, older children without higher education often worked at home in family businesses, whereas younger ones, particularly sons, were sent to college for the prestige of the family. Takashi Maeyama examines the formation of three social classes by 1958: the "old middle class" (63 percent), comprising primarily the self-employed in family business, mostly Isseis and older (and Japanese-speaking) Niseis, who lacked formal Brazilian education; the "new middle class" (20 percent), namely salaried employees in occupations requiring professional and technical skills, made up of younger Portuguese-speaking Niseis and Sanseis; and the "working class" (17 percent), made up of wage laborers, including students holding such jobs.[54]

Across the Pacific, the Japanese government turned to emigration again, in order to resolve the overpopulation of postwar Japan. Kaigai Ijū Kyokai (Association for Overseas Emigration) was established in Tokyo in 1947, after self-paid *yobiyose* (immigration sponsored by relatives who are citizens or permanent residents of Brazil) had already resumed in 1946.[55] After the war, five million veterans and repatriates returned to the defeated Japan of 1945–1946, with sharp food shortages and a high birth rate, and their number reached 6.3 million for 1945–1969. Upon the enactment of the San Francisco Peace Treaty (April 28, 1952), postwar Japanese immigration to Brazil began during President Vargas' third term (1951–1954). The so-called Tsuji immigrants (named after Kotaro Tsuji, and comprising 10 families, or 54 persons) arrived in Rio de Janeiro on the *Santos Maru* on February 11, 1953, to cultivate jute in the Amazon basin. They were followed by the "Matsubara immigrants" (after Yasutaro Matsubara, a personal friend of Getúlio Vargas, and comprising 22 families, or 112 persons). They arrived in Santos on the Dutch ship *Luis* on July 7, 1953, and departed for their destination of Colônia Dourados in Mato Grosso do Sul state.[56]

With the demise of the Ministry of Colonial Affairs (1929–1942), the Ministry of Foreign Affairs of Japan took charge of postwar emigration with the opening of two national emigrant centers in Kobe (1952) and Yokohama (1956). In 1954, Nihon Kaigai Kyokai Rengōkai (Federation of Japan Overseas Associations, or Kaikyoren) was established as the ministry's extradepartmental body.[57] In 1955, the Bureau of Immigration was established within the Ministry of Foreign Affairs. To improve the image of state-sponsored postwar mass emigration, the ministry banned the official use of the term *imin* (immigration and immigrants; literally, "to move the nation"), claiming that the term connoted the prewar notion of emigrants as *kimin* (those "abandoned" by the state), and replaced it with *ijū* (overseas emigration) and *ijūsha* (those who emigrated overseas).[58] In the same year, Nihon Kaigai Ijū Shinko Kabushiki Kaisha (Japanese Cooperation to Promote Overseas Immigration Ltd.) was established in Tokyo with loans from three major US banks. In the following year the new cooperation opened its two local agencies in Rio de Janeiro under Brazilian law: Imigração e Colonização Ltda. (Colonization and Immigration Ltd., JAMIC) for immigration and colonization; and Crédito e Financiamento Ltda. (Credit and Finance Ltd., IJYUSHINKO) for credit and funding.[59]

In Brazil, Japanese-language newspapers were back in business, and Japanese language education was resumed in November 1947. In the early 1950s, Japanese descendants in Brazil remained sharply and bitterly divided between *kachigumi* and *makegumi*. In response to a request from São Paulo City for support for and financial contributions to its celebration of its four hundredth anniversary, held in 1954–1955, the first postwar Japanese association emerged as Nihonjin Kyoryokukai (Japanese Association for Cooperation) under the leadership of Kiyoshi Yamamoto (1892–1963) on December 8, 1952. Yamamoto successfully campaigned in Brazil and Japan to collect sufficient funding for the construction of a Japanese pavilion at Ibirapuera Park (1954).[60] Yamamoto, a University of Tokyo graduate, had come to Brazil in 1926 as an elite businessman, not an immigrant, and after the war, with a PhD in agriculture from his alma mater (1946), emerged as a leader of the Japanese Brazilian intellectuals' movement to inform Japanese descendants in Brazil of Japan's defeat. Yamamoto had also played a crucial role in Japanese property-owners' movement to cancel the Brazilian government's freeze on Japanese assets during the war.[61] In 1955, upon the completion of the special festivities for the city, Yamamoto successfully dissolved the Kyoryokukai and reestablished it as the São Paulo Nihon Bunka Kyokai (Japanese Cultural Association of São Paulo), with its headquarters in Praça da Liberdade. It was moved in 1962 to its present location at Rua São Joaquim 38, and in 1968 was renamed Burajiru Nihon Bunka Kyokai (Brazilian Association of Japanese Culture). Known as Bunkyo, it has functioned until the present day as the official national center for Japanese Brazilians. As Bunkyo's first president (1955–1963), Yamamoto led Japanese Brazilians in São Paulo to celebrate the fiftieth anniversary of Japanese immigration to Brazil on June 18, 1958, which Prince and Princess Mikasa of Japan attended. Under Yamamoto's leadership, the first national survey of the Japanese Brazilian population was conducted under the direction of Teiichi Suzuki, an elite prewar immigrant lawyer.[62] Yamamoto also worked toward the construction of the Nihon Bunka Sentā (Center for Japanese Culture), known as the Bunkyo building, in which Bunkyo has been located since 1964, and the MHIGB has been housed since its inauguration in 1978.[63]

After the war, Japanese Brazilians came to perceive their community differently, no longer as the prewar *hōjin skakai* (Japanese society) but as the postwar *colônia japonesa* (Japanese colony), including the Brazilian-born (Niseis and Sanseis), who were estimated to have already outnumbered the Japanese-born (Isseis/prewar immigrants) by 1949.[64] The first Japanese Brazilian politician came from the city: born and reared among the Japanese in Liberdade, Yukishige Tamura (1915–2011) graduated from Universidade de São Paulo (University of São Paulo, or USP) Law School in 1939, became the first Japanese Brazilian city councilman in 1948, proceeded to the São Paulo State Legislature in 1951, and was elected the first Japanese Brazilian deputy in 1955. Yukishige Tamura was soon followed by other elite Nisei men: João Sussumu Hirata, Ioshifumi Utiyama, Shiro Kyono, Diogo Nomura, Antonio Morimoto, and Paulo Nakandare, all from São Paulo, as well as Minoru Miyamoto and Antonio Yoshio Ueno, both from Paraná.[65] With the passage of time, the name *colônia japonesa* shifted to *colônia Nikkei*, and during the late 1950s to *colônia* only, with "Nikkei" increasingly omitted. Accordingly, in January 1960, Bunkyo changed the title of its newsletter from *Kaihō* (News on the Association) to *Colônia*.[66] Japanese Brazilian intellectuals, especially those of Japanese birth, who actively participated in ethnic Japanese organizations and/or associations, began to identify themselves as *colôniajin* (those of the *colônia*) to distinguish themselves from the Japanese in Japan.[67] Throughout the 1960s, Japanese-language newspapers, such as *São Paulo Shimbun, Paulista Shimbun,* and *Nippak Mainichi Shimbun,* reported and celebrated the achievements of elite Niseis, not only in politics but also in law and academia, such as Kazuo Watanabe, Kokei Uehara, Nobue Miyazaki, and Kenkichi Fujimori.

During the 1950s and 1960s, the Niseis in the city established their own voluntary associations, commonly known as "Nisei clubs." According to Maeyama, Nisei clubs were the urbanized version of *seinenkai* for the Japanese in the countryside; Japanese Brazilian youth in the city joined such clubs around the age of fifteen and dropped out once they got married. In 1965–1967, there were more than four hundred Nisei clubs active in São Paulo City for young Japanese Brazilians' sports and cultural activities, through which they found suitable marriage partners among themselves.

Nisei clubs were exclusively for Japanese descendants and were divided sharply by class: the largest and most elitist was the Associação Cultural e Esportiva Piratininga (Piratininga Cultural and Sports Association, known as the Piratininga Club), and some others were formed exclusively for college students and graduates, whereas the less-educated Niseis, who continued to work in their family businesses, formed and participated in their own clubs. The Piratininga Club was established in 1950 with eight hundred members in the building of the former Pinheiros branch of Taisho Elementary School. By contrast, less-educated Niseis' clubs established their federation as the Associações Unidas de São Paulo (United Associations of São Paulo, AUSP), with fifteen executive members, all Japanese descendants, and headquarters located in the aforementioned Bunkyo building. The AUSP hosted sport events, beauty contests, and big parties. At a committee meeting on April 18, 1967, the executive members discussed the participation of non-Japanese Brazilians in their upcoming sports events, and eventually voted to include them for soccer but not for table tennis.[68]

By 1980, many Niseis had attended the prestigious USP, where tuition for students was free (and still is), and had become lawyers, medical doctors, dentists, pharmacists, engineers, and architects. Educated Japanese Brazilians had come to identify themselves as "not a social group but a cultural group," and one that was in the speedy process of full assimilation.[69] During the military regime (1964–1985), some of the educated Niseis actively participated in guerrilla/terrorist movements against the military government.[70] Curiously, however, there has been no mention of these activists in any official publications in commemoration of Japanese immigration to Brazil and the history of Bunkyo. According to Masao Daigo, the guerrilla/terrorist movements in Brazil were reported at length in Japanese Brazilian newspapers but were treated as "events in Brazilian society that were not directly related to the Nikkei community," even though some Niseis were involved.[71]

Japanese Brazilians had become increasingly mixed with Brazilians racially and culturally. In 1987–1988, while only 6.3 percent of the Niseis were racially mixed, 42 percent of the Sanseis and 61.64 percent of the Yonseis were. At the same time, 59.19 percent of Japanese Brazilians identified themselves as Catholics.[72] Ironically, this is around the time when Japanese Brazilians' "return" labor migration to Japan began to take place on a large scale, because of Brazil's troubled economy and hyperinflation. The 1980s came to be known as Brazil's "Lost Decade," which caused the breakdown of its small middle classes. In 1988–1989, the minimum monthly salary in Brazil was $40 to $50 and the inflation rate reached 1,000 percent a year.

However, the average wage in Japan was eight to ten times higher than in Brazil, and by working in Japan for two years one could save $150,000 to $200,000 toward the purchase of a house and/or car, which were regarded as the symbols of one's middle-class position in Brazil.[73]

In the mid-1980s, many South Americans of Japanese descent—not only from Brazil but also from Peru, Argentina, and Paraguay—began migrating to economically booming Japan as foreign guest workers. It is estimated that in 1985 some 13,800 Japanese Brazilians went to work in Japan.[74] Since the beginning, Japanese Brazilians have always constituted the majority of Japanese descendants working in Japan. In 1994, there were almost two hundred thousand Latin Americans of Japanese descent living in Japan, of whom approximately 70 percent were from Brazil.[75] In both Brazil and Japan the new "return" labor migration and migrant came to be known as *dekassegui* in Portuguese, derived from the Japanese word *dekasegi*, which refers to seasonal labor migrations as well as migrants from rural Japan to major cities such as Tokyo.

In Brazil, *dekassegui* started predominantly with immigrants and Niseis who held Japanese citizenship, most of whom spoke Japanese fluently. It spread to younger generations lacking proficiency in Japanese beginning in June 1990, when the Japanese government partially amended the Immigration Control and Refugee Recognition Act to allow Japanese descendants up to the Sanseis and their spouses of any ancestry, together with their unwed, minor Yonsei children, to work in Japan in all types of employment. The Niseis became eligible for the three-year "visa for a spouse of the Japanese national and so on" (commonly known as the "spouse visa") and the Sanseis and their unwed minor Yonsei children for the "long-term resident visa," either for a year or for three years. As a result, in the following years, the number of *dekasseguis* going from Brazil to Japan rose quickly, from 67,300 in 1990 to 250,000 in 1997. The estimated amount of money Brazilians sent back to their families in Brazil amounted to $240 million in 1995, and $190 million in 1996.[76] Despite the collapse of Japan's "bubble economy" in 1994, followed by a long-term economic downturn with high unemployment rates, the number of incoming Brazilians steadily increased, and the total number of Brazilians in Japan continued to grow until the end of 2007.[77] Japanese sociologists Naoto Higuchi and Kiyoto Tanno argue that during Japan's long-term recession in the late 1990s, Brazilians were forced to compete with other peripheral workers, such as Japanese women and elderly people. Thus they came to be marginalized in the secondary labor market as a "flexible and disposable workforce," especially at larger firms, where the majority of them worked, through indirect employment mediated by recruiting agencies, which profited from establishing a "just-in-time" labor delivery system. As a result, demand for and supply of Brazilian workers were always on the increase.[78]

In Japan, all foreign guest workers, including Japanese Brazilians, were supposed to perform hard manual labor characterized as the 3 K's: *kitanai* (dirty), *kitsui* (difficult), and *kiken* (dangerous). Japanese Brazilians have added two more K's—*kibishii* (harsh) and *kirai* (hateful)—to make "5 K's." As of 1990, the typical *dekassegui* worker worked more than ten hours a day, with at least two hours' overtime work for 25 percent more than the hourly wage. Many also worked night shifts and on weekends and holidays for better wages. Not all of the *dekasseguis* were blue-collar workers; some male college graduates found jobs as systems engineers in Japan.[79] In the mid-1990s approximately half of Japanese Brazilian workers in Japan, both men and women, still worked on assembly lines, while others worked in the construction industry, as well as in the service industry, including hotels, hospitals, and golf courses.[80] The majority of Japanese Brazilians came to be concentrated in such prefectures of central Japan as Aichi and Shizuoka, followed by Mie, Gifu, Gunma, Nagano, Kanagawa, and Saitama. At the same time, because of Japan's prolonged recession, Japanese Brazilians dispersed geographically throughout most of Japan in search of employment.[81]

In Japan, the local Japanese did not accept Japanese Brazilians as their equals, socially or culturally. For the Japanese population, these Japanese Brazilians were cheap foreign guest workers and/or descendants of long-forgotten emigrants. In return, Japanese Brazilians, many of whom perceived the Japanese as cold, separated themselves from the local Japanese population to a considerable degree, forming ethnic Brazilian enclaves, commonly called "Brazil Towns," in various small and middle-sized industrial cities in Japan, such as Hamamatsu in Shizuoka prefecture, Toyota in Aichi, and Oizumi in Gunma.[82] Within the Brazilian enclaves, Japanese Brazilians spoke Portuguese, published their own Portuguese newspapers, and operated Brazilian restaurants, nightclubs, and bars with Afro-Brazilian samba music. For instance, Oizumi's famous "samba parade" began in 1991 at the initiative of a leader of the local Japanese community, and the majority of its participants were *dekassegui* Brazilians.[83] Yet back home, most Japanese Brazilians, who identified themselves as middle class, did not care about carnival parades, which they perceived as what "the poor" do, as *Nikkey Shimbun* editor-in-chief Masayuki Fukasawa maintains.[84] Japanese Brazilian sociologist Angelo Ishi also notes that "when compared to Brazilians in general," Japanese Brazilians "as a group appeared to lack interest in samba and carnival," but they suddenly began to "appreciate samba nights and organize carnival parades in dance halls and city festivals all over Japan."[85]

Over the years, the number of *dekassegui* repeaters increased. In the last few years of the 1990s, I kept hearing the stories of Japanese Brazilians who had lost their *dekassegui* savings in new businesses they had started in São Paulo and had chosen to go back to Japan to make more money. In a survey conducted with *dekassegui* returnees in Brazil by São Paulo City's Centro de Informação e Apoio ao Trabalhador no Exterior (Center of Information and Help for Emigrant Workers, CIATE) from June to December 1999, 67 percent of 793 respondents had been to Japan as *dekasseguis* more than once.[86] Furthermore, their transnational migration pattern changed significantly from individual, temporary migration (while leaving family behind in Brazil) to permanent, family-unit settlement in Japan. The number of Japanese-born Brazilian children increased rapidly, from 1,725 in 1994 to 3,820 in 1998.[87] In addition, whereas at first most *dekassegui* workers had lived among Japanese Brazilians in Brazil, beginning in the early 1990s many of the migrants were not accustomed to the Japanese language or to Japanese customs. Such shifts inevitably resulted in serious new issues of assimilation and acculturation for these migrants and their non-Japanese Brazilian spouses, including language acquisition and schooling for their (often racially mixed) children.[88]

Dekassegui was attributable chiefly to the deeply troubled national economy of Brazil, which had excessively high inflation rates in the late 1980s. In 1988, the individual average annual income was $2,160 in Brazil, ten times less than that in Japan ($21,600).[89] A great number of Brazilians of all ethnicities and races migrated to various parts of the First World. As of 1991, according to *Veja*, Brazil's major weekly news magazine, some 630,000 Brazilians were living and working as immigrants in other countries: 330,000 in the United States; 150,000 in Japan; 45,000 in Italy; 20,000 in England; 12,000 in France; 7,000 in Canada; 6,000 in Australia; 5,000 in Spain; and 25,000 in other countries, including Switzerland, Belgium, the Netherlands, and Israel.[90] Brazilians in Japan were exceptional in the sense that they constituted approximately 10 percent of all Japanese Brazilians in Brazil as of 1991, and also in that they were documented workers and their families had legitimate visas, unlike others working outside Brazil, who were predominantly illegal immigrants.

Dekassegui created lucrative new business opportunities among Japanese Brazilians. In 1990, there were 230 travel agencies specializing in *dekassegui* in the Liberdade district alone, and in 2006, the total number of Japanese Brazil travel agencies, *dekassegui* travel agencies, and *dekassegui* temp agencies still amounted to 100.[91] Tadao Ebihara, a postwar industrial immigrant (1968) and *dekassegui* travel agency owner, told me that he had sent some 150 workers a month to Japan in 1994–1996.[92] There were some *dekassegui* specialty agencies, such as those for women who wanted to work as caregivers in Japan. For instance, in 1987, Tsuruyo Sugimoto (b. 1928), a prewar child immigrant, bought a package that included job training in São Paulo City, a one-way air ticket to Tokyo, and job placement as a caregiver in Tokyo for a total of 350,000 yen. She bought the package from an agency in Liberdade owned and run by a Japanese Brazilian woman who, in a successful collaboration with a former chief nurse at Tokyo's Red Cross Hospital, found employment for their clients. Upon arriving in Tokyo, Tsuruyo Sugimoto was required to pay her loan back to the agency in the next five months as an automatic monthly deduction from her salary.[93] Such loans by *dekassegui* agencies to *dekassegui* workers (called *tatekae* in Japanese) became a common custom, which enabled more people without enough cash to buy plane tickets to migrate to Japan for work.

In São Paulo City, it was commonly said that each *dekassegui* recruiter ("promoter") could make $1,000 or 10,000 yen for each new recruit.[94] Some *dekassegui* returnees became employees at *dekassegui* agencies, and others set up their own agencies. In the mid-1990s, even regular Japanese Brazil travel agencies in São Paulo City got involved in the sale of plane tickets to Brazilian workers traveling to Japan. Until the global recession began in 2008, new workers continued to arrive from Brazil, sustaining the *dekassegui* middleman business in Brazil. As Higuchi and Tanno point out, labor contractors generally preferred to bring in new (and therefore "unspoiled") workers directly from Brazil, rather than recruit "old" Brazilian workers already in Japan, who, according to the contractors, "easily changed jobs, tended to neglect their duties, and were often absent from work at factories."[95]

My informants have claimed that by the end of the twentieth century almost every Japanese Brazilian family in São Paulo City had at least one member or relative who was working or had worked in Japan. In fact, among my informants, the number of *dekasseguis* in a family tended to reflect the class position of the family as a whole, not necessarily an individual's educational level or class position. It was also commonly noted that if a household was earning the average wage of a Brazilian middle-class family, approximately US$1,000 a month, none of the family members would migrate to Japan as *dekasseguis*.[96] This suggests that the long-prevalent image of Japanese Brazilians as a successful urban middle class may have been an illusion. Furthermore, as a result of *dekassegui*, Japanese Brazilians' well-known enthusiasm for higher education and urban professional occupations declined notably. Even some professional Japanese Brazilians with college degrees, including medical doctors, dentists, engineers, and lawyers, chose to work as manual laborers in Japan during the early years of the *dekassegui* boom, although many came back in a year or two to resume their careers after they had saved enough money to purchase real estate.

I was often told by Japanese Brazilians in São Paulo City that one of the "positive" aspects of *dekassegui* was that it equalized Japanese Brazilians from diverse class backgrounds when all of them became foreign manual laborers and made the same wages in Japan, in the same way they believe all Japanese immigrants started out as *colonos* many years ago. Needless to say, the Japanese immigrant population was diverse from the beginning.[97] Nor did Japanese Brazilians form a community in Japan that transcended their original class positions. Young Japanese Brazilians from families with relatively limited means opted for *dekassegui* work in Japan rather than college education in Brazil as the route to financial gain. Such is the case of Wagner M. Horiuchi (b. 1970), a Nisei born to postwar immigrants. Upon his father's passing, Horiuchi decided not to attend college and went to work in Japan in 1987–1991 to support his mother and two younger sisters. Back in Brazil, he married a white Brazilian woman and had a child, and then went back to Japan to work again in 1995–1996.[98] Thus some young Japanese Brazilians delayed college or dropped out of college to work in Japan, and others have simply given up the chance of higher education forever. This inevitably decreased the educational level of the Brazilian *dekassegui* population in Japan.[99]

Dekassegui survived and even thrived in Japan's prolonged recessions with record-high unemployment rates that began in the last few years of the twentieth century. In fact, the number of those who decided to live in Japan permanently with their Japanese-born children increased over the years. At the end of 2006, 312,979 Brazilians were registered in Japan; in addition, 18,000 Brazilians held dual citizenship. Of the total of some 330,000 Brazilians living in Japan, approximately 290,000 were regarded as working people, including at least 13,200 who were unemployed.[100] The number of Brazilians registered at Japan's Ministry of Foreign Affairs continued to grow and reached 316,967 at the end of 2007.[101]

In 2008, Brazil witnessed a series of nationwide festivities on the centenary of Japanese immigration. Throughout the month of June 2008 major Brazilian TV stations aired special programs and news segments on Japanese immigration and Japanese Brazilians. Many TV commercials and newspaper and journal advertisements carried images of Japanese immigration and Japanese Brazilians. Many special publications on Japanese immigration to Brazil were on sale at every newspaper stand (*banca*) in São Paulo City. The streets of Liberdade were filled with Brazilian TV reporters, visitors, and tourists even on weekdays. During the festivities for the centenary, Brazilians were enthusiastically watching *O Japão no Brasil* (Japan in Brazil), as São Paulo's TV station Rede Record titled its six-segment documentary series for its news program, *Jornal da Record*. *Folha de São Paulo* and *O Estado de São Paulo*, two major São Paulo newspapers, repeatedly published special issues in commemoration of the centenary. Whereas the previous celebrations in each decade starting in 1958 had been Japanese-driven, it was Brazilians, the Brazilian government, and Brazilian mass media that got heated up for the centenary. By contrast, the Japanese government's official response was cordial but not particularly enthusiastic. Brazil and Japan used the same logo designed for the centenary celebration, but the latter eliminated the word *imigração* (immigration) and replaced it with *intercâmbio* (interchange): Ano do Intercâmbio Japão-Brasil (The Year of Interchange between Japan and Brazil). This inevitably caused some discontent among the prewar immigrants, who felt their history of immigration to Brazil was not respected by their own homeland.

On April 12, 2008, São Paulo City began to renovate Liberdade's *bairro oriental* as Caminho de Imperador (Street of the Emperor), and the Liberdade branch of Banco Bradesco (Bradesco Bank) was to have its exterior remodeled to resemble Osaka Castle by June 18, 2008. Once completed it was to become a new exotic tourist attraction. TV Rede hosted a nationwide "Miss Centenary" contest with Amauri Jr, a popular Brazilian TV personality, as its host, and on May 17, 2008, twenty-six-year-old Sansei Karina Eiko Nakahara was crowned at the finals held in São Paulo City. Nakahara is from Moji das Cruzes, São Paulo; graduated from USP's School of Dentistry; and practices dentistry in Arujá. Not surprisingly, she is a *mestiça*, born to a Nisei father and a white Brazilian mother; as *Nikkey Shimbun* reports, some 90 percent of all Japanese Brazilian beauty contestants are *mestiças*.[102] But the selection was unusual in the sense that the prize went to an older professional woman who had graduated from Brazil's top institution. From May 21 to July 18, 2008, Banco Real (Royal Bank) held a special exposition, *Japão em cada em um de nos* (Japan in Each One of Us), at its main branch on Avenida Paulista.

Three memorial ceremonies for Japanese immigrants were held in São Paulo City on June 17 and 18, 2008. The first was held on June 17 at Iberapuera Park, in front of the Monument in Homage to the Late Japanese Immigrants, which had been inaugurated on August 23, 1975, by Burajiru Todōfukenjinkai Rengōkai (Federation of the Prefectural Associations of

Japan in Brazil, or Kenren), established in 1966 in São Paulo City. The ceremony was hosted by Kenren and the Federacão das Escolas de Budismo do Estado de São Paulo (Federation of Buddhist Schools in the State of São Paulo, Butsuren). For the centenary, Bunkyo chartered a special bus for those who wished to attend the ceremony. The officiant at the ceremony was Reverend Yomei Sasaki, a prominent Buddhist monk in Brazil of Jōdo Shinshū, the most widely practiced branch of Buddhism in Japan. On the morning of June 18, the "Day of Immigrants" in São Paulo, the archbishop of São Paulo hosted a special Catholic mass in Portuguese at the Sé Cathedral (not at the usual São Gonzalo Church at Praça São Mendes of Liberdade), which was well attended not only by Japanese Brazilians but also by Brazilians in general. In the afternoon, Butsuren hosted a special Buddhist memorial ceremony at the large Celso Furtado Auditorium of Anhembi Park, not at the Bunkyo Auditorium, where it would have been held any other year. The Buddhist ceremony was followed by an interfaith celebration in the same Anhembi Auditorium later in the afternoon.

For the centenary, each prefectural association in Brazil received a special monetary contribution from the corresponding prefectural government in Japan. In return, the association welcomed a group of special, important visitors from the prefectural office in Japan and hosted special events to entertain them. For instance, Yamaguchi Prefectural Association in Brazil took its eight guests to Campinas, São Paulo, for a one-day excursion; on another day the association's president, Nobuyuki Hironaka (1944–2012), a postwar immigrant, entertained all eight guests at his home and successful flower farm in Atibaia, São Paulo; and the prefectural association held a special dinner in the guests' honor on the evening of June 20, 2008, at Casa do Portugal, a Portuguese restaurant in Liberdade. The association's officeholders, all postwar immigrant men, were present (without their spouses) to entertain the special visitors from their home prefecture, also all men. Unfortunately, general attendance was not good, except for elderly members, who received a 50 percent discount. Several Niseis in their late twenties and early thirties who had studied in Yamaguchi prefecture on its prefectural fellowships were obligated to help entertain the visitors, many of whom were prefectural government officers. Not surprisingly, there were two male Japanese politicians who represented the prefecture in the national Diet and were soliciting votes through *zaigai senkyo* (the absentee-balloting system for Japanese citizens overseas), which had become effective in May 2000.[103]

The highlight of the centenary was the special national ceremony held at São Paulo City's Anhembi Sambadrome on June 21 and 22, which was reported to have drawn approximately fifty thousand in total. On June 21, despite the gray skies and constant rain, some thirty thousand people attended the all-day event. At 4:30 P.M. the festivities climaxed with the appearance of Crown Prince Naruhito of Japan, who paraded through the stadium in a car before showing up on the stage with other special guests for the ceremony. Enzo Yuta Nakamura Onishi, a three-year-old boy from Paraná, and his paternal Issei grandparents lighted the friendship fire with a torch sent from the former Emigration Center of Kobe and carried by many celebrities in Japan and Brazil. Enzo is the first Rokusei (sixth-generation Japanese Brazilian) and a descendant of a *Kasato Maru* immigrant; he was supposed to represent the one-hundred-year Japanese Brazilian history for the ceremony, but he is exceptional in the sense that his family has never intermarried. Many elderly prewar child immigrants were among the audience, including Taro Mushino (1919–2009), Hiromi Yamashita (1914–2010), and Tokuichi Hidaka (b. 1926), the *kachigumi* members who murdered some of the prominent *makegumi*—all attending the ceremony to see the crown prince.[104]

Conclusion

At the highlight of Brazil's centenary festivities in June 2008, retired Nisei architect Iossuke Tanaka (chapter 3) characterized all of the enthusiasm among Brazilians as "just a temporary boom"; they would "forget all about it once the centenary is over." Tanaka added, "What Brazilians have got enthused about as Japanese culture this year does not seem to be the same as what the Japanese have kept as their culture in Japan. What Brazilians long for or are interested in is the Edo period, such as geisha and *kabuki*. That is the reason why nobody talks about Japan's advanced science technology for the centenary." He noted that the popularity of Japanese food was permanent rather than temporary, "but they [Brazilians] talk about sushi and sashimi only."[105] *Veja* had reported in 2004 that Japanese cuisine was becoming extremely popular among Brazilians in major Brazilian cities; in São Paulo City, there were six hundred Japanese restaurants, which outnumbered the five hundred *churrascarias* (traditional Brazilian barbeque restaurants).[106] By 2008, the majority of sushi chefs (*sushiman*) had already been replaced by *nordestinos,* migrant men from the northeast.[107] It took a long century for Japanese culture to finally be embraced in São Paulo.

Yet the centenary did not bring a "happy" ending to Japanese Brazilians in Japan. Ironically, in the same year, 2008, Japanese Brazilians in Japan were forced to deal with the global recession that started that year, and the number of Brazilians began to decline, from 312,582 in 2008 to 267,456 in 2009. In April 2009, the Japanese government began to sponsor the repatriation of Latin Americans of Japanese descent, with funding of 300,000 yen to the applicant and 200,000 yen to each family member, on the condition that they would not be allowed to reenter Japan for the next three years. The program was criticized internationally for its "paid deportation" of Brazilian workers and their families. By the end of March 2010, when the program was ended, a total of 22,403 had applied for paid repatriation, of whom Brazilians constituted 92 percent. At the end of 2010, 230,552 Brazilians were registered in Japan. That is, within two years of the start of the global recession, more than a quarter of Brazilians in Japan had gone back to Brazil. The Great Tohoku Earthquake (March 11, 2011) had a further impact on Brazilians in Japan: 3,882 Brazilians went back to Brazil in the three months following the quake, and the Brazilian government paid their return passage to Brazil. The number of Brazilian residents in Japan continued to decline: a total of 175,410 were registered at the end of 2014.[108] Once again, Japanese Brazilians were on the move, from Japan back to Brazil this time.

Chapter Two

PREWAR CHILD IMMIGRANTS
AND THEIR JAPANESE IDENTITY

The imperial family has been a very special presence here in Brazil.
The present-day (Heisei) emperor came to Brazil a few times when he
was still the crown prince [Akihito], and I was very honored to meet
him through Esperança Fujinkai. I had something to say to Princess
[now Empress] Michiko: "I am a naturalized Brazilian citizen, but I am
always Japanese." She smiled at me. Well, I became a naturalized citizen
in 1978. My husband had already done so. Our three sons are all Brazilians. I felt strange about being the only Japanese in my family, so I went
to the consulate general of Japan to ask for dual nationality. They told
me that that I would have to give up my Japanese citizenship to become
a Brazilian. This has been the biggest hardship in my life. I felt great pain
when I did the paperwork to get rid of my Japanese nationality, telling
myself this was just on paper and that I would be Japanese forever.

—*Sumiko Mizumoto, a tanka poet, 2001*[1]

In the late afternoon of June 19, 2001, Sumiko Mizumoto narrated her
story to me at her famous gift shop, Casa Mizumoto, located near the
Liberdade metro station. On the right side of the wall inside her office was a
large framed photo of the Japanese imperial family, about which I had just
asked her. Mizumoto's narrative demonstrates her inner conflict, caught
between being a member of her Brazilian family and her own Japanese identity. Mizumoto was born in Abashiri City, Hokkaido, in 1920 and immigrated with her birth family, the Satos, to Brazil in June 1932 on the *Rio de
Janeiro Maru*. Her late husband, Tsuyoshi Mizumoto (1920–1989), also a prewar child immigrant, was a highly reputed businessman in São Paulo who
became the first president of the Liberdade Shōkōkai (Association of Merchants in Liberdade; 1974–1989). In the year following his death, Tsuyoshi

Elderly Japanese Brazilian women of Liberdade Shōkōkai dancing on the main street of the *bairro oriental* of Liberdade, São Paulo City, for their Tanabata Festival, July 8, 2001. Photo by author.

was decorated by the Japanese government. Even though she "had no public life" and "lived in her husband's shadow," Mizumoto herself became well known among Japanese immigrants in São Paulo City, not only as a tanka poet and teacher but also as the president of Esperança Fujinkai (1975–1978 and 1983–1994). In 1995, Mizumoto herself was decorated by the Japanese government.

Mizumoto's narrative makes us wonder what it means to be Japanese in Brazil for her and for other prewar child immigrants. In the 1930s they were rather pejoratively called *Burajiru sodachi* (those who grew up in Brazil) and *jun*-Nisei (quasi-Nisei) and were often regarded as "not smart," because the adult immigrants were very critical of their Japanese-born children's gradual Brazilianization.[2] How important has it been for prewar child immigrants to be Japanese in Brazil? How has their Japanese identity changed over the years, either collectively or individually? How do they understand gender and family in relation to their mediated Japanese identity? This chapter also examines prewar child immigrants' own discourse on quasi-Nisei identity.

Katsuo Uchiyama (1910–2004), a prewar adult immigrant (1930) who became the editor-in-chief of *São Paulo Shimbun*, writes that Japanese descendants in Brazil have felt they shared a common destiny with the emperor system, and that the intense and prolonged *kachi-make* (victory-defeat) conflicts were finally settled when they learned that the emperor system had survived the defeat of Japan after all.[3] But at the same time, the imperial family's survival was interpreted by *kachigumi* as strong evidence of imperial Japan's "true" victory. Whether they accepted Japan's defeat or not, many prewar immigrants' Japanese identity has been closely connected to emperor worship until the present day. For many years, it remained a common custom for Japanese immigrants in Brazil to hang *goshinyei* (an imperial portrait) at home, as well as in public places. They did so even when they lived in *colono* cottages on coffee plantations in the early stages of their settlement in rural Brazil. The prevalent custom of bowing to an imperial portrait disappeared in postwar Japan under the US occupation (1945–1952), after the "Humanity Declaration" by Emperor Shōwa (Hirohito) on January 1, 1946. By contrast, in Brazil, emperor worship not only continued to prevail among the Japanese but was even strengthened in some areas, as the ideological backbone for the *kachigumi* to justify their terrorism and other activities. As a result, Japanese Brazilians remained severely divided for years to come, especially in the major rural Japanese agricultural settlements.[4] In order to unite them, Kiyoshi Yamamoto, as Bunkyo's founder and its first president, concluded that the attendance of imperial family members was necessary for the successful celebration of the fiftieth anniversary of Japanese immigration to Brazil. Thus the visit of Prince and Princess Mikasa came to be realized.[5] Even today the Burajiru Nikkei Rōjin Kurabu Rengōkai / Associação dos Clubes de Anciões do Brasil (Association of the Brazilian Nikkei Clubs for the Elderly, or Rōkuren) in São Paulo City proudly displays large framed portraits of the Meiji emperor, as well as of the Showa emperor and empress, in its main conference room on the second floor. Those portraits must have been brought in when the association was established in 1975, already thirty years after the war.[6]

Prewar child immigrants longed for a true belonging to Japan, exemplified by their emperor worship. In the late 1980s, some relatively well-to-do child immigrant women in their sixties chose to go to Japan as *dekasseguis* to work as private caregivers at hospitals for half a year or for a few years, even though they did not have to work for money. They say they had a great time traveling in Japan for fun with the money they had earned there.[7] Even today, elderly Japanese descendants, especially prewar immigrants, often refer to Brazil as a *santō koku* (third-class country) while praising Japan as an *ittō koku* (first-class country). This attitude has been most prevalent among immigrant men who do not regard themselves as successful, especially in financial terms. There is another twist in the politics of position for the Japanese in Brazil: while referring to the United States as another "first-class country," they emphasize the moral superiority of Brazil over the United States for its alleged "racial harmony" or "lack of racism," buying into Brazil's national ideology of "racial democracy."[8] Japanese immigrants often say, "Brazil is such a wonderful country. We the Japanese have been well accepted. There is no racism here in Brazil, unlike the case of the United States." In such comparative arguments, Japan and the United States are economically superior to Brazil, which is still morally superior to the United States.

Prewar Japanese immigration to Brazil took a very specific form of family migration (chapter 1). It was usually the patriarch, not always the official head of the immigrant family, who made the decision to immigrate, and his wife, as well as (some of) his children and aging parents, had to obey his decision.[9] Even though almost all prewar immigrants were registered officially as farmers on the passenger lists, and the majority of them were indeed so, the proportion of nonfarmers and/or nonrural residents rose after state-sponsored emigration began in 1924.[10] In fact, Mizumoto's birth family, the Satos, had never farmed in Japan. Mizumoto's father owned a lumber company and would travel to Karafuto, a prefecture of the Great Japanese Empire (present-day South Sakhalin, Russia) to buy lumber, which he sold to Japanese paper companies. In the Great Depression, the family business did not do well, and Mizumoto's father decided to immigrate to Brazil only to find he was not eligible to head his family because he was already fifty-one years old. Luckily, he had three sons older than Mizumoto, and his oldest son, Hakuzo, then twenty-six, married in a great hurry in order to head the Satos to Brazil. Eventually the Satos made a family of seven: Mizumoto's parents; her oldest brother and his new wife; one of her older sisters, Kimi (b. 1909); Mizumoto herself; and her younger sister, Tomoko (b. 1922). Two young adult sons and one young daughter remained in Japan.[11] As Mizumoto's case demonstrates, in large families, all of the members rarely immigrated together.

By contrast, Shizu Saito's birth family, the Hashimotos, was young and small at the time of their immigration to Brazil in 1933. As an oldest child, Saito was born and grew up in Taiwan under Japanese occupation, where her father worked for a Japanese sugar refinery company. The Hashimotos had a reasonably comfortable life in Taiwan, where Saito attended a Japanese elementary school, taught by Japanese teachers sent from Japan: "I had to quit school at the age of ten, when I was in the fourth grade. That was hard on me. I did not have the chance to master the Japanese language in school. Neither my Japanese nor my Portuguese is good enough. I wanted to attend a Japanese girls' high school in Taiwan, where we could have stayed until I reached adulthood. We lived in Shika but could do anything in Tainan, which had a big market. We had a good life there. That was the best time for my mother." The Hashimotos left Taiwan at the end of 1932 for their three-day passage to Japan. They stayed at Saito's uncle's house in Yaizu City, Shizuoka prefecture, for six months, during which time her father visited the prefectural office many times to arrange their immigration to Brazil. At the time of emigration, the Hashimotos made a family of five: the two parents, Shizu, her six-year-old brother, and a fourteen-year-old male cousin. Her cousin did not stay with the Hashimotos in Brazil; upon arrival he took off on his own and the family lost one male adult laborer. Saito's mother was pregnant and her younger sister was born on their immigrant ship in 1933. As a result, the Hashimotos ended up having only two workers, the parents, while Saito was required to take care of her baby sister, as well as her younger brother, without any formal schooling in Brazil.[12]

Immigrants began to construct new prefectural identities even before departing for Brazil. Prospective emigrants arrived in Kobe by train or ship from various parts of Japan for their scheduled embarkation to Brazil. After the opening of the Asylum of Emigrants in Kobe in 1928, they all were required to stay there for ten days of training as well as medical examinations to screen out those with trachoma, who were not allowed to immigrate to Brazil. At the asylum emigrant families from the same prefecture shared accommodations, which were modeled after the immigrant ship and nicknamed "shelves for silkworms." They shared rooms for the entire voyage of some forty or fifty days and began to bond as shipmates, regardless of their regional origins, through their daily activities and through special social events, such as the ceremony of crossing the equator. Upon arriving at the port of Santos, many immigrants were transferred on special trains to the Hospedaria do Imigrante (Asylum of Immigrants) in São Paulo City, where they would spend a few days before heading toward the plantations, each of which was identified by the name of a railway line and the train station at which the immigrants would get off. Others were sent directly from Santos to their assigned plantations by train, when the asylum was packed with immigrants as well as with migrants from northeast Brazil, as happened often after the late 1920s.[13]

Mizumoto's birth family, the Satos, was assigned to a large coffee plantation, Fazenda Chantebled of the Noroeste line, owned by a Brazilian politician, who hired a German overseer and a Japanese interpreter. There were around forty immigrant families, including Italians, working on the same *fazenda*. The Satos and all of the other families from Hokkaido on the same voyage were assigned to the Fazenda Chantebled. Saito's birth family, the Hashimotos, was assigned to an old, worn-out coffee plantation located between Minas Gerais and São Paulo states, where coffee cultivation did not flourish. Saito describes how she came to bond with other immigrants from the same prefecture: "We arrived on the *Africa Maru*, on which we the immigrants were grouped by each prefecture of origin for the assignment of rooms. There were a dozen families from Shizuoka on the same ship, and all of us got settled on the same plantation. That was better because we had been together on the ship and we spoke the same dialect. In March of the same year, the next group of Japanese immigrants arrived on our plantation, and they were all from Fukuoka."[14] It was on the coffee plantations that Japanese immigrants came into daily contact with the non-Japanese population. Tsuruyo Sugimoto (b. 1928), arriving in Brazil from Miyazaki in 1936, remembers her first coffee plantation, where she and her family had to work for their two-agricultural-year contract:

> It was an Italian coffee plantation of the Paulista line. A medical doctor invested his money in the plantation. There was a manager and an overseer, both of whom were quite competent. The *fazenda* was full of *gaijin*, with only ten Japanese families. It was a large estate. We, the Japanese, worked very hard, and they were so pleased with us that they took in Okinawan immigrants for the following year. Thanks to our idealistic plantation owner, we did not have to work on Saturdays and Sundays, so we went to work for the Japanese in a nearby estate where they grew cotton. They had finished their labor contracts and rented the land for cotton cultivation.[15]

Note that a given coffee plantation did not keep taking in Japanese immigrants from the same prefecture. For the sake of convenience, each intake grouped workers from the same prefecture, who spoke the same regional dialect and shared relatively similar customs. In the larger framework of labor control, however, the Japanese on the same plantation had to come from different prefectures so that they could not too easily unite in resistance against the planters. Of course, exactly the same "divide and conquer" mechanism worked with European immigrants, who had arrived earlier, as well as with Brazilian migrant workers. Each group had its own living area, and their cultural, national, and racial differences were emphasized. For instance, Italians were given better land and work than the Japanese. And whereas Brazilian workers were under the supervision of an Italian immigrant man, a black Brazilian man oversaw the work of Japanese immigrants. Furthermore, unlike Brazilian workers and European immigrants,

Japanese immigrants were provided with an interpreter. Such interpreters were supposed to represent the interests of Japanese immigrants, but they were paid by Brazilian planters during their stay on the plantations, and had arrived in Brazil originally as employees of KKKK and therefore remained instruments of the Japanese government to control Japanese immigrant labor for the planters. This made life even more complicated for Japanese immigrants.[16]

For most immigrants, plantation life itself was much harder than one could have imagined. The experiences of Masashi Sugimoto (1917–2016), Tsuruyo's husband from Hokkaido, were different from hers. He and his family arrived in Brazil in 1931, and, with seven other Japanese families from the same immigrant ship, were assigned to a German-owned coffee plantation in Cafelandia of the Noroeste line. They all had to work on Saturdays to catch up with the assigned work on the plantations or be penalized. After eight months of *colono* labor, Masashi Sugimoto's family paid a penalty for breaking their two-agricultural-year labor contracts and moved away from the coffee plantation. After twenty days in São Paulo City, with the help of BRATAC, they moved to Fukuhaku-mura, a Japanese agricultural settlement in Suzano, São Paulo, on November 18, 1931, after having purchased their own land there for suburban agriculture.[17] Many other prewar immigrants, including Tsutomu Akahoshi (b. 1921) and his family from Kumamoto prefecture, ran away from the assigned coffee plantations at night, without completing their labor contracts.[18] According to Iossuke Takana, who studied all of the prewar immigrant passenger lists housed at the Museu Histórico da Imigração Japonesa no Brasil (Historical Museum of Japanese Immigration to Brazil, or MHIJB), most of those who ran away from their plantations did so within half a year or a year of arrival.[19] Of course, many were caught and forced back. For instance, after losing two of his three young children, Shigeichi Sakai (1901–1984), a college-educated prewar immigrant, did not find any hope in his *colono* life and ran away one night from the plantation one night with his wife and their only surviving child, without completing their one-agricultural-year labor contract. The Sakais were caught on their way to another plantation where he had been offered a job to teach Japanese children. They were eventually released after Sakai's younger brother testified that Sakai was too weak to work on the plantation. Sakai's aging father cursed him, saying that he was no longer his son.[20]

Mizumoto's birth family, the Satos, were able to complete their one-agricultural-year *colono* contracts and moved on to Colônia Hirano in Cafelandia, but it "went broke" and they "got lost." By accident, the Satos got into contact with a former fellow *colono* worker who had run away from their first plantation. He was looking for workers, so they followed him and moved to Bastos. Unfortunately, their new land was not good, so the Satos moved again after a year to another plantation, where they stayed two years. They kept moving in rural São Paulo, where they grew cotton. The Satos thus relocated themselves four times until they finally settled.[21] The Hashimotos, Saito's birth family, moved several times also; as the family head, Saito's father kept in touch with their shipmates and, by visiting with them, found a better settlement to move to next.[22] Among my prewar immigrant informants, each *colono* family moved at least four or five times until they settled as small independent farmers, either owning or renting sufficient land for agricultural production. This fits with Seichi Izumi's finding that each prewar Japanese immigrant family moved an average of 4.8 times.[23] In contrast, Japanese Brazilian censuses of 1958 indicate that the average number of resettlements per family among prewar immigrants was 3.4, lower than Izumi's sampling in 1952.[24] Networking with those from the same prefecture, shipmates, and former coworkers, immigrant families kept relocating in search of better wages and living conditions in order to become successful independent farmers so that they could save enough money to return to Japan. According to Hiroshi Saito, there were three major courses of relocation for prewar Japanese immigrants after competing their *colono* contracts. The first was to become independent coffee producers by sharecropping and eventually purchasing pieces of land (*lotes*) in areas along the Noroeste and Paulista lines. The second was to rent land for vegetable production and eventually become independent farmers in the suburbs of São Paulo City and along the Central line. The third was to become renters and then independent farmers in mixed agriculture in the interior, in areas along the Sorocabana and Paulista lines, northern Paraná, and the interior along the Araraquara line.[25]

There was an old Japanese saying among Japanese immigrants in Brazil: "If five Japanese get together, they build a school." Once they finally settled down, albeit often with the full use of their older children's labor, the majority of Japanese immigrants wanted to get their younger children, both Japanese-born and Brazilian-born, educated as Japanese, as they hoped they would eventually go back to Japan. Saito herself had no chance of schooling in Brazil, but her younger brother was able to attend a Japanese school on their second coffee plantation for a short time, since her father was hired there to teach Japanese children for half a day. The school was "just a regular house," and only a dozen Japanese students attended it. Her mother had to work alone in the mornings when her father taught, but he joined her in the afternoons.[26]

Kazuyo Yoneda (b. 1925), her parents, and her two younger sisters arrived in Brazil in 1935. They were her maternal aunt's *yobiyose* immigrants from Kumamoto prefecture. Upon arrival in Brazil they moved into the Colônia Prejão, a Japanese agricultural settlement established in 1915 by Ken'ichiro Hoshino, which later became Álvares Machado. According to Yoneda, almost all residents of Colônia Prejão were Japanese who were landowners, and they were passionate about their children's education. There was already a *grupo escolar,* where she learned Japanese until noon and Portuguese until 1 P.M. every day for two years until she was forced to quit her schooling to take care of her three younger sisters at home. It was a big school with financial support from the Brazilian government. By contrast, all *camaradas* (wage workers on a farm or plantation) were Brazilians who did not know how to write their own names: "They did not go to school in the countryside. They began to work with hoes when they were children and would go to drink in town with their families on Sundays. They had a miserable life. There were many Brazilian *camaradas.* On Sundays, they all, including women, went to town to drink *pinga* (sugar cane brandy) at bars. Then they returned home, terribly drunken."[27]

Tsuruko Kikuchi was only one year old when she and her family arrived in Brazil in 1926. When she was around seven, Kikuchi and her birth family moved into Fazenda Boa Vista of the Noroeste line, where an elementary school had been just built.

> We had a Portuguese class in the mornings, had lunch, and took a Japanese class in the afternoons. We got up early and went to school when it was still dark. More and more Japanese moved in as the *colônia* was formed. Among them, some family heads taught at the school. *Gaijin* children could also attend the school, and we had some Italians. They came to learn Portuguese when they were young but did not graduate. Well, Italians rented land there, made money, and moved out. After they moved out, the Japanese usually moved in. We had a *seinenkai* and held a sports meeting. If the Japanese built a school, they would soon make a playground with 200-meter tracks, next to the school. We had our sports contests among ourselves, and our winners went to São Paulo's state championships.[28]

Even after the outbreak of the war, Kikuchi and others could go to school in secrecy. Furthermore, her family subscribed not only to a Japanese-language newspaper published in São Paulo City but also to several magazines imported from Japan. Her older brothers would ride a horse twelve kilometers to the town to pick up those Japanese magazines for their family.[29]

As Japanese immigrants stayed on in Brazil much longer than they had planned, they came to be concerned about their children getting married. There is an old Japanese saying in Brazil: "A young woman is worth three contos." Potential brides were always in short supply, especially before Japanese state-sponsored immigration to Brazil began in 1924. "Three contos" refers to the average amount of betrothal money the bride's father was to receive from the groom's family for the loss of one adult laborer. Tomoo Handa maintains that three contos were equivalent to an adult laborer's wages for three years and concludes that the patriarch would be willing to approve of the marriage if the groom and his family were doing well enough to pay a suitable bride price. He adds that there were other immigrant families who refused to let their daughters marry at all, saying that they needed their labor and could not afford to lose it.[30] Of course, nobody would have had to pay betrothal money in the case of marriages with local Brazilians. In rural, agricultural areas, the socioeconomic position of prewar Japanese immigrants was so low that the marriage partners available to their children were poor local Brazilians known as *caboclos,* who were "little educated and culturally different," according to Izumi.[31] Therefore even impoverished Japanese immigrants positioned themselves above these Brazilian workers and did not allow their children to marry any Brazilians for family honor in the good name of the Japanese.

Furthermore, prewar immigrant parents expected their children's marriages to be arranged as *miai,* based on each family's social standing, as was customary back in Japan. The Japanese were against their children dating even among themselves. An extreme case occurred in 1948 in the town of Álvares Machado as reported by Kiyoshi Shima; a young Nisei man killed his Nisei girlfriend and her Issei father and then committed suicide because his girlfriend's father had forced the couple to break up.[32] Yoshie Miyano (b. 1924), a prewar child immigrant from Saitama, remembers the elopement of a neighbor's daughter back in Bastos during the early 1940s. The young woman, an only child, fell in love with a young Japanese man of whom her parents did not approve, so they had to elope to be together. Of course, Miyano's own marriage to her prewar immigrant husband was arranged and acknowledged properly. Her husband used to work as a *viajante* and would walk in front of her house in Bastos. He had known one of her classmates, and her father got to like him. After they were married, the Miyanos moved from Bastos to Tupã in 1950, where they owned and ran a successful store selling musical instruments.[33]

Kazuyo Yoneda's marriage was also arranged, albeit for a different reason. Her birth family, the Ishidas, needed an adult man to marry into their family and work for them. With four young daughters and high medical bills for a chronically ill mother, the Ishidas were struggling financially, and an acquaintance suggested to her father that Kazuyo's marrying would solve the problem. Her father wanted his oldest daughter's husband to be a *yōshi* (a son-in-law who takes his wife's family name legally). "Of course, there was no such thing in Brazil," and Kazuyo had to take her husband's last name, Yoneda. She was nineteen years old, and her husband, who had arrived in Brazil at the age of twenty, was already thirty. Even though her husband refused to change his last name, he moved in with the Ishidas and worked with them in farming, while quarreling constantly with his father-in-law; it pained Yoneda a lot to be caught between them all the time.[34]

Prewar interracial unions took place most commonly between young Japanese women and "Brazilian" *camaradas,* who were usually unskilled migrant workers from the northeast employed by the Japanese immigrants. Of course, immigrant parents, who were very strict about their young daughters' sexual behavior, did not allow such unions, and usually the young women were disowned in public and/or soon disappeared from the sight of the Japanese and lived among the lower-class Brazilian population, as Handa writes,

> In the old days, the Japanese in Brazil were just temporary migrant workers, namely the lower class on a social scale. Therefore many of those whom the Japanese came into contact with were the even further lower-class workers whom they hired. Those men were kinder to women than Japanese men were. They were called *camaradas,* and one would be socially disgraced if s/he eloped with a *camarada.* Parents would never allow such unions to be recognized socially, so elopement was the only means for the couple to be together. Men could still be treated as members of the Japanese community, but women who eloped with *camaradas* fell down into the Brazilian lower classes and never showed up in front of Japanese immigrants.[35]

Tsuruyo Sugimoto maintains that the Japanese trusted "*camaradas* too much" so that "when they became independent farmers and built houses they let *camaradas* move in with themselves to live in the same house." Thus "mistakes" took place between young Japanese daughters and the *camaradas.* She recalls the most beautiful girl in the village eloping with a dark-skinned man: "She did not want to run away. She got pregnant. Babies were born out of all such unions. Such women must have left the community permanently."[36] But were such unions really only "mistakes"? Yasuto Shigeoka (1925–2016), a prewar child immigrant, recalls an episode during the early 1940s in the Japanese *colônia* of Presidente Prudente, São Paulo, where the Shigeokas had become pioneers in the cultivation of peppermint:

> When a young woman ran away with a *gaijin*, all the men of the *colônia* got together and took the woman back. She ran away with a *camarada*. All of us looked for her everywhere possible for a week and finally found them hiding in a cottage on a mountain. She came back looking down and she was no longer a virgin. We took her to a doctor [for a medical examination of her hymen] and when he came out and waved his hand to us, who were waiting outside [the doctor's office], the woman's father fell down in despair. In the *colônia*, we had a very strong consciousness as the Japanese. We believed we had better raise all of our children as good Japanese.[37]

Thus, women's "sexual behavior (or rather lack of it) reflected upon the men associated with them," borrowing the words of Sonya Lipsett-Rivera in her study of honor in colonial Mexico.[38] In the case of prewar Japanese immigrants in rural São Paulo, a young woman's loss of virginity to a "Brazilian" man shamed not only her father and family but also all of the Japanese men in the community. Shigeichi Sakai writes about three cases of interracial relationship in the countryside, just after the war, between young Japanese women and black *camaradas* whom their parents had hired as field hands. Those interracial couples all eloped and disappeared from the Japanese community. One of the three cases concerns an only child in a well-to-do cotton-farming family. Their daughter spoke Portuguese fluently, cared dearly for her parents, and took care of their family business. Her parents wanted to choose the best possible Japanese man to marry into the family as her husband but could not find the ideal son-in-law. At that time, the parents hired more than ten *camaradas* for farming, and the daughter eloped with the leader of the workers, just after she turned twenty-five.[39] Hiroshi Saito maintains that such elopements prove that "patriarchy had come to lose its effect as an organizing principle" among the Japanese in rural Brazil. In other words, "the institution of family had been internally destroyed" by young daughters' refusal to obey male authorities.[40]

In 1941, Mizumoto moved to São Paulo City. As a young Japanese woman, Mizumoto was not supposed to move on her own; her husband-to-be, Tsuyoshi Mizumoto, came to get her to move to be with him. Tsuyoshi was also a child immigrant; he had arrived in Brazil at the age of nine when he and his family emigrated from Okayama prefecture. Both were twenty-one when they married. It was not exactly an arranged marriage, since they had known each other; Mizumoto's older sister, Kimi (Wakamatsu), had taught Tsuyoshi as her student in an advanced elementary course (*kōtōka*) at Bastos' Japanese school after he had finished a *grupo escolar*. In 1935, Tsuyoshi left Bastos for São Paulo City to work and study. According to Mizumoto, she and her husband got married "out of necessity"; "I knew him and heard that he was doing well in the city. I decided to move to the city since nothing good had happened in the countryside."[41]

In the city, Tsuyoshi Mizumoto had attended Myojō Gakuen (Rising-Star School), established in 1934 by Koichi Kishimoto (1898–1977) in the Pinherios district. Kishimoto, a Rikkokai immigrant, was Tsuyoshi's former teacher back in the countryside. Myojō Gakuen had a *kinrōbu* (branch of hard work) that ran a cleaning business using its students' unpaid labor, where Tsuyoshi worked for two years. In 1938, he and his two brothers opened their own cleaning business, Tinturaria Aurora, in the upper-class residential neighborhood of Perdizes and started to employ Japanese-descendant youths from Bastos. Their younger sisters and other young women cooked for the employees while attending Myojō Gakuen's sewing school. That was when the Mizumotos got married. With the capital they had accumulated from their cleaning business, the Mizumoto brothers started their first gift shop, Casa Mizumoto, in Pinheiros in 1948 and, by buying a business from an old Japanese acquaintance, opened the second shop in Liberdade in 1958. Throughout the 1940s Mizumoto devoted herself to her three young sons as well as to her husband's family business. With the passage of time, the rest of the Satos moved to the city.[42]

As it turns out, Mizumoto was one of many Japanese immigrants who moved into the city in 1941, the year that Japanese urbanization became pronounced. In fact, already by 1940, the number of those whose "color" was "yellow" totaled 45,136 in São Paulo City, constituting 18.3 percent of the "yellow" population of the entire state of São Paulo.[43] By the time Tsuyoshi arrived in 1935, the Japanese had already formed three "Japan Towns" in the city: Cantaleira (for the São Paulo municipal market), Pinheiros (where the Cotia Agricultural Cooperative's warehouses were located), and the oldest Conde neighborhood. In the city, many Japanese immigrant men became *feirantes* (merchants who retail their wares in large open-air markets for consumers), *quitandeiros* (greengrocers), and vegetable and grain traders. As a result, there were more and more young Japanese men arriving in the city in the late 1930s and early 1940s to look for better economic opportunities. Yoshiro Fujita (1920–2014), who immigrated to Brazil in 1934 with his parents as his older brother's *yobiyose*, worked on a coffee plantation in São Paulo for a year, moved with his family in 1935 to Assai, Paraná state, and then in 1938 moved to São Paulo City on his own. He immediately found a job at Hachiya Shōkai (Hachiya and Co.), the biggest Japanese import company in Brazil, and while working full-time he attended a school of commerce to become a certified accountant with a degree in accounting in 1945. Masugi Kiyotani (1916–2012) and his family, who had emigrated from Hiroshima in 1926, moved to the city in 1940. In 1944, he married Tumoru (b. 1921), a prewar child immigrant from Fukuoka (1930), and they ran a *quitanda* in the Bella Vista district for four years and seven months to support their family.[44]

Tsuyoshi Mizumoto was one of the many prewar Japanese immigrants who made it in cleaning and dyeing service (*tintureira*), with his siblings' "free" labor, and eventually all of the family members ended up living in the city. Before long the Japanese "drove away" Brazilian cleaners and dominated the business.[45] Hirofumi Ikesaki (b. 1927), owner of Ikesaki Cosmetics in Liberdade, began to work at a Japanese cleaner in 1947 when he arrived from Bastos. After learning sufficient skills in cleaning, he started his own cleaning business with his older brother, Kazuhito Ikesaki (1920–2008).[46] According to Rokurō Kōyama, the Japanese constituted two-thirds of the 1,500 *tintureiros* already in the city by the end of the 1940s. In the 1950s, the term *tintureiro* became interchangeable with "Japanese," and the popular song "Xótis do Tintureiro" (Cleaner's Song) recorded by Dupla Ouro e Prata in 1958, which made fun of Japanese immigrant cleaners, became a huge hit among Brazilians.[47]

Sumu Arata (b. 1915), as a single man, moved to the city in 1947 to open a store selling men's ready-to-wear clothes in Pinheiros after he and his two brothers had co-owned a business selling fabrics in the town of Cafelandía of the Noroeste line for ten years. Masayuki Mizuno (b. 1924), a prewar child immigrant (1933) from Nagoya City, Gifu prefecture, moved from the countryside to the city on his own in 1947, when he and thirty-six other young men of Japanese descent applied for two openings at the newly established *makegumi* newspaper *Paulista Shimbun*. Mizuno was surprised to learn that most of the other applicants were Brazilian junior and senior high school graduates, who were having a hard time in their job search since Brazilians refused to hire any "Japanese" for fear of the *kachi-make* conflicts. Mizuo was hired, despite his lack of formal education.[48]

Yasuto Shigeoka, as a second son, had attempted to move to the city at the age of eighteen, but his older brother, Kasuke, did not allow him to do so because his family needed Shigeoka's labor in agriculture. Shigeoka finally moved to the city in 1947 at the age of twenty-two and took up a two-year apprenticeship with a Spanish carpenter. From 1947 to 1955, he lived in a Japanese *pensão* (boarding house) named Asahi in Liberdade, owned by the Higakis. All thirty of the Asahi residents were "Japanese" men from the countryside, and 80 percent of them were learning vocational skills as mechanics. After Shigeoka made it as a carpenter, Mrs. Higaki asked him to marry one of her Nisei daughters and run the business with one of her sons; she offered 600 contos, but he did not hesitate to decline her proposal, because, as he says, "My father used to say no real man should marry into his wife's family [as *yōshi*] if he had three bottles of rice bran [to feed himself]." Such a marriage would have dishonored Shigeoka's family. In 1955, after working in the city for eight years, Shigeoka finally married Mineko, a childhood Nisei friend from Prudente Presidente, and in the same year the rest of the Shigeokas (his father, Kasuke, and his wife with their eight children) moved to the city to live with them. Soon Yasuto and Kasuke Shigeoka opened their carpentry business.[49]

Like Tsuyoshi Mizumoto, Ikesaki, and Shigeoka, young adult single immigrant men without any capital tended to move to the city on their own to look for better economic opportunities. Photography was another popular occupation among Japanese immigrant men in the city. Following his younger brother, Yoshiaki Umezaki (b. 1923) moved from the Noroeste zone to São Paulo City in December 1949 and ran his own photo studio until his retirement in 1988. Yasumi Nakayama moved from Colônia Tiete to the city in 1951 with his aging father and three younger sisters, after his mother's death from breast cancer (1949); her treatment had exhausted all of their resources. In the city, Nakayama worked as a typesetter for a few Japanese-language newspapers, but it did not pay him well enough. His younger sisters worked as seamstresses at home. Nakayama met his Nisei future wife, Michiko (b. 1934), a friend of one of his younger sisters, and they got married in 1962. With three children to support, Nakayama ran a photo studio from 1966 to 1987, while Michiko worked as a seamstress at home.[50]

Prewar child immigrant women seldom moved to the city on their own, especially before the end of the war. Shizu Saito had married in 1940 and moved to the city in 1941, with her husband and her newborn baby boy. Shizu's marriage to Hiroshi was arranged in a hurry by Hiroshi's older brother-in-law, as Hiroshi's mother, Michie, was dying of cancer. On their immigrant ship, one of Hiroshi's older sisters had fallen in love with a young immigrant man from Shizuoka, Shizu's home prefecture, and they had married upon arriving in Brazil. Through such kinship and prefectural networks, Shizu was chosen as Hiroshi's wife. She was eighteen, and he twenty-two, and they met in March 1940 and got married three months later. Their first child was born in April 1941, and the family moved to the city within three months later, as Hiroshi found employment at Hachiya

Shōkai. Michie died soon afterward, and in 1943, Hiroshi's father, Torao, and younger brother moved in with the Saitos in the Ipiranga district, saying that they could not make a living in agriculture without Hiroshi's labor. Their arrival made the family finances more difficult to manage, and Shizu, who was pregnant with her second child, had to take care of Torao at home until he died of cancer.[51]

It was important for young Japanese immigrant women to receive proper bridal training, which reflected a family's position among the Japanese once they had settled down as independent farmers. Toshi Yamane (b. 1921), who had arrived in Brazil at the age two, finished her four-year primary education in the countryside and moved to the city in 1937 to work as a live-in maid for a wealthy *fazendeiro* (coffee plantation owner) family. That was because her older half-brother (1909–1962) from her mother's previous marriage wanted her to gain "education, such as sewing skills." Having completed his middle school education in Japan, he had been hired as a teacher for Japanese immigrant children on a coffee plantation, where he got to know its Brazilian *fazendeiro* and his German Brazilian wife and eventually asked them to hire Yamane at their home in the city so that she "would be educated, such as in sewing." Thanks to her employers' support, Yamane started at a *genário* (junior high school) at the age of sixteen and even completed *colégio* (senior high school) in the early 1940s. She wanted to attend college or become a nun but, as "the oldest child of the Yamanes," she felt responsible for her family's finances. She found a job at a French agrochemical company that was looking for a bilingual secretary for its business selling insecticides, livestock medicine, and vaccines for cows and chickens to Japanese farmers. Back in the 1940s and 1950s, all of Yamane's coworkers were white Brazilians; very few Japanese Brazilians worked in offices. Never married, Yamane worked at the company for thirty years until her retirement in 1980; she was able to purchase a large house for her family in the 1950s and to support her parents and three younger brothers.[52]

After the war, sewing became an important trade for Japanese women. In 1947, when her birth family moved to Arujá, São Paulo, for suburban agriculture, Tsuruko Kikuchi was sent to São Paulo City to live with her older sister-in-law's younger sister to learn how to sew while working as an unpaid assistant. Her mistress was "a highly paid seamstress who worked from morning to night, without doing any cooking." Kikuchi states, "She had no other seamstresses and did all the work on her own. I was her assistant. Eventually I learned how to make patterns and finish sewing every kind of cloth. She gave me a certificate in sewing." Afterward Kikuchi worked as a full-time maid for one of her shipmates, a big business owner, who taught her all the necessary housekeeping skills. A year later, Kikuchi's marriage was arranged with one of the men who were working for her employer's business. She was twenty-three years old, and her husband, also a prewar child immigrant, was thirty. After the birth of her three children, Kikuchi saved enough money to buy a sewing machine and worked as a seamstress at home, with her husband often away as a *viajante*: "I had to go to a factory to take orders and brought them back home. I learned how to embroider blouses and made good money. I used to sew from 11 P.M. to 1 A.M. every night."[53]

Haruko Fujiotani, another prewar child immigrant woman without any formal schooling (introduction), began to work at a ceramics factory in Mauá, São Paulo, when she was thirteen or fourteen years old. After a few years her family sent her to Santo André, São Paulo, to work as a live-in maid for a Japanese family with a cleaning business, because her maternal grandmother insisted that she needed to learn the trade of sewing. Fujitani worked on the promise that she would be taught how to sew by a member of her employer's family in exchange for her "free" labor. She stayed there for a year and went back to live with her family, where she began to work as a seamstress with a sewing machine that her maternal uncle bought for her. Fujitani worked as a seamstress to support her birth family until she married at the age of twenty-three.[54]

In the early 1950s, Sumiko Mizumoto began to get involved in new activities as a tanka poet and a member of Esperança Fujinkai, through both of which she came to know many other prewar child immigrants of similar backgrounds. Of course, her new activities as a full-time home-maker were made possible by her husband's financial successes as a busi-nessman. Casa Mizumoto continued to do well in Pinheiros, and in 1958, Tsuyoshi opened his second store in Liberdade. In the following year he founded Brazilian Branch of Shochiku Film Company (of Japan) and opened a movie theater, Cine Nippon. He also became an executive of Shochiku Film do Brasil, which distributed Japan's Shochiku movies all over South America. That enabled Mizumoto to travel to Japan with Tsuyoshi a dozen times, during which Sumiko enjoyed watching *kabuki* (traditional Japanese theater) in Tokyo and sightseeing in Kyoto and Nara.[55] Tsuyoshi's business thrived as São Paulo City's new "Japan Town" (which was to be officially renamed *bairro oriental* in 1975) of Liberdade developed after the opening of Cine Niteroi (1953), a Japanese movie house with a hotel, bar, and restaurant by Kazuyoshi Tanaka (1909–1979), a prewar immigrant from Ehime prefec-ture, who had become a very successful grain trader in São Paulo.[56]

Prewar child immigrants wrote passionately about their experiences and identities in haiku, tanka, and other forms of traditional Japanese poetry, as well as essays and fiction in Japanese. Mizumoto chose tanka, a traditional Japanese poem of thirty-one syllables, as an important means of literary self-expression. Kiyotani, another prewar child immigrant, began to compose tanka in his midteens when he was in the countryside working on the plantations. During the 1930s, some of Kiyotani's early tanka poems were published in *Nippak Shinbum,* a newspaper owned by Rokurō Kōyama. According to Kiyotani, prewar immigrants with limited Japanese language education and rather poor vocabulary in Japanese found it easy to use tanka poetry to describe their daily life, because of its familiar rhythm of five-seven-five-five-seven syllables and the "shortness" of thirty-one syllables. In the late 1920s and early 1930s, there was a Japanese literary boom, including tanka writing, among the prewar immigrants, which culminated in the foundation of the journal *Yashiju* (Palm Trees) in 1938.[57] *Yashiju* has remained the only Brazilian journal specializing in tanka until the present day. Like Kiyotani, Mizumoto and her Sato siblings began to compose tanka in the countryside. In the city, Mizumoto's tanka teacher was Yoshio Takemoto (1911–1983), a prewar immigrant from Okayama prefecture (1930) who cofounded *Colônia Bungaku* in 1965 with Japanese anthropologist Takashi Maeyama (b. 1933).

In 1952, Mizumoto joined Esperança Fujinkai: "I wanted to learn something new. I began to take cooking lessons at Fujinkai—Brazilian, Italian, and Chinese. Then one day I was asked to join the administration." Mizumoto wrote in 1975,

> We, the quasi-Nisei, have spent many more years here in Brazil than in Japan, where we were born. I think we all have done much mental self-training for many years in order to accept all customs in this country. Yet we have always been holding on to our Japanese thinking. Furthermore we can never leave the world of the Japanese language. . . . Most quasi-Niseis have struggled to live in a place without much sunlight. Following our Issei parents [to Brazil], we were thrown into another culture with various other ethnic groups, where we have lived without much social skill or personal freedom.[58]

At that time most of the eight hundred or so Esperança Fujinkai members were quasi-Nisei women in their fifties who had become mothers-in-law and, even as widows, chose not to live with their married Nisei children or their families. Many such quasi-Nisei women used the association's meetings and gatherings as opportunities to speak the Japanese language with other quasi-Nisei members as much and as freely as possible. Thus they enjoyed their Japanese ways of thinking, separated from the Portuguese-speaking world to which their Brazilian-born children and young Sansei grandchildren belonged.[59]

One wonders who have identified themselves as quasi-Niseis. How is the term itself defined? And in what historical context has the term been used? Hiroshi Saito, who arrived in Brazil at the age of fourteen, identified himself as a quasi-Nisei. According to him, the quasi-Niseis arriving in Brazil between the ages of six or seven and fifteen or sixteen were treated as Japanese even though they did not possess any Japanese consciousness; they are "neither Isseis nor Niseis" but "those who exist between the two generations and connect them with each other."[60] Another self-identified quasi-Nisei, Kiyotani maintains that the quasi-Niseis share the "eternal feelings of hunger" for Japan and Japanese culture, so that they have managed to perfect their reading and writing in Japanese, often without attending schools in Brazil.[61] In short, not all prewar child immigrants can be classified as quasi-Niseis and/or identify themselves as such. For instance, Kokei Uehana (b. 1927), former USP professor of engineering and Bunkyo president (2003–2009), is well known for always identifying himself as "a Brazilian who was born in Japan"; he was born in Okinawa and arrived as his older brother's *yobiyose* immigrant in Brazil in 1936 at the age of nine.[62]

In 1970, Bunkyo's newsletter, *Colônia,* hosted a roundtable discussion on the quasi-Niseis titled "The Buried Generation Speaks." The panelists were six self-identified quasi-Niseis in their forties and fifties—Atsushi Imoto, Masuichi Omi, Kiyoshi Kato, Chikako Hironaka, Yoshiro Fujita, and Kinuko Fujiwara—and the panel was chaired by another and older self-identified quasi-Nisei, Tomoo Handa (1906–1996). This was a great line-up of the prominent Japanese immigrant intellectuals at the beginning of the 1970s. Except for Kato, a graduate of the Universidade Presbiteriana Mackenzie (Mackenzie Presbyterian University) in architecture, all of the participants had little formal education in Brazil but had taught themselves to achieve the highest level of language skills in Japanese not only in speaking but also in reading and writing. Masuichi Omi, a well-to-do merchant in São Paulo's municipal market, later served as the seventh Bunkyo president (1983–1990). The two women, Hironaka and Fujiwara, both married to prominent Japanese immigrant men, were listed as a poet and a certified professor in Japanese flower arrangement, respectively.[63] The *Colônia* editor Susumu Miyao (1930–2016) also attended the discussion as "an observer." Miyao was the second son of prominent Rikkokai immigrant Atsushi Miyao

(1892–1971) and a *kihaku* Nisei who was educated in Japan (1940–1953), with a bachelor of arts in philosophy from Shinshu University.

At their discussion, the panelists differentiated quasi-Niseis first, from other child immigrants who arrived in Brazil before they were nine years old; second, from the Niseis of the same generation, who grew up in the same Japanese environment with them; third, from other child immigrants who were immersed in the Brazilian cultural environment immediately upon arrival; and lastly, from postwar child immigrants, who seemed to be adjusting more easily to Brazilian life. Being forced to move to Brazil after they attained the age of discretion, the quasi-Niseis "share a common longing for Japan," said Kiyotani.[64] The panelists acknowledged that they all once suffered from inferiority complexes as quasi-Niseis but concluded that they may well be "more Japanese than Isseis," while "understanding both Japanese and Brazilian ways."[65] Miyao asked whether the panelists were representative of "the buried generation"; they were the elite quasi-Niseis, who had been "elevated to the highest ranks," whereas many others in the countryside had not even learned how to express themselves in Japanese or Portuguese.[66] Imoto, as "the least elite of all of the panelists," responded to Miyao that quasi-Niseis were "sacrificed for the sake of their families," without being integrated into Brazilian society. Therefore, all quasi-Niseis suffered from the "invisible sense of loss," whether they became successful or not.[67]

In 1975, Maeyama published a critical essay titled "Colônia's literature" in *Colônia Bungaku*. He characterized the journal's self-identified quasi-Nisei authors as "victims without victimizers" and maintained that their literature had never been one of resistance or accusation but "of suffering and patience," which failed to "transform a writer's fate into his/her privilege."[68] Maeyama's understanding of quasi-Nisei expressions of victimhood seems to be accurate, but he missed the most important point about why they wrote in Japanese and made so much effort to acquire the language. Rather than creating their own genre, they wanted to prove themselves "true" Japanese, or even "more" Japanese than the Japanese, to those who had ridiculed them as "those who grew up in Brazil" or "Brazilian heads."

By 1970, some quasi-Niseis had been able to obtain social positions to express themselves. Prewar male child immigrants now in their forties and fifties, with proficiency in Japanese, had replaced the aging prewar adult immigrant men in the important positions of the "*colônia*"—agricultural cooperatives (Kiyotani), banks (Hironaka's husband Jin), and organizations and associations (Handa), as well as in São Paulo's municipal market (Omi), where Japanese remained the lingua franca. Ethnic Japanese businesses in

Liberdade continued to thrive. In accordance with their husbands' social ascension, some prewar female child immigrants, most of whom were full-time homemakers, found opportunities to make themselves socially visible as wives and mothers through writing and women's social activities among Japanese immigrants in the city. Bunkyo's newsletter, *Colônia*, published an article on aging prewar immigrants' retirement plans in 1961, and then in 1965 a series of articles concerning the common problems of aging Isseis.[69] In 1975, Rōkuren was established in São Paulo City for aging prewar immigrants who had finally retired with some financial resources to enjoy themselves in their last years.

By 1970, it had become much easier for Japanese immigrants to travel from Brazil to Japan. For one, the number of new Japanese companies operating in Brazil peaked during Brazil's economic boom in the early 1970s: 43 in 1972, 72 in 1973, and 52 in 1974.[70] Such increase of capital investment in Brazil created more commercial traffic between Brazil and Japan by air, and air travel became more affordable for upper-middle-class Japanese Brazilians. In 1968, Varig, Brazil's national airline, started its first direct flight to Japan and aired its first TV commercial targeting Japanese immigrants traveling back home, using the theme of Urashima Taro, a popular Japanese folktale hero, returning to Japan, with a jingle sung in Portuguese by Rosa Miyake, a Nisei woman singer/TV personality. The 1970 World Exposition in Osaka provided an additional incentive for prewar immigrants traveling to Japan to pay their respects to their ancestors' graves for the first time since they had immigrated to Brazil years earlier. That year, Japan Air Lines began to charter special flights for such travelers, although it did not establish direct flights between Tokyo and São Paulo until 1978.[71] The "visiting-Japan-boom" dramatically increased the number of Brazilian visitors in Japan: 3,042 in 1968, 7,949 in 1970, and 8,067 in 1973.[72]

Chikako Hironaka (1922–1998), mentioned above, traveled to Japan with her husband in 1974 for the first time since her immigration in 1934. Visiting the homeland that she had left at the age of nine, Hironaka surprised herself by "constantly missing the *colônia*," while referring to Japan as "a place, which I may visit again, but where I will never live." Yet Hironaka found herself becoming increasingly attracted to things Japanese as she got older, thinking that prewar quasi-Niseis were reputed to be "more Japanese than the Japanese in Japan." Her quasi-Nisei friends agreed with her in wanting to go to Japan as many times as possible for the money they could have spent to travel to Europe; their "hunger" for Japan turned out to be much more complicated than Isseis' homesickness or Niseis' longing for Japan. Hironaka had two sons who were born in the early 1940s and had grown up in the city, and both attended the USP School of Medicine in the 1960s. In 1976, one of them decided to marry a college-educated white woman; although Hironaka knew he had been dating the woman, the decision still shocked her and made her recognize him as a Brazilian.[73]

Hironaka's sentiment was surely shared by Mizumoto, who, after having traveled to Japan a dozen times, stated, "I feel very Japanese whenever I go to Japan." In April 2001, Mizumoto participated in Kenren's "visiting home" tour to Japan. To begin with, she and other participants in the tour visited with *dekassegui* Brazilians in Oizumi and Nagano. While others enjoyed sightseeing in Kyoto and Nara, Mizumoto flew on to Okinawa for three days of sightseeing on her own. She rejoined the others to attend the ceremony in Kobe on April 28, 2001, for the inauguration of the Japanese Emigrants Monument, which features a married couple and their young son, all dressed in Western clothes, happily departing for Brazil. The boy is pointing in the direction of Brazil and a bright future. Kobe's city council welcomed all of the Japanese Brazilian guests with a luncheon and a harbor tour. The special ceremony, which started with a whistle at 5:55 P.M., the time at which the *Kasato Maru* had departed for Brazil, moved Mizumoto "a great deal." Thinking that this might be their last visit to Japan, Mizumoto and a friend visited Lake Kawaguchi to see Mount Fuji at sunrise before moving on to Tokyo to join others.[74]

In June 2001, Mizumoto talked passionately about Esperança Fujinkai. She never used the term "quasi-Nisei"; instead she made a distinction between Issei and Nisei members:

> Our annual membership fee is low, and when it peaked, we had one thousand members in São Paulo. Then depression started and we lost members. Also, many Isseis are dead. Many Niseis have joined also. Our new president [Misue Kumagai] is a Nisei. Niseis are well educated and have their own community. Isseis did not have opportunities to be educated; they get by with the Japanese language only. Niseis feel sorry for not being able to speak Japanese. Yes, they get along with Isseis. Isseis are old now and have backed off. In that sense they are very Japanese. Isseis make *salgadinhos* [snacks] for Esperança and sell them at a weekly bazaar. Such homemade *salgadinhos* sell very well, and the profits are donated to various institutions for charity. This way, Isseis are still making a significant contribution to Fujinkai. Niseis know that the association would not work without the Issei members.[75]

Esperança Fujinkai itself had changed. By 1998, its membership had dropped further, to 670.[76] Under a new Nisei president, Nisei members had been

Japanese Emigrants Monument with the inscription "From Kobe to the World, Departure by Sea, Full of Hope," Kobe, Japan, July 24, 2010. Photo by author.

recently recruited. By then almost all of the prewar immigrant members were those who had arrived as children. In other words, "quasi-Nisei" no longer worked as a collective social category/label in contrast to their parents' generation. That, of course, does not mean that quasi-Nisei identity has lost importance at a personal level. Hironaka, for instance, continued to express her quasi-Nisei identity in her tanka and essays, even in her last years. In her last essay (1993), she wrote, "All of us who are called quasi-Niseis share the same inner conflict and deep-seated grudge after having been transplanted in a foreign land as young plants without wanting to and then having been forced to be rooted in the ground as Japanese seeds."[77]

Even though it is no longer in daily use, the term "quasi-Nisei" has remained important to many prewar child immigrants who are now in their eighties and nineties, such as Fumio Oura (b. 1924), to express their Japanese identity in Brazil.[78]

Conclusion

The year 2008 was very special for many prewar child immigrants. It turned out to be a rewarding year in particular for Saito, whose late husband, Hiroshi Saito, the first MHIJB director and USP professor, was honored on many special public occasions for his contributions to the studies of Japanese immigrants in Brazil. On the morning of June 20, 2008, the *bairro oriental* of Liberdade was packed with those eagerly waiting to welcome Crown Princess Naruhito and holding national flags of Brazil and Japan. A dozen of the elderly were representing Rōkuren. The prince was scheduled to visit Bunkyo first to hand an imperial donation to Koei Uehara, Bunkyo's president, for the MHIJB, and then to parade in a car escorted by the federal police through Rua Galvão Bueno to Praça da Liberdade, where a group of elderly Japanese immigrants were seated as special guests for the occasion. Saito and her good friend Alice Sachiko Shimizu (b. 1922), also a longtime Esperança Fujinkai member, were very exited to see the prince up close at the front of Bunkyo after having waiting there for an hour or so. Mizumoto was there also, escorted by her "Brazilian" maid, but her dementia had gotten far worse and she could no longer recognize many of those she used to know.

Early in the afternoon of July 3, 2008, I stopped by Esperança Fujinkai in the Bunkyo building to bid farewell to Saito and Shimizu, knowing that they were scheduled to attend the monthly directorial meeting. That was where I had met them for the first time in January 1998. To my surprise, Saito did not sit with Shimizu at the meeting; in fact, they sat on opposite sides of the conference room. Next to Saito was another longtime Issei member, Chisako Ohta, whom Saito had known for years without realizing until recently that they had been shipmates. As it turned out, members were following the association's unwritten rule: "Isseis and Niseis never sit together at our monthly meetings. We have always made two separate lines," as Saito explained to me. Saito and Simizu were the same age, but, unlike Saito, Shimizu is a Nisei who was born in rural São Paulo and grew up in Assai, Paraná. That was the last time I saw Saito. Saito lived alone and independently in her own home until she collapsed of a severe stroke, which killed her on the following day, March 11, 2009. Mizumoto passed away on August 23, 2011. Both long outlived their successful husbands. After all, Mizumoto and Saito lived honorably among the Japanese in São Paulo as the respected widows of prominent Japanese immigrant men, as well as the proud mothers of their successful Brazilian children.

Chapter Three

NISEIS AND THEIR BRAZILIAN IDENTITY

I think my generation of Niseis had more familiarity with the Isseis. There are the so-called quasi-Niseis between the Isseis and us, the Niseis. We the Niseis also tried to distance ourselves from the Isseis at the same time. Shigeaki Ueki and Kazuo Watanabe have come back to the Nikkei society after having distanced themselves for many years. Back in our old days the Nikkeis had been perceived as a pure cyst. After the end of the war, especially after Japan grew economically, people became less prejudiced against the Japanese. The younger generation of Niseis did not have to fight in the way we had to.

—*Iossuke Tanaka, a retired architect, 2008*[1]

Japanese Brazilians are stereotyped as "honest," "responsible," and, most characteristically, "guaranteed,"[2] which greatly concerned Iossuke Tanaka (1933–2009), a retired Nisei architect. On June 25, 2008, I met with Tanaka for his second interview, when he gave me a copy of a newspaper article titled "'Garantido' Shōkō" (Small Thoughts on "Guaranteed") by Masayoshi Norichika, a prewar child immigrant who arrived in Brazil in 1934. Norichika maintains that "Japanese" and "guaranteed" were used interchangeably in rural São Paulo, because prewar Japanese immigrants, who were not used to Brazilian culture and customs, would ask local Brazilians whether their contracts or appointments were indeed "guaranteed," and Brazilians began to make fun of the Japanese for repeating the question. Therefore "guaranteed" originally referred to those who were suspicious of Brazilians, inflexible, or resistant to acculturating or assimilating.[3] According to Tanaka, there is another origin of the term: when prewar Japanese immigrant farmers peddled their vegetables and their Brazilian

68

customers would ask if their commodities were "fresh and all right," they would reply, "It's guaranteed." Thus Brazilians began to say, "The Japanese say 'guaranteed' for everything." It was always a "term of contempt," and Tanaka and his generation of Niseis were constantly insulted as "guaranteed." It frustrated him greatly that many Japanese descendants regarded it as a compliment, without knowing the history.[4]

Many Niseis of Tanaka's generation, who were born in the 1930s and 1940s, grew up among the Japanese in the countryside and moved to the city during and after the war for higher education and/or urban employment. How did prewar immigrant parents perceive their children? What were the Niseis expected to achieve for themselves and/or for their families? With whom did they associate? How did they choose their marriage partners? What did Tanaka and some other older Niseis "fight" against and/or for? And how? How have they come to identify themselves? And how have gender and class determined their experiences and self-perceptions?

According to Hiroshi Saito, the generational distinction between Isseis and Niseis was rarely used by the Japanese in Brazil before the end of the war, as prewar immigrant parents, who identified themselves as overseas Japanese in Brazil, regarded their children, including those born in Brazil, solely as Japanese.[5] Yet prewar immigrants referred to their children as *Burajiru sodachi* (those who grew up in Brazil) and *Burajiru umare* (Brazilian-born), both of whom were perceived together pejoratively as "Brazilian heads" in contrast to "Japanese heads." Accordingly, until the 1930s, the term "Nisei" had also been used by prewar immigrants to refer to the "Brazilianized and therefore ruined."[6] That does not mean that Niseis identified themselves in the same way they were perceived by Isseis. Furthermore, Niseis themselves never constituted a homogeneous group; their individual positions reflected their Issei parents' educational backgrounds in Japan and their families' socioeconomic positions in Brazil.

By the early 1930s, Japanese and Japanese Brazilian students enrolled in middle schools and above had emerged in São Paulo City and found themselves caught between Brazilian nationalism under President Getúlio Vargas and imperial Japan's aggressive militarism and ultranationalism. In 1934, Japanese-descendant students founded their own voluntary association, São Paulo Gakusei Renmei / Liga Estudantina Nipo-Brasileira de São Paulo (League of Japanese Brazilian Students in São Paulo). In 1934, as anti-Japanese sentiment peaked and the Brazilian government severely restricted Japanese immigration (chapter 1), the consulate general of Japan in São Paulo started a Japanese-government-sponsored fellowship program to recruit Niseis who were Brazilian citizens or naturalized Brazilian citizens, with the intention to transform them into "the good Japanese" in Brazil. The Japanese government hoped that they would participate in Brazilian politics on behalf of Japan, as they were elite Brazilian citizens. Naturally, Gakusei Renmei members were selected preferentially for such fellowships.[7]

With financial support from the consulate general, Gakusei Renmei hosted speech contests, organized sports and cultural events, and published its monthly newsletter, *Gakusei,* in Portuguese, as well as the periodical *Gakuyu/O Amigo dos Estudantes de São Paulo* twice a year, mainly in Japanese and partly in Portuguese.[8] These two publications were discontinued in August 1938 under the Estado Novo's stricter control of publications by foreigners, and Gakusei Renmei began to publish *Tradição* as of June 1939. There were 15 founding members, all men, and the majority were Japanese-born and had arrived in Brazil in their early teens. Those who established and joined this student association, both Japanese-born and Brazilian-born, identified themselves as *dai*-Nisei ("the second generation"), regardless of birthplace, by contrast to *dai*-Issei (the first generation). The association's members grew from 105 in October 1934 to 141 (including only 20 women) in June 1935, and they constituted around 90 percent of all "Japanese" students in the city.[9] As of 1936, 233 out of nearly 300 Japanese-descendant students studying in the city held membership in the association.[10] There was no woman among the founding members in 1934, but women participated in the association, and some even became officeholders. In its seven-year history, no woman became president, but three women, all Brazilian-born, were elected as vice presidents from 1938 to 1940.[11]

Before the outbreak of the war, the Niseis held dual nationality, and in the eyes of imperial Japan they were all subjects of the emperor. This does not mean that all Niseis perceived themselves as such. In fact, Gakusei Renmei's *dai*-Nisei members, both Brazilian-born and Japanese-born, identified themselves first and foremost as Brazilians. This is clearly exemplified by José Yamashiro (1913–2005), a main editor for *Gakusei* and *Transição.* Born to Okinawan immigrant parents in Santos, Yamashiro, as a proud Brazilian citizen, had fought in the Constitutionalist War in 1932. Furthermore, as a USP student in chemistry, despite his father Ryukiti's strong wish, Yamashiro refused to apply for the Japanese government's fellowship program. That was because the program's political agenda did not go with his Brazilian identity—even though he could barely afford to pay for his college education and eventually dropped out of college.[12]

In 1935, Cassio Kenro Shimamoto, Gakusei Renmei's president and one of its founders, published in *Gakusei* an essay in Portuguese, which was published in *Gakuyu* in Japanese translation in the following year. In his essay, Shimamoto wrote, "How could we love the unknown country [Japan]? We love Brazil. That is because Brazil is our homeland."[13] Shimamoto's statement was taken as an unforgivable offense to imperial Japan by the consulate general of Japan in São Paulo. Accused of being disrespectful to the emperor, Shimamoto and his administration were forced to resign. Furthermore, all of the fellowship students were advised to leave Gakusei Renmei immediately. Most of them chose their fellowships over Gakusei Renmei, but many would regain their Renmei memberships later.[14] As of 1937, under Vargas' Estado Novo, which severely restricted and almost prohibited rural education in foreign languages, a greater number of the *dai*-Nisei youth were expected to arrive in the city for better formal education. Thus in September 1938, Gakusei Renmei published in *Gakuyu* a special guide to six Japanese dormitories in the city for *dai*-Nisei college students.[15] Around the same time, with the increase of Nisei students in the city, Gakusei Renmei's leadership and membership shifted from Japanese-born to Brazilian-born *dai*-Nisei, who were also called "pure Niseis."

In 1938, a new journal in Japanese titled *Bunka* (Culture) published a roundtable discussion with five self-identified *dai*-Nisei men (three Japanese-born, including Tomoo Handa, and two Brazilian-born Gakusei Renmei members, João Sussumu Hirata and José Yamashiro), held at Tomiya, a traditional Japanese restaurant in São Paulo City. The meeting was chaired by two Issei male intellectuals, Zenpachi Ando and Kikuo Furuno, and observed by a Brazilian, Mario Miranda of USP Law School, as a "student of Japanese culture." While praising traditional Japanese culture, the *dai*-Nisei all agreed with the Issei intellectuals about the *dai*-Issei's "lack of cultural life" or "low standard of culture" in Brazil. Interestingly, Handa Tomoo, who was to become a prominent quasi-Nisei intellectual after the war (chapter 2), identified himself as a *dai*-Nisei during the 1930s, and, together with two other prewar child immigrants and the two Niseis mentioned above, "observed the *dai*-Issei in almost the same way as Brazilians did."[16]

Gakusei Renmei was eventually dissolved at the outbreak of the war in December 1941, when it still had fifty-six full members.[17] In the same year, João Sussumu Hirata (1914–1974), who had been elected as the league's seventh president in 1939, graduated from USP Law School and departed on the last prewar Japanese ship to Japan as a Japanese government fellowship student at the University of Tokyo. Hirata turned out to be one of some fifty young Niseis, both men and women, stuck in Japan during the war. Among them fifteen men were drafted by the Japanese government, and six died in the war.[18] Hirata, who was not drafted, could not return to Brazil until

1951, by when *dai*-Nisei identity had disappeared and been split into (pure) Niseis and quasi-Niseis according to birthplace, with the rapid growth of a (pure) Nisei generation after the termination of prewar Japanese immigration. Tanaka belonged to this Nisei generation, who had to survive the hard times of the 1940s and 1950s as "children of the Japanese" in São Paulo.

On April 18, 1932, the Tanakas, from Hiba province, Hiroshima prefecture, departed Kobe on the *Rio de Janeiro Maru,* which arrived in Santos on June 2, 1932. The family was composed of Takekazu (b. 1900) and Sadako (b. 1908), their son Kaoru (b. 1926), and Sadako's fourteen-year-old brother, Hideo Yokoyama (b. 1917). Accordingly, the family labor force was calculated as "three adults and a quarter" on the passenger list. The family had a one-agricultural-year *colono* contract with Plinio Janqueira and his brother as the *fazendeiros* of Fazenda Santa Cecilia near the train station of São Joaquim da Barra of the Mogiana line. Tanaka was born there in 1933 as the second oldest of the family but the oldest of its five Nisei children. Upon completing the *colono* contract, the Tanakas moved to Androdina of the Noroeste line, and then to Mirandópolis to work as *colonos* for a Japanese immigrant *fazendeiro* on Fazenda Matuda; there were already many Japanese *fazendas* in the Noroeste zone.[19] In 1939, when Tanaka was six years old, the family moved to Moji das Cruzes, São Paulo, for his formal schooling. Kaoru had begun his elementary school education in 1937 and therefore was left behind to complete it in care of Hideo Baba (1908–2000), a prominent Rikkokai immigrant from Fukushima.

By the time Tanaka began to attend a *grupo escolar* in Moji in 1939 or 1940, Japanese language education had already been banned under Vargas. In the countryside, the law was enforced strictly, but the rule was loosely applied in suburbs such as Moji, and therefore the Japanese there managed to maintain an informal Japanese school with twenty to thirty children until the war began, according to Tanaka. Tanaka attended the school for a while until his family moved again to start over as independent suburban farmers. Eventually his family moved to the town of Moji, where Tanaka's father worked as a vegetable trader in its municipal market. During this time, Tanaka had a Japanese tutor who taught the Japanese language to a group of five or six children. But his father's middleman business did not go well, because of the war, and he moved his family to Suzano, where he engaged in suburban agriculture, an egg ranch, and charcoal making. Concerned about the poor quality of formal education in the countryside, his father sent Tanaka alone back to the town of Moji for his primary education; it had a newly established *shōgakusha* (Japanese children's dormitory for study), where twenty-five students were taught the Japanese language and were forced to memorize the Imperial Rescript on Education by the Meiji emperor. In 1945, Tanaka finished his four-year elementary school education in Moji das Cruzes.[20]

Tanaka's old friend Atsushi Yamauchi, Bunkyo's eighth and first Nisei president (1991–1999), was born in 1931 as the oldest child in his family in the town of Araçatuba, São Paulo, but grew up in northern Paraná. His father, Yasufusa Yamauchi, a young schoolteacher from Fukushima, arrived in Brazil as a single Rikkokai immigrant, with a dream of becoming a successful *fazendeiro*. Unfortunately, São Paulo's declining coffee economy directly affected the immigrant life of the Yamauchis and many others. Many immigrants in São Paulo were forced to shift from coffee to cotton production, but others, including the Yamauchis, moved to northern Paraná for coffee cultivation. In Paraná, Yamauchi's father bought a plot of virgin woods in Rolândia, twenty-five kilometers from Londrina. He did all of the necessary deforestation on his own in their first settlement, and that damaged his health; he hired *camaradas,* and after paying their wages there was no extra money left for the family. Two younger brothers were born but died during these difficult years. By the time Yamauchi began his schooling in 1941, his family's finances were looking up. A baby girl was born when he was nine years old, and he babysat her every day after school, while his father taught him Japanese at night. In northern Paraná, there were few "Japanese" children attending even *grupos escolares,* as their labor was needed for farming. Yasufusa Yamauchi was exceptional in valuing the education of his children more highly than anything else.[21]

What about Nisei women's formal education in rural Brazil? Tiyoko Oba, born in 1928 as the fourth of five children, finished primary school in Parada de Taipas, São Paulo, during World War II, when Japanese language education was banned. None of the five children in her family was able to receive any higher education in the countryside. Yukie Yano was born in 1931 to the Uedas, an immigrant couple from Kochi prefecture, who eventually settled in Cotia, São Paulo, for potato farming. Yano was born there as the oldest of six children and attended Cotia Nihonjin Shogakko (Japanese Elementary School of Cotia) until the fourth grade (1938–1942). Eiko Kanazawa (1932–2010) was born in Malíria, São Paulo, and grew up in Bastos, where her mother and stepfather engaged in sericulture. She attended schools up to the third grade of *grupo escolar* and the second grade of a Japanese language school, which was then closed because of the war. During the war, Kanazawa, her mother, and her younger sister moved to the city to operate a cleaning business with her godmother in the Santo Amaro district of São Paulo City.[22]

Generally speaking, Tanaka's generation of Niseis, who were born in the countryside, had a much better chance to receive formal Brazilian primary schooling than prewar child immigrants, many of whom were counted as workers immediately after immigration (chapter 2). As Brazilian citizens, most of the Niseis, both men and women, whom I met in São Paulo City had attended *grupos escolares*. However, for a long time rural areas and even suburbs of São Paulo City had no schools above the four-year primary education. Only Niseis who grew up in Bastos, such as Watanabe (b. 1936) and Ueki (b. 1935), had the advantage of finishing the Brazilian junior high school education (*genário*) that was established there in 1939, and had a much better chance to receive a high school or college education in the city.[23] Therefore it was inevitable for Nisei children to move to the city for a vocational or junior high school education once they completed their primary education in the countryside. Some Nisei men were able to do so, but Nisei women were expected to marry and have families.

Upon completing his primary education in Moji das Cruzes in 1945, Tanaka moved directly to São Paulo City on his own; he passed a competitive entrance examination to attend a state technical high school for men: Escola Técnica Estadual "Getúlio Vargas" (São Paulo State Technical School "Getúlio Vargas," or GV), whose curriculum comprised a four-year junior and a three-year senior high school education. From the time of its establishment (1911), GV was known for its willingness to take immigrant children and had its own dormitory and cafeteria for students. As a state school, GV offered all of its students not only full tuition fellowships but also free lunch and a snack, as well as small allowances. Tanaka was, in fact, one of many young Nisei men starting the school in 1945; some 70 percent of Tanaka's class was of Japanese ancestry. The rest of his class consisted of "whites of European ancestries, largely Italians." It is at GV that Tanaka met Yamauchi, who had just arrived in the city in December 1945 upon graduating from the *grupo escolar* in Paraná. Having suffered greatly from health problems, Yamauchi's father believed his son had better learn a trade to make a living.[24] In the 1950s there were already Niseis on the GV faculty, including Riki Miyao, himself a GV graduate (1947) and the oldest son of Atsushi Miyao.[25]

Because young Nisei sons were needed as unpaid labor for the family, not many immigrant families in the countryside could afford to send them to the city for higher education. As *Paulista Shimbun* reported in 1950, in the last few years of the 1940s, the number of Niseis attending junior high schools increased dramatically, and in the suburbs of São Paulo City, half of those who had just graduated from elementary schools rushed to take entrance exams for junior high school. That indicates that after the war, Issei parents who had decided to stay in Brazil permanently became dedicated to the Brazilian education of their Nisei children, mostly sons. *Paulista Shimbun* also listed nineteen Japanese student dormitories in the city and added that there were many other smaller accommodations for students. Like Tanaka and Yamauchi, whose fathers wanted them to learn a trade to make a living, other young Nisei men who grew up in the countryside began to attend vocational training schools in the city, which were exclusively for men. In 1949, when more than 80 percent of the "Japanese" in Brazil were registered to remain engaged in agriculture, Japanese descendants constituted two-thirds of the fifteen hundred GV students, and half of the students at Escola Prática de Agricultura de Pirassununga (Practical Agricultural School of Pirassununga).[26]

There were no equivalent public middle-level institutions for young Nisei women to learn a trade after they finished primary school education in the countryside. For a long time Japanese Brazilian women's education was limited largely to domestic training, such as sewing and cooking. The Japanese regarded sewing as "as an essential part of women's knowledge as homemakers," and therefore sewing skills were perceived more as an important part of bridal training than as a trade.[27] This was, of course, a reflection of prewar immigrant parents' strongly gendered perceptions of their Nisei children's education. Japanese anthropologist Seiichi Izumi's sampling of Japanese Brazilians in southern Brazil for 1952–1953 demonstrates a strong tendency for parents to expect their sons to receive a middle school education or higher and for their daughters to attend sewing and cooking schools with only a primary school education.[28] Thus the majority of young Nisei women's lives were clearly centered on marriage and family rather than on individual social climbing, as was the case with men. After all, women were expected to marry out and produce offspring for their husbands' families. It was not worth investing limited resources in a daughter's formal education. Rather, making them more desirable wives-to-be among the Japanese could bring the families not only prestige and honor but also useful kinship networks and some financial benefits in both the short and the long terms. In rural Brazil, even in the early 1950s, it was rare for Japanese descendants to date; marriage was usually arranged by matchmakers, and the amount of betrothal money, varying between 10 and 50 contos, was based on the financial power of each family. No betrothal return was necessary, but the bride's family paid to prepare her for the wedding and for a

Japanese-style marriage. It was common for the eldest son and his wife to live with his parents, who often renovated and expanded their house before their son's wedding.[29]

Tanaka graduated from GV in 1952 as an engineering major, but reentered GV to study architecture and finished his second high school diploma in 1954. After failing USP's entrance exams twice and finishing his three-month training at a reserve officers' cadet school, he finally began his undergraduate studies in 1957 at the USP School of Architecture (Faculdade de Arquitetura e Urbanismo, or FAU).[30] According to Tanaka, many Japanese Brazilian students were already enrolled in the USP School of Engineering (Escola Politécnica, or Poli). When Tanaka started college, there were thirty freshmen in FAU, of whom five were of Japanese descent, including two women. Other Japanese Brazilian students in architecture came from more or less the same background as Tanaka, and all chose to attend USP because they did not have to pay tuition. The rest of Tanaka's class was all white, with no black students. It took seven years for Tanaka to graduate from college; Bunkyo awarded him college scholarships (1958–1960), and he supported himself working as a part-time Bunkyo employee as well as a freelance illustrator and a translator of Japanese movies for Portuguese subtitles.[31]

Yamauchi graduated from GV in 1954 and moved into the Casa de Estudantes "Harmonia" ([Japanese Brazilian] Student Dormitory "Harmony") in São Bernado do Campo, São Paulo, which was established by Burajiru Rikkokai (Rikkokai of Brazil). One of the other residents who moved in for the same year was Watanabe, who would start USP Law School in 1955.[32] Yamauchi started his undergraduate studies in 1955 at Mackenzie University as a double major in electrical and mechanical engineering. Yamauchi begun to learn judo (modern Japanese martial arts) in the city and eventually became the president of the students' judo association. Back then judo was practiced by Japanese descendants only, and therefore Yamauchi's association was predominantly of Japanese ancestry. Through judo, Yamauchi got in touch with Bunkyo and became a member in 1957. At Mackenzie, there were 160 students enrolled in engineering in his entering class, including ten Japanese Brazilians, all Nisei men. According to Yamauchi, back then women rarely got into engineering, but, as at USP, there were some Japanese Brazilian women majoring in architecture at Mackenzie.[33]

After the end of World War II there was a new trend among the Niseis toward getting a Brazilian higher education. The majority of Nisei college students were concentrated in law and sciences, most notably engineering, medicine, and dentistry. Law students attended school for half a day while working at law firms for the rest of the day, whereas in the sciences classes were held for the entire day. Therefore, according to Tanaka, "one needed to go to law school if s/he had to support him/herself. Plus, one could attend a night school for law."[34] From 1936 to 1948, a total of 87 Japanese Brazilians graduated from USP, including 19 in medicine, 18 in law, 17 in pharmacy, 12 in engineering, and 11 in dentistry. By contrast, as of April 1949, 99 Japanese Brazilian students were enrolled at USP, including 33 in engineering, 16 in medicine, and 10 in agriculture. Out of the 165 students who passed Poli's entrance examination in 1949, nine were Japanese Brazilians, including Kohei Uehara.[35]

Nobue Miyazaki (b. 1931), a retired Nisei woman USP professor, graduated from USP in 1958 as an ethnology major. According to Miyazaki, back then Nisei women were expected to have primary education only in the city. Her Nisei boyfriend broke up with her as soon as he learned she was going to college: "There were Niseis like him, with this kind of old-fashioned idea about women."[36] Miyazaki's report accords with a 1957 interview with To-mie Higuchi published in Bunkyo's newsletter, *Kaihō*. Higuchi was a proud mother of two Nisei USP graduates: a twenty-four-year-old son, Tsunehiko, an engineering major, and a twenty-year-old daughter, Ritsuko, a major in pharmacy and dentistry. Higuchi said she wanted her son to be useful to the nation of Brazil after studying engineering in Japan on a Japanese government fellowship, but she preferred that her daughter, who was employed at a research institute, "become a full-time homemaker, not a female scholar or career woman."[37] One may never know whether Higuchi expressed her honest opinion, but her interview at least reveals gendered norms among Japanese Brazilians in São Paulo City during the 1950s.

Some Nisei women were allowed or even encouraged to study in certain areas at a college level, mainly to learn a trade. For instance, Midory Kimura Figuchi (b. 1936), who grew up in Paraná as the seventh of eight children born to prewar immigrant parents from Kagawa prefecture, moved with her family to São Paulo City at the age of fifteen. She worked during the day and attended schools at night. She graduated from USP at the age of twenty-one with a major in public health and began to work as a nutritionist at public hospitals. She married at twenty-three and took a few years off to raise two infant sons (born in 1963 and 1966), but went back to work with strong support from her husband and mother-in-law. She also hired a live-in maid, a young migrant woman from Bahia, for ten years, who took care of her young sons at home. Figuchi cultivated a successful career with the state government of São Paulo and eventually became the director of the Museu da Imigração do Estado de São Paulo (São Paulo State Museum of Immigration). It should be noted that Figuchi is the only Nisei child in her family who attended college.[38] Another Nisei woman, Shizue Higaki Arai (b. 1935), the oldest child of the Higakis, a well-to-do business-owning family in Liberdade (chapter 2), began her undergraduate studies at USP in 1956 as a pharmacy major. Her incoming class in pharmacy contained twenty-five freshmen, eighteen of which were Niseis. Some of her professors were also Niseis, but none of them had doctorates yet. Arai graduated in 1960, and after working at a clinic and a number of pharmacies, opened Farmácia Galvão Bueno in 1963, in the same year she married. While running her own pharmacy, Arai raised her four children (born in 1964, 1966, 1968, and 1973), all college graduates who are now married to Japanese Brazilians. Her younger sister did not become a pharmacist herself, but married a Nisei pharmacist, and they also opened their own pharmacy on the same street.[39] According to Senichi Adachi (chapter 4), Bunkyo's longtime secretary-general, the easiest way for Japanese Brazilian women to earn wages was to become seamstresses, but

> Nisei women became nurses and pharmacists. There were many Japanese pharmacies since they could start business with a small capital. Those who did not possess a certificate had to use one from a Brazilian pharmacist by making a contract for a monthly payment. Those Japanese pharmacy owners found it ridiculous to pay a lot of money to those Brazilian pharmacists, and therefore encouraged their daughters to attend college to become pharmacists so that they could make more money now that they not only had no need to lease a license but also could rent it to others.[40]

Yamauchi conducted a nationwide survey in 1957, with Tanaka's help, on Japanese Brazilians who had graduated from college by 1956 for Bunkyo's commemoration of the fiftieth anniversary of Japanese immigration to Brazil (1958). According to Yamauchi, the number of Japanese Brazilian college students rose quickly in the mid-1960s.[41] During the late 1960s, Japanese Brazilians already constituted approximately one-tenth of undergraduate students in the state of São Paulo, where they made up only 2.5 percent of the population. That means that already one out of ten Japanese Brazilians was attending college.[42]

It was in their college days that both Tanaka and Yamauchi got involved in the activities of the Piratininga Club (chapter 1). In 1957, Yamauchi was recruited by one of the Club's thirty-one founding members, and he recruited Tanaka in 1958. According to Tanaka, their members included women and men, and the membership was not exclusive to college students and graduates. At the same time, they all belonged to the middle classes and sufficient financial means for such "cultural" activities. Otherwise, Tanaka says, "they would have become a financial burden for the club activities."[43] On June 22, 1960, the Piratininga Club officially declared its "independence" from Bunkyo when its representatives were called into a meeting with Bunkyo's president and two vice presidents. Bunkyo's administration was very concerned about the Piratininga Club's plan to build a hall, which was perceived as a critical obstacle to Bunkyo's own plan to construct the Center for Japanese Culture ("Bunkyo building," chapter 1). President Kiyoshi Yamamoto started the meeting by acknowledging that, perceiving the Niseis as still children, Bunkyo had failed to recognize the new Nisei leaders over the last five or six years. He went on to state that Bunkyo expected the Piratininga Club to collaborate with it on the center, which would be theirs in the end. Then the vice presidents, both prewar immigrants, demanded that Piratininga drop its building plan so as not to compete with Bunkyo's fundraising. Piratininga Club president Yaginuma, Vice President Watanabe, and three trustees (Jorge Onodera, Shigeaki Ueki, and Isao Imano) refused to accept this request that they give up their building plan, which had begun five years earlier. They maintained that their club's primary aim was to "educate the Nisei without sufficient Brazilian consciousness and to transform them into good Brazilians," and therefore the club could not cooperate with Bunkyo, whose primary missions were the introduction of Japanese culture to Brazil and the enlightenment of the Isseis.[44] In short, the Piratininga Club made it clear in public that elite Niseis did not need Bunkyo's parental approval.

Both Yamauchi and Tanaka were recruited into the Piratininga Club for their excellent Japanese language skills, which its Department of Culture needed for its "cultural caravans" to rural Japanese settlements in São Paulo and Paraná states. According to Tanaka, ten to twenty students formed a group to visit the countryside, where they had roundtable discussions with rural Japanese Brazilians, and did sightseeing in the areas during the day:

> Back then at the end of the 1950s and beginning of the 1960s transportation was not developed and the communication system was primitive. They [the rural Japanese descendants in the countryside] were so taken by the fact that the students came to visit with them that they were eager to hear what they had not known and to teach us the students what we did not know yet. I felt like I had learned a lot. We students felt like our perspectives had widened when we came back from our two-week caravans.[45]

Yamauchi participated in two "caravans" (1958 and 1959) with Tanaka, Uneno, and Watanabe, as well as his Mackenzie classmate Tadayoshi Wada. According to Yamauchi, intermarriage was often brought up as a topic for roundtable discussions with the rural Japanese Brazilian population, including the youth, but their immigrant parents were completely against it, valuing their Japanese "purity of blood."[46] Toshio Sonehara, a Nisei architecture student who participated in the Piratininga Club's thirteenth fifteen-day caravan to the Alta Paulista zone in July 1959, also stated that the Isseis in the countryside were against their Nisei children's intermarriage with white Brazilians. Yet he also noted Issei parents' changing attitudes toward their Nisei children. First, the Niseis were now proudly hosting *bailes* (dance parties) in most of the rural ethnic Japanese settlements, where the Isseis had never allowed them to do so. Second, the Isseis wanted to understand the Niseis' ways of thinking, how different the Niseis were from the Isseis, and on what the Isseis and Niseis could agree, rather than telling the Niseis to learn Japanese and not to marry white Brazilians. Now the Japanese language and intermarriage were perceived as "Niseis' own problems," rather than problems for both Isseis and Niseis.[47]

Members of the Piratininga Club were also engaged in charitable activities. According to Tanaka, club members traveled to the post of Santos in groups of ten to thirteen to interpret for newly arrived immigrants at the inspection of their luggage every time an immigrant ship arrived.[48] Tanaka also directed and starred in Piratininga's fundraising production of *Sanshō Dayū* in 1961. In the same year, Piratininga Club members, including Tanaka, Yamauchi, and Imano, held a roundtable discussion with a group of male Japanese students from Sophia University in Tokyo, who were visiting Brazil.[49] Unlike other Nisei clubs, the Piratininga Club put special emphasis on cultural activities and had a Department of Education, which was, in fact, a preparatory school for the junior high school entrance exams. In 1965, some three hundred children, including Brazilians of no Japanese ancestry, were attending the school.[50]

During the 1960s, the majority of the educated Niseis continued to intermarry among themselves, mainly though their own Nisei networks. Most of the Piratininga Club members in Tanaka's generation married Japanese Brazilians. For instance, Watanabe married Nisei Yoshimi Moriyama, a graduate of a senior high school in commerce and the third daughter of Rikkokai immigrant Heishiro Moriyama. Tanaka married a *kihaku* Nisei in 1962 at the age of twenty-nine, when he was still in college. Having finished her junior high education in Japan, his wife was working at the Cotia Agricultural Cooperative. They got married counting on his wife's full-time

income, but the cooperative forced her to quit her job as soon as she notified her boss of her upcoming marriage. In 1969, at the age of thirty-eight,
Yamauchi married a college-educated Nisei woman (b. 1942), who had studied education at a graduate level on a fellowship at a Japanese university.[51]

Throughout the 1960s, ethnic-class endogamy remained largely a
norm among the educated Niseis. Yamauchi attributes the young Niseis'
endogamy in the 1950s and 1960s to Issei parents' pressuring them strongly
not to marry "Brazilians." "Back in the 1960s," she says, "one would be kicked
out of home by his parents if s/he married a 'Brazilian,' and there were
many who were, in fact, kicked out."[52] Yamauchi's observation accords well
with a statement made by Adachi:

> When I came to Brazil in 1956 there were very few "international marriages."
> Japanese parents disowned their children who married Brazilians. The maga-
> zine *Manchete* reported that a Japanese immigrant man committed hara-
> kiri for having a daughter who married a *gaijin*, thereby shaming his family
> name. Back then it was not allowed for the Nikkeis to marry Brazilians. It
> was like that in the 1950s and 1960s, here in the city. At that time the Nikkei
> community was predominantly Issei, and Niseis did not yet express their
> own opinions.[53]

Bernardo Y. Shinohara is more than a decade younger than Tanaka and
Yamauchi. In his midtwenties, Shinohara, a Pontifícia Universidade Católica de São Paulo (Catholic University of São Paulo, PUC) graduate with an
MBA from Fundação Getúlio Vargas (Getúlio Vargas Foundation, FGV),
married an elite Nisei (b. 1943) with a BS from USP and an MS from Miyazaki University (Japan), both in chemistry. Both were born and had grown
up in São Paulo City. Shinohara maintains that at that time the educated
Niseis still married largely among themselves.[54]

Yet the rate of interracial marriage had been growing. For the years
1958–1962, 14.1 percent of male Japanese Brazilians (2.7 for immigrants, and
18.4 for the Brazilian-born) and 7.4 percent of females (4.6 for immigrants,
and 7.6 for the Brazilian-born) were married to "Brazilians." This gender
differentiation seems quite extreme; it is possible that not all of the women
who married out were included.[55] And there is no way of knowing what was
going on in São Paulo City specifically, since the data are not broken down
by regions or localities. By the mid-1960s, the incidence of interracial marriage by the Niseis was being discussed, often as a critical problem for the
ethnic Japanese community, in Bunkyo's newsletter, *Colônia*.[56] According
to a 1965 survey conducted by *Paulista Shimbun*, some 40 percent of the

Niseis approved of such marriages.[57] Of course, this does not necessarily mean that educated Niseis were actively seeking "Brazilians" as their marriage partners. Nisei woman Nail Muramatsu stated (1965), "I would not oppose other Niseis' intermarriages but I myself would hate to marry a Brazilian. I do not feel comfortable with Brazilians and I am afraid that they do not understand the true goodness of the Nikkei."[58] The same tendency is observed among the one hundred educated Niseis (sixty-nine men and thirty-one women) born to Rikkokai immigrants as of 1966. Among them twenty-four (twelve men and twelve women) were married, and most of the married women were full-time homemakers. Nineteen were married to educated Niseis; four (three men and one woman) to "Brazilians."[59]

It is most likely that in the 1960s interracial marriage was still understood generally by educated Japanese Brazilians in the city as marrying down in socioeconomic terms, for example to *caboclos*.[60] In a roundtable discussion on marriage for *Colônia,* nine educated single Nisei men and women in their twenties discussed how important it was for them to find marriage partners of equal educational and economic standing, while mentioning that the majority of intermarried Japanese had married non-Japanese Brazilians who were "lower than middle class." They concluded that the Niseis, themselves included, were not ready for interracial marriages, and that they found suitable marriage partners at Nisei clubs.[61] Nisei Hiroshi Ikuta, with a doctorate in agriculture (1961), also maintained in 1965 that it was preferable for the Niseis to marry among themselves, while assuming that intermarriage would pose few problems for Sanseis and Yonseis.[62] This accords with twenty-year-old Nisei woman Tsuyako Hirai's statement (1957) that the educated Niseis had not yet gained much familiarity with individual educated white Brazilians, nor had they collectively reached a socioeconomic level that enabled them to marry white Brazilians of equal socioeconomic standing by the mid-1960s, a time when Japanese Brazilians in São Paulo commonly quoted a saying in Portuguese: "*A cara não ajuda*" (The [Japanese] face does not help).[63]

By around 1970, intermarriage became more accepted in the city. Yamauchi maintains the 1970s were the decade when Issei parents felt they could no longer prevent their educated Nisei children from marrying "Brazilians." In the 1970s, Shinohara's younger sister, a medical doctor, married a white Brazilian of the same educational background. Tanaka's youngest sister, who became a nurse, married a white Brazilian man of Hungarian descent. Both of Chikako Hironaka's sons, USP-educated medical doctors, married college-educated white Brazilian women (chapter 2). Sandra Akahoshi, a Nisei (b. 1944) born to prewar immigrants from Kumamoto, herself married a child immigrant man also from Kumamoto, who joined her family business in hairdressing. However, her younger sister, a USP-educated medical doctor, married a white Brazilian medical doctor, and her younger brother, a college-educated engineer, married a white Brazilian woman.[64]

This is when gender started to determine the pattern of Japanese Brazilians' intermarriages more sharply. Shizu Saito maintains that Nisei women "used to obey their parents well" and that "it was much more common for Nisei men to marry non-Nikkei women, not vice versa." Masami Takiyama (b. 1949), a Sansei woman, was not allowed to marry her white Brazilian boyfriend, a fellow law student; her late mother's sisters persuaded her father not to allow her to intermarry. Yet some years later her father allowed her younger brother, his only son, to marry his *morena* (light-skinned Afro-Brazilian) girlfriend, whom she says he adores. Takiyama herself has never married; she even gave up her law practice in Brazil and worked in Japan for eleven years to fulfill the financial needs of her family. Emi Ito (b. 1944), two of whose eight siblings (one older sister and one younger brother) intermarried, was not allowed by her prewar immigrant parents to marry anybody; she was chosen in her childhood by them to become their caretaker, although she received a college education in the city. Respecting her parents' wishes, Ito has never even dated.[65]

While there are no quantitative data available, I have often heard from Japanese Brazilians that intermarriage was much more common among Japanese Brazilian men than among their female counterparts. While I have met many prewar immigrant parents whose sons married white Brazilian women during the 1970s and 1980s and who therefore have mixed grown Sansei grandchildren, I have also encountered many less-educated Nisei women, born in the 1930s and 1940s, who chose to marry postwar Japanese immigrants during the 1960s because, they say, they did not want to marry "Brazilians" or even Niseis; they positioned "new Japanese" (chapter 4) above Brazilians and the Niseis.

In the mid-1960s Bunkyo's newsletter, *Colônia*, published a series of interviews with educated Niseis who had become successful professionals mainly thanks to Tanaka, who remained a part-time editor for the newsletter while attending USP. Tanaka conducted many interviews with educated Niseis and also coordinated and participated in roundtable discussions with them. In short, Tanaka functioned as a cultural hinge between the Issei members of Bunkyo and the educated Niseis, who identified themselves as Brazilians first and foremost. Unlike himself and Yamauchi, both of whom became members of Bunkyo's executive committee in 1975, many educated Niseis "distanced themselves from the Issei." Susumu Miyao (chapter 2) stated in 1969 that Niseis were "new Brazilians." "Many Niseis had some contact with the Nikkei *colônia* but were not living their lives within its framework," he said. In fact, most were indifferent to the *colônia*, which, in Miyao's opinion, "would disappear naturally" when the immigrant generation died out.[66]

It was commonly said during the 1960s that Niseis were neither Japanese nor Brazilians; they were "half-finished." In 1965, a journalist from Japan's *Asahi Shimbun* reported on Japanese descendants in South America. According to the reporter, the Niseis in São Paulo resented their Issei parents for not understanding that they were not Japanese but Brazilians. At the same time they were not really Brazilians, either. While they struggled to escape the Isseis' influence, they were still emotionally "Japanese." For instance, some young Niseis in São Paulo held a meeting to reflect on the Niseis' tendency to call meetings among themselves whenever they were concerned about something, and concluded that they, as Brazilians, should advance themselves in Brazilian society. But as soon as the meeting was over, they all went to dine at a Japanese restaurant that they frequented. The Japanese reporter visited the Piratininga Club and interviewed its thirty-five-year-old president, Isao Imano, a Mackenzie-educated architect. Imano spoke eloquently of the club that fought passionately against the Isseis in order to prove what the Niseis could accomplish on their own. The reporter characterized the Piratininga Club to Imano as "half-finished" in the same way as the Niseis were; it worked as a "good means of defense for the Niseis from the countryside, of offence against the Issei in speaking as the representative of Niseis, and of gradual self-transformation for the Nisei." He concluded that "The Nisei were fighting their own inferiority complex carried from their parents' generation."[67] But what he described as an "inferiority complex" is, in fact, the complexity of Nisei identity. In 1966, a male secretary-general of a Nisei club stated it would be more helpful for the Niseis, who "were clearly Brazilians," to learn English rather than Japanese. A young Nisei woman trustee of the same Nisei club added, "We the Nisei form a club among ourselves but that is not because we do not like Brazilians. It is a matter of feeling as if we still have a 'Japanese tail.' Such Nisei clubs will all disappear in our children or grandchildren's generation."[68] Time would prove that she was mistaken (chapter 6).

By the beginning of the 1960s, funding became available for college-educated Niseis to study in Japan. In 1958, Nobue Miyazaki became the first Brazilian recipient of Japan's Ministry of Education fellowship and studied at the University of Tokyo in 1958–1962 for a PhD in anthropology under Seiichi Izumi. Yamauchi received a one-year fellowship (1960–1961) from

Plant Kyokai in Rio de Janeiro for his professional training in Japan. Kenkichi Fujimori (b. 1929), who immigrated to Brazil at the age of four and graduated from USP in physics in 1957, was awarded a Bunkyo fellowship and spent five years and eight months at Tohoku University. He received a PhD in 1963 and returned to Brazil with a Japanese wife, an elite Tsuda Women's College graduate. *Kihaku* Nisei Yojiro Hama, second son of Rikkokai immigrant Rokuro Hama, finished his Brazilian middle school and college education at USP, and studied with Hideki Yukawa for a PhD (1966) in physics at Kyoto University. Kazuo Watanabe (b. 1936) graduated from USP Law School in 1959, worked as a lawyer for the South Brazilian Agricultural Cooperative for two years, and became the first Japanese Brazilian judge in 1962. In 1965, Watanabe was chosen as one of five recipients, all men, of Japan's Ministry of Foreign Affairs fellowships for "excellent Nisei with social activities for more than ten years."[69]

Why did the educated Niseis want to study in Japan, while identifying themselves as Brazilians? How did they perceive Japan and the Japanese? How did they identify themselves in Japan? Identifying herself as "a Brazilian who is proud of being a child of the Japanese," Nobue Miyazaki says that she never liked the Japanese lifestyle, such as tatami mats and public baths, and that she has never wished to live in Japan permanently.[70] In 1961, upon his return from Japan, Yamauchi stated that he could not stand the smell of public bathrooms in Japan and that he observed the Japanese holding strong feelings of inferiority toward white foreigners.[71] During half of his fellowship year in Japan, Yamauchi was forced to serve as guide and translator for a very wealthy white Brazilian man who did not speak Japanese, but he had a great training in electrical engineering at Hitachi Corporation for the rest of the year. He was offered a job at Hitachi's headquarters in Japan but declined it, saying that as a Brazilian he would prefer to be hired at Hitachi do Brazil.[72] Upon returning to Brazil after studying architecture at Kyoto University on a two-year fellowship from Japan's Ministry of Foreign Affairs, Toshio Tomimatsu published an essay in *Colônia* in 1962, in which he wrote that the Japanese's alleged high cultural level was doubtful and that the Japanese spoiled their children in the name of democracy and individualism.[73]

In 1965, *Colônia* hosted a roundtable discussion on the Niseis' perceptions of Japan, chaired by Teiichi Suzuki, an elite prewar immigrant lawyer (chapter 1), with participation by six young college-educated Niseis (two men and four women) who had lived in Japan on fellowships for a year or two. Only one, Toshio Furuhata, who studied Japan's industrial policies at Saitama University, was positive about Japan for its advanced technology.

The other five were extremely critical of Japan and the Japanese, and one of them (Renate Kono), a medical school graduate, as a Brazilian "saw nothing good" in Japan. All five agreed that the Japanese lacked honesty and sincerity and discussed how badly they were treated in Japan. Akiko Hachiya noted that she was surprised that everybody in Japan was Japanese, and that in her third month there she was so relieved to see a "white person" for the first time that she "wanted to rush to shake hands with the person." Eventually all of the discussants agreed that they would like to visit Japan again as tourists but never wished to live there permanently.[74] They consistently placed Brazil in a position superior to Japan.

A decade later, in 1974, *Colônia Bungaku* hosted its first Nisei roundtable discussion, chaired by Nisei lawyer Antonio Nojiri, at a popular Japanese restaurant in Liberdade. Participants were five top Nisei professionals, a lawyer and four PhDs, two women and three men: Ryuzo Dohi, Kenkichi Fujimori, Nobue Miyazaki, Nina Mabuchi, and Takeshi Ohara. Whereas the three men on the panel, and the chairman, were in science, medicine, and law, and all were married with children, the two women, both USP professors in the humanities and social sciences, were single with no children. The two women's comments reveal how differently women's higher education was perceived: while Miyazaki stated that the *colônia* was generally against Nisei women's college education, Mabuchi maintained that it was common for women to study at three-year teacher's colleges to become primary school teachers, rather than attending senior high schools and universities. Then the panelists began to discuss the following critical points. First, they commented that prewar immigrant parents' enthusiasm for their children's higher education was a means of social climbing, which was supposed to benefit the Isseis in the end. Second, they criticized the younger generation of Japanese Brazilians, who did not understand their "beat *gaijin*" attitudes in their younger days and who did not behave themselves and even cheated on exams at USP. Lastly, they presented critical self-reflections on their own generation of Niseis, who "had their own thoughts but did not have their own Nisei organization" and therefore were "not united," as in the case of the Isseis.[75] Their discussions suggest that the Nisei elites, who had moved up the social ladder individually, continued to struggle to find their own place in Brazilian society. Caught between the prewar Japanese immigrants and the younger Niseis and Sanseis, they found themselves neither Japanese nor Brazilian, without having formed any collective identity.

Educated Niseis born in the 1930s and 1940s have identified themselves as Brazilians first and then as children of the Japanese. But how have the less-educated Niseis of the same generation perceived themselves? How critically has class determined their experiences and affected their self-perceptions? Yukie Yano, a devout adherent of Sōka Gakkai, one of Japan's so-called New Religions, identifies herself as Japanese. Yano has less than a four-year elementary school education. She had five surviving younger siblings, all with only a four-year primary education. Her marriage to a prewar immigrant from Kochi Prefecture in 1952 was a *miai*, and she had three children by him who were born in 1954, 1955, and 1957. Even though Yano herself married a Japanese immigrant and claims that back then the Japanese married only among themselves, two of her younger brothers, born in 1934 and 1936, married working-class "Brazilian" women, while her younger sister, another Sōka Gakkai adherent, married a Japanese Brazilian man through their shared religion. After her husband's passing in 1959, as "nobody would marry you if you had three children," Yano raised her children on her own, and all of them married Afro-Brazilian migrants from Pernambuco and Bahia, whom she characterizes as "*dekasseguis* from the North."[76]

The same pattern of interracial class endogamy is observed among two of the younger Nisei brothers of a prewar child immigrant, Haruko Fujitani (introduction). Except for her oldest younger brother (b. 1941), an engineer with a college degree, who is married to a Nisei woman, all of Fujitani's siblings had only a four-year primary education. Her second younger brother, Mario (b. 1944), joined Sōka Gakkai at the age of eighteen and moved out of his parents' house. He was single for many years but eventually married a much younger Japanese Brazilian woman of the same religious faith, with whom he had a daughter in 1995. Fujitani's younger sister, Yuko Hanada (b. 1947), a hairdresser, is married to a much older Nisei truck driver with three daughters. The two youngest brothers, Hiroshi (b. 1951) and Takashi (b. 1954), who co-own a mechanic shop each had multiple marriages to working-class "Brazilian" women.[77]

Working-class Japanese Brazilians have many family members, including their "Brazilian" in-laws, who have been to Japan as *dekasseguis*. Yano's second younger brother and his family have been in Japan since the early 1990s, and two of her three children and their families have been gone since the mid-1990s. In 2004, Yano herself traveled to Japan for the first time to work as a caregiver at a hospital in Saitama prefecture. Some of Haruko Fujitani's nieces and nephews, including Yuko Hanada's youngest daughter, have been in Japan for years, and one of her nieces married a local Japanese man in the 1990s. Some of her "Brazilian" ex-in-laws, such as Hiroshi's ex-wife and Takashi's former son-in-law (son of his second wife, an Afro-Brazilian woman from Bahia), have also gone to Japan as *dekasseguis*. My Japanese Brazilian informants have told me that certain non-Japanese

Brazilians looked for Japanese Brazilians to marry solely for the sake of *dekassegui* work in Japan.

Hisahiro Inoue (b. 1938) is a less-educated Nisei whose command of Japanese is impeccable, although he maintains he does not know how to write nor read it well enough to understand many difficult Chinese characters. Inoue identifies himself as Japanese, not Nisei. According to Inoue, Brazilian birth in itself does not determine whether one is Nisei; the Niseis have "a particular way of thinking that comes from their upbringing." He claims that his Nisei friend Akio Ogawa (b. 1942), a USP-educated businessman, is a Nisei. So are his two youngest sisters, who graduated from college in the city. However, his other male Nisei friend in his Japanese theater group is a "Japanese," as he himself is. Since 2004 Inoue has held a top administrative position at the Sindicato dos Permissionários em Centrais de Alimentos de Estado de São Paulo (Union of Licensees in State Food Supply Center of São Paulo State). Inoue was born in Avalé, São Paulo, as the fourth of twelve children to prewar immigrants from Miyazaki prefecture who arrived in Brazil in 1934. The Inoues moved to Moji das Cruzes (1946) and to Itapapeceria da Serra (1949), where the Inoues were engaged in suburban agriculture, such as tomato farming. Inoue's parents raised all twelve of their children (one Issei and eleven Niseis) as Japanese and did not allow them to speak Portuguese at home: "When I was fourteen or fifteen years old, I finally talked back to them. 'Why do you two get mad when I speak Portuguese? Is it wrong for me to speak my own country's language?' They finally stopped scolding me for speaking Portuguese."[78] In 1958, at the age of twenty, Inoue moved to the city on his own to work at the São Paulo municipal market in the Cantareira district. Within two years, Inoue and his second-oldest brother opened their own store there but could not make much money. Through his vegetable vending business, Inoue met a young Nisei woman at the same educational level, a daughter of a tomato farmer and a relative of his former employer. He chose to be baptized in 1961 before his church marriage with his Nisei fiancée, a Jehovah's Witness. His Portuguese name, Rogério, which he uses at work, was given at baptism by his Japanese godparents. In 1962, Inoue and his wife moved to Três Lagoas, Mato Grosso do Sul, where dam construction was employing a few thousand workers. Inoue made a living by transporting vegetables from São Paulo's municipal market to Três Lagoas until 1969, when he returned to São Paulo City with his family and began to work at the Companhia de Entrepostos e Armazéns Gerais de São Paulo (Company of General Warehouses of São Paulo).[79]

Inoue and his wife have two college-educated Sansei children who were born in Três Lagoa in 1965 and 1966, and two racially mixed Yonsei grandchildren. Inoue strongly resents the way he and his siblings were raised by their Japanese parents and says he did not want his children to marry Japanese Brazilians. Never married, Inoue's son, an engineer, has a daughter with his white Brazilian ex-girlfriend. Their daughter, who works at the Bank of Brazil in São Paulo, has a son by her white Brazilian ex-husband. In 1991, Inoue, who holds dual nationality, and his Nisei wife left for Japan as *dekasseguis* and worked on an assembly line for a small plastic parts company in Hyogo prefecture, near Himeji City. Inoue stayed on there through the Great Kobe Earthquake in 1995 and returned to Brazil in 1998. In Japan, Inoue and his wife were joined by one of his younger sisters (b. 1944) and her postwar immigrant husband, as well as by their daughter and her husband. Upon returning to Brazil, Inoue invested most of his *dekassegui* savings in a *fazenda* but lost almost all of it when it went bankrupt. Inoue says today that when he lived in Japan he "made every effort to behave himself"; he "was a Brazilian at the factory but behaved like a Japanese outside the workplace." He claims that he "became white" when he was in Japan.[80]

Like Inoue, all of his siblings married Japanese descendants, except for the youngest two, both daughters, born in the early 1950s, who have never married. They moved to the city with their parents in 1962 and always lived with them. Their father passed away in 1970, but their mother did not allow either of his youngest sisters to marry anybody but Japanese Brazilians. One of them was once engaged to a Nisei man, but their mother broke their engagement, saying she did not like him. Thus Inoue's two youngest sisters had to devote themselves to their mother, while holding full-time white-collar jobs, until she died in 2006 at the age of ninety-four. Inoue and his other siblings seem not to have lent a hand to their college-educated youngest sisters, especially during their mother's last years. In fact, he and three other less-educated older siblings left for Japan in 1991 as *dekasseguis,* and two of them have never been back to Brazil since then. Referring to the illness of one of his youngest sisters, Inoue commented, "All women are made to give birth, and they get sick if they do not do what they are supposed to do."[81] Such a comment is often made even today by less-educated Nisei men of Inoue's generation, who still repeat what they learned from prewar immigrants back in the countryside.

Less-educated Niseis distinguish themselves from the college-educated Niseis of their own generation, who managed to live in Brazilian society as urban professionals. In their politics of identity, the difference is not of class (blue collar vs. white collar) but of culture ("Japanese" vs. Nisei). Whereas none of Yano's family members received higher educations, and although they mixed with working-class Afro-Brazilians from early on, Inoue and his siblings show a sharp class division within the same family, in relation to each member's extent of assimilation in Brazilian society. The family could not afford to give the first seven children (six sons and a daughter) higher educations, but the next three (all sons) graduated from college, albeit not in São Paulo City, and none of those younger sons has gone to Japan as a *dekassegui*. Only the two youngest children received college educations in the city, but because of their gender they got caught in daughterly obligations to their aging parents, despite or because of their college educations and white-collar jobs. Their rural working-class Japanese family background did not allow them to leave their Issei parents in order to join the Brazilian upper-middle class individually. Midory Figuchi criticizes gender relations in the Japanese diaspora, "I think many Nikkeis continue to live with the cultural components from the old Era of Meiji, when their grandparents and parents immigrated to Brazil. Nikkei women still follow and obey the old social notions and cultural traditions, which Japan itself lost many years ago. They want to be good homemakers, first and foremost, taking care of their husbands and children, while remaining oppressed under patriarchy."[82]

There is a strong tendency among the college-educated Niseis born in the 1930s and 1940s, who identify themselves as Westerners, to look down on Japan and the Japanese, as well as "Orientals" and the "Orient," as culturally backward, while admiring Europe and the United States. Figuchi, for instance, states, "I would very much like to learn the Japanese language, literature, and history, but I am not interested in visiting Japan. My mother could not stand dirty public bathrooms in Japan and because of that she came back to Brazil earlier than she had planned. It seems like Japan is still culturally backward."[83] The educated Niseis also buy into the Brazilian notion that "money whitens" and have "whitened" themselves. Even though many of them engaged in ethnic-class endogamy back in the 1960s and early 1970s, they have come to regard Japanese Brazilians' racial mixing as strong evidence of their assimilation into Brazilian society.

Delma Arashiro (b. 1943) is a Nisei pharmacist and pharmaceutical company owner of Okinawan descent. She is the second youngest of nine siblings in São Pedro, São Paulo, but grew up in Rio Claro, and moved to the city in 1962 for her college education at USP. In the late 1970s, Arashiro married a white Brazilian engineer, but he passed away after six years. In

1988, she married her second husband, a white Brazilian TV art director. This is his third marriage; his two previous wives are upper-middle-class white Brazilian women. Arashiro and her husband are both adherents of *candomblé*, an Afro-Brazilian religion. Among her six surviving siblings, her younger sister, an architect, is married to a white Brazilian, whereas their five older brothers "naturally" married women of Okinawan descent, except for one who became a medical doctor, studied at the University of Tokyo's Medical School, and married a Japanese Brazilian woman. Arashiro identifies herself as white and discusses the meanings of whiteness in Brazil: "It is more possible for prejudice to disappear here in Brazil than in the United States. In the United States, all the races—blacks, Asians, and Latin Americans—are all separated. But that is not the case of Brazil. A big difference lies in [the power of] money. Money makes anybody white, more or less." Arashiro, who has no children herself, has unofficially adopted three young black boys, the children of her sister's maid, in order to support their future higher education so they can "whiten" themselves.[84]

Yuriko Matsuno (b. 1946), a USP Law School graduate, met her Nisei husband (b. 1938) at the Bastos Nisei Club in São Paulo City, which Watanabe had cofounded. They dated and got married in 1971 upon her graduation. Matsuno says she is "more Japanese than Brazilian"; she was born and grew up in Bastos among the "Japanese" and finished her junior high school education there. She attended a senior high school in Tupã, São Paulo, for two years, and finished her senior year in São Paulo City after she and her family moved there for her father's job. She was interested in studying English and German literature in college but her family made a strong objection: "That is not right. It's not worth it. You have got a brain to pass the entrance exam to the Law School." She studied tax law at USP but has never practiced, after all; instead she got married and has remained a full-time homemaker. According to Matsuno, many college-educated Nisei women of her generation did not pursue a career; "Nobody made a career out of college."[85]

As a member of a *kachigumi* family, Matsuno's husband had once "returned" to Japan after the end of World War II but came back to Brazil three years later. Matsuno says her husband and his family have remained "typically Japan but the old Japan." Becoming a medical doctor, he expected her to be a full-time homemaker. As an elite Nisei couple, Matsuno and her husband have surely "whitened" themselves and their Sansei children; as an obstetrician and gynecologist, her husband developed a thriving career in private practice. "Interestingly," Matsuno says, "the majority of his patients are white women. I think they look for 'Japanese' doctors, who are reputed

to be honest." Her son never liked Japanese descendants and always preferred white women. Matsuno thinks that is because neither Matsuno nor
her husband wanted to socialize Japanese Brazilians or participated in any
ethnic Japanese organizations. While her husband speaks Japanese well and
likes things Japanese very much, Matsuno "did not want to be anywhere
Nikkeis gathered," while saying, "I like European culture very much. I love
anything European." Yet Matsuno and her husband were shocked when
their son, who became a medical doctor, married a white Brazilian woman
who is also a medical doctor. This would seem to be perfect class endogamy
for Mastuno, who does not like things Japanese, but she says she wanted
her son to be "Japanese" and wanted him to marry a "Japanese" woman, as
she "wanted her family to be Japanese"—a clear example of multiple identities in conflict. Matsuno states, "White women seem to be more open than
daughters of the Japanese, who are more reserved. I've always thought this
is the reason why Japanese Brazilian men have preferred the other race."[86]

Matsuno is one of the elite Nisei women who joined Esperança Fujinkai in 2001. They were, in fact, recruited through Nisei women's personal
networks under the new Nisei president, Mitsue Kumagai. Not surprisingly,
these Nisei women are full-time homemakers and do not belong to the
same social circle as professional Nisei women of their generation, such
as Miyazaki, Figuchi, and Arashiro, whom I also interviewed. When she
joined Esperança Fujinkai, Matsuno wanted to seek a position in its administration. Another new Nisei member, Erica M. Yamaoka (b. 1949), coordi-
nates karaoke on Thursdays. She was also born in Bastos, where her father
worked as an accountant for the Bastos Agricultural Cooperative and her
mother ran a bridal training school for young Japanese Brazilian women.
In 1958, she and her family moved to the city for the Nisei children's formal
education. Out of five children, only Yamaoka and one other received college educations, but all had high school educations in the city and are doing
well financially; there is nobody in her birth family who is gone as a *dekassegui*. Yamaoka is married to a Nisei engineer with two grown children, and
all of her siblings married Japanese Brazilians also, as "they wanted to."
Like Mastuno, Yamaoka has never been particularly interested in Japan
or Japanese culture. She has traveled to Europe and the United States as
well as all over Brazil, but she has never been to Japan. She says she would
go there as her very last trip when she travels to other Asian countries such
as Thailand.[87]

Yamaoka's Nisei friend Emília Riccio joined Esperança Fujinkai in
order to sing *enka* songs on karaoke. Riccio was born in the city and married an Italian Brazilian. Yamaoka says Riccio is "very different from those

who grew up in the countryside," like herself.[88] I did not have a chance to interview Riccio, who did not show up for two appointments. Nisei Hiroko Nakama (b. 1940) told me a story of her older Nisei sister, who was born in 1931, educated in the city at a French Catholic school, and eventually graduated from a teacher's college (*escola normal*). According to Nakama, her older sister is like a "Brazilian"; she married an Italian Brazilian, never liking Japanese descendants. Yet once she became a widow, her sister began to mingle with Japanese Brazilians. Nakama says she does not understand why her sister wants to be with Japanese Brazilians in the end.[89]

Around the beginning of the 2000s, I began to hear stories from many of my informants about Nisei men divorcing their "Brazilian" wives after many years of marriage. Senichi Adachi attributed it to food: "As they grow older, they begin to miss what they got used to eating at home, and that is the reason why they divorce their Brazilian wives. By now, Brazilians have begun to eat some Japanese food, and some even eat raw fish. There are still some Nikkei men who divorce their Brazilian wives over their difference in daily diet."[90] Nisei Sandra Akahoshi told me a similar story about her younger siblings, born in the late 1940s, both of whom are college graduates and hold well-paid jobs as urban professionals. Her USP Medical School–educated sister, a radiologist, married a white Brazilian psychiatrist who also graduated from USP Medical School, and had a daughter and a son, but the marriage did not last. Their daughter is also a medical doctor, who graduated from her parents' alma mater and is "as intelligent as her parents are." Akahoshi's younger brother, an engineer, married a white Brazilian woman and then separated from her but eventually got back with her because of their only child's illness. She attributes her younger siblings' marital problems to food: "My sister was used to Japanese food and loved it, but her husband did not like any of those. That was difficult. Living is eating. Marriage with Brazilians is a very complicated business. My brother also loved Japanese food and has got more luck because his wife really likes Japanese food. This is easier."[91]

Akio Ogawa, Inoue's friend, never thought about himself as a Nikkei when he was younger. Ogawa married a less-educated white Brazilian woman but subsequently divorced. In college, his Nisei women classmates did not regard their Nisei male classmates as good enough and chose to date more senior students and professors. Ogawa says that he and many other educated Nisei men of his generation dated and married their "Brazilian" secretaries and receptionists because "those women passionately pursued Japanese Brazilian men." Once married, Ogawa was expected to take care of his wife's parents and siblings financially. Ogawa maintains that it was a mistake for him and many other Nisei men to marry Brazilian women of lower social classes. In the late 1990s, Ogawa eventually remarried a much younger, college-educated Japanese woman, who came to study in Brazil as an exchange student in 1988.[92]

In the early 2000s, a small number of retired elite Niseis, predominantly men, suddenly began to participate in Bunkyo and other Japanese Brazilian organizations and associations in the city; they seemed to be "returning" to "the Nikkei community" after having distanced themselves from it for thirty or forty years. Interestingly, their "return" coincided with Japanese Brazilians' preparations for the upcoming centenary on Japanese immigration. Already in the mid-1990s, during Yamauchi's presidency, Bunkyo began to face major financial problems stemming from two external factors. The first was the demise of two major Japanese Brazilian agricultural cooperatives and a bank that had supported Bunkyo financially for many years: the Cotia Agricultural Cooperative, the Southern Brazil Agricultural Cooperative, and the Bank of South America.[93] The second was Bunkyo's loss of many members due to *dekassegui,* which reduced the Japanese Brazilian population. Yamauchi, as the first Nisei Bunkyo president, failed to carry out successful fundraising for its formal celebrations on the ninetieth anniversary of Japanese immigration to Brazil. As a result, Bunkyo quickly lost its position of importance among Japanese Brazilians. In 2002, Kazuo Watanabe, known as the elite of the Nisei elites of his generation, was asked to intervene in Bunkyo's internal financial problems, and officially took on the title of coordinator of Bunkyo's Committee for Reforms. To start with, in April 2003, Watanabe had all sixteen trustees resign and replaced them with new members of his choice. Under Watanabe's leadership, Bunkyo started with Kokei Uehara, a retired USP engineering professor, as its tenth president, and five vice presidents, all born in the 1930s: Eiji Denda, Tomoko Higuchi, Ryomei Yoshioka, Tadayohi Wada, and Osamu Matsuo. These are four elite Niseis, including one woman, and one postwar immigrant, all retired. Kokei Uehara served in Bunkyo's presidency for two terms under Watanabe's leadership and became the president of the Committee on the Centenary. According to Watanabe's definition, it does not take Japanese ancestry to be a Nikkei, as he maintains that "anybody can become a member of the *colônia* if s/he is interested in the Nikkei community which shares and inherits excellent Japanese culture and spirit, regardless of Japanese ancestry."[94]

Yamauchi maintains that some 80 percent of Japanese Brazilians living in São Paulo City have nothing to do with any Japanese Brazilian associations and organizations, and those retired elite Niseis, who have "returned to the Nikkei community," are truly a minority. Yamauchi adds that they desire public recognition, usually decorations from the Japanese government.[95] In fact, both Uehara and Watanabe were decorated by the Japanese government in 2001 and 2011, respectively. However, Shinohara, a Nisei elite younger by a decade, states that he "does not understand why Watanabe and other elite Nisei men wanted to be in the *colônia*" and that Bunkyo is "an unattractive association that has nothing to offer."[96] As *Nikkey Shimbun* reported in 2005, those elite Niseis who "returned to the colônia" in the first few years of the 2000s are the "model Brazilians, who advanced themselves by pushing other Brazilians aside," and the "brains of which the *colônia* is proud." Yet, as Fumio Oura points out, these elite Niseis, who were born in the 1930s, belong to the generation "who developed a strong consciousness of renouncing Japan after its defeat" and "tried to save themselves by identifying themselves as Brazilians." As a result, they have a "complicated mental structure."[97]

Takeshi Horie of *Nikkey Shimbun* cites an interesting episode. One evening, after a meeting at Bunkyo, Watanabe and other elite Nisei members decided to dine together at a local Japanese restaurant, where all chose to have "curry with rice," a popular family meal in Japan. At the dinner table, Watanabe casually mentioned that it would be tastier to crack a raw egg over the curry dish, and all of the others followed him, even though Watanabe did not mean to have them do so.[98] It shows that Watanabe has retained such a strong "Japanese" taste in food over the years and that other Nisei elites did not find it strange to eat a raw egg, which Brazilians/ Westerners do not do. Watanabe is also known as an excellent go (traditional Japanese chess) player, a skill he learned from his Nisei high school classmate in São Paulo City. Furthermore, he is a big fan of Aki Yashiro (b. 1950), a famous Japanese female *enka* singer, with a large collection of her CDs.[99] This accords with what I have heard in São Paulo City about what elite Nisei lawyers born in the late 1930s and early 1940s do for entertainment: they get together to sing Japanese *enka* on karaoke. Watanabe and other elite Niseis of his generation seem to share a similar personal taste in popular food and music, which may be attributed to the way they grew up among the Japanese in the countryside. As prewar Rikkokai immigrant Hideto Futatsugi, headmaster of Casa de Estudantes "Harmonia," recalled in 1978, whenever fried chicken was served as a meal, the Japanese Brazilian students of "Harmonia" a quarter century earlier would throw the bones on the floor without thinking. Growing up in the countryside, where Japanese farming families had meals in an unfloored part of the house, they were accustomed to tossing chicken bones to their dogs. Those

Japanese Brazilian students also shared solid Japanese language skills. Futatsugi characterized them as "somewhat unsophisticated but very sensitive in a Japanese way."[100] In fact, Watanabe and Yamauchi lived together in "Harmonia" in 1954–1955, and they belong to this older generation of elite Niseis. What Watanabe and his old Nisei friends have been doing at Bunkyo under fancy political rhetoric since around 2002 may not be so different from what they did at the Piratininga Club in the 1950s and 1960s: primarily socializing among themselves. After thirty or forty years of individual career advancement in Brazilian society, on reaching the age of retirement they finally "released" their long-suppressed Nikkeiness/Japaneseness and shared familiar Japanese food and music with other old Nisei friends of the same socioeconomic standing.

Conclusion

The centenary of Japanese immigration to Brazil provided opportunities for older elite Nisei men to create and/or reclaim their Nikkei identity, as in the case of a famous journalist, Jorge Okubaro (b. 1946), an editor of *O Estado de São Paulo*. Okubaro did not identify himself as a Nikkei until 2007, when he published a book on his immigrant father and his family with the title *O Súdito (Banzai Massateru!)*.[101] Okubano is a Nisei of Okinawan ancestry and, like Olga Futemma (see chapter 5), always had a strong ethnic Okinawan identity. During Brazil's military regime, Okubaro became a political militant and was imprisoned for a few months. After being released from the prison, he dropped out of Poli and studied journalism at USP. He hid his record of imprisonment for many years to protect his family's honor until he gave a public lecture at Centro de Estudos Nipo-Brasileiros in June 2011.[102]

Kiyoshi Harada (b. 1941), a prominent Nisei lawyer, edited and published *O Nikkei no Brasil* in 2008 for the centenary. Harada, a USP Law School graduate in 1967, was born in Marília, São Paulo, to prewar immigrants from Kumamoto. The book's contributors are all elite Niseis of his generation, predominantly men, including Watanabe. The book also includes interviews with prominent Japanese Brazilians. In chapter 2, which he authored, Harada describes how well the Nikkei had come to be integrated into Brazilian society and culture.[103] Yet, according to *Nikkey Shimbun*, Harada stated in a public lecture in São Paulo City on May 29, 2008, "The Nisei in Brazil are more Japanese than the Japanese in Japan."[104]

Watanabe also spoke of the centenary: "The whole of Brazil celebrated the centenary." He said that he felt "respected and loved" when he was interviewed in his office by a Japanese professional photographer from Japan on October 9, 2008.[105] Watanabe claimed he had "never experienced any racial discrimination" during the twenty-five years he served as the very first Japanese Brazilian judge for the São Paulo State Court of Appeals. Yet he mentioned having been told, at the time when he was studying, that "the Nikkeijin [people of Japanese descent] could never pass the exam to become a judge," and concluded, "It was like a dream for the state of Brazil to accept anybody who *looked Asian*."[106] Not surprisingly, Watanabe was well aware of Brazilian racism while he was busy "whitening" through individual social climbing; only after his retirement has he been able to reunite with some of the other educated Nisei men of the same class and educational background.

According to Watanabe and other elite Niseis, being Nikkei in Brazil is cultural, not racial. And culturally the elite Niseis are superior to the Japanese in Japan because they are more Japanese than the Japanese themselves are. Having survived and even thrived as "special Japanese" among the Brazilian elite, the elite Nisei men born in the 1930s and 1940s may well feel strong emotional connections only with one another. Having distanced themselves from "ordinary" Japanese Brazilians and their ethnic organizations and associations for many years, they did not just "come back" to Bunkyo, *colônia,* or the "Nikkei society" for the centenary. Rather, they created their own space to share their collective identity. In this way, they have been able to position themselves as elite Brazilians among Japanese Brazilians, who take much ethnic pride in them as their "elite Niseis."

Unlike most of his old friends of the Piratininga Club, Iossuke Tanaka had never left Bunkyo or the Nikkei community in São Paulo. That does not mean Tanaka did not struggle harder than others who had separated themselves from the general Japanese Brazilian population; Tanaka's search for self took a more internal form than that of Watanabe and others, who succeeded as "model Brazilians." Tanaka stated, "I can be Japanese and Brazilian, but it is up to each situation. Many of us, the Nisei, feel that we do not have a spiritual home. We are unfortunate in this regard, but at the same time fortunate, as we understand what it means to be Japanese and Brazilian at the same time, even though not perfectly."[107] Tanaka wrote in a lengthy handwritten letter of May 12, 2009:

> As a Nisei, I have no home to "long for from afar." That's why I can never imagine how the old prewar immigrants really felt when they finally went home after the end of the war. As I said before, I visited my father's hometown in 1989. His old house was still standing there, although it was falling apart.

On a small hill near the house there were my ancestors' graves with stones, big and small, as burial markers. Some stones were relatively new so that I could read the names of the deceased, but others were so old that they did not look like burial markers. But while looking at those stones, I felt like something was warming up inside myself as I was finally finding what I had been looking for for many years. What is it that I found then? That is probably that I have Japanese blood in myself.[108]

Neither Brazilian nor Japanese, Iossuke Tanaka, as an elite Nisei, seems to have accepted that he belonged in his "spiritual home" deep inside himself—in the invisible "Japanese blood" that only he could feel.

Chapter Four

POSTWAR IMMIGRANTS AND
THEIR NEW JAPANESE IDENTITY

My husband is also an immigrant who was brought by his parents. He was forced to move. He always wonders how his life would have turned out to be if he had stayed in Japan. He still seems to regret it. He visited where he and his family used to live and says he would have been much better off if they had not left Japan. My oldest sister says the same thing. I do not have the same feelings as they do. I do not feel that I was forced to come with my family. I was only nine years old and do not remember any of my friends. Of course, we are all treated as Japanese here in Brazil. My husband says that in Japan the Japanese come up and say, "You are from Brazil, aren't you?" He feels sad being treated as a Brazilian. He speaks Japanese well and has a Japanese face, but they can always tell he is from Brazil as a *dekassegui*.

—*Sachiko Tomino, the secretary-general*
of a Japanese language school, 1999[1]

On June 25, 1999, I was visiting with Sachiko Tomino (b. 1953), a postwar child immigrant, for her first interview. Since 1994, she had been working at the Curso de Língua Japonesa Bunkyo (Bunkyo Japanese Language School), as its secretary-general after having spent eighteen years as a full-time homemaker. Tomino was married to another postwar immigrant (b. 1946), and they had two Nisei children, twenty and seventeen years old. Tomino said, "I think I am Japanese, but they think I am Nisei. My true friends are Nikkeis. I have three really good friends, all of whom are postwar child immigrants. My husband also thinks he is Japanese." Her husband and his family (parents, a younger sister, and two younger brothers) had immigrated from Hokkaido first to the Dominican Republic in 1956 and, after living there for seven years, moved to Brazil, with a

Dominican-born youngest son. With *colono* contracts, the family first settled on a coffee plantation in rural São Paulo and then all moved to São Paulo City. Tomino's husband graduated from a technical school there and worked as an engineer for years, but after his company went bankrupt in 1989, he could not make a smooth transition to his new company and became unemployed. In 1990, Tomino's husband began his *dekassegui* in Japan and was working in Shizuoka prefecture at a computer parts company on the night shift at the time of Tomino's first interview in June 1999. I followed Tomino and her story until June 2005, by which time she had divorced her husband.

In 1962, Sachiko Tomino arrived in Brazil on the *Brazil Maru* from Iki Island of Nagasaki prefecture, with her parents and two older sisters, aged fifteen and thirteen. During the war, Tomino's father, as a single man, had been drafted and sent to Manchuria as a soldier. He came home after the war but never stopped dreaming of moving somewhere such as Manchuria for large-scale farming; he was easily swayed by the Japanese government's advertisement on emigration to Brazil. Tomino's father applied to Kaikyoren, which screened applications for state-sponsored family immigration to Brazil. Before emigration, he also bought land in Amazonas state through JAMIC in order to engage in the booming cultivation of black pepper. Unfortunately, his big dream did not come true in Brazil; soon the family gave up on farming and moved to Manaus, capital of Amazonas, where they made a living in vegetable vending for ten years. In Manaus, her oldest sister met and married a Japanese immigrant who lived in São Paulo City. Soon her middle sister followed her there by marrying his younger brother, with whom she ran a cleaning business. In 1973, Tomino and her parents eventually moved to São Paulo City, where they made a living with a *quitanda*. Tomino is the only one in her birth family who was able to receive a formal Brazilian education; she graduated from a junior high school in Manaus and finished her senior high school education in São Paulo City, where she also worked at two Japanese companies, Ataka Sangyo and Sanyo. She met her husband through a friend of her oldest sister and got married in 1978, becoming a full-time homemaker, while giving birth to a son (1979) and a daughter (1982). Tomino had a relatively comfortable life until her husband became unemployed and opted for *dekassegui*.

In the early 1980s, postwar immigrant men became the first group to migrate to Japan as *dekasseguis;* most of them went to Japan on their own while leaving their families behind in Brazil, as a temporary solution to their financial problems. That often ended up turning into a long-term separation of family members across the Pacific, which often resulted in the gradual demise of patriarchal rule and the dissolution of marriages and/or families, as Tomino's case illustrates.

Postwar Japanese immigrants, long known collectively among the Japanese for their "unwillingness to participate in the *colônia*," often characterize themselves as "individualistic with much petit-bourgeois consciousness" and maintain that they do not have such a strong community-oriented mentality as their prewar counterparts did.[2] Postwar immigrant men and women brought to Brazil "new" values and ideas from postwar Japan, which often created various conflicts with prewar immigrants and their descendants, and confirmed or challenged patriarchy in the diaspora.

Japanese emigration was resumed in 1952 upon the enactment of the San Francisco Peace Treaty on April 28. On January 18, 1953, 51 Japanese men arrived on a Dutch ship in the port of Santos—all single, young adult self-paid *yobiyose* immigrants. They were soon followed by Tsuji and Matsubara immigrants (chapter 1) and 248 sericulture immigrants sponsored by Paulista Sericultural Cooperative (1954). Rikkokai resumed its function as an agency for overseas immigration, and for the postwar period, some 1,210 Rikkokai immigrants arrived in Brazil.[3] The Japanese government began to sponsor the emigration of Okinawans in 1957, even though postwar Okinawa was occupied by the United States until 1972. As a result, the number of Okinawan *yobiyose* immigrants entering Brazil increased rapidly, with 1,430 in 1957, and 1,830 in 1958.[4] Meanwhile, Japanese companies began to advance to Brazil on a large scale, starting with Doi and Astoria Ceramics Industries in 1953. Japan's capital investment in Brazil resulted in the establishment of two steel manufacturing companies as major joint ventures between Brazil and Japan: Usinas Siderúrgicas de Minas Gerais S.A. (Steel Mills of Minas Gerais Corporation, Usiminas) in Belo Horizonte, Minas Gerais (1958), and Ishikawajima do Brasil Estaleiros S/A (Ishikawajima Shipyards of Brazil Corporation, ISHIBRAS) in Rio de Janeiro City (1962).[5]

Japan's state-sponsored single male emigration began in the mid-1950s, mainly in order to fulfill the economic needs of younger sons of small farmers/landowners, who continued to struggle to survive financially in overpopulated Japan and wanted to start a new life overseas. Cotia Agricultural Cooperative had grown, with more than five thousand members by its twenty-fifth anniversary in 1952, and, suffering from a shortage of young male adult labor of Japanese descent, it turned to immigration from Japan. From 1955 to 1968, 2,295 young single adult immigrant men arrived as Cotia *seinen*, plus 313 Cotia immigrants who arrived in family units.[6] On June 9, 1956, 22 young male agricultural workers arrived in Brazil as the first group of Sangyo Kaihatsu Seinentai (Young Men's Corps for Industrial Development), and a total of 207 young adult men immigrated to Brazil under this program by 1962, when it was terminated. Not all state-sponsored immigrants were contracted to engage in agriculture in Brazil. In 1961, industrial immigration also started with Japanese state subsidies, targeting young mechanics and craftsmen, and around 1,350 Japanese men arrived under this program for the next twenty years.[7] In addition to agricultural and industrial immigrants, small numbers of college graduates were directly employed by some major Japanese Brazilian companies, as in the case of Sachio Akimoto (b. 1937), who arrived in Brazil as an employee of the Bank of South America, to which he had applied through Japan's Fuji Bank.[8]

Japan's postwar immigration to Brazil peaked in 1959 (at 7,041) and 1960 (at 6,832), but the number declined quickly afterward, due to postwar Japan's emergence as a world economic power with the Summer Olympics in Tokyo (1964). During the first fifteen years of postwar immigration the Japanese government made loans to emigrants for their overseas travel expenses, and after five years' grace each immigrant was obligated to repay his/her loan to the government over the next fifteen years by annual installments. As of April 1, 1966, the Japanese government began to subsidize emigrants' passages to Brazil fully, while exempting previous ones from repayment.[9] Japanese immigrants entering Brazil totaled 53,657 by 1993, when the Japanese government finally terminated its state-sponsored emigration. Postwar immigrants constitute approximately one-quarter of the Japanese immigrants who have entered Brazil since 1908.[10]

Brazilians called all postwar Japanese immigrants *japonês(a)*, as they had done with prewar immigrants and their descendants. After all, the "Japanese" were all the same in the poplar Brazilian mind. Among my postwar male immigrant informants, Hiroshi Komori (1929–2015) and Yasuo Shiobara (b. 1936), who immigrated to Brazil in 1957 and 1964, respectively, did business with "Brazilians" only, but they differed in their ways of dealing with Brazilian perceptions of the Japanese. Komori's narrative reveals that he was not bothered at all when his business partners called him *o japonês*, not by his name. By contrast, Shiobara has always taken it as an insult, saying that his "inferiors, especially blacks" often called him that. In 1990, when a black engineer made fun of him for being Japanese, Shiobara talked back to him, "You are neither my employer nor professor. Why do you say such things to me?" Surprised at his strong reaction, the engineer shut up immediately.[11]

Postwar immigrants differ from their prewar counterparts in a few important ways. First, 93.9 percent of prewar immigrants were recruited by emigration companies, whereas only 5 percent were *yobiyose* immigrants, who were "sponsored" by relatives and acquaintances living in Brazil. The rest, who constituted 1.1 percent, were those who had already immigrated to Brazil and were returning after a short absence. By contrast, more than half of postwar immigrants (51.2 percent among those who arrived in Brazil by 1963) came as *yobiyose* immigrants.[12] It should be noted, though, that *yobiyose* immigrants are divided into two categories: "special *yobiyose* immigrants," whose emigration was sponsored by the state, and "ordinary *yobiyose* immigrants," whose passages were paid by the immigrants themselves or those who summoned them to Brazil.[13] The rest of the postwar immigrants (48.8 percent) belong to two other categories: "immigrants for employment" (33.6 percent) and "settler immigrants" (15.2 percent). Settler immigrants corresponded roughly to prewar "owner-farmers," who constituted 8.9 percent of prewar immigrants. Second, because of the change in Brazil's immigration policy, the proportion of single immigrants increased considerably, from 3.9 percent for the prewar period to 15.5 percent for the postwar period, virtually all men (99.7 percent).[14] Third, whereas the majority of prewar immigrants ended up staying in Brazil permanently (chapter 1), around half of the postwar immigrants appear to have returned to Japan.[15] For instance, two-thirds of some 1,200 postwar Rikkokai immigrants returned to Japan. Hisashi Nagata (b. 1929) maintains that most postwar immigrants arrived with enough money to buy a return passage to Japan, and they returned home if things did not work in a year or so.[16]

Within the Japanese diaspora in Brazil, postwar immigrants were pejoratively called Japão Novo (New Japan) in Portuguese by their prewar counterparts, and in Japanese were called *shinrai imin* (newly arrived immigrant), *shin imin* (new immigrant), *shin imin-san* (Mr./Mrs./Ms. new immigrant), and, in the case of single young men, *shinrai seinen* (newly arrived young men). Prewar immigrants, once pejoratively called Japão by Brazilians and *imin-san* by the Japanese in Japan, especially in Kobe before departure for Brazil, perceived and treated many newcomers from their homeland with the same or even worse contempt.

Upon arrival in Brazil, many postwar immigrants had to get in direct contact with prewar immigrants as their "patrons" in Brazil for their labor contracts, which created various levels of cultural clashes and interpersonal conflicts. After all, there had been little direct communication among the Japanese between Brazil and Japan for over a decade until postwar immigration began. Still divided among themselves over the defeat of Japan, during the 1950s many prewar immigrants in Brazil could not even imagine how much and how quickly Japan and the Japanese had changed after the war; some postwar immigrants called them "provincial" and *Burajiru boke* (outdated after spending many years in Brazil).[17] In return, some prewar immigrants treated postwar immigrants with what the famous Japanese critic Soichi Ōya, who was traveling in Brazil in late August and September of 1954, called a "sergeant spirit." Ōya wrote, "One cannot deny that old [prewar] immigrants feel that they have established themselves by enduring all the hardships in life so that they want newly arrived [postwar] immigrants to suffer in the same way."[18] The same opinion was expressed by six elite Japanese male college students who visited Brazil in 1956 as a caravan of Hitotsubashi University led by Hitotsubashi alumnus and novelist Shintaro Ishikawa (governor of Tokyo, 1999–2012). They reported that many prewar immigrants expected newly arrived postwar immigrants to suffer the same hardships they had gone through, and it was regrettable that the Japanese seemed to exploit other Japanese in Brazil.[19] According to Senichi Adachi,

> Postwar immigrants had a very had time with prewar immigrants, who said, "They do not work and we have to teach them how to work harder." Postwar immigrants regarded prewar immigrants as backward, with the spirit of noncommissioned officers who bully soldiers. Prewar immigrants regarded postwar immigrants as spoiled and therefore wanted to retrain them with "whipping of love." Many postwar immigrants could not put up with the *fazenda* life in the countryside and ran away to the city, where they got into fights with others on the streets. Japanese-language newspapers published exaggerated articles on such fights and then prewar immigrants tended to conclude that postwar immigrants were no good.[20]

Komori and many other *shinrai seinen* were treated with deep suspicion after a young Cotia *seinen* killed his patron/employer, a prewar Japanese immigrant.[21] Japan's *Yomiuri Shimbun* reported on the arrest of twenty-year-old Chikara Miki, who committed the murder on December 13, 1957, and stated that the Cotia Agricultural Cooperative blamed the Japanese government for its sloppy selection of prospective emigrants. By then the cooperative had accepted 1,340 young male immigrants, including drug addicts, those with sexually transmitted disease, and mental patients, 6 of whom had already been deported back to Japan, with 16 more to follow.[22]

In the end, out of a total of 2,295 Cotia *seinen* immigrants, some 30 committed suicide in Brazil.[23] Adachi states that, arriving at the age of eighteen, many "got depressed clinically and that became a problem for the Nikkei community" so that eventually, with funding from the Japanese government, a mental institution was constructed for their rehabilitation.[24] Goro Tamura (b. 1932), himself a *Cotia seinen*, states that those young men, fresh out of high school and with no work experience, were simply not ready for their new life in Brazil and could not adjust to the new environment. He immigrated in 1960 at the age of twenty-eight, with a college degree.[25]

It is the young male self-paid *yobiyose* immigrants without labor contracts who became the first to move to São Paulo City. Senichi Adachi (1931–2003) was one of them. He immigrated to Brazil in 1956 for health reasons; originally from Hokkaido, he had become very ill with acute pleurisy when he was a student at Meiji University in postwar Tokyo and needed to recuperate in a place with a warm climate and abundant food. Thus Adachi asked a remote relative in Rio de Janeiro to sponsor his immigration to Brazil. His relative/sponsor, who was engaged with his family in suburban tomato farming, found Adachi rather useless as a farmer. At his suggestion, Adachi moved in May 1957 from Rio de Janeiro to São Paulo City, relying on the advice and help of his shipmate, Mr. Arakawa, a Waseda University graduate. Arakawa introduced Adachi to Takuji Fujii, Bunkyo's secretary-general, who hired him immediately as Bunkyo was busy preparing for the fiftieth anniversary of Japanese immigration to Brazil in 1958. At Bunkyo, Adachi was visited by many prewar Japanese immigrants, who wanted to ask him if Japan had won the war. At the same time, they often told him, "None of you guys is good. You are all drunkards and nonworkers." "Back then," Adachi states, "the Nikkei *colônia* was in huge chaos due to the continuing *kachi-make* conflicts. Bunkyo was founded in order to unite Japanese descendants in Brazil as a community and was recognized by the Brazilian government as an official organization." According to Adachi, the Brazilian government maintained that "the Japanese did not assimilate":

> Therefore Nikkei leaders used to urge us to assimilate ourselves. I did not understand what they meant by assimilation. I did not know whether it referred to true cultural transformation into Brazilians or a rather superficial acculturation, which enabled us to make friends with Brazilians. Prewar immigrants said to us, "Throw away all of your clothes and shirts that you brought from Japan with yourselves. You would not be able to assimilate otherwise. You must all learn how to speak Portuguese." It was a reflection of assimilation policies promoted by the Brazilian government. We the Japanese were told not to form a large group among ourselves. Some Nikkei congressmen cautioned us that DEOPS [Departamento Estadual de Ordem Política e Social de São Paulo (São Paulo State Department of Political and Social Order)] were watching and might come to arrest us any time.[26]

In October 1956, before Adachi arrived in São Paulo City, Bunkyo had already set up a department of employment counseling; by then some seven hundred single young male *yobiyose* immigrants had quit farming in the countryside and moved to the city to look for new jobs. About the increasing concentration of *shinrai imin* in São Paulo City, Takuji Fujii wrote in 1959 that the majority of these *yobiyose* immigrants had arrived in Brazil and moved to the city without the knowledge of their employees/sponsors; they were college graduates, college dropouts, or high school graduates, without any experience in farming, and they quickly gave up on the countryside because it lacked entertainment. More than 70 percent of the job seekers whom Bunkyo helped from October 7, 1956, to June 15, 1959, were so-called *shinrai imin,* who were legally unemployable since they had not finished their two- to four-year labor contracts and did not even know that they needed to apply for work permits.[27] Meanwhile, in São Paulo City some postwar young male immigrants constantly got into fights with Nisei men in public and committed crimes against other Japanese Brazilians. Japanese Brazilians' hostility toward young postwar immigrant men peaked on June 3, 1962, when three young immigrant men broke into a Japanese Brazilian household in Liberdade, where they severely beat a homemaker and her two daughters, and ran away to northeast Brazil. The homemaker died several days later.[28] Katsuzo Yamamoto, a successful prewar immigrant, observed how greatly this crime had "shaken the Nikkei *colônia*," especially prewar immigrants, who were extremely nationalistic as Japanese.[29]

Adachi met his wife, Yukiko (b. 1935), in São Paulo City at a Japanese *pensão* in Liberdade, where both of them lived. Yukiko is a Nisei from Bastos who is fluent in Japanese and "more Japanese" than Adachi himself. She had already obtained a certificate as a sewing teacher back in Bastos and intended to polish her sewing skills in the city. Knowing how to type, Yukiko worked at a German-owned company and continued to do so for two years after marriage until her first child was born in 1962.[30] Komori, a Nihon University graduate and veterinary science major (1956), arrived in Brazil in 1957 as a self-paid *yobiyose* immigrant. He married a Nisei daughter of a prewar Japanese immigrant pharmacy owner who had hired him. It seems that his marriage was arranged by his wife's Issei mother. Goro Tamura met and married a Nisei woman. Susumu Ozawa (b. 1936), who arrived in 1957 as a member of his uncle's immigrant family from Nagasaki, moved alone in 1962 from Amazonas state to São Paulo City, where he fell in love with Nisei Sakiko Uda (b. 1940) and eventually persuaded her to marry him in 1969, with her father's blessing. Together the Ozawas built a very successful jewelry and souvenir business in Liberdade during the 1970s. But other postwar immigrant men were not so lucky, as in the case of Masaru Takanashi, a junior high school gradate in Mie prefecture who once lived in the same *pensão* as Adachi. Takanashi says that the most painful thing he had to endure in Brazil was that his marriage proposal to his Nisei girlfriend was declined by her prewar immigrant parents, who wanted her to marry a college-educated Nisei man.[31] Adachi states that there were many similar cases:

> They [prewar immigrants] thought we [postwar immigrant men] were lazy and therefore thought we did not deserve their precious daughters. Many people were treated that way. They thought their daughters would be better off with college-educated Nisei husbands, who were all called *dotor* [doctor]. Most were told that they were not allowed to marry their Nisei girlfriends, since they were vagabond *shinrai seinen*.[32]

Semanário Nikkei reported (1966) another reason: Issei parents had suffered a great deal as immigrants in Brazil and did not want their daughters to go through the same hardships by marrying immigrant men, whereas young Nisei women wanted to marry men with stable means, whether they were Isseis or Niseis.[33] In the end, more than 40 percent of the total postwar single male immigrants married Nisei women whom they had met in Brazil.[34]

Approximately one-quarter of the total single postwar immigrant men in Brazil married "bride immigrants," Japanese women arrived directly from Japan.[35] Their marriages had to be legally registered in Japan before their departure for Brazil in order for them to receive state funding for their emigration from the Japanese government, as well as for them to be allowed by the Brazilian government to immigrate to Brazil as legitimate family members of immigrants. It was the Japanese government's responsibility to transport bride immigrants safely to their husbands in Brazil. As a Kaikyoren employee, Takeshi Nagase (b. 1936) was ordered in 1962 to work as assistant director for the voyage of the *Argentina Maru* to South America under the supervision of a director from the Ministry of Foreign Affairs. The ship carried around four hundred immigrants from various parts of Japan, including ten or eleven "bride immigrants." As one of his official duties, Nagase was specifically instructed by the ship's director to "protect bride immigrants" from the many available single young men, immigrant men and the crew, on board. Nagase had to patrol the ship day and night to make sure there would be no affairs involving bride immigrants going on during the voyage.[36]

Some marriages between postwar immigrant men in Brazil and Japanese women in Japan were arranged through kinship, as in the case of Misako Kuroki, who was asked by her aunt to marry her cousin who had immigrated to Brazil as a Cotia *seinen*. Kuroki agreed to do so at her mother's strong suggestion on the ground that her father was hospitalized for depression and her older brother's new wife had moved in. Thus she arrived in the port of Santos on August 13, 1959, and her wedding was held two days later.[37] Other marriages were arranged between strangers through correspondence and the exchange of photos between prospective marriage partners who had never met in person; new wives arrived in Brazil as bride immigrants whose major role was to "support their husbands." Noriko Shimada maintains that, in contrast to "war brides," who were portrayed negatively, state-sponsored "bride immigrants" were presented widely in Japanese mass media as "well-educated, urban young professional women," with special emphasis on their important spousal role in helping young Japanese men succeed overseas.[38]

Cotia *seinen* had four-year labor contracts with their employers, and many wanted to marry and have families as soon as they became independent farmers. In 1959, twelve "bride immigrants" for Cotia *seinen* arrived in Brazil, the first of five hundred such immigrants.[39] Setsuo Yamaguchi (1930–2004), Reiko Uehara's fourth-oldest brother, played an important role in recruiting bride immigrants. Born as one of nine children to the head of a local agricultural cooperative in Nagao prefecture, Yamaguchi had immigrated to Brazil in 1955 as a Cotia *seinen,* and became very successful in flower cultivation in Atibaia, São Paulo. He married one of the first twelve Cotia bride immigrants. In 1962, he became the first president of the newly established Cotia Seinen Renraku Kyogikai (Cotia Seinen's Council for Communication and Discussions), and he and the vice president visited Japan in 1963 for business. That was when Yamaguchi told his parents in Nagano that one of his two single younger sisters should move to Brazil to "help" him. The youngest sister, aged eighteen, refused to move to Brazil, and her parents told twenty-two-year-old Reiko to go. As a daughter, she "felt obligated to obey." As it turned out, Setsuo Yamaguchi wanted her to marry his business partner, also from Nagano (1931–1990), who had spent two years as an agricultural trainee in Brazil and returned to Japan but agreed with Yamaguchi to go back to Brazil provided he could do so as a married man. Thus Reiko's "destiny" was decided by two patriarchs for the sake of their business. Reiko Uehara arrived in Brazil in 1964 and worked in her husband's business of chrysanthemum and later fruit cultivation in Atibaia for the next twenty-six years.[40]

But in postwar Japan, some other young women did not act so passively. As the "old-fashioned" Reiko Uehara has noted, time was already changing for young Japanese women as Atibaia became "full of bride immigrants" in the late 1960s.[41] One of these was Isoko Terada, who arrived in 1968 on the *Argentina Maru* as the wife of Michio Terada, a successful flower farmer. The couple had never met in person. Interviewed at home in 1999, Isoko stated, "I myself chose to come. Nobody else told me to do so. My parents made strong objections for three years but I still came. . . . I am a farmer's daughter and I wanted to farm with my husband." As a Cotia *seinen* form Nagano, Michio Terada had arrived in Brazil in 1961 at the age of twenty-four with a labor contact with Setsuo Yamaguchi as his patron. The Teradas' flower cultivation business in Atibaia grew successfully over the years, and their three sons all graduated from college—the oldest one in agriculture, to inherit the family business, and the two younger ones in engineering.[42]

Like Isoko Terada, some young Japanese women actively chose to become bride immigrants out of "longing for life in a foreign country." Those women usually turned to agencies that recruited and even trained young women as prospective bridal immigrants, most prominently Kaigai Joshi Kenshu Sentā (Women's Training Center for Overseas Migration) in Fujisawa City of Kanagawa prefecture. This center was established in 1954 by Miyoko Konami (1909–2006), a graduate of Nihon Women's College, and her husband, Kiyoshi Konami, a retired professor of agriculture at the University of Tokyo, with the support of the Ministry of Foreign Affairs. Junko Ōshima, for instance, spent forty-five days there in 1966 as a trainee and departed for Brazil in November 1967 as the wife of a Tokyo University of Agriculture graduate who had already immigrated to Brazil. As of 1986, approximately one hundred former bride immigrants who had completed the six-week bridal training at Konami's center were living within the jurisdiction of the consulate general of Japan in São Paulo.[43]

Taeko Sase (b. 1932) writes that, as a young single woman, she became so "obsessed" about moving to Brazil that in 1958 she learned of Rikkokai and visited its headquarters to ask whether there would be any way for a single woman to immigrate to Brazil. She was allowed to participate in Rikkokai's training courses and other activities with its members, all men, to wait for a chance to come along. Eventually she was recommended to marry a Rikkokai immigrant to Brazil. Her husband-to-be was carefully chosen, and she corresponded with him for a short period, without meeting him; in August 1959, Sase departed for Brazil and became Rikkokai's first bride immigrant.[44] In 1960, Rikkokai itself established its own agency,

Minamijujikai (The Southern Cross Association), to recruit young women
to marry Rikkokai immigrants in Brazil. Yasuko Tanaka, for instance, remembers Rikkokai members distributing bills on the streets of Tokyo in
February 1960, asking, "Are there any brides-to-be who would like to go
to Brazil?" She joined Minamijujikai and married a Rikkokai immigrant to
move to Brazil. Thus, from 1959 to 1970, sixty bride immigrants arrived
in Brazil as members of Minamijujikai.[45] Yumiko Hibino immigrated to
Brazil in 1959 through Japan's Zenkoku Nōgyo Takushoku Kumiai Ren-
gokai (National Federation of Agricultural Associations for Colonization,
Zentakuren), which collaborated with Cotia Agricultural Cooperative in
recruiting bride immigrants. Hibino maintains that she chose to become a
bride immigrant because "no single Japanese woman could move to a foreign county on her own back then."[46]

Rather surprisingly, in the mid-1980s, some young Japanese women
were still turning to bride immigration to migrate overseas. As of 1986 a
total of some forty single women, aged nineteen to thirty, from diverse
regional and class backgrounds were taking a six-week training course at
Konami's center at a fee of 130,000 yen. The center continued to receive four
hundred applications per year from prospective grooms in South America,
among whom eighty or ninety men were allowed to register after a rigorous
screening, mainly for financial status and abilities, which were most important for a successful match, according to Konami. More surprisingly,
despite the fact that more and more women chose to study and/or work
overseas, Konami wrote as late as 1986, "Women cannot migrate to overseas without marrying men," while advocating such properly arranged marriages to successful husbands overseas as the primary source of women's
happiness.[47]

Needless to say, not all of the bride immigrants stayed in Brazil. Many
who chose not to stay married to their husbands in Brazil returned to Japan.
Masako Okino, who arrived in Brazil in 1968 with three other bride immigrants on the same immigrant ship, says she is the only one still remaining in Brazil; the other two went back to Japan almost immediately. In
Yasuko Tanaka's group of eleven bridal immigrants, two soon dissolved
their marriages and returned to Japan.[48] Those who did not have money to
buy passage to Japan needed to find ways to support themselves, but it was
difficult for them to find employment in Brazil. According to Adachi:

> By that time, large Japanese Brazilian companies such as Cotia had become
> Brazilian corporations, where all official documents had to be in Portuguese.
> Those corporations hired Nisei women who knew how to type. Of course,

that was not the case of Issei women, who did not speak Portuguese. The fortunate ones found work as secretaries in Japanese, but there were not many jobs as such. The Nikkei *colônia* back then was still predominantly Issei and therefore there were many Japanese-style restaurants, such as Aoyagi and Akasaka, and all of their customers were Issei men, who tended to be very strict about proper Japanese manners, such as the usage of chopsticks and movement of ceramic cups. That is where the bride immigrants found employment in the end. That is the only place they could work at [without having legal papers].[49]

Interestingly, some well-to-do prewar immigrant men, especially wealthy potato farmers, ended up providing the "new" Japanese women with financial opportunities that enabled many of them to work and save money, with which some eventually went back to Japan on their own. These women continued to rely on patriarchy for their survival, even after they escaped from the marriages they did not want to keep.

For state-sponsored immigration in family units, as in the case of prewar immigration, it was usually the patriarch who made the decision to migrate. Kiyoshi Shima found that among the immigrant families he interviewed on the *Brazil Maru*, departing Kobe on September 27, 1955, this was true for around 86 percent.[50] Tomino's father chose to migrate to Brazil, dreaming of large-scale farming. His wife and three young daughters could not help but follow him, even though his fifteen-year-old daughter, an excellent high school student who wanted to continue to study, made strong objections. Being rather poorly informed about Brazil by postwar Japan's state propaganda, even some relatively well-to-do men dreamed big and unrealistic dreams and inevitably made their family members pay the price for their decisions. For example, Katsuko Sumida's father, as an eldest son of a well-to-do family in Maebashi City, Gunma prefecture, was not allowed to immigrate to Brazil before the war, but moved with his own family to Manchuria in 1940–1941. In 1953, after the passing of his father, he finally relocated himself and his entire family (wife, two daughters, and a son), except his oldest and married daughter, to Macapá, Amapá state, where many hardships awaited them. The family suffered for years to come, and today Sumida (b. 1931) is the only surviving member of her immigrant family; she took care of her mother until her passing in 2002, by which time not only her father but all three of her younger siblings had passed away. After working for Lutheran missionaries and their hospital in southern Brazil, Sumida went to Japan in 1962 and graduated from a nursing and midwifery school there, as it turned out to be much more difficult for her to attend an equivalent nursing school in Brazil. She came back to Brazil in December 1969, four days before her father's passing, and worked as a nurse and eventually as a head nurse at a major hospital in São Paulo City for years until her retirement in 1994.[51]

Another well-to-do family paid the price for the big dream of its patriarch, who had been to China during the war. On December 4, 1956, Japan's *Yomiuri Shimbun* reported on the emigration of Yoshinori Ōkawa, a wealthy farmer in Kagawa prefecture and the 1952 recipient of the first prize in rice cultivation in Japan, and his family on the *Burajiru Maru* (with a total of 711 emigrants). Ōkawa had accumulated much property, including nineteen rental houses, all of which he gave to his younger brother, who was to succeed as head of the family. At that time Ōkawa's eldest daughter, Teruko (now Moriyama), was a first-year nutrition major at Showa Women's College in Tokyo but dropped out of college and moved with her family to Guamá, Pará state, where her father intended to engage in large-scale rice cultivation. She says they moved to Brazil "for her father to make his dream come true." Her four younger siblings, three brothers and a sister, aged sixteen, twelve, nine, and seven, could not receive any formal education in Brazil. After many years, finding no hope in the future of farming in Brazil, all three of her younger brothers and their families moved to Japan as *dekasseguis* and have settled down there permanently.[52]

Emiko Arakaki (b. 1954) had to follow the decisions of her father as a daughter and later those of her husband as a wife. As a result, she moved many times between her native Okinawa and South America, and among Bolivia, Argentina, and Brazil. Her father owned a successful wholesale business in Okinawa but decided to move to Bolivia in 1962 to make money. Her father's ambitions moved his family (wife and five children) to Bolivia in 1964, and they lived in Colônia Okinawa for two years, except her older brother, who was sent back to Okinawa as the eldest son, who was expected to receive a college education. The family moved back to Okinawa in 1966, and then again to Bolivia in 1968. From Bolivia, as many other postwar Okinawan immigrants did, her father immigrated to Argentina, accompanied only by Arakaki, who is the second child and oldest daughter, while the rest of the family went back to Okinawa. From Argentina, in 1971, rather than going back to Bolivia, where he still owned land and a house, Arakaki and her father moved to São Paulo City, where her cousin ran a successful business in the Okinawan community of the Vila Carrão district. The rest of her family, except for her oldest brother, moved from Okinawa again to join Arakaki and her father, and the family ran a sewing business (*custura*) for many years. Arakaki's father "made her and her three younger siblings move around for his ambitions to make more money." In São Paulo City, Arakaki met and married an Okinawan man who was visiting his relatives, her neighbors. Because of his occupation as a member of Japan's Defense Military Forces, in 1981, after the birth of two daughters in Brazil (1979 and 1981), Arakaki accompanied her husband back to Okinawa and lived there for five years until 1986, when her husband decided to move to Brazil to start his own business. Thus the Arakakis returned to Brazil and joined Arakaki's birth family in Vila Carrão, where they started their own business.[53]

Kazuya Matsuhira (1937–2014), an eldest child, had to obey his father's decision; he had graduated from high school and was studying for his college entrance exams when his father suddenly decided to immigrate to Brazil in 1956. Matsuhira began his interview by stating, "What I really want to say most of all is that I did not choose to come to Brazil in order to venture overseas. The majority of postwar Japanese immigrants in Brazil did not choose to come; they were brought here for the convenience of their parents." Matsuhira is originally from Sadowara City, Miyazaki prefecture, where his grandparents had arrived as domestic migrants from Uwajima City, Ehime prefecture. After the passing of his maternal grandfather, his father, who married into the Matsuhiras and worked as a local merchant, realized that he would not be able to give all six of his children college educations and therefore decided to move to Brazil for a better life. His maternal grandmother obeyed the new patriarch's decision. Thus the Matsuhiras settled as *colonos* on a coffee plantation in Cafelandia, São Paulo, but coffee did not grow well on their worn-out land, and by paying the penalty to the *fazendeiro* they moved out for suburban tomato farming in Piedade, São Paulo.[54]

Kazuko Ezawa (b. 1929) moved to Brazil to support her older brother. She was educated at a prewar women's high school in Yokohama City and never married in Japan, a fact that she attributes to the great shortage of eligible single men in Japan caused by the war. At the age of twenty-nine, Ezawa arrived in Brazil in 1958 with her older brother and his family, who had once migrated to Kushiro, Hokkaido prefecture, to work on virgin forests in the late 1950s. Finding no hope in the future of Hokkaido for farming and seeing people there immigrating to Brazil, Ezawa's older brother decided to do the same. However, having four young children, he and his wife needed to have one more adult family member to receive state subsidies. Ezawa's older brother wanted to take his eighteen-year-old younger brother, but he had just graduated from high school and did not want to go to Brazil. Ezawa agreed to go with her brother and his family to facilitate their state-sponsored immigration. Together they were assigned as *colonos* to a German-Brazilian-owned coffee plantation in northern Paraná. With no previous experiences in farming, Ezawa soon became a nanny for the plantation owner's new baby, and because the baby needed medical treatment, Ezawa moved with his family to the Santana district of São Paulo City.[55]

Kiyoe Sekiguchi (b. 1937) and her three young children (born in 1966, 1968, and 1971) had a very comfortable life in Japan because of her husband's well-paying job at Japan's Maritime Self-Defense Force. Sekiguchi's husband (b. 1937) had sailed on submarines to many ports all over the world and wanted to immigrate to Brazil. He almost gave up, since he had no relatives in Brazil and knew nobody there. Sekiguchi made his dream come true. When the Sekiguchis were living in Yokosuka City, Kanagawa prefecture, where her husband was stationed, Sekiguchi read in a Japanese newspaper an article about a successful immigrant man visiting from Brazil and found out where he was staying. Then she went to ask him to summon her and her family as his *yobiyose* immigrants. Thus the Sekiguchis immigrated to Brazil in December 1971, when the youngest child was only seven months old. Unfortunately, things did not work out for the Sekiguchis in Brazil. Her husband could not find a job as a sailor in Santos. Sekiguchi had to support her entire family by working at a bank for a small salary, while her husband became a bartender at a nightclub. Eventually, in 1979, Sekiguchi's husband was hired by a Japanese company, Eidai, and the entire Sekiguchi family moved to Belém, Pará, for his job in the Amazon. Within about a year, Sekiguchi and her children moved back to São Paulo City for the children's higher education, leaving her husband alone working. The Sekiguchis got a divorce in 1986, after her husband had a baby by his young "Brazilian" girlfriend. After moving his entire family to Brazil, he did not make it in Brazil after all, and Sekiguchi thinks he must have moved back to São Paulo City or gone back to Japan with his new family.[56]

I have encountered a few cases in which women made the decision for the entire family to move and/or negotiated a deal to gain what they had wanted in the first place. Teiko Saeki (b. 1945) and her family gave up a comfortable living in Hiroshima City in order to immigrate to Brazil in 1959, solely because of her older sister, Kaneko, who, at eighteen, insisted on moving to Brazil even if she had to do it on her own. That was simply because Kaneko had read an article published in *Fujin no Tomo* (Women's Friend), a liberal women's magazine founded by famous woman educator Motoko Hani, in which immigration to Brazil was idealized and promoted for women. She had just graduated from an elite private women's high school and was already accepted at its sister college, but she refused to listen to her parents. Saeki's college-educated father eventually moved himself and his family to Brazil to accompany his oldest daughter; he sold his house and other properties and bought land for farming in Mato Grosso do Sul through JAMIC. As a result, at the age of thirteen Saeki dropped out of a public junior high school and immigrated to Brazil despite her relatives' objection. Thus one daughter's pursuit of her dream forced another daughter to sacrifice herself. Another case I encountered is a man in his early sixties who had been forced to drop out of college by his widowed mother, who wanted him to immigrate with her to Brazil, where his older sister and her husband had already settled. He did what his mother wanted him to do and eventually married a Nisei woman, whom he says his mother "bullied to death." Eventually, his mother went back to Japan with his older sister and her family, and he was left in Brazil with his two motherless children, whom he raised on his own.[57]

With language barriers to deal with and little capital to invest, many postwar immigrant families moved to São Paulo City and followed much the same path that prewar immigrants had paved. Tomino and her parents did vegetable and fruit vending as *feirantes,* while Tomino's middle sister, Yasuko Hashida, joined her husband and his family in a cleaning business. Yasuko Tanaka and her late Rikkokai immigrant husband supported themselves and their two Nisei children as *feirantes* for twenty-five years.[58] Hiromi Ono (b. 1954) and her family (parents and three older siblings) arrived in Brazil in 1960 as the *yobiyose* immigrants of one of her father's remote relatives, who was a *feirante* in São Paulo City. Upon arrival, the Onos immediately started their *feirante* business in the Penha district. Within ten years, Ono's parents were able to buy a house in the Santana district, and the family moved there. The Onos continued to be engaged in vegetable vending until the parents' retirement. Ono's three older, Japanese-born siblings graduated from high school or professional school, while she and her five younger Brazilian-born siblings all graduated from college in São Paulo.[59]

After engaging in suburban tomato faming in Piedade, São Paulo, for a few years, Matsuhira and his family moved to the city in 1962. According to Matsuhira, the "Japanese" in the city worked as either *tintureiros* or *feirantes* in the 1960s. Cleaning service was popular among those who had young daughters, and young men were hired for delivery and taking orders from their customers. Matsuhira himself could not bear the thought of cleaning, as it required such hard labor, "like an octopus eating its legs." Fortunately, there were many jobs available for postwar young male immigrants such as Matsuhira. He held a dozen different jobs for the next ten

years: reporter for *São Paulo Shimbun,* employee of Cotia Agricultural Cooperative, merchant dealing in rice and beans, salesman for Amino Futon,
researcher for JAMIC, flower cultivator, *feirante* in flowers, florist, and taxi
driver until 1973, when he was hired for a survey on postwar industrial immigrants by JAMIC, which became part of the Japan International Cooperation Agency (JICA) in 1974. Around the same time Matsuhira married
his wife, who had also come to Brazil as a young adult daughter of a postwar immigrant family, and their two Nisei daughters were born in 1974
and 1975.[60]

Many other young men found jobs at branches of Japanese companies
that ventured into Brazil in the late 1950s and 1960s. Toshio Hata (b. 1932),
from Nagano, quit the job he had held at Tokyo Gas for ten years and arrived
in Brazil in 1960 as a self-paid *yobiyose* immigrant. His sponsor was one of
the founding members of Cotia Agricultural Cooperative. After working
as an announcer for Radio Santo Amaro, the first Japanese-language radio
station, and marrying a postwar immigrant woman from Hokkaido, Hata
worked at a the Brazilian branch of a Japanese ceramic company for the next
thirty-two years.[61]

Yasuo Shiobara (b. 1936), an industrial immigrant through Ibaraki
prefecture's emigration society, arrived in 1964. Just before departure, Shiobara met and married a woman his own age. His wife arrived later in Brazil
as a Minamijujikai immigrant of Rikkokai in July 1964. His immigration
was sponsored by a Japanese Brazilian company, Cherry Musenn (Cherry
Radio), but, wanting to get into Brazilian society for his career, within three
months he broke his labor contract for a much-better-paying job at a Brazilian company, Aluno, for which he worked for the next three years. Shiobara
maintained a successful career as an engineer in Brazil until his retirement
in 2003.[62]

The majority of postwar women immigrants lived their adult lives as
full-time homemakers, at least after marriage. Tomino, for instance, became a full-time homemaker after marriage in 1976 and remained so until
1994. After finishing her labor contract, Kazuko Ezawa opened a dressmak-
ing shop with a woman friend in Liberdade and kept running the business
for ten years after her friend returned to Japan, while lodging and supporting her three nephews through higher education in the city. In 1970, she
married a much older and wealthy prewar immigrant merchant, through
a matchmaker, and became a full-time homemaker. Hiroko Nakama immigrated to Brazil in 1960, but she is actually a Nisei born to a couple who
had arrived in Brazil in 1930 as BRATAC employees, not as immigrants. In
São Paulo City, Nakama attended a French Catholic school until 1950, when

she and her family moved back to Hokkaido at her father's insistence. By 1960, all of her family members except her father returned to Brazil; she had graduated from a high school in Hokkaido and "had forgotten Portuguese." Back in Brazil, Nakama, "fresh out of Japan" in her perception, thought it would be "the best for her to marry an Issei man." While working at Ishiburas in Rio de Janeiro she met and married a postwar immigrant from Okinawa in 1966 and abandoned her original plan of attending college in Brazil. They moved to São Paulo City as her husband's job at Cotia Agricultural Cooperative. Back then she "thought she was Japanese, as her husband is, but later realized she is not." Nakama stayed at home to raise her two daughters until the early 1990s, when she began to work as a bilingual translator in Portuguese and Japanese for prospective *dekasseguis*.[63]

Tomino's husband is one of the many postwar immigrant men who lost well-paying jobs during the 1980s and chose to go back to Japan at least temporarily for work. By the beginning of the 1980s, Japan's economy was booming and the number of prospective immigrants to Brazil had declined drastically. However, Brazil's economic boom of 1968–1973 (the "Brazilian miracle") was followed by a great recession in the 1980s. Brazil was facing economic crises and high unemployment, and the Brazilian government began to take drastic measures to protect Brazilian companies and Brazilian workers. In 1980, Brazil pressured the Japanese government to close its two local agencies that rendered financial aid to Japanese immigrants in Brazil: JAMIC and Nihon Kigyo Enjo Kabushiki Gaisha (Japan's Company to Support Enterprises Ltd.), to which the Japanese government had contributed one billion yen each year. In 1981, both of the agencies were dissolved. Japan's *Yomiuri Shimbun* reported that with the termination of available funding from Japan, 1,400 Japanese farming families in Brazil who still needed financial support would be "abandoned."[64]

Suddenly it became much more difficult for Japanese men to be allowed to immigrate to Brazil as industrial workers. Indeed, to protect Brazilian workers, Brazilian companies began to fire Japanese industrial immigrants, who had been hired to train Brazilian workers and held well-paid, prestigious positions in the name of ODA (Official Development Assistance) through JICA. According to Shiobara, himself an industrial immigrant, many industrial immigrants returned to Japan in the 1980s.[65] Akio Koyama (b. 1941), another industrial immigrant (1967) and president of the Associação dos Imigrantes Tecno-Industriais no Brasil ([Japanese] Industrial Immigrants' Association), maintains that in the 1970s at ordinary factories middle-ranked engineers were earning forty times more than unskilled workers. Therefore it was more cost-effective to fire one engineer than ten factory workers, and many out-of-work Japanese immigrant men chose to become *dekassegui* workers in Japan to support their families.[66] Tomino's husband was one of them. Furthermore, in the early 1980s many Japanese companies began to close their Brazilian branches, and that stranded many of their "locally hired" postwar immigrant employees.[67]

Meanwhile, their homeland emerged as the world's super economic power during the early 1980s. That is the reason why Tomino's oldest sister and husband, who had to leave Japan as children, wish that they could have stayed on in Japan. Some of those who were struggling financially in Brazil chose to work in Japan with the intention of bringing their savings back to Brazil. Already in 1983, Nisei Andrea Yumi Minami's Japanese-born older brother (b. 1958), who arrived in Brazil in 1961, went back to Japan as a single man for his *dekassegui* in Hamamatsu. Minami says her Issei brother and others who went to Japan as *dekasseguis* in the early 1980s were able to save much money because of the great income difference between Brazil and Japan.[68]

Exactly in the same way, *dekassegui* resulted in the "disappearance" of many Japanese *feirantes*, who had once dominated the open-air markets (*feiras*) of São Paulo City. For instance, Yasuko Tanaka and her husband closed their *feirante* business in the mid-1980s, when he went to work in Japan on his own. Japanese journalist Tomonori Omiya quotes one of his Japanese Brazilian friends in São Paulo City in 1992, when Brazil's unemployment rate was 17.8 percent: "The current value of one's salary had declined to one-third or a quarter of what it used to be in the 1960s. Salaries do not catch up with inflation. Ordinary people have become poorer and poorer. One can have a comfortable life if he works in Japan as a *dekassegui*. Furthermore, work for *feirantes* is very hard."[69]

Matsuhira lost his job at JICA's São Paulo office when its Department of Immigration was terminated in 1981 because of the changes in immigration policies in Brazil and Japan, but was immediately hired by the consulate general of Japan in São Paulo for its Department of Immigrants. Other postwar immigrant men were not so lucky. Many of those who lost their jobs during the 1980s were around fifty years old and had ten more years to go before retirement, with their Brazilian-born children who had not yet finished their schooling. As a result, like Tomino's husband, many moved to Japan alone and sent remittances. During the late 1980s and early 1990s, many postwar immigrant men felt ashamed of being *dekasseguis* back in Japan. Even though they were fluent in Japanese, Japan and the Japanese that they used to know in the 1950s and 1960s were no longer there, and they were forced to deal with a cultural shock as foreign guest workers. Many refused to contact any of their family members or relatives in Japan, while others were ignored or rejected by them.[70]

Tomino's husband began his *dekassegui* work in 1990 and went back and forth between Brazil and Japan for more than ten years until he became too depressed to work. According to Tomino, her husband, who "speaks Japanese very well and has a Japanese face," got hurt terribly in Japan whenever the local Japanese came up and said, "You are from Brazil, aren't you?" and could not adjust well to his *dekassegui* life in his homeland. In order to speak Portuguese, he joined an evangelical Brazilian church at the suggestion of his younger sister, who is well off because of her Issei husband's business in Brazil. Meanwhile two of his three younger brothers, both Japanese citizens, also went to Japan as *dekasseguis,* when each turned thirty-five as a single man. Tomino says the youngest one, the only college graduate in her husband's family, will never come back to Brazil permanently.[71]

Nisei Hanae Yukimura's postwar immigrant husband from Hokkaido also opted for *dekassegui.* He is one of the many postwar immigrants whose small businesses went bankrupt in the late 1980s and early 1990s. He had immigrated to Brazil in 1957 as a *yobiyose* sponsored by a major Japanese Brazilian bank. He co-owned and ran a successful telephone appliances business from 1974, but his business went bankrupt in 1990. In the following year he went to Japan to work on an assembly line at Suzuki Automobile for eleven months, during which he never contacted his older sister in Ibaraki prefecture. He came back with savings of $7,000, with which, together with loans from her older sisters, the Yukimuras ran a grocery store in Liberdade from 1993 to 2000, while all three of their sons finished college and got started in good careers.[72] Yukimura's husband was lucky to have his Nisei wife's business skills and her older sisters' financial resources. Many others had no way of making it back in Brazil. After closing their candy store in the district of Santa Cecilia, Nisei Natsue Sakagami (b. 1938) and her postwar immigrant husband (b. 1937) went to Japan as *dekasseguis* together in 1991. This was Sakagami's second and her husband's first *dekassegui* in Japan; they rented a house from their company in Tokyo and had much fun on weekends. In 1995, after three years and eight months in Tokyo, Sakagami returned to Brazil on her own, while her husband continued to work in Japan until 2005. During his many years of *dekassegui* work he never contacted his family in Kagoshima, while coming back to Brazil every two years to renew his permanent residency.[73] He maintained his family and home in São Paulo, where he could enjoy his retirement rather comfortably.

Some postwar immigrant men may have felt not only shame but also guilt about being involved in *dekassegui* business. In December 1997, I met a postwar immigrant man in his early sixties, who was working a small, modest "Japanese" hotel in Liberdade. He was working there without any pay but in exchange for one room and three meals a day, as one of his legs was disabled and he was constantly in great pain. In Brazil, he had married a Nisei widow with a young boy, while becoming a certified jeweler in São Paulo City. When his business hit bottom because of Brazil's hyperinflation, he went to Japan as a *dekassegui* and saved a good amount of money. His work was greatly appreciated by his employer, and he was promoted to an overseer for Brazilian workers. He also made a fortune in recruiting and trading Japanese Brazilian workers in Japan as if he "had become a slave trader." In the end, he was seriously injured in a railroad accident; his life was spared but one of his legs was critically damaged. He said that it was his inevitable "punishment" for having "treated his own people in the way he had." He managed to come back to Brazil, where he found himself homeless. His Nisei wife had been dead for some years, and his stepson, whom he said he had not treated well, would not take him in.[74]

Dekassegui did not make much negative psychological impact on postwar immigrant women who chose to work in Japan as in the case of their male counterparts, who had been main breadwinners in Brazil. Postwar immigrant women, many of whom were full-time homemakers in Brazil, were not only able to move to their homeland even on their own, they also enjoyed new economic opportunities and freedoms that they would not have had in Brazil. The most lucrative job for women up to 1998, when Japan's state-sponsored medical insurance system changed, was working as private caregivers at hospitals. That is what both Natsue Sakagami (mentioned above) and her older Issei sister, Yoshie Miyano (chapter 2), did in 1989, and Tsuruyo Sugimoto (chapter 2) did in 1987–1988. Tomino's middle older sister, Yaeko Hashida (b. 1947), worked as a caregiver at Ichikawa Hospital of Chiba from March 1989 to December 1989 and upon return, with her savings, attended Akahoshi Beauty School and became a barber.[75] I also met a postwar immigrant woman who worked as a caregiver (a private one first, and then a certified "helper" after 1998) in Japan for fifteen years (1989–2004). She had arrived in Brazil in 1960 as a wife of a college graduate who was hired by Nomura Farm in Paraná as its manager. After living in São Paulo City as a full-time homemaker for many years, she went back to Japan as a *dekassegui* as soon as her youngest son began his college education.[76]

Other postwar immigrant women worked on assembly lines. Kiyoe Sekiguchi (mentioned above), after losing her job as a manager at a popular Japanese sushi restaurant in Liberdade, worked at a subcontract company for Fuji Film in Aichi from 1987 to 1991 to support her youngest child's higher education. Fortunately, she went to Japan with her oldest son (b. 1966), who took a leave of absence from Poli to earn enough money to buy a house for his upcoming marriage. Sekiguchi, needing to send all of her pay to her youngest son, was able to rely on her oldest son for her living expenses as long as he was there with her. She was "very disappointed in herself" when she had to work at a factory in Japan, where she had been born to a well-to-do family and had worked only as a white-collar worker before marriage. Sekiguchi maintains that back then one could save enough money to buy a house in São Paulo City if s/he worked as a *dekassegui* in Japan for a year. Most importantly for Sekiguchi, her story had a happy ending. All three of her children are USP graduates with very successful careers. The youngest child (b. 1971) chose a rather unusual career path: after graduating as a veterinary major, he decided to become a sushi chef and is now the proud owner of a Japanese restaurant, Hinodê, which Sekigushi bought for him.[77]

Hiromi Ono's older Issei sister was twelve years old when she arrived in Brazil. She became a very successful hairdresser with wealthy Brazilian customers but could no longer do the work because of health problems. As a forty-year-old single woman, she moved to Japan as a *dekassegui* in 1989, married a local Japanese man, and has settled permanently back in Japan. Ono (b. 1955) herself returned to Japan in 1999 for the first time since immigration in 1960, but not as a *dekassegui;* she had to accompany her aging father, who wanted to see his sister in Tokyo for the last time. She had to stay in Japan with her father for three months, during which she began to work at factories.[78] Emiko Arakaki, mentioned above, used to co-own a family business with her younger brother in the Okinawan district of Vila Carrão. In the late 1990s, Arakaki's husband, who "could not stay in Brazil due to some trouble in the business," moved to Japan on his own and worked as a steeplejack in Osaka City, where he died in an accident. Meanwhile, Arakaki's business in São Paulo City went bankrupt, and in 1998 Arakaki first moved back to Okinawa with her two Nisei daughters, both high school graduates, then, after two months, settled in Hamamatsu, where her older brother and his family had lived since 1978. In 1999, Arakaki and her daughters began to work on assembly lines. Eventually, with her business skills and language proficiency, Arakaki started a small business and emerged as an important spokeswoman among Japanese Brazilians in Hamamatsu, especially for the education of Brazilian children.[79]

Some postwar immigrant women found ways to challenge the existing patriarchy in the diaspora. For instance, Tomino, who was forced to become a main breadwinner for her family in 1994, hired a lawyer and got a divorce in 2003, with her Nisei children's strong support, even though she was not sure of her financial future. In 2002, Tomino described how "Japanese" she was compared to her USP-educated Nisei daughter; whereas she herself wanted to serve her man, her daughter wanted to have her man as a servant. Her divorce did not mean her independence from patriarchy; she told me seriously and repeatedly that she needed to find a man younger than seventy who would like to support her financially.[80]

Reiko Uehara, raised "to treat men with due respect," put up with her much older "feudalistic" husband for twenty-six years, attributing his being "such a patriarch" to his prewar education in Japan. Despite his successful business in flower and fruit cultivation, her husband did not like Brazil and talked about returning to Japan every day, and eventually they decided to leave Brazil. In January 1973, Uehara and her young sons, who were six and eight years old, arrived in Ueno City, Nagano prefecture. She rented a house, enrolled her sons in a local elementary school, and found a full-time job for herself. In March of the same year, however, her husband arrived, insisting that they should all go back to Brazil with him. He complained to Uehara's parents, "Reiko does not care about me or my hard work. She had been talking about Japan all the time and eventually left me." Her parents believed his story and forced her and her sons to go back to Brazil. Her husband died of cancer in 1990, when both of her sons were still in college. In 1991, Uehara moved from Atibaia to São Paulo City, where she worked at a Japanese Brazilian travel agency. All of her co-workers were Niseis who spoke Japanese fluently but could not read or write it. She "did not get to know any of them and felt lonely, having lunch alone every day." When she was thinking of quitting her job, she was contacted by Jiro Manabe (1916–2011), Rōkuren's third president (1991–1995), about its secretary-general position. Manabe was a prewar immigrant (1937) from her home prefecture of Nagao, and she accepted the job offer despite its much lower salary and the association's financial chaos. For the next eighteen years, until her retirement in 2009, Uehara had to deal with patriarchy and sexism at work from the association's elderly immigrant members. She was constantly condemned for her gender ("women cannot possibly do the work") by not only male but also female members, most of whom had no formal education either in Japan or Brazil and who would "never think men and women are equals." In November 1999, the association's new president, also a prewar immigrant man who was growing senile, tried to convince Rōkuren's three vice presidents and trustees to fire Uehara, albeit without success, and in May 2000 at a board meeting took votes on her resignation from all of the voting members, a majority of whom voted to keep her. The president resigned in great anger and went to *São Paulo Shimbun,* whose editor-in-chief, Katsuo Uchiyama, repeatedly criticized her in print. Reiko Uehara lived only among the Japanese in Atibaia and later in São Paulo City. After retirement, she was able to continue to live comfortably in financial terms, thanks to the savings she and her late husband had accrued, but, as she said in 2001, "I would be in trouble if I were alone, because of my lack of language skills in Portuguese. I am afraid I am a heavy burden for my children, but I cannot help it."[81]

Hiroko Nakama had to fight very hard for her daughters against her postwar immigrant husband, who believed that, as women, they did not need any higher education. With Nakama's support and encouragement, both of her daughters (b. 1973 and b. 1976) attended top private schools in the city, graduated from prestigious public universities, and became successful professionals.[82] Eventually she divorced her husband in 2004. Unlike Tomino, Nakama had developed her career during the 1990s as a professional translator and was capable of making a living on her own. Furthermore, unlike Uehara, Nakama would not need to rely on either of her children for her life in Brazil, as she was equipped with excellent proficiency in Portuguese.

Some postwar immigrant women, often divorcées or widows, not only supported themselves and their children but also succeeded in their own businesses, although that does not always mean that they resisted patriarchy in the diaspora. At the same time, unlike their well-known male counterparts, especially those who had become presidents of prefectural associations in Brazil, such as Hikoji Yamada (b. 1937), Yataro Amino (b. 1937), and Sadao Onishi (b. 1943), postwar immigrant businesswomen do not seem to have sought out leading positions in male-dominant Japanese Brazilian associations. Kiyoe Sekiguchi became a successful business owner after many years of financial struggle, mentioned above, without ever having a patron or "living like a man." She never belonged to a Japanese Brazilian association and "could not be a typical quiet grandmother" like her Sansei daughter-in-law's grandmother, a prewar child immigrant.[83]

Yoko Yoshida (b. 1932) claims, as Sekiguchi does, that she has "nothing to do with the Nikkei community," adding that she has done everything on her own. Yoshida and her husband, a half-Russian former professional baseball player, arrived in Brazil in 1955 as self-paid immigrants. Together they opened the very first Japanese nightclub in São Paulo City, but their business did not do well. They had a daughter in 1956, but divorced in 1957. Yoshida supported herself and her infant daughter by working at a traditional Japanese restaurant, Aoyagi, for two years, where she was able to network with some of her well-to-do customers for her future business. With no credit history, no banks would lend to her, but with high-interest loans from two elderly prewar immigrant Japanese women, Yoshida and her best friend opened and co-owned a bar and found many customers among Japanese male employees temporarily posted at the São Paulo branches of their Japanese companies. Even after Yoshida's business partner and her family returned to Tokyo, Yoshida stayed on and managed her entertainment business alone until 1986. Meanwhile her Nisei daughter attended Colégio Dante Alighieri (Dante), an elite private school on Avenida Paulista, graduated from Mackenzie University as an art major, and married a well-to-do Nisei medical doctor. At Dante in Yoshida's daughter's class, no student "with a Japanese face" was enrolled, and there were only two Japanese descendants: Yoshida's daughter, who did not look like her, and "a half-Japanese" female student who looked like "a typical white Brazilian girl." Yoshida made every effort for her daughter to receive a higher education so that she would belong to "a cultured world with a high class," rather than creating "a world she and her daughter could belong to together." Yoshida, who never remarried, has been determined to spend her last years at a nursing home in São Paulo City that she can afford to pay for without relying on her married daughter.[84]

Mari Tozuka (1931–2015) was born and raised in Beijing, China, where her father, a medical doctor, had a private practice. She and her family moved back to Japan in 1945 after the war. Her older half-brother had been drafted by the Japanese government, captured by Russians, and ended up spending several years in a camp in Siberia. At the age of fifteen, Tozuka began to work as a professional ballet dancer to support herself and her family in Tokyo. In 1958, her parents had immigrated to Brazil with her younger sister and brother but, ten years later, came back to Japan permanently. At their suggestion, Tozuka decide to immigrate to Brazil in 1973 for the sake of her husband, Yupo Tozuka, an Ainu wood sculptor from Hokkaido, and their two children, who were subjected to prejudice and discrimination in Japan because of their Ainu ancestry. The Tozukas' passages on the *Nippon Maru* were subsidized by the Japanese government since Yupo was recruited by Japan's Yaohan Department Store as an industrial immigrant for its São Paulo City branch in the Pinheiro district. Soon after they settled, Yupo quit his job at Yaohan and Tozuka became a breadwinner for the family by teaching ballet, flamenco, and tango, and touring with her Italian Brazilian tango partner. After many years of alcoholism and depression, Yupo went back to Japan alone and died at the age of fifty-five.[85] Tozuka's son (b. 1965), an FAU graduate, commuted between Brazil and Japan for his business in used music albums, while living with her mother in her apartment. Her daughter (b. 1968) returned to Japan with ambitions in acting as soon as she graduated from high school. As a well-known dancer and dance teacher in São Paulo, Tozuka was regarded as a sort of celebrity among older Japanese Brazilians, but, at the same time, because of her gender, background, and lack of financial resources, she seems to have always been perceived as a half-outsider.

Mikiko Nagashima (b. 1944), owner of a specialty shop in Liberdade, had to immigrate to Brazil at the age of thirteen with her family in 1958, dropping out of a junior high school in Yamaguchi prefecture. Her father, a prewar immigrant who had returned to Japan before the beginning of the war, decided to immigrate to Brazil again, with his wife and three children, as his wealthy sister's *yobiyose*. As the oldest child, Nagashima never attended school in Brazil, whereas her two younger siblings both graduated from Brazilian universities. Nagashima married a young postwar immigrant man from the same prefecture, and they had a son (b. 1968) and daughter (b. 1972). Because of her husband's domestic violence, in combination with her family's extreme poverty, Nagashima left him and moved with her two young children to São Paulo City. She found a job at a Japanese Brazilian institution for children with mental disabilities but was fired on the ground that the institution could not allow her children to mingle with those who were institutionalized. At the age of thirty-one she accepted a proposal of common-law marriage from a sixty-seven-year-old retired prewar immigrant man, and together they started a business; they drove to the countryside with Japanese food and other goods not only in São Paulo but Mato Grosso do Sul and Minas Gerais as well. After making a fortune, they decided around 1988 to specialize in tools and clothes for "gateball," a form of Japanese croquet. Nagashima's husband passed away in 1998, but her business has continued to thrive owing to the popularity of the sport among elderly Japanese Brazilians throughout Brazil.[86]

Lina Mitsuko Nishimoto (b. 1974) has been able to break out of patriarchy in the diaspora by eventually moving back to Japan on her own. As a young daughter she was forced to move to Brazil in 1988; after having lived in Japan for nearly twenty years, her Nisei father suddenly decided to return to Brazil permanently, with his Japanese wife and their two Japanese-born daughters: Nishimoto and her older sister (b. 1970), both Sanseis on their father's side. Nishimoto and her family lived a comfortable life in Osaka City, which "they had to abandon," due to her "*gaijin*-like" father's decision to return to Brazil. Her mother was "quiet and would be wherever her family were, without complaining." Nishimoto had to drop out of school in the eighth grade to move to Brazil, and obtained a high school diploma at the age of twenty-one. In São Paulo City, Nishimoto felt "uncomfortable with the *gaijin*" and did not wish to marry her well-to-do Japanese Brazilian dentist boyfriend, who did not speak Japanese: "I would hate it if my children were Brazilians. I would hate to have Nikkei children." In 1997, Nishimoto went to Japan to work at a ski resort in Nagano prefecture for several months and isolated herself from Japanese Brazilians: "Nikkeijin have overpopulated Shizuoka and Nagano. I do not like *dekasseguis* because they refuse to see how wonderful Japan is. They go to Japan without learning the Japanese language and complain of Japan." In 2000, she moved back to Japan on her own, married a Japanese man, and became the mother of a Japanese child in 2001. By so doing, she reclaimed her Japanese identity. Nishimoto was, in fact, ahead of her time. In the early 2000s, many Japanese-born Brazilian children began to "return" to their unknown homeland. Nishimoto stated in 1998, "I came to feel more comfortable here once I learned how to communicate in Portuguese. Until then I used to cry out of sadness. I think I survived all of it just because I was only fourteen and I could not go back to Japan by myself."[87] Nishimoto's story makes us wonder how Japanese-born Brazilian returnees would come to identify themselves in the end. Like Nishimoto, they were too young to move back to Japan on their own, but unlike Nishimoto, who holds dual nationality because of her Japanese mother, they cannot go back to Japan with a Japanese passport.

Tomino told me repeatedly that both she and her husband considered themselves Japanese. It was so important for her husband to be Japanese that during his *dekassegui* it hurt his feelings terribly when the local Japanese could tell that he was from Brazil. Being Japanese seemed to be important for postwar immigrants; all thirty-three of my postwar immigrant informants remained Japanese nationals with Japanese passports at the time of their interviews. Some of them, especially men with higher educations in Japan who had arrived in Brazil in the 1950s, were extremely critical of postwar Japan. Those educated immigrant men, now in their eighties, demonstrated a strong tendency to ascribe "problems" in present-day Japan to the US-imposed democracy and postwar Japanese education.

Elite postwar immigrant man Masatake Suzuki (b. 1932), a Waseda University graduate who immigrated in 1959, writes that Isseis/immigrants are "definitely Japanese, not the Nikkeijin," and that "certain Niseis claim wrongly that they [Isseis] have been assimilated in Brazil and therefore have become the Nikkeijin themselves." Focusing on adult men's experiences only, Masatake Suzuki examines competitions and tensions between Niseis and postwar immigrants in the process of getting ahead, as well as over Nisei women as marriage partners. For instance, at the Bank of South America, there was a long history of competition and conflict over the bank's leadership between college-educated postwar immigrants hired from Japan and elite Niseis; in the end, the prewar Issei leaders gave it to their Nisei offspring. He claims that elite Niseis destroyed all of the Japanese Brazilian corporations and businesses the old prewar Isseis had established. He explains that prewar immigrants disregarded postwar immigrants and gave their businesses to the Niseis, who were not ready to take on the task, although he admits that one may wonder whether postwar immigrants would have been able to keep the businesses running, either.[88] Masatake Suzuki's own elite male consciousness and understanding of Japanese Brazilian history are clearly expressed in his biography of Teiichi Suzuki (no relation to himself). He states that history and culture have been created by a small number of elites, "never by the 'silent majority' or masses involved in their grass-roots movements," and maintains that Teiichi Suzuki was one of the "chosen elites," who "lived their lives for the sake of culture, education, and social welfare." By contrast, he asserts, the majority of immigrants valued only secular wealth and social climbing.[89]

Hisashi Nagata is another elite postwar immigrant man; he is the fifth son of Shigeshi Nagata, second president of Rikkokai (chapter 1), and himself the former president of the Brazilian Associaton of Rikkokai. In 1952, at his father's request, Nagata and his younger brother traveled to Brazil to see whether postwar immigration was possible for Rikkokai members. Nagata was already engaged to his wife, an elementary school teacher in Japan, who arrived in Brazil a few years later to marry him. During his interview in June 2010, Nagata criticized me severely for my lack of "political" interest in Japan and strongly advised that I subscribe to Nippon Hōsō Kyokai (Japan Broadcasting Corporation, or NHK), Japan's equivalent of PBS.[90] What Nagata was referring to is NHK's international simultaneous broadcasting, called "NHK World Premium," by which viewers can watch the same programs as in Japan. In March 2000, NHK began to air the program in Brazil and, as of April 2008, its subscribers amounted to 380,000 households, approximately 270,000 Japanese Brazilians.[91] Postwar immigrants, both men and women, were always attentive to NHK broadcasting, and their daily conversations often started with the weather in Japan, as reported on NHK news, or, especially in the case of women, NHK's daily fifteen-minute morning drama series. But at the same time, postwar immigrants tended to be much more critical of Japan, the Japanese, and Japanese language and culture than their prewar counterparts were. Since their own departure for

Brazil, Japan and the Japanese had come to be "rotten," a change they claimed to have experienced when they visited Japan for business, pleasure, and/or *dekassegui* work. For many postwar immigrants, Japan was still a major part of their reality, not the imagined homeland that prewar immigrants had longed for with much nostalgia. A postwar immigrant woman told me repeatedly that Japan and the Japanese owed much of their postwar economic development to postwar immigrants in Brazil, and that the Japanese in Japan should have been grateful to them for what they did for the younger generations of Japan. It is an interesting logic to connect from a nation's past to its present though one's own experiences as an emigrant. NHK's daily broadcasting has given postwar immigrants the illusion of belonging to Japan while living in the diaspora.

CONCLUSION

Postwar Japanese immigrants were forced to cope with many political and socioeconomic changes in Brazil, as well as the rise and fall of the postwar Japanese economy. As Nagata and Goro Tamura point out, returning to Japan was always an option for the majority of postwar adult immigrants, in case things did not work out in Brazil. Rapid technological advancement made Japan much closer to Brazil and more accessible for the "Japanese" in Brazil. In the early 1970s, during Brazil's economic boom, few imagined returning to Japan for work, but in the 1980s many postwar immigrants men, like Tomino's husband, began to migrate back home as *dekasseguis*, especially for the sake of their children's higher education in Brazil. For many—not all—it was a bitter and shameful return.

Arriving either as members of immigrant families or as "bride immigrants," postwar immigrant women were expected to support their men as daughters, wives, and mothers under patriarchy, though some businesswomen were able to stand on their feet, as divorcées and widows, by detaching themselves from Japanese Brazilian men and their patriarchal rule. Even though Tomino probably continued to rely on patriarchy for financial reasons, even after divorce, she expected her Nisei daughter to be as successful and independent as her son would be. And however patriarchal they remained (or became in the male-dominant Japanese diaspora), many postwar immigrant men expected their Brazilian-born children, both sons and daughters, to succeed as educated Brazilians.

Senichi Adachi's narrative exemplifies this point. His children all graduated from college and have succeeded professionally: his son (b. 1962), a Poli graduate, became an engineer, and both of his daughters (b. 1967 and

b. 1971) became dentists. At the time of his interview (2002), only his older daughter was married, and he was not very pleased with her choice of a younger Japanese man from Japan as her marriage partner:

> I hoped that my daughter would marry a man who was educated in Brazilian schools, but she married a Japanese man who came from Japan. I said, "Why are you marrying a Japanese? You used to speak ill of the Japanese all the time." She used to say, "I do not like Isseis. They are not kind to women. I will marry a Nisei." When I made objections against their marriage two years ago, she said, "I've dated Nisei medical doctors but all of them lack a sense of responsibility and are unreliable. By contrast, Isseis keep their word. I can depend on them. That is the reason why I decided to marry my Issei boyfriend." I replied, "How would you explain about all the shortcomings of the Isseis you used to talk about?" She just said, "I don't remember." I bet love is blind. My daughter grew up with her Brazilian friends, but she says she cannot get along with them; she has Japanese ways of thinking, after her parents.[92]

As a postwar immigrant father, Adachi wanted his daughter to marry a successful Japanese Brazilian man—ironically, exactly what prewar immigrant parents had wanted for their Nisei daughters, whom many single postwar immigrant men of Adachi's generation wished to marry. Times had changed. As an educated professional Brazilian woman, Adachi's Nisei/Sansei daughter did not need her Issei father's approval for her own marriage, nor a husband to support her financially; she refused to buy into patriarchal rule, either in her "Japanese" family or in the diaspora.

Chapter Five

NISEIS, SANSEIS, AND THEIR
CLASS-GENDER IDENTITY

When I started school, they said, "The Japanese have slanted eyes and crushed faces," and I did not like being Japanese. Not only Nikkeis but also other Brazilians do not want to mix with blacks. We see them being discriminated. I had a black friend from the first grade to high school. She graduated from college. At school another friend did not invite her to a birthday party. She is from the middle class but her family did not have much money. Her parents had education, though. Her mother is black and her father is Portuguese, so she is a *mulata*. Yet she was not accepted. Black women cannot protect their rights without organizing their own associations. Nikkei women do not do so. They do not complain. That is not just an image; in fact, they do not complain.

— *Christina Sakura Oda, a former*
research scientist, 2001[1]

In the early morning of June 20, 2001, Christina Sakura Oda and I met at a small coffee shop in the middle-class residential district of Aclimação, near Oshiman Gakuen / Colégio Oshiman, an elite private Japanese Brazilian primary school. Oda drove her five-year-old son, Nasser Ken, to the school from her parents' home in the working-class suburban district of Pirituba every morning and agreed to meet with me for an interview on this particular day after she dropped him off. She would have to come back to pick him up in the afternoon. Thus she was spending a few hours each day just to transport her son to and from school.

"Yes, I am a Nikkei," states Oda. "My consciousness came from my parents. I did not like it when I was a child. I wished I were the same as (white) Brazilians." In her school days, Oda was ridiculed for her "Japanese face," and saw her classmates not accepting her mixed, middle-class

Afro-Brazilian friend for her race. Yet Oda did not complain. Her statement that Japanese Brazilian women "do not complain" accords with Edna Roland's statement that Japanese Brazilian women are "negatively stereotyped as submissive," while their male counterparts are stereotyped "positively as excellent workers" (chapter 1).[2] This was the world she was part of as a Brazilian. Oda also belonged to the "Japanese" world on weekends, when she attended a Japanese language school and socialized with Japanese Brazilians only.

Oda was born in São Paulo City in 1964 as the second child of a prewar child immigrant father and a Nisei mother, which makes her a Nisei/Sansei. During the early 1950s each of her parents had moved from rural São Paulo to the city, where they met and married in 1962. Oda graduated from USP as a veterinary science major and worked for three years as a research scientist at the Cotia Agricultural Cooperative's agricultural laboratory for disease prevention. In May 1992, she quit her job and left for Japan to marry her then fiancé, a Universidade de Moji das Cruzes graduate in phyical education, who had been working as a *dekassegui* in Hamamatsu City, Shizuoka prefecture. Her older sister, Luiza Kaoru (b. 1963), a PUC graduate in geology who used to work at Bank of Brazil, had already been working on an assembly line for a major watch company in Nagano City since January 1990. Once in Japan, Oda expected to obtain gainful employment as a research scientist but soon found that to be impossible. After spending a month with her fiancé in Hamamatsu, where he worked as a plasterer, Oda moved alone in June 1992 as a *dekassegui* worker to Aichi prefecture, where she began to work at a plywood factory. She and her fiancé still spent every weekend together but eventually broke up in October 1992. Oda attributes their breakup to her own negative feelings toward him because she "had left everything she loved, including her job, back in Brazil to be with him," even though she "knew it was wrong of her to blame him for her own decision."

In July 1995, Oda married a Sansei high school graduate from Rio de Janeiro, whom she had met as a fellow *dekassegui* worker in Hamamatsu. Their only child, Nassar, was born there in the following year. Her husband and all of her in-laws are "very Brazilian"; they eat "rice and beans every day," and none of his family members is a college graduate. Oda's husband moved to Japan in the same year as she did; all of his family members had settled "back" in Japan permanently, and his older sister's husband started and owned a *dekassegui* temp agency in Hamamatsu. He is also eight years younger than she is, and she was afraid her parents might be upset about their age difference. Interestingly, her father had no problem with their age difference; he was more concerned about his son-in-law's lack of college education.

In March 2001, after nine years of *dekassegui* in Japan, Oda came home with Nasser to live with her parents in São Paulo City, while her husband stayed behind in Japan to work. She wanted to find a professional position back in São Paulo City but quickly learned that she needed to get herself retrained in her field after many years of absence. Meanwhile, her Japanese-born son had a hard time adjusting: "We got him a nanny when he was seven months old. She was a neighbor and is an elderly Nikkei woman who speaks Japanese only, so he grew up speaking it with her. Yes, he spoke Japanese only. At the age of two and half he started to go to a nursery in Hamamatsu, where only Japanese was spoken." In São Paulo City, Nasser could not get used to a nearby preschool with Brazilian children. Oda and her parents "felt so bad for him" that they took him out of the school after two months and then enrolled him in Oshiman Gakuin, where both Portuguese and Japanese are taught, but that turned out to be very expensive, and time-consuming for her. Oda concluded her interview by stating, "I wish *dekassegui* had never happened. Because of the poor Brazilian economy, Brazilians have been migrating to other countries. The Nikkei have been going to Japan, but Brazilians go to the United States, for instance, to New York and Miami. Many will never come home."[3]

Like Oda, some of the Niseis and Sanseis who were born in the 1950s and 1960s and grew up with and among "Brazilians" in the city were born to prewar child immigrants and Niseis without higher education. Others were born to postwar immigrants (chapter 4). Many Niseis and Sanseis of this generation attended reputable universities, aiming at becoming successful upper-middle-class Brazilians. In other words, their parents believed in the possibility of their individual social climbing through formal education. Some attempted to deny their Japaneseness and/or rigorously resisted what was expected of them as "Japanese." At the same time, many women, willingly or reluctantly, acceded to patriarchal rule; they chose to remain single to become their parents' caretakers and/or work in Japan as *dekasseguis* to satisfy the financial needs of their families. One may wonder whether Oda and many other educated Nisei and Sansei women of her generation ever resisted the structure of gender inequality in the diaspora.

While struggling financially, Oda's parents were always passionate about their children's higher education, regardless of gender. Oda and her siblings attended only public schools, but back then public school education was much better than it is now, and her younger brother, Rodrigo Jun (b. 1968), even passed a very competitive entrance exam to study at the

Young Oshiman Gakuen students dressed as Brazilian peasants for their *festa junina* (festival of June), June 23, 2001. Photo by author.

Escola Tecnico Federal (Federal High School of Technology). Oda's parents expected all three of their children to graduate from reputable universities and become urban professionals. After all, many college-educated Niseis had already succeeded in Brazilian society, and Oda's parents did not see any obstacles that would prevent their children from advancing themselves as Brazilians. In their parents' view, college education in certain fields, such as practical science and law, should have secured their children's financial future in Brazil.

As early as 1950, *Paulista Shimbun* reported on "the breakdown of 'cysts,'" owing to the social advancement of Japanese Brazilians in Brazilian society.[4] By the late 1950s, according to Senichi Adachi, Japanese Brazilians had become "popular as employees. They have been reputed as honest and hardworking. They work hard even when they are not supervised."[5] The documentary filmmaker and film critic Olga Toshiko Futemma (b. 1951), a Nisei woman of Okinawan descent, critiques these seemingly positive stereotypes:

> In the 1950s, Japanese immigrants held a good image. Western Brazilians viewed the Japanese with admiration—they were the best workers in the countryside, and the best vegetable vendors and *tintureiros* in the cities, and regarded as educated people. But that attitude that the rich held was also

authoritarian. I always knew it. They did not want to create any sense of competition with the Japanese.[6]

There would have been no competition with Brazilians if the Japanese had "known their place." Brazilians could accept and tolerate a small number of elite "Japanese" as exceptions to the rule, such as Kazuo Watanabe (chapter 3), who had become an "exceptional" Japanese, never a threat to racial hegemony. However, with the increasing number of educated Niseis rapidly moving up the social ladder, competition among white-collar workers intensified, and social pressure against Japanese descendants grew. According to Takashi Maeyama, this pressure stemmed from the fact that Japanese Brazilians had neither capital to invest nor Brazilian-type familial social networks.[7] Maeyama notes that during the 1960s Japanese Brazilians were frequently called "ugly but intelligent" (*feio, mas inteligente*) and it was said that they "smell but do not stink badly" (*cheia, mas não fede*).[8] These attributes made them racial inferiors, even though they could be tolerated and even appreciated for some "good" qualities, such as intellectual abilities that even white Brazilians might not "naturally" possess.

Until the early 1960s it was not difficult for the elite Niseis of Iossuke Tanaka's generation to climb the social ladder individually. However, by the time Futemma started her undergraduate education at USP, the situation had begun to change. Brazilians' general attitude toward Japanese Brazilians was well represented in the famous graffiti allegedly written on the wall of a bathroom at USP: "Kill a Japanese if you want to get into USP." In 1976, Futemma's contemporary, Edmundo Sussumu Fujita (1950–2016), a USP Law School graduate who also did postgraduate studies in law at the University of Tokyo on a Japan's Ministry of Foreign Affairs fellowship, passed the entrance exam of the Rio Branco Institute (the Brazilian government's diplomatic academy in Brasília, IRBr) at the top of six hundred applicants. Thus he became Brazil's first diplomat of Japanese ancestry. Edmundo Fujita is the oldest son born to prewar child immigrant Yoshiro Fujita (chapter 2) and his Nisei wife. He has two younger brothers (born in 1953 and 1956), both engineers, who succeeded to the family business. His wife, Ligaya, whom he met at a summer seminar for international students in the United States in 1971, is an elite Philippine, with a PhD in political science from the University of Denver.[9] In April 1978, when a Brazilian journalist attributed the nonexistence of black diplomats in Brazil to racism, Brazil's Ministry of Foreign Relations (Itamaraty) denied the accusation, citing the fact that Edmundo Fujita had passed the exam for Rio Branco at the top of the class. When fifty-eight-year old Nisei congressman Diogo Nomura

(1920–2005) was interviewed by Japan's major newspaper, *Yomiuri Shimbun,* in 1978, he commented that Japanese Brazilians were always referred to as Niseis, while Brazilian-born children of European immigrants, including President Ernest Geisel, a child born to a German immigrant father and a first-generation German Brazilian mother, were "naturally" regarded simply as Brazilians. Nomura continued, "Those born in Brazil are all Brazilians. Brazil expects us all to be Brazilians." Thus, according to the article, "the Nikkei who located themselves at the center of Brazilian society disciplined themselves as 'Brazilians' rather than 'Nikkeis.'" The article concluded with Edmundo Fujita's alleged comment to friends that, as a Brazilian, he "would prefer not to be sent to Japan as a diplomat."[10]

Olga Futemma was born to prewar Okinawan immigrants, both with no formal schooling, either in Okinawa or in Brazil. At the end of the 1940s, the Futemmas moved from Campo Grande, Mato Grosso do Sul, where many prewar Okinawan immigrants had settled, to São Paulo City, as one of their sons needed medical treatment for malaria. In São Paulo City, her father worked as a vegetable vendor for the municipal market. The Futemmas lived among Okinawan descendants in the Vila Carrão district, where Futemma was born and grew up with Okinawan music and culture. At the same time, her father took her to Liberdade every Saturday for the Japanese cinema until she turned thirteen, when she moved on to Hollywood movies. She is the youngest of six children (including two older siblings who died back in Campo Grande) and the only one who attended and graduated from college. As a patriarch, her father worked day after day and took care of her mother. Futemma states, "He preserved the romance of being a Japanese man or being the Oriental. In relation to the fact that he was neither Japanese nor Brazilian, I felt much fear for my father." Futemma majored in journalism at USP during the military regime, which strongly affected her political and social consciousness in relation to her national identity. She was interested in studying art in college but "had to think about financial security, safety, and money," and chose journalism instead; she needed to support not only herself but her immigrant parents while studying. For Futemma, "school represented Brazilian society," which separated her from her daily life as a daughter of poor, uneducated prewar Okinawan immigrants. While pursuing her career, Futemma chose to live with her white Brazilian boyfriend, who was separated from his wife, and had two sons by him in the late 1970s, which created much anguish for both of her parents, who wanted her to marry an Okinawan descendant. Even though among Okinawan descendants "there was a lot of pressure against marrying a Japanese man," according to Futemma, "it would still have been much better if

I had chosen to be with a 'Japanese' man."[11] As it turns out, all of her siblings married Japanese Brazilians of non-Okinawan descent.[12] Of the factors contributing to her marginality, Futemma regards being a woman as the most important, adding, "To be an Okinawan descendant is inside myself." She had a hard time with Japanese Brazilian organizations and associations when she tried to make a documentary on the eightieth anniversary of Japanese immigration to Brazil. She attributes the difficulty to her lack of language skills in Japanese as well as to such Japanese Brazilian institutions' discriminatory treatment of her as an Okinawan descendant. Even though it was surely "a painful experience" for her, Futemma concludes, "It was wonderful for me to converse with the generation of journalists who have passed away since then about the first wave of immigration."[13]

Futemma's longtime relationship with her partner dissolved in 2000, and she moved out of their place, where her two sons continued to live. As of 2002, both of her sons were dating white Brazilian women:

> My sons think that they are Brazilians but enjoy very much getting in contact with Okinawan culture whenever possible. My older son took a Japanese language course a long time ago, but he dates a German descendant, and so does my younger one. My sons have much more benevolence from the world than I did, but they do not participate in cultural events nor understand Okinawan culture as I do. Well, it's a loss. I have had more freedom than my mother did, but missed the chance to learn her culture. It's a loss. We keep losing.[14]

While Futemma articulates her position as a minority Brazilian woman of Okinawan descent, Suely Harumi Satow (b. 1953), a Sansei social psychologist with a PUC PhD, talks about her position of marginality from a different position. Satow was born with cerebral palsy in Suzano, São Paulo, to prewar child immigrants as the oldest of four Nisei children. When she was three, she and her family moved to São Paulo City for the medical treatment she needed. In the Santana district, Satow's parents became successful merchants in electronic appliances, and Satow and all three of her younger siblings received higher educations at elite institutions in the city. One of her younger sisters studied medicine at USP–Ribeirão Preto and became a pediatrician. She married a white Brazilian medical doctor of Spaniard and Portuguese ancestries, and the oldest of their three children studied business administration at FGV. Satow's other sister finished the Escola Superior de Propaganda e Marketing (Superior School of Propaganda and Marketing, ESPM) but became a full-time homemaker.

Her younger brother graduated from FGV and works as a business administrator. Thus Satow's family came to be well "whitened" through the power of higher education.

Satow articulates the meaning of the term "whitening": "Here [in Brazil] the Japanese and blacks are respected only for having money or social statuses, sometimes those they purchased." She continues, "I think the Japanese are still very closed among themselves within *kaikan* [an umbrella term for Japanese Brazilian associations], and that they think essentially of becoming rich and of having a lot of money, and that is the most important for them." Satow maintains that Japanese Brazilians "are rarely interested in social problems": "They do not study philosophy and social sciences often. They seldom show up in movements of struggle for citizenship, as those of us with physical deficiencies do, for example." Therefore, "when the Japanese deal with people with disabilities, they just put us into institutions or appropriate residences, which Brazilians rarely do." Until 1995, Satow had been the only "Japanese" with a disability participating in the Ibero-American Congress on the Handicapped.[15] Satow has been hampered in advancing in her profession due to her disabilities: "With my scholarly credentials, I can be a journalist, university professor, or therapist, but my condition of disability 'bars' my possibilities. It's prejudice."[16] For her comparative study of prejudice, Satow collaborated with an Afro-Brazilian woman psychologist, Eneida Almeida Reis, who states, "We don't talk about our sentiments. She has been regarded as stupid and mentally ill. I have been called *negrinha* [little black girl], *brincadeira* [joke], and *puta* [whore]. That's how we became friends."[17] Satow, who never married, has continued to fight the odds as an educated Brazilian woman, beyond and above her Japanese ancestry. As exemplified by Futemma and Satow, some educated Nisei women who were born in the early 1950s began to struggle to find their place as Brazilians during the 1970s, while resisting patriarchy in the Japanese diaspora. Unlike many others, they did not remain "quiet" as Japanese Brazilian women and chose to identify themselves as Brazilians.

During the late 1970s, when she was in high school, Oda thought about marrying a "Brazilian" but never dated any. At a *cursinho* (college preparatory school), she met her ex-fiancé, also a Nisei/Sansei, and she never dated anybody else in Brazil. After she broke up with her fiancé and stayed on in Japan as a *dekassegui*, Oda did not want to marry a local Japanese, as she felt uneasy about staying on in Japan. According to Oda, her older sister Luiza is "very Japanese"; "Japan suits her personality very well," for she is "very quiet and never complains about anything." Yet Luiza has stayed single and by doing so "has avoided whatever complications in life."[18]

However, their younger brother, Rodrigo, the youngest and only son in her birth family, dated white Brazilian women only, without ever belonging to any Japanese Brazilian associations. Rodrigo attended several top colleges: USP in biology, Faculdade de Tecnologia de São Paulo (São Paulo College of Technology, FATEC) in computer science, Universidade Estadual de Campinas (State University of Campinas, UNICAMP) in biology, and again USP in business administration, from which he finally graduated in 1998 at the age of twenty-nine. Rodrigo has had a successful career at Petróleo Brasileiro (Petrobras), a semipublic Brazilian multinational energy corporation. Unlike his sisters, he has never been to Japan, as a *dekassegui* or otherwise.

The traditional norm of ethnic endogamy among Japanese Brazilians in São Paulo City loosened during the 1970s. According to Atsushi Yamauchi (chapter 3), intermarriage was "tolerated" in the 1980s, as Japanese Brazilian parents regretfully said "We cannot help it," and eventually came to be "completely accepted" by Japanese Brazilians during the 1990s.[19] In 1987–1988, 42.5 percent of married Japanese Brazilians of both sexes in São Paulo City had non-Japanese Brazilian spouses. Unfortunately, there is no breakdown of these intermarried Japanese Brazilians by gender or class, or of their "Brazilian" spouses by gender, class, or color. Interestingly, the percentage of intermarried Japanese descendants was even higher for all of Brazil (45.9 percent).[20] Japanese Brazilians' rate of intermarriage was much higher than that of white Brazilians (15.9 percent [men] and 21.3 percent [women]); and even those lighter-skinned Afro-Brazilians ("brown") (28.9 percent [men] and 25.2 percent [women]), as far as the 1991 Brazilian national censuses are concerned. In fact, it was close to the rates of interracial marriages among darker-skinned ("black") Afro-Brazilians: 51.1 percent (men) and 41.1 percent (women). Furthermore, white Brazilian women are more likely to outmarry than their male counterparts, whereas white Brazilians, both men and women, choose the lighter-skinned Afro-Brazilians over the darker-skinned ones.[21] To my knowledge, there is no statistical study available on distinctive patterns of Japanese Brazilian's intermarriage regarding the gender of intermarried Japanese Brazilians and the colors of their "Brazilian" spouses, but Japanese Brazilians do not seem to have followed the tendencies found for white Brazilians, based on my informants' observations.

Koichi Mori claims to have found some distinctive patterns among intermarried Japanese Brazilians by gender: Japanese Brazilian men tend to marry non–Japanese Brazilian women of all class backgrounds; it is not rare for college-educated Japanese Brazilian men to marry lower-class non–Japanese Brazilian women, such as domestic maids, who have no formal education. By contrast, according to Mori, college-educated Japanese Brazilian women tend to marry educated men of the same class background: "First of all, they look for Japanese Brazilian men, and only if they cannot find a suitable one do they marry non-Japanese Brazilian men of equal socioeconomic standing."[22] This may well suggest that educated Japanese Brazilian women prefer class endogamy to ethnic endogamy.

Sachiko Tomino (chapter 4) states that at the Curso de Língua Japonesa Bunkyo her Japanese Brazilian students are "highly mixed" and "some 80 percent of the racially mixed students have 'Japanese' fathers and 'Brazilian' mothers." Furthermore, Tomino maintains, as Mori claims he has observed, that almost all of the college-educated Japanese Brazilian fathers of her students are married to non-Japanese Brazilian women of differing socioeconomic standing:

> They [Japanese Brazilian men] have been attracted to the beauty of Brazilian women. Such women were working as receptionists when they began to work. Japanese Brazilian men long for blonde-haired secretaries. Some others married maids who were working for their families, believing that they were beautiful. Also, thinking that the Japanese Brazilian men are wealthy, Brazilian women try very hard to seduce them. Oftentimes Japanese Brazilian fathers, dressed up very nicely, bring their children to this school at the beginning. Then after a while mothers show up to ask about their children. I am always surprised to see these mothers are the lowest of maids—*bahianas* [migrant women from the state of Bahia].[23]

Tamiko Hosokawa, editor-in-chief of the Japanese-language magazine *Bumba*, also claims that Japanese Brazilian men "tend to get a huge crush on blonde women and end up marrying them"; "they cannot tell the difference between educated and uneducated women."[24] I have heard not only from Tomino but also from many other Japanese Brazilians that "Brazilian" women are all after Japanese Brazilian men's money and want to seduce them into marriage. A prewar child immigrant woman (b. 1923), for instance, said to me in 2001 of her Sansei grandson in his early twenties: "He has been always chased around by Brazilian girls and he has never been left alone. They say, 'Japanese men are good safety boxes.'"[25]

Unlike Japanese Brazilian men, white middle-class Brazilians have always preferred to marry white middle-class women, while choosing women of color as sexual partners.[26] "The vital apotheosis of the dark-skinned woman as a lover is widely recognized" in Brazil, according to Carl N. Degler, who quotes a famous Brazilian aphorism: "White women

for marrying, mulatto women for fornicating, black women are for service."
A Brazilian novelist told Degler in 1968, "It is not easy to meet a white man
married to a black woman. Generally, the opposite occurs," because interracial marriage would lower the position of the white man but raise that of
the black man.[27] Then why have educated Japanese Brazilian men been
marrying uneducated women of African descent, including migrant
women who work as maids for their families? According to my Japanese
Brazilian informants, unlike white middle-class Brazilian men, who "know
how to treat" interracial affairs, Japanese Brazilian men sometimes marry
young domestic maids, especially if pregnancies are involved, under pressure from their parents, who expect their sons to be "responsible" for their
unborn grandchildren. Such educated Japanese Brazilians have not fully
understood the norms of race and gender relations in Brazil; ironically,
while busy "whitening" themselves through college education and urban
professional jobs, they have not learned the meaning of their newly acquired and therefore vulnerable "whiteness" in Brazilian society. Meanwhile, such intermarriage with educated Japanese Brazilian men has
worked effectively as an important means of "whitening" for uneducated
young Afro-Brazilian women. Tomino states that educated Japanese Brazilian fathers, not Japanese Brazilian mothers, have their racially mixed children enrolled in a Japanese language course.[28] This suggests that Japanese
Brazilian men may identify and raise their racially mixed children as
Nikkeis, despite their own choice of intermarriage. In this sense, the mixed
families headed by Japanese Brazilian men may remain Nikkei, whereas
mixed children born to Japanese Brazilian mothers and "Brazilian" fathers
may have grown up with weaker Nikkei identity.

Until the early 1990s, Japanese Brazilians' intermarriage tended to
take place much more frequently between Japanese Brazilian men and
"Brazilian" women than otherwise. Tomino and many other Japanese Brazilians claim that, as a result, educated Japanese Brazilian women have
tended to remain single, without finding suitable marriage partners among
their male counterparts. For years, many "Japanese" parents seem to have
been successful in preventing their daughters from marrying "Brazilian"
men and kept them with themselves under patriarchal rule. In my observation, it was more often mothers, rather than fathers, who intervened directly in their daughters' marriage decisions for their family honor or in
the name of family. Mothers needed to make their daughters ideal brides
desired by "Japanese" men. If a daughter failed to contract a sociably desirable or at least acceptable marriage, her mother might have preferred to
keep her single so that she would be able to care for her aging parents to

the very end, as the case of Hisahiro Inoue's two youngest college-educated sisters illustrates. Having such a self-sacrificing and devoted daughter was regarded as honorable for the Japanese immigrant mother, who would never have expected her son to remain single for her own and her husband's sake.

Junko Oshima, a postwar immigrant woman, argues that many pre-war child immigrant women and older generations of Nisei women were "feudal," in effect saying, "Women should not get higher education since educated women do not marry."[29] This may well suggest that one reason many Japanese Brazilian men have preferred to marry less-educated Brazil-ian women is to preserve their male authority. Tamiko Hosokawa main-tains that Japanese Brazilian men are "timid and have no guts" and "cannot communicate with educated women."[30] Amelia Yagihara (b. 1958), a college-educated professional Nisei woman, states that Nisei men of her generation wanted to marry Japanese Brazilian women but felt inferior to educated ones. In order to feel superior to their wives, "they married women of lower social levels, including cleaning women from Bahia, who strongly appealed to them sexually."[31] Such Nisei men inherited an old Japanese notion of gender from their immigrant parents of rural Japan, according to Reiko Uehara, who also maintains that even in postwar Japan it was commonly said that no man would marry a woman educated above a women's junior college.[32] By contrast, according to Yagihara, younger, educated male San-seis and Yonseis date and marry educated Japanese Brazilian women of the same social class (chapter 6), and, as a result, it has become "fashionable" for the educated Nisei women of her generation to date younger Sansei men, who are not threatened by highly educated professional women.[33]

Even though college education has been understood by Japanese Bra-zilians as the best means of individual social climbing, educated women have not always been given any greater freedom of personal choice in life than their less-educated counterparts. As chapter 3 explains, it was com-mon for an older generation of educated Nisei and Sansei women not to be allowed to marry equally educated white Brazilian boyfriends, as in the case of Sansei Masami Takiyama. While her former boyfriend has been suc-cessful as a judge in Brasília, Takiyama eventually became an agent at a *dekassegui* travel agency in Liberdade, while taking care of her aging father and living with him and her older sister and her family.[34] Rosa Aiko Utimura (b. 1956), a Sansei graduate of the Universidade Paulista who works in the administration of a state institution, dated three white Brazilian men in college but has never married, while living with and taking care of her aging parents. Utimura's parents have never received any financial support from their older children, a daughter and two sons, all college-educated and married to Japanese Brazilians with children, and have relied on Utimura only. Utimura claims that reliance on a single child is neither sexist nor distinctively Japanese, as a male Brazilian friend of her age does the same thing—it is simply that pensions are not enough for retirees in Brazil.[35] But she does not explain why she became the designated support and caregiver.

In São Paulo City, I have encountered few cases in which a single Japanese Brazilian man has been designated as the sole caretaker of his parents. However, over the years I have often observed aging Japanese Brazilian parents relying on one (or two) of their Nisei daughters, especially college-educated ones. I know of one case in which a college-educated, married Nisei woman in her fifties took daily care of her mother and her mother-in-law, both in their eighties and both afflicted with dementia, at the same time; her prewar immigrant father was well but could be of no help, and her Nisei husband and his two brothers did not render any help to their own mother. As an only child, Mariana Fujitani (b. 1958) has remained single and always lived with her prewar child immigrant parents in their house, even though she has had a successful career as a reference librarian at a reputable public university and owns her own apartment (introduction).[36] It is most likely she will take care of both of her parents in their last years, as her mother did for her prewar immigrant parents. Despite or because of their higher educations, these Nisei and Sansei women have remained unattached to anybody but their parents, by design or choice, thereby confirming female subordination to male authority in their Japanese Brazilian families.

Oda's narrative demonstrates clearly that she had more than one reason for moving to Japan, becoming a *dekassegui* worker, and staying on there as such. As a college student, Oda wanted to go to Japan, but could not afford to study there, even on a fellowship, since she had to start to work as soon as she graduated, due to her family's financial situation. Oda graduated from USP in 1989 and began to work as a research scientist at Cotia Agricultural Cooperative's laboratory, where she specialized in mushrooms, among other things.[37] Coincidentally, this was the year that Fernando Collor de Mello became the first democratically elected president of Brazil in twenty-nine years and embarked on his economic policies (the "Collor Plan") to deal with Brazil's hyperinflation, which had risen to 1,764 percent a year. As a result, there were not enough jobs even for elite college graduates until 1992.[38] Mikiko Nagashima's Nisei son (b. 1968) did not get a job offer when he graduated from Poli in 1991, and therefore chose to study engineering at Kyoto University on a Japan's Ministry of Education fellowship. He then worked at a major Japanese company in Osaka City for the next ten years until he eventually came back, as a single man, to be enrolled in USP School of Medicine, while helping his mother with her business. Masako Sakamoto's college-educated Sansei nephew (b. 1962) quit his job as an engineer in 1994 and succeeded to his family business in Liberdade, attributing this move to his "low" salaries as a professional.[39]

Oda loved her job as a research scientist in São Paulo City, but her and her family's financial situation kept deteriorating for the next few years. Her fiancé was already in Japan, and he kept telling her to come to join him. Furthermore, she believed that her credentials would get her a professional position in Japan.[40] Unfortunately, Oda's decision to go to Japan in 1992 permanently changed the course of her life. As soon as she realized that she could not find a professional job in Japan, she chose to work as a *dekassegui*, which paid her ten times better than working as a professional back in Brazil. She ended up staying on in Japan for nine years. In return, her career in Brazil was gone forever—though, of course, no one knows whether she could have maintained her career if she had stayed in Brazil. Her employer, the Cotia Agricultural Cooperative, went bankrupt in 1994, and she would have been unemployed and might have opted for *dekassegui* if she had not been able to find another job immediately.

A similar story was narrated by Nisei Marcelo Shuji Yoshimura (b. 1958), who grew up in Liberdade, where his family owned a *pensão* for Japanese Brazilian students. He is fluent in Japanese; he grew up speaking it with his grandparents. As a college graduate in management Yoshimura worked at a Brazilian branch of Japan's Mitsubishi Bank but quit the job and started his own hamburger shop in Liberdade. His business went very well, with many college students as his customers, but after five years it went bankrupt because of Brazil's hyperinflation in the late 1980s; he had borrowed money to remodel his shop and could not pay it back because the interest rate was increasing daily. Yoshimura went back to work as a banker again, this time at Itaú Bank, where he was promoted to auditor. Then his former boss at Mistubishi Bank contacted him for possible *dekassegui* work on behalf of his cousin, a *dekassegui* in Hamamatsu, whose company wanted to hire more Japanese descendants from Brazil. Yoshimura and his wife arrived with forty-five-day tourist visas in January 1990. Yoshimura stated, "I had just got married and we thought we would go to Japan as a honeymoon and save money by working for a few years, but it has been twenty years, and our two children were born here in Japan. Salaries were excellent. In Brazil I had worked at banks only, and manual labor was very hard on me at factories in Japan." In Hamamatsu, Yoshimura was hired by a subcontract company of Yamaha Motorcycles, where he worked at an assembly line for wheels: "They were very heavy, and I worked all the time without sitting down. I had three to four hours' overtime work every day." During his first two years as a *dekassegui* Yoshimura earned and saved a lot of money but lost all of it by hosting a carnival in Hamamatsu and inviting a samba band from Tokyo.[41]

Like Oda and Yoshimura, many, but not all, college-educated Nisei professionals chose *dekassegui* in the last few years of the 1980s and the early 1990s, before the collapse of Japan's "bubble economy." *Dekassegui* transformed such college-educated Japanese Brazilian professionals into blue-collar foreign guest workers in middle-size industrial cities of central Japan. Oda could have come back to Brazil when she broke up with her ex-fiancé. Instead, she kept working in Japan for the next nine years, during which time she got married and had a child. Oda's marriage to her much younger and less-educated Sansei husband in Hamamatsu in July 1995 would not have taken place if she had not gone to Japan as a *dekassegui*. It is widely said among Japanese Brazilians in São Paulo City that during their *dekassegui* in Japan many college-educated Japanese Brazilian women have married younger, less-educated Japanese Brazilian men; this would rarely have happened if they had stayed on in Brazil, where they would have been regarded as "marrying down." However, this perception cannot be applied to the *dekassegui* context in Japan, where men gained much more earning power than women as unskilled manual workers: women have been always paid less by 100 to 300 yen per hour than men, depending on the kind of manual work, regardless of educational level. In the mid-1990s, the basic wages of *dekassegui* Brazilian women were 20 to 30 percent lower than those of their male counterparts for similar jobs, according to sociologist Keiko Yamanaka: "Such gender inequality in wages is institutionalized in almost all occupations in Japan . . . , so it is not surprising that this discriminatory practice is applied even more stringently to immigrant women workers."[42]

For instance, in 2001, Nissen, a *dekassegui* travel agency in São Paulo City, advertised job opportunities in Japan for 1,200 to 1,400 yen per hour for men, and 900 to 1,100 yen per hour for women. Another agency, Asahi, advertised jobs at an hourly wage of 1,300 yen for men between the ages of eighteen and thirty-five at Juji Sangyo-Suzuki, and 1,000 to 1,250 yen for women at Bell Tec Inc. In 2005, Nissen advertised jobs in Japan at 1,000 yen per hour for women, and 1,400 yen per hour for men, while Nibras Tourism's advertised rates were 800 to 1,100 yen per hour for women and 1,000 to 1,400 yen per hour for men.[43] The ideal figure of a *dekassegui* worker in Japan always took a masculine form, and younger adult men were regarded as most valuable in Japan's Nikkeijin labor market. Therefore ethnic endogamy across original class lines among Brazilian *dekassegui* workers in Japan was largely a reflection of their new reality, in which men's larger earning abilities promised a restoration of patriarchy.

As in the case of a niece of Fujitani's (introduction), I often heard in São Paulo City that many less-educated single female Japanese Brazilian *dekassegui* workers married local Japanese men and settled down in Japan permanently.[44] Such marriages have often been talked about in São Paulo City as women's success stories, although I never heard anything concrete about their Japanese husbands. A staff member of the Hamamatsu Foundation for International Communication and Exchange maintains that many Nisei women who arrived as *dekasseguis* are married to local Japanese men.[45] According to the statistics on international marriages in Japan collected by Japan's Ministry of Health, Labor, and Welfare (1970–2009), for the year of 1995 there were 741 marriages contracted and registered between Japanese and Brazilian nationals, of which 579 (77.1 percent) were between Japanese husbands and Brazilian wives. However, the number of such international marriages declined and gender gaps narrowed and evened out over time, with Brazilian men slightly outnumbering Brazilian women as the spouses of Japanese nationals in Japan. In 2009, there were 563 marriages contracted between Japanese and Brazilian nationals: 273 between Japanese men and Brazilian women, and 290 between Brazilian men and Japanese women.[46]

Reiko Uehara maintains that Nisei women who were raised by their old-fashioned Issei parents "treat men with due respect," and that is the reason Japanese men in Japan want to marry such Nisei women.[47] Yagihara's younger sister, a graduate of USP–Porto Alegre in agriculture, worked in Paraná and studied the cultivation of persimmons in Fukushima prefecture on a prefectural fellowship. A famous Japanese researcher on persimmons fell in love with her and, soon after her return to Brazil, came to propose to her. As a result, Yagihara's sister went back to Japan and has settled down in Fukushima permanently, even though she was "embarrassed about herself, thinking she looked like as a Nisei woman who married a Japanese man during her *dekassegui*."[48]

While the majority of male *dekassegui* workers were not college graduates, typically single and college-educated Japanese Brazilian women, most often the oldest daughters, tended to choose to work in Japan for their families, for example, to buy real estate for their aging parents and pay college tuitions for their younger siblings. There has also been a strong tendency

for Issei parents to spend most of their limited resources on the higher education of their children, without making any sound financial plans for their
own retirement. In their last years, they could not help depending financially on at least one of their children, usually a daughter. Oda's older sister,
Luiza, decided on *dekassegui* to buy a house for her parents, who had never
owned any real estate and were struggling to pay their rent due to Brazil's
hyperinflation. In January 1990, at the age of twenty-six, Luiza quit her job
as a banker in Brazil and has been working at a factory in Nagano City ever
since. Her father describes her as "such a dutiful daughter," whom he and
his wife "can never thank enough for what she has done" for them. It has
never been clear to me whether the parents would have expected Rodrigo
to make any career sacrifices for the family or whether Luiza would have
been praised her self-sacrifice if she were a man; she may have acted on an
unwritten code of gender in patriarchy. By May 1992, when Oda moved to
Japan, a new house had been built, all thanks to the money Luiza had saved
and borrowed from her Japanese Brazilian friends in Japan, and the entire
family, except for Luiza, had moved in. Luiza will not return to Brazil until
she retires, while becoming vested in her pensions in Japan. Oda's best
friend, Patrícia Matoba from Londrina, Paraná, gave up her career as a pharmacist to work in Japan for her three younger siblings, all of whom were in
college when their father passed away. Oda and Matoba worked together
on an assembly line in Aichi from June to December 1992, and at the same
pinball parlor in Hamamatsu from January 1993 until Oda's return to Brazil
in March 2001. By then Matoba's brother had become an obstetrician and
gynecologist, one sister a pharmacist, and the other sister also a medical
doctor. With no money left, Matoba had to keep working in Japan to save
money for herself. Her own career in Brazil had been long buried in the
past, like Oda's. According to Oda, Matoba's siblings are "very grateful and
feel bad for her"—though they seem to have been willing to depend on her
financially all those years.[49]

Many of my informants in São Paulo City told me that one could
earn the equivalent of his/her annual salary as an urban professional in São
Paulo City by working as an unskilled manual laborer in Japan for only
a month. According to Amelia Yagihara, some older Japanese Brazilian
employees of Bank of Brazil were able to take "vacation leaves" from work
for a year and a half or two; they went to work in Japan on their vacation
time and resumed their jobs/careers upon return.[50] Shigeru Kojima, a research staff member of the Japanese Overseas Migration Museum (JOMM)
in Yokohama (chapter 7), states that the Japanese were shocked to learn
that there were medical doctors and lawyers among the early waves of

Brazilian *dekassegui* workers in Japan.[51] Many of the earliest college-educated *dekassegui* migrants, who went to Japan before 1990, had concrete financial goals within a certain time frame and were able to resume their careers upon return. Such is the case of Masashi and Turuyo Sugimoto's older Nisei daughter, Sueli, a dermatologist with a degree from the Federal University of Rio de Janeiro, and her college-educated Nisei husband, an engineer. They realized that even with their double incomes as a medical doctor and an engineer they would never be able to buy an apartment in São Paulo City and figured out that they could save enough money to do so if they worked in Japan for two years. At Masashi's suggestion that they should work at something "very Japanese," they chose to work on an assembly line at a *kamaboko* (boiled fish paste) factory in Shiogama City, Miyagi prefecture, for 1987–1989. In their second year, Sueli was able to receive advanced medical training as an intern at Tohoku University Hospital twice a week while working at the factory. Upon returning home in 1989, the Nisei couple immediately resumed their careers and bought a nice apartment in the city, as they had planned.[52]

There were also younger Japanese Brazilians who suspended their undergraduate studies in Brazil for *dekassegui* and were able to resume their educations and move on into careers. In 1987, Kiyoe Sekiguchi's older son (b. 1966), as a senior at Poli, worked as a *dekassegui* at Fuji Film in Mie prefecture to buy a house for his future marriage. He came back after a little more than a year and resumed his undergraduate studies. He graduated from USP, got a job at a Dutch bank, and married his Nisei fiancée as he had planned.[53] Isabel Natsumi Yonamine (b. 1965), a Nisei Okinawan woman, is another example. Yonamine was born and grew up in the Okinawan neighborhood of Vila Carrão, with her parents working as vegetable vendors in the municipal market. Her narrative centers on her family and gender: "I know my parents liked my younger brother better because he is the eldest and only son. I wanted to show my parents that I was good, although I am a girl." When she got into Mackenzie University as a business administration major, her mother said, "A girl does not need college education. We will not pay for you." Yonamine worked during the day while attending college at night. As postwar Okinawan immigrants who resented Japan and the Japanese very much, Yonamine's parents did not allow her to date any Japanese Brazilians. Yonamine recalls, "When you are young, you want to do the opposite of what your parents say you should." She first dated a Sansei, and her parents "did not leave her alone." She ended up dating "Brazilians" and married one of them at the age of twenty-two, and she was surprised to see how "the family of *gaijins* would like to get you into their lives." Her white Brazilian husband of Portuguese and Italian ancestries did not attend college, and her parents therefore did not want her to marry him. In 1989, Yonamine and her husband went to Japan as *dekasseguis* in Kanagawa prefecture, where they had their only daughter in 1994, after three years of fertility treatment. They returned to Brazil in 1995 and soon their marriage dissolved. Yonamine resumed her undergraduate studies and graduated from Mackenzie, while her ex-husband remained unemployed. When I interviewed her in 2002, Yonamine was studying at Mackenzie for her master's degree in finance.[54]

Dekassegui provided other educated Niseis with a temporary solution for their problems in life. Gustavo Akitoshi Kobayashi (b. 1965), a Nisei graduate of the Universidade Estudual Paulista (State University of São Paulo, UNESP) at Presidente Prudent in cartographic engineering, went to Japan as a *dekassegui* upon graduation in 1993. He had to suspend his undergraduate studies for two years to work in his family's business in agriculture when his father was terminally ill, and found it very difficult to catch up with his studies at an advanced level when he returned to college after his father's passing. Losing all his self-confidence in the professional field he had once chosen, he could not think of pursuing a career in Brazil and decided to make money to start a business on the land he had inherited from his late father. In 1994, with savings of 2,000,000 yen, he returned to São Paulo City. He did not know what to do for the next six months but found a job at Gendai, the first fast-food sushi restaurant in São Paulo City, which was advertising jobs as sushi chefs for "Niseis with no previous experience, yet willing to work." All of Gendai's employees were of Japanese ancestry, but there was a critical shortage of sushi chefs with the necessary "Japanese face," as many young Japanese Brazilians had gone to Japan as *dekasseguis*. Kobayashi found out that he really liked working as a sushi chef, and he continued to work there for five years. In 1998, Kobayashi married his long-time girlfriend, Carolina (b. 1972), a Sansei/Nisei physical therapist, whom he had met at college in 1991:

> After getting married we realized we could not have the same days off from work. We did not have enough time to spend together. Then my wife began to say she wanted to go to Japan for work but I myself did not want to go back to Japan. But when she said she wanted to go, I began to think I could not live like this any longer; I liked my job but I worked too much. My income was all right but I could not save any money. But rather than the money itself, I did not like the way I was living my life—as an escape. I once

thought about opening my own sushi business and consulted with a friend but it did not work out.[55]

In 1999, Carolina suggested to Kobayashi that they should go to Japan as *dekasseguis* soon after splitting up with her two Japanese Brazilian business partners in their physical therapy clinic. She had never been to Japan before; in her childhood she did not like being of Japanese descent and refused to learn Japanese. Carolina's Nisei father does not speak Japanese at all and eats Brazilian food only, whereas her mother, a postwar child immigrant is "more like a Brazilian." Kobayashi stated, "I am afraid in a real sense Carolina escaped from her reality by going to Japan just because she could not do her work here in Brazil. But at least we could be together." With no job prospects in Brazil, they became *dekassegui* repeaters. Kobayashi planned on repeating *dekassegui* until he turned fifty, remarking, "It would be the very best for us to work in Japan for a year and to come back to Brazil for the next year so that we can go to school. In addition to Japanese, my wife takes lessons in swimming and violin. I take classes in office work and ceramics. I like craftwork."[56] They worked in Japan as manual laborers temporarily in order to enjoy their urban upper-middle-class lifestyle in Brazil. As Kobayashi stated repeatedly during his interview, *dekassegui* became his way of "escape" from his troubled professional life as a Brazilian. However, the savings he and Carolina had made out of their *dekassegui* work became a source of pride for them as educated middle-class Brazilians in São Paulo City.

Ricardo Takashi Ninagawa (b. 1967), a Nisei/Sansei, was twenty-nine years old in 1996 when he went to Japan as a *dekassegui* for the first time. He had dropped out of USP twice, as a physics and biology major, and made a living in music by playing an electric bass guitar for several years. Then at the age of twenty-five he passed an entrance exam at USP for the third time as a pharmacy major. Not enjoying that field, he dropped out of USP again one year short of graduation and went to Japan as a *dekassegui*. In Japan, Ninagawa worked on assembly lines for four years, during which, as a typical *dekassegui* worker, he moved three times in search of better-paying jobs: "I worked in rural Hyogo prefecture first as an ordinary factory worker. This is a common job for *dekasseguis*. A month later I moved to another place, with a better pay. I was making 1,000 yen per hour for the first place but 1,300 yen per hour for the second one in Gifu prefecture. I stayed there for a year and a half."[57] During his first *dekassegui*, Ninagawa had no idea what Japan was; he was busy working all the time. He was not particularly interested in Japan or his being a Japanese Brazilian. In 2000, when he was working at Toyota Group in Gifu prefecture, his postwar immigrant father passed away suddenly without any financial planning. Ninagawa came back and gave all of his savings to his mother, who had been a full-time homemaker, while his younger brother (b. 1977) was still in college. He was back home in São Paulo City for three years, during which he studied and took an exam in order to work as a low-ranking judicial clerk.

In 2003, Ninagawa went back to Japan for his second *dekassegui* after he had passed the exam and found out where he was ranked among those who made it. He worked in Japan for two years to save money for himself: "First I worked at SONY in rural Guifu, and then moved to Yatomi City, Aichi prefecture, twenty kilometers away from Nagoya. I worked at a small company called Okamura Seisakusho. They paid me 1,250 yen per hour, plus tons of overtime work, which was good. I worked twelve hours a day." Being fluent in Japanese, Ninagawa enjoyed talking with the Japanese, but, he says, "Fellow Nikkeis workers did not like it if I talked much with the Japanese. Most of them spoke Portuguese only, with just a little bit of Japanese to get by. Yet a few spoke better Japanese than I do. That was my personal choice; I wanted to experience more culturally by interacting with the Japanese if there were any opportunities. But the Nikkeis did not like it and called me a traitor. On the other hand, the Japanese accepted us as long as we did a good job."[58] In June 2005, Ninagawa was working at a Japanese Brazilian association in Liberdade only in the afternoons, waiting to be called in for his new job. Ninagawa was fortunate to obtain a reasonable job, which most other college-educated fellow *dekassegui* returnees would not have been able to do.

Masashi and Tsuruyo Sugimoto's two youngest Nisei children, now in their fifties, who are college graduates in engineering and physical therapy, have not been back to Brazil since the mid-1990s, when they began *dekassegui* work in Japan. They have been working at the same *kamaboko* factory in Shiogama, Miyagi prefecture, where their older sister and her husband had worked back in 1987–1989. Both of them have remained single and "missed the chance to return to Brazil," according to Masashi.[59] Back in 2001, Masashi and Tsuruyo had traveled to Japan and visited with and befriended their children's employer, who is their age, and they are proud of their Nisei children's willingness to help the local Japanese after the Great Tohoku Earthquake (2011).[60] As in the case of Oda and Luiza, there are no professional positions or reasonably paying jobs in Brazil for the younger children of the Sugimotos should they wish to return after many years in

Japan. I've heard many times in São Paulo City that there are no jobs in Brazil for job seekers who are over thirty years old.

It should be noted that *dekassegui* never "homogenized/equalized" Japanese Brazilians in Japan, at least in the sense that was understood among Japanese Brazilians in São Paulo City (chapter 1). As unskilled blue-collar part-time workers, they did the same manual work on assembly lines and were paid the same hourly wages, regardless of differing class positions back in Brazil, and in the eyes of the local Japanese population, they might all have appeared the same. But in reality class continued to differentiate them. Angelo Ishi (b. 1967), a Sansei sociologist and professor at Musashi University in Tokyo, points out that, first, educated Japanese Brazilians faced professional identity conflict as blue-collar workers in Japan, where they found no upward social mobility. One of Ishi's informants said to him that he would fall into depression when he compared his intellectual job in Brazil to his manual work in Japan: "I don't suffer because my work is heavy, but I cannot stand it because it is manual labor, too simple for me." Second, they suffered from "what could be called a class identity conflict" in Japan, where they occupied "the lowest position in the host society's social pyramid." Thus, they turned to weekend leisure activities among Brazilians and middle-class patterns of consumption in the "land of yen," where they bought cars and houses. Ishi continues, "Self-realization now takes place on weekends (or during other free time), in spaces outside the workplace (such as ethnic enclaves or on returning to the homeland), and with Brazilian, not Japanese, friends and compatriots."[61]

Dekassegui Brazilians had their own politics of identity among themselves. What they used to be back in Brazil could be validated and used in certain situations. As Ishi explains, "A male factory worker in Japan can, when he comes to meet a Brazilian woman, provide a self-introduction using his 'original' social condition: 'I'm a lawyer (in Brazil).'" This is the same form of positioning many Japanese immigrants practiced in Brazil, and some still do by fabricating their family lineages and/or previous lives back in Japan to exaggerate their social status. But since most *dekasseguis* meant to return home to resume their lives, what they would have been back home inevitably carried a more realistic appeal to others. With the capital they had earned as *dekassegui* workers, some aspired to move up in the host society but were critically limited by their marginality in Japanese society; they usually moved up on a social ladder from blue-collar workers to Brazilian store owners, but "because their clientele is composed mainly of Brazilians, they are inactive in local (Japanese) society and not (yet) fully recognized as members of 'high society' by host Japanese." Thus, one's position among Brazilians in Japan is determined not only by one's background in Brazil but also by one achieved among Brazilians in Japan. At a collective level, this was an important process of alienation in the host society with a deepening *saudade* (yearning) for the homeland, according to Ishi.[62] It should be noted that Ishi's arguments center on male *dekassegui* Brazilians in Japan; his study does not concern gender inequality or the reconstruction of gender relations. How did Oda, for instance, deal with her inner conflict between being a college-educated professional woman in Brazil and being a female *dekassegui* worker in Japan? How did her gender determine her experiences in Japan? How has she reconciled herself with her lost goal of self-realization?

In May 1992, when she arrived in Japan for the first time, Oda was "not surprised that the Japanese all looked alike but was surprised that they all spoke the same language."[63] Despite her being a *japonesa pura* with amazing fluency in the Japanese language, the local Japanese could tell Oda was not Japanese; she was "either a foreigner or Brazilian" in their perception. Although she is not racially mixed, according to Oda, the local Japanese could not even tell she was a Japanese descendant, even though some thought she was Japanese until she spoke Japanese. Oda maintains, "The more Japanese you look and the better you speak Japanese, the less discriminatory treatment you receive from the Japanese. The racially mixed have a harder time, and so do those who do not speak Japanese." According to Oda, the Japanese did not begin to discriminate against Brazilians until Brazilians started getting together among themselves as their number began to increase rapidly. I heard similar stories from other *dekassegui* returnees in São Paulo City in the first few years of the 2000s.

In Japan, Oda never felt she herself received any discriminatory treatment from the local Japanese, but observed what was going on with other Brazilians in Hamamatsu:

> We have a national-chain supermarket, Ito-Yokado, in Hamamatsu, near the train station, which regularly made an announcement to their customers: "Please take caution of foreigners who are here in the store." It was around eight years ago [1993]. That became a subject of public discussion. Also, [in June 1998] a Brazilian journalist [Ana Bortz] visited a jeweler in Hamamatsu. There she was shown some items but when she said she is Brazilian she was no longer welcomed. Some Brazilians did terrible things in Japan; being unemployed, those committed petty crimes and stole some things. But, of course, that does not mean that all Brazilians would do such things. So that is the problem for the Japanese.[64]

Andrea Yumi Minami (b. 1962), a Nisei woman (chapter 7) remembers during the 1990s a security officer always following her white Brazilian husband at department stores in Hamamatsu whenever she went shopping with him and their young children.[65]

Unlike many other *dekassegui* workers, who moved to different cities and kept changing jobs constantly in search of better wages and more overtime work, Oda worked at the same pinball parlor, which ran two stores in Hamamatsu. Each store hired some twenty Brazilians, together with Chinese part-timers on student visas. She made deliveries in a van for the hourly wage of 1,000 yen per hour, which was much better than her previous factory wage of 850 yen per hour for women. Oda also discusses Japanese Brazilians' patterns of socialization in Japan: "Brazilians were always saying that the Japanese, not only women but also men, are cold. The Chinese were saying the same thing. I did not have a chance to make personal friends with the Japanese. Yes, Brazilian Nikkeis socialize with other Brazilian Nikkeis. Well, I should not say that there is no chance for us to socialize with the Japanese. It is easier for Nikkei men to socialize with Japanese men. It is difficult for Nikkei women to make friends with Japanese women, I think."[66] Oda's discussion of gender here is noteworthy. It is always easier for men to move to a new country; for men it means a movement from one form of patriarchy in their homeland to another form of patriarchy in the host society. Even though both men and women have to deal with racism and other biased perceptions and discriminatory treatment, men's positions are always less restricted than women's, as men are able to locate themselves over women under patriarchal rule. As a Japanese Brazilian woman in Japan, Oda made only one Japanese woman friend, a full-time homemaker with two young children, at a *kōdan* (public housing complex) where she and her family lived. This was the only local Japanese who invited Oda to her apartment. Oda also describes how Brazilians behaved in Japan and how she understood Japan in comparison with the Nikkei *colônia* and Brazil:

> Both Brazilians and Japanese live in the same company-owned apartment complexes, but the Japanese do not want to be where Brazilians congregate. At the [company] cafeteria Brazilians are loud and making much noise. They like playing music very loud and they do not try not to bother others. That is the reason why they are not liked. I think Japan is the opposite of Brazil. Even here in Brazil, I thought that the *colônia* was different from Brazil. It was stern, unlike Brazil. Then Japan turned to be even more stern than the *colônia* was.[67]

Hiromi Ono (b. 1954), a postwar child immigrant (1960) told me a similar story involving one of her college-educated Nisei younger brothers in Kanawaga prefecture, where he worked as a *dekassegui*. One day he and a few other Japanese Brazilians took a local train together, and when they sat next to each other, a young Japanese woman called them *gaijin* and left her seat to get away from them as quickly as possible. Ono could not believe the story: "They are all *pure Japanese*, not mixed at all. How could she treat them like that?" All three of Ono's younger Nisei brothers, who had dated only "Brazilian" women in São Paulo City, married Japanese Brazilian women in the end. One of them decided on *dekassegui* work in Japan when he graduated from college as an engineer and could not get a good job in Brazil. He worked in Japan for three years and returned to São Paulo City, where he bought a house with his *dekassegui* savings and found a very good job as an electrical engineer.[68]

Being categorized as Brazilians and discriminated against by the local Japanese inevitably created collective Brazilian identity among Japanese Brazilians in Japan. In other words, Japanese Brazilians became Brazilians by contrast to the Japanese in Japan only by going to Japan. At the same time, it is important to note that being Brazilian means different things to each individual Japanese Brazilian in Japan. Many chose to date and marry among themselves partly because as *dekasseguis* they intended to return to Brazil in the end. Minami has three brothers: one older Issei brother (b. 1958), who arrived in Brazil at the age of two, and two younger Nisei brothers. All went to Japan as single *dekasseguis* and married Japanese Brazilian women while working in Hamamatsu.[69] Thus, like Oda and her husband, many single adult Japanese Brazilians practiced ethnic endogamy in Japan.[70]

But not all Japanese Brazilians in Japan separated themselves from the local Japanese and lived only among themselves. During his first *dekassegui* in 1993, Gustavo Kobayashi, with dual nationality and fluency in Japanese, felt displaced among Brazilian *dekassegui* assembly workers in Japan. At Yasuzu Kōgyo, a subcontract company for Suzuki Motor Cooperation in Kosai City, Shizuoka, he worked with twenty-two other Japanese Brazilian workers from Paraná and Pará, none of whom spoke Japanese or was a college graduate. After six months there without overtime work, he was recruited to work in Kumamoto prefecture for the next seven months for better pay and many hours of overtime. He enjoyed getting to know the local Japanese there.

As discussed, Kobayashi resumed his *dekassegui* work in 1999, together with his wife, Carolina. In Gotenba City, Shizuoka prefecture, both of them worked at a small auto parts factory, on assembly lines. Kobayashi recalls, "It was very difficult for us to live among Brazilians in Shizuoka, due to their bad reputation. The Japanese do not disturb others, and that is their best quality," and "I do not have much to do with other Brazilians, unless they think like we do." For Kobayashi and Carolina, the best thing about working in Gotenba City was making friends with their local Japanese coworkers, as Kobayashi had done in Kyushu on his first *dekassegui*. But they had hardly any overtime work, so Kobayashi got another job by calling a temp agency:

> We moved to a *bentoya* [shop selling takeout lunches] in Tokorozawa, Saitama. My hourly wage went down by 100 yen, but it was rather high for lunch-box packing—1,200 yen per hour. Usually it is only 1,000 per hour. My wife worked at the same place. We could have only two hours or so of weekly overtime work in Gotenba, but we got four or five hours in Tokorozawa. I did not like the work, but that was still a job, so I was determined to work there for a year. In the end, we stayed there for three years—at the same *bentoya*.[71]

Kobayashi and Carolina returned to Brazil in 2002. Carolina did not want to return to Brazil, as "she likes the Japanese and does not like Brazilians; she wanted to stay in Japan longer since she thought she could not go back to Japan again." But at the same time they did not want to live in Japan permanently. Back in São Paulo City, Kobayashi worked at a sushi restaurant again, but Carolina was so depressed for a year that she did nothing. For the following year she worked part-time while learning Japanese, but she had "no foundation in Japanese and did not comprehend the language at all." In 2006, Kobayashi and Carolina went back to Japan and worked at a *bentoya* in Miki City, Hyogo prefecture. This was a job they got through a *dekassegui* agency in Liberdade, and they stayed at the same place for one year and ten months until they returned to Brazil in 2007. In July 2008, they went back to Japan for their third *dekassegui* together.

In Japan, Kobayashi and Carolina always avoided other Brazilians and socialized instead with their Japanese coworkers as well as with other local Japanese who took interest in another culture. According to Kobayashi, with the passage of time, the number of uneducated Brazilians had increased in Japan, and that caused problems: "*Dekasseguis* do the same work but that does not mean we are all the same. Brazilians can see who and what other Brazilians are." Interestingly, he did not see class stratification among the local Japanese; he seems to have understood semiurban working-class Japanese, especially middle-aged female part-time workers, as the nation of Japan, whom he positioned above less-educated Brazilians in Japan.

Separating themselves from other Brazilians and mingling with the local Japanese might well be Kobayashi and Carolina's way of protecting their upper-middle-class Brazilian pride; they avoided facing the reality that they were longtime *dekassegui* repeaters with no careers back home. Kobayashi was still fully aware that he was different from the Japanese, who told him he was "too honest and blunt," and felt more comfortable with Brazilians in Brazil, a feeling he attributed to his native Portuguese language.[72]

Ricardo Ninagawa's total of six years (1996–2000 and 2003–2005) as a *dekassegui* in Japan strengthened his Brazilian identity, though he admitted, "There have been more and more bad guys among the *dekasseguis* in Japan, as Japanese newspapers have been reporting. It's shameful." Ninagawa was born to a college-educated postwar immigrant father and a *kihaku* Nisei mother who had returned to Brazil in 1953. He spent his early childhood in Liberdade among the Japanese, speaking Japanese only until he started kindergarten in Belém, Pará state. Nevertheless, he does not think of himself as a Japanese descendant and is "simply a Brazilian." As of 2005, both of his younger sisters were married to white Brazilians, while his younger brother, the youngest in the family, who had become a lawyer, remained single. Ninagawa states, "The distinction between Nikkeis and non-Nikkeis has become blurred these days. I will not think of such a thing when I get married."[73]

In other cases, Japan became a source of pride for educated *dekasseguis* who came to identify themselves as Nikkei. Isabel Yonamine says she literally fell in love with Japan: "Japan is so beautiful, and we are Nikkeis. We have our country Japan, an image of Japan, and an image of hard workers in the country that reached its prosperity after the war." Even her postwar Okinawan immigrant parents came to love Japan and Japanese culture and identify themselves as Nikkeis after many years of *dekassegui* in Japan (1989–2001). Upon returning to Brazil, they bought a house with their savings and were able to live comfortably on the rent, while enjoying watching Japanese broadcasting on NHK every day. All three of Yonamine's younger siblings are long gone to Japan as *dekasseguis* since around 1990; her younger brother dropped out of college, while her younger sisters did not attend college at all. In Japan her sisters are married to an Okinawan and a Sansei Brazilian, whereas her brother married and divorced a white Brazilian and is now married to another one.[74]

Back in São Paulo City, Yonamine first worked at a *dekassegui* agency and then co-owned a *dekassegui* agency in Vila Carão with two male returnees. Yonamine spoke of her *dekassegui* days in Japan: "Well, my face, I look Japanese. I would say, 'I'm sorry. I am a Brazilian and I do not understand Japanese very well.' My Japanese friends said, 'You do not speak Japanese but you have the demeanor of the Japanese.' Well, people liked it. That is not Brazilian. You have to respect the people there and the traditions of the country." According to her, "the Japanese and Nikkeis are honest, hardworking, and trustworthy. That's why Brazilians want to marry Nikkeis. One receives more respect if s/he has the Japanese face." Identifying herself as a "Nikkei mixed with Okinawans," Yonamine maintains that Brazilians have "good racism" toward Japanese descendants, who are "well respected." "Here in Brazil," she says, "there are two types of education: white and black, and the Japanese are more white. Well, Nikkeis are better compared to whites than to blacks."[75] Refusing to acknowledge her marginal position as a minority Brazilian woman, Yonamine relies on her newly founded ethnic pride as a middle-class Nikkei through her experiences in Japan.

Conclusion

In the 1970s and 1980s, some college-educated Nisei and Sansei women began to challenge patriarchy or social injustice by breaking off ties with the male-dominant Japanese Brazilian organizations and associations, while others continued to accede to patriarchy to serve the needs of their families as dutiful daughters, despite their higher educations and professional positions. By the end of the 1980s, college education no longer guaranteed Japanese Brazilians a comfortable upper-middle-class life in São Paulo City, and many chose to migrate temporarily to Japan, where wage differentials redefined gender relations among Japanese Brazilians as foreign guest workers, regardless their differing levels of formal education.

In 2005, after several years of failed attempts to find a reasonable job in São Paulo City, Christina Oda left for Japan with Nasser to be reunited with her husband, who had refused to return to Brazil. Thus Oda resumed her life in Hamamatsu and enrolled her son in a private Brazilian school there. Realizing that its curriculum was weak, she sent Nassar back to her parents in March 2007 to prepare him for higher education in Brazil. He was only eleven years old then. Since then Nassar has been living with his maternal grandparents and attending good private schools in São Paulo City. In 2011, he graduated from a junior high school and started his high school education. Meanwhile, Nasser has traveled to Japan to visit his parents in Hamamatsu almost every year, while keeping in touch with them daily via Skype.

Oda's decision was not a common one among Japanese Brazilians residing in Japan. On the ground that her husband and his family had already settled in Japan permanently, she could have chosen to have her Japanese-born son finish Japanese schooling in Japan up to university level. But from a historical perspective, what Oda has been doing for her son is nothing new; before the outbreak of World War II some well-to-do prewar immigrant parents sent their young Brazilian-born children, all holding double nationality, to Japan for Japanese education, which they believed was much better than Brazilian education. After the war, those Niseis returned to Brazil permanently. They are the *kihaku* Niseis. Also, in the 1940s and throughout the 1950s, some Nisei children were sent on their own from the countryside to São Paulo City for higher education (chapter 3). Among them elite Niseis emerged in Brazilian society during the 1960s, when Oda was born.

Oda has been fortunate to have a solid support system for Nasser's formal education back in Brazil; her parents are in reasonably good health, very attentive to Nassar, and very enthusiastic about his higher education. Remaining single, Rodrigo acts as Nasser's guardian, has been doing all of the paperwork for him, and comes home every Sunday to spend time with him. Oda may want her son to grow up like Rodrigo, not her own husband. Back in 2001, Oda did not talk much about her husband; she said she liked him very much, adding that she thought he "would change" once they got married, but he did not.

In December 2007, Oda's parents accompanied Nasser to visit with Oda and her husband in Hamamatsu, and Luiza in Nagano City. In Hamamatsu, for the first time, Oda's father met Nasser's former nanny, an elderly former immigrant woman. She was very surprised to hear that Oda is an elite USP graduate who used to work as a research scientist in São Paulo City; Oda had never talked about her past in Brazil. One can only guess why she kept silent. It does not seem that her husband and his family cared about her college education or former career back in Brazil. Probably most of her coworkers are not college-educated, either. Her background, in combination with her fluency in Japanese, could have become cultural capital among Japanese Brazilians in Hamamatsu only if she were a man. But that does not mean that she could just fit in among other *dekassegui* workers as long as she kept quiet about her background. For her first nine-year-long *dekassegui,* her best friend in Japan was Patrícia Matoba, who had also given up her career to help her younger siblings. As Kobayashi points out, doing the same kind of manual work in Japan never makes Japanese Brazilians into a homogenous group.

Oda has never complained. Through *dekassegui,* Oda and many other educated Niseis and Sanseis of her generation permanently lost their place as urban professionals in Brazil. In a sense, what Oda has been doing for her son is the same as what her parents did for her and her siblings— investing her earnings in his education for his future as an educated Brazilian, without pursuing her own career. Yet, unlike her parents, Oda graduated from Brazil's top institution to become a professional scientist, and even though she gave up her professional position and goals in Brazil permanently, she is proving at least to herself that she is still an educated Brazilian, unlike many other Brazilians in Japan; she has kept her upper-middle-class pride alive in her own way. Her ultimate self-realization depends on her Japanese-born son's future achievements as an educated Brazilian. In São Paulo City, Nasser has continues to carry his mother's dream of self-realization within himself.

Chapter Six

SANSEIS, YONSEIS, AND
THEIR RACIAL IDENTITY

It is not a good thing to be mixed. This is my personal opinion. I believe Japanese culture cannot be passed on to a next generation if racial mixture progresses further. I have few Nikkei friends. There is definitely racism [against Japanese Brazilians]. I believe the Japanese have separated themselves from Brazilians culturally so that they would not feel discriminated against by them. That is their strategy. I've thought about it before. While being a Nikkei is a physical thing for me, I have taken in such a Japanese tradition as a family heir for my identity. This is my personal strategy.

—*Hugo Shinji Murakami,*
a college student, 2008[1]

On June 26, 2008, I interviewed Hugo Shinji Murakami, a nineteen-year-old second-year USP student. He is a *mestiço*, born in 1989 to a college-educated Nisei father and a white Brazilian mother. Murakami identifies himself as a Nikkei, stating that that he would have perceived himself differently if he had looked "more Brazilian." He does not use his Portuguese first name and goes by his Japanese middle name. Murakami possesses impeccable skills in speaking, reading, and writing Japanese; he learned the language from his late paternal grandmother, a prewar immigrant from Yamanashi prefecture, who used to be a Japanese language teacher. In his childhood, especially after his parents' divorce in 2001, Murakami became very close to his paternal grandparents. His late grandfather, a prewar immigrant from Fukui prefecture, was "very strict" but confided in him "as his only grandson he liked." Murakami regards himself as "the only heir" of his paternal Japanese family, and maintains it would be ideal for him to marry a "pure Nikkei" woman to retain "Japanese blood" in the family, adding that he "would not mind marrying a *mestiça* if she is very pretty."

In his schooldays, Murakami was the only "Japanese" and was called *japa* wherever he went, and there was a "Brazilian" boy who bullied him constantly: "Children are so cruel that they discriminate against other children. This happens to almost all Nikkeijin. I thought I was bullied because I am Japanese but now I am proud of being a Nikkei." When he entered a private senior high school, he had one Japanese Brazilian classmate, who was born to a Chinese father and a Japanese mother. When Murakami was a freshman, there were six second-year Japanese Brazilian students in the same class, none of whom understood Japanese except for a male student with whom Murakami made friends. They "separated themselves from Brazilians," which was "not a cultural or ethnic issue but that of grouping," according to Murakami. "They did not understand the Japanese language but were interested in Japanese music only, such as J-Pop, which is identical to Western popular music, except for its Japanese lyrics." When he went to USP to take his entrance examination, Murakami saw "Brazilian" students call a male Japanese Brazilian student *japa olho puxado* ("slanted-eyed Jap") and keep yelling at him, "Open your eyes, Jap!"

At the time of his interview Murakami's own friends were almost all "Brazilians," predominantly male, including his best friend of Middle Eastern ancestry, an electrical engineering major at a state university, whom he had known since childhood. As of 2008, Murakami had only two Japanese Brazilian friends, both young women. One was a twenty-five-year-old Nisei of Okinawan descent, who spoke Japanese, was very interested in Japan, participated in Okinawan Brazilian associations, and played *taiko* (a traditional Japanese drum). All of her other friends were Okinawan descendants. Like Murakami, she preferred to be called by her Japanese middle name, Natsumi, not by her Portuguese first name. She had been to Japan for *dekassegui* several times. The other was another USP student, who did not speak Japanese; she had "no ties to the Nikkei community" but had many Japanese Brazilian friends. She preferred to be called by her Portuguese first name, Alexandra. Murakami spoke critically of other young Japanese Brazilians socializing among themselves: "Members of young Nikkei associations, such as Seinen Bunkyo, do not speak Japanese, so I do not understand why they get together in the way they do."[2]

The upper-middle-class Sanseis and Yonseis born in the 1970s and 1980s have struggled to define and redefine their positions under the fluid racial hegemony in Brazil. Many were born to college-educated parents, attended private schools, and have attended and/or graduated from reputable universities. They had no financial need to work in Japan, but some have been able to take advantage of *dekassegui* without letting it determine their life course or career plans. While many refused to identify themselves as Nikkeis and continued to intermarry with white Brazilians to "whiten" themselves, others, including some of the racially mixed, chose to affirm themselves collectively as Nikkeis and practiced ethnic and/or racial endogamy. Definitions of Nikkeiness vary from individual to individual, and gender has also determined young self-identified Nikkeis' identities and actions in their daily interactions with "Brazilians." Who are "true Brazilians" in their definition? What has "the Japanese face" signified for the upper-middle-class Japanese Brazilian youth in São Paulo City?

Japan's emergence as the world's leading economic power improved the collective self-perception of younger generations of Japanese Brazilians in São Paulo City. Such positive sentiments were shared by the fourteen upper-middle-class Japanese Brazilians, all *paulistanos* (persons from São Paulo City), ranging in age from seventeen to twenty-eight, who were invited in July 1997 to participate in a roundtable discussion hosted by a Japanese Brazilian magazine, *Japão Aquí* (Japan Here), for its article "Japanese or Brazilian: How Do the Young Nikkei Feel?"[3] During the late 1980s, Eduardo Seiji Tamura (b. 1972) and his fellow young Sanseis "suddenly felt superior to Brazilians and longed for Japan"; Japan's economic prosperity helped them feel proud of being "Japanese" in Brazil.[4] In the early 1990s, the Sansei youth all felt ambivalent about having some of their family members working as manual laborers in Japan. Eduardo Tamura states, "Among friends, we said, 'Oh, your father is living in Japan,' even if it were for *dekassegui* work. We did not use the term *dekassegui*, and one did not say how his father got to work there. But when he bought a new car, he said, 'Of course, my father has been working in Japan.'" When he was enrolled in a *cursinho* at the age of nineteen, Tamura himself wanted to go to Japan "just because everybody was going there." As FATEC students, he and his Sansei friends often wondered whether they should go to Japan for work, but they all ended up staying on in Brazil, except for one friend who went to study in Japan on a prefectural fellowship.[5]

Eduardo Tamura is the second oldest of four Sansei children, all of whom became exceptionally high academic achievers. His Nisei father was always very passionate about their higher education, although both of his parents finished only the four-year primary education. Eduardo's older brother graduated from FATEC four times with four different degrees and obtained an MBA from FGV. After dropping out of FATEC twice, Eduardo himself graduated from the Universidade de Nove de Julho (July the Ninth

University) as a marketing major and completed his MA in marketing communication at ESPM. Eduardo's younger brother, who studied at the Federal Technical High School, as Oda's brother Rodrigo did, graduated from UNICAMP as a mechanical engineering major, and earned a MS in engineering at the Instituto Tecnológico de Aeronáutica (Technological Institute of Aeronautics, ITA). His younger sister graduated from USP and finished her PhD at UNICAMP, both in Japanese.

Unlike Eduardo Tamura and his siblings, many young Japanese Brazilians chose to go to Japan for *dekassegui*. For instance, postwar child immigrant Yaeko Hashida's Nisei son went to work in Japan in 1990, when he was a nineteen-year-old college student. After working in Japan for three years, he came back, finished his college education, got a job at IBM, and married a Nisei/Sansei woman, a college graduate in pharmacy, in 1999.[6] Ana Sakagami (b. 1973), the only child of Nisei Natsue Sakagami and her postwar immigrant husband (chapter 4), suspended her undergraduate studies at PUC in 1995 and worked in Japan for two and a half years as a caddy on a golf course. In Japan, Ana had a baby boy by her *mestiço* boyfriend, a fellow *dekassegui* worker, but, back in Brazil, she finished her college education in business administration (2000) and then another degree in accounting (2001).[7] While working as a *dekassegui* agent in Liberdade, Natsue raised her grandson Alberto by hiring a *bahiana* as her live-in maid. In 2001, Ana began to work for a major US company in São Paulo City, and in 2002, passed a competitive exam to be hired by the federal government and moved with her son to Illéus, Bahia, for her new job.

Yonsei Christina Agari (b. 1971) suspended her undergraduate studies to work as a *dekassegui* in Japan for three years. She lived there alone and worked on an assembly line for twelve hours a day. She came back, resumed her undergraduate studies, and graduated from the university. Then she went to Japan again, this time to study on a Miyagi prefectural fellowship for a year. After coming back from Japan, Agari joined Seinen Bunkyo in 2000 through Daniel Tateno, president of Seinen Bunkyo (2000). She became Seinen Bunkyo's vice president in 2001 and was chosen to be its first woman president in the following year, while working in marketing for a store for domestic utensils, and enjoying playing *taiko* as her hobby.[8] As of 2006, at the age of thirty-five, Agari, "being crazy about Japanese culture," was working at a Japanese Brazilian NGO in São Paulo City for those with mental disabilities.[9]

Edwin Hideki Hasegawa (b. 1982), a Sansei, was a business administration major at USP when he decided to take a leave from school to work in Japan for fifteen months, because he "just wanted to go to see Japan."

According to Hasegawa, working on an assembly line in Japan was very hard on him physically. Furthermore, he had to live among Brazilian *dekassegui* co-workers, whom he did not get along with, due to their different educational backgrounds. He ended up speaking Portuguese with other Brazilians in Japan and had no chance of improving his Japanese language skills. Hasegawa graduated from USP and has been employed as a systems analyst by the Serviço Nacional de Aprendizagem Comercial (National Service of Commercial Learning), an education management industry, in its São Paulo headquarters.[10]

Sansei Sabrina Mayumi Akiyoshi (b. 1983) went to Japan as a *dekassegui* in 2000, with her mother, her older sister (a USP student), and younger sister. Her father stayed behind on his own in São Paulo City, refusing to admit that his business was in trouble. At seventeen, Akiyoshi had just graduated from high school, whereas her older sister suspended her college education for *dekassegui,* and her younger sister, still in high school, needed to continue her schooling at a private Brazilian school in Japan. Her mother, already retired, decided to work in Japan to make money to save her father's troubled business, and all three daughters decided to help their mother. The Akiyoshis settled in Mie prefecture, where Akiyoshi worked on an assembly line at a factory, as the youngest worker in her section. Her original plan was to work there for two years, but, fearful of losing the chance for a college education, she returned home in a year and a half and enrolled herself in a *cursinho.* After "studying days and nights for half a year," at the age of nineteen, she passed a competitive college entrance exam to major in pharmacy and biochemistry at Universidade Estadual Paulista–Araraquara. In January 2001, Akiyoshi went to Japan again to spend a month with her mother and sisters and then took her younger sister with her back to Brazil; they were worried that Brazilian high school education in Japan was not good enough for college education in Brazil. Akiyoshi's younger sister lived with her in Araraquara, São Paulo, studied for college entrance exams, and then eventually graduated from college. Akiyoshi's mother and older sister did not come back until 2004, by which time they had saved the money they had planned on. While her older sister resumed her studies at USP, her mother began cancer treatment but passed away soon after. Akiyoshi herself graduated from college in 2007 and was employed by a pharmaceutical company. She was back in Japan from April 2009 to March 2010, when she studied at Kyushu University on a Fukuoka prefectural fellowship. Her older sister, who finally graduated from USP, married a Japanese Brazilian in 2011.[11]

Many young Sanseis have been able to take advantage of *dekassegui* in order to travel, live, and work in Japan, either temporarily or permanently. In 2006, Newton Hirata, a Sansei (b. 1974) originally from Paraná, was completing his PhD in political science at USP, while his two brothers were working in Toyohashi City, Shizuoka, and Okazaki City, Aichi. Both were married and still working in Japan as of May 2012. His older brother, a college-educated engineer, began his *dekassegui* work in Japan after having lived as a student on a Fukuoka prefectural fellowship for a year, as many other prefectural fellowship students have done. Hirata's older brother, being career-oriented, would be willing to move to any other country where he could find a better opportunity. By contrast, his younger brother started *dekassegui* work at the age of seventeen as soon as he graduated from high school, and at the age of thirty-six (in 2012) he was most likely to stay on in Japan permanently.[12]

Eduardo Tamura and his wife finally visited Japan in July 2005 for the first time to spend two weeks there solely for pleasure. They also visited with his wife's two brothers and their families in Kanagawa prefecture. Like Hirata's brothers, Eduardo's two brothers-in-law, both college dropouts, were in Japan as *dekasseguis*. One of them had already decided to stay on in Japan permanently, but the other had yet to make the decision where to raise his young child. In Japan, Eduardo "tried to find his identity." He says, "When I was younger I used to think I was more Japanese than Brazilian, but now I surely believe that I am a Brazilian, who respects more deeply the way the Japanese think to do everything." He and his wife also visited with Japanese Brazilians who did not wish to come back to Brazil after living in Japan for many years. After seeing them living in Japan, Eduardo himself thought about working in Japan: "The image was really different. I used to think there was no time to do anything but heavy and stressful jobs. True, there are no good jobs [for *dekassegui* workers], but Japan seems to be a kind of Wonderland. In Japan, we can walk with pockets full of money. There are lots of high-quality products, such electronic equipment as PCs and sound systems. Compared to Brazil, Japan is a real paradise."[13] No matter how difficult their work situation might be, just living in Japan may have boosted each *dekassegui* worker's self-esteem; living and working legally in the "Land of Yen" has been a special privilege granted only to Japanese descendants.[14] Interestingly, Eduardo makes two contrasting comments on his "Japanese face." In Japan, the Japanese were very kind to him and he did not have to tell them he was a Brazilian because they could "see it in his face." But on his return flight on Japan Air Lines from Tokyo to São Paulo, a "true Brazilian man, if there were anything like that" made fun of him and other Japanese Brazilian passengers, *dekassegui* returnees, for their lack of skills in the Japanese language despite their "Japanese face." Eduardo is saying that in the same "Japanese face" the Japanese see Brazilianness and Brazilians see Japaneseness. In other words, he has no fixed, half-and-half Japanese Brazilian identity; his ascribed identity depends on context. In the end, Eduardo Tamura identified himself as "a real Brazilian, who fell in love with Japan."[15]

Murakami is a product of intermarriage. Murakami's father, Paulo Takashi (b. 1951), wanted to become an astrophysicist but chose to study engineering in college instead in order to make a living. According to Murakami, his father is fluent not only in Japanese but in English. At work his father is known only by his Portuguese first name, but he is Takashi among his family members and friends. Murakami's parents met at work, where his father was an electrical engineer and his mother an accountant, and they married in 1983. Murakami's mother (b. 1960) is a white-collar worker without a college degree, who is "very white with green eyes, and not racially mixed at all." Murakami's father does not like anything related to Japan or the Japanese and has never belonged to any Japanese Brazilian associations; he was raised as a Japanese by his prewar immigrant parents and was not allowed to speak Portuguese at home. Murakami's paternal grandfather was, in fact, a stern *kachigumi* and was imprisoned three times as a member of Shindō Renmei. Murakami understands some of his father's actions, including intermarriage, as "a revolt" against his rigid Japanese upbringing. Murakami thinks his mother simply fell in love with his father as a person, regardless of his Japanese ancestry. When Murakami was twelve, his parents divorced and his father moved out to live with his aging parents. Later, Murakami's father married another white Brazilian woman of Portuguese descent, with a PhD in literature, whom he had met on Internet dating site, and they have a young daughter, Sayuri.

Murakami can be understood as a successful result of his Nisei father's individual "whitening." First, his father got a college education and moved himself up in Brazilian society as an engineer, because "money whitens." With the power of a higher education and an urban professional position, he married a white Brazilian woman and produced offspring "whiter" than he is. In the logic of the older generation of educated Niseis (chapter 3), somebody like Murakami, a Sansei born to a college-educated father and a white Brazilian mother, should have been "a true Brazilian." In a typical Japanese perception, Murakami is only half Japanese (and the Japanese Brazilian usage of *mestiço/mestiça* emphasizes the non-Japanese ancestry and therefore racial/ethnic otherness), but, in the Brazilian mind, Murakami, whose skin color is definitely "white," looks "Japanese" because of his "Japanese face," according to Murakami himself, and therefore he is no different from any other "Japanese" in São Paulo.

Other *mestiços* can escape being categorized as "Japanese" and treated or bullied accordingly if they do not have "the Japanese face." In short, they can simply pass as "white" Brazilians, like three *mestiço* participants in the aforementioned roundtable discussion for *Japão Aqui* (1997): Katia Cristina Fudalhes Weber (b. 1970), Patrícia Yakabe Malentaqui (b. 1980), and Douglas Yakabe Malentaqui (b. 1977). Unlike Murakami, all three were born to white Brazilian fathers and Japanese Brazilian mothers, identified themselves as "completely Brazilian," and maintained that they had never experienced any prejudice or discrimination as Japanese Brazilians. Weber, a twenty-seven-year-old architect, was born to a father of Italian and Polish descent. She married a Brazilian man of no Japanese ancestry, and their four-year-old son was "more mixed" than Weber herself, and, being called *japa neguniho* ("little black Jap"), he "suffer[ed] more prejudice" than she did. By contrast, seventeen-year-old Patrícia and twenty-year-old Douglas preferred to date and marry Japanese descendants. Douglas had always preferred to date women who were at least "partly Japanese descendant," like himself. He maintained that being "Japanese" was not a matter of race or anything physical but was psychological, involving matters such as "quality of sincerity." Patrícia stated that she wanted to have a child by a Japanese Brazilian man, even though she "attracted all sorts of Brazilian men."[16]

Murakami has the choice of "whitening" himself still further by marrying a white Brazilian woman and producing offspring who would be three-quarters white and one-quarter Japanese, as many others have already done. The logic of whitening is exemplified by Sansei Keiko Nakahara Alvarenga, president of Organização Educational Nippaku (Japan-Brazil Educational Organization), a private Japanese Brazilian nursery and elementary school. She married an educated white Brazilian man, a successful banker. Their mixed Yonsei son, who has succeeded to her business, married a white Brazilian woman. And, according to Alvarenga, their son is "a Gosei, who looks *very white*."[17] As discussed in previous chapters, the rate of Japanese Brazilians' racial mixing grew increasingly higher over the years and came to be regarded as a common practice by the end of the twentieth century. Eduardo Tamura states, "What is interesting in Brazil is that the Nikkei, including Sanseis and *mestiços*, mix with anybody and produce their offspring. There is no barrier for mixing. Black soccer players and musicians, who make a lot of money, mix with anybody also. Therefore

Brazil is becoming extremely mixed."[18] Note that he compares Japanese Brazilians to Afro-Brazilians with respect to their shared practice of racial mixing with white Brazilians, even though he may not be fully aware of what he is really talking about—the meaning of "whitening" for persons of color in Brazil.

During the 1990s, both men and women of Japanese descent began to date and marry "Brazilians" at almost equal rates. By 2000, however, intermarriage had become more common for Japanese Brazilian women, on the assumption that marriage between "Brazilian" men and Japanese Brazilian women works better than the other way around. Wagner M. Horiuchi, who once married a white Brazilian woman after coming back to Brazil from *dekassegui* work in Japan, states that Japanese Brazilians, both men and women, are attracted to white Brazilians.[19] However, Eduardo Tamura admits, "In my generation no matter how much we said we liked *gaijins* and we made friends with them, we tried to marry Nikkeis in the end." He characterizes Japanese Brazilian women as "quiet and hardworking" and explains, "What is bad is that Nikkeis would not truly get along with non-Nikkeis later in life. Even if I feel I am completely Brazilian now, as I age, I might become much more Nikkei if I had married a blonde woman. I was afraid of not being able to use the Japanese language when I was studying very hard and networking with the Japanese and Japanese companies; I did not want to throw everything away by marrying a non-Nikkei woman."[20] In 2004, Eduardo married a college-educated professional Japanese Brazilian woman (a UNESP graduate in nursing). He says, "We speak Portuguese only at home, but she does not mind hearing me speak Japanese and talk about Japan. Non-Nikkei women might not like it. I did think about these issues before I got married. Before that I thought I would marry a Taiwanese beauty or anybody else who was not a Nikkei." Thus he decided on his marriage partner mainly out of professional concern. His younger brother married a white Brazilian woman upon graduation from UNICAMP but got divorced. According to Eduardo, as did his younger brother, those who attend elite universities such as USP and UNICAMP tend to date and marry among themselves, beyond race or ethnicity.[21]

Sansei Kulara Kawamura's case fits in this group. Born in 1976 to a Nisei father, a dentist who has a private practice in the middle-class district of Jabaquara, and a Nisei mother, a teacher, Kawamura always dated white Brazilian men, except for one *mestiço*, and in 1999, as a USP graduate in biology, was dating Paulo, a twenty-eight-year-old USP graduate in business administration of Italian and German ancestries. Her family seems to have been "whitened" well. Two of her paternal uncles married white Brazilian women, one Jewish and another Spanish, while her paternal aunt became a medical doctor. Kawamura and her three younger siblings grew up with live-in maids, and all attended reputable public universities (FATEC, UNESP, and USP). She and her father practiced Allan Kardec's spiritualism. Even though Kawamura thought her paternal grandfather would want her to marry a Japanese, her father would not have any problem with her inter-marriage. At the same time, as of 1999, Kawakami had three good female friends of nine years' standing, all "Japanese." She says, "It is always easier to make friends with the Japanese than with other descendants."[22]

Alice Minemura is also a Sansei woman (b. 1977), who, in 1999, was pursuing her MA in history at the Universidade Paulista while dating a younger white Brazilian man, who had a four-month-old baby with his ex-girlfriend. Unlike Kawamura's Nisei parents, both of Minemura's Nisei parents had received only four years of elementary education back in the countryside. Her father (b. 1941) is a retired mechanic, and her mother (b. 1949) is a seamstress and hairdresser. Her older sister (b. 1975) married a maternal cousin in Campinas, São Paulo, who had spent two years in Japan as a *dekassegui* and then completed his college education back in Brazil. One of Minemura's female cousins married an "Italian," but no one in her family married a "person of color." Minemura always dated white Brazil-ians, except for one young Japanese Brazilian man, whom she saw only for a month and characterized as "very Japanese and timid." Her parents wanted her to marry a "Japanese," and she wished to continue to live with them even after marriage.[23]

During the 2000s, I saw many interracial couples involving Japanese Brazilians in public, more frequently a Japanese Brazilian woman with a "Brazilian" man than otherwise. I also constantly heard from my Japanese Brazilian informants of different generations that intermarriage would work much better between Japanese Brazilian women and "Brazilian" men than vice versa. According to Marisa Kinoshita, Japanese Brazilian women are "always exotic and mysterious" to Brazilian men.[24] Nisei businessman Akio Ogawa, who was once married to a less-educated white Brazilian woman (chapter 3), states that intermarriage lasts only in the case of Nisei or Sansei women and Brazilian men. That is because "Brazilian men treat women more kindly" than their Japanese Brazilian counterparts.[25] Accord-ing to Tamiko Hosokawa, there is a high divorce rate between Japanese Brazilian men and Brazilian women, but it is said that Brazilian men tend to live longer if they have Japanese Brazilian wives. "Nikkei women know how to be patient, and therefore Brazilian men look for Nikkei women to marry," Tamiko Hosokawa says.[26] He continues,

Brazilians tend to think that most young Nikkei women are *ugly* but at the same time they certainly admire something originally Nikkei as beautiful. It seems like they treasure something characteristically Japanese as precious beyond the *ugly* face of Nikkei women. Brazilian men look for kindness and patience in Japanese women because Brazilian women are selfish. They like quiet and selfless women like Japanese ones. . . . They [Nikkei women] are not as quiet as Japanese women but much more so than Brazilian women. Brazilians find Nikkei women mysterious; they are not always looking for money only.[27]

Tamiko Hosokawa's description of Japanese Brazilian women as "ugly but kind and patient" accords perfectly with the prevalent perception of them among Brazilians as social inferiors, and repositions them as ideal wives for Brazilian men. In this logic, Japanese Brazilian women can be freed from their ethnic gendered duties among Japanese Brazilians but continue to accede to the structure of gender inequalities in Brazilian society, in which they are expected to serve Brazilian patriarchs with their "kindness and patience," which is "naturally" attributable to their ethnic Japanese womanhood. Thus intermarriage does not enable Japanese Brazilian women to escape from patriarchal rule, even outside the Japanese diaspora.

Eduardo Tamura was born and grew up in Guarulhos, São Paulo, and attended private schools in the city where there were only one or two Japanese Brazilian students in the same class. There were five or six Japanese Brazilians in the same *cursinho*, but there were many when he got into college at the beginning of the 1990s. Back then most of the Asian students at FATEC were of Japanese descent, and therefore FATEC was nicknamed FATOQUIO (After Toquio—Tokyo). USP had a similar proportion as FATEC. Eduardo states, "Nikkeis get together among themselves, and walk together. It seems that there is *an invisible power* that bonds us together. When I was in college and was walking alone, all of a sudden other Nikkeis showed up and began to talk to me. We would get together among ourselves. One of them said, 'Why does a Nikkei want to talk to other Nikkeis?' It happens often. For instance, at USP, FGV, and Mackenzie University, Nikkei students get together among themselves."[28] Eduardo's choice of the words "invisible power" here is interesting, given that Japaneseness is recognized "visibly" through "the Japanese face."

In fact, in the late 1980s, some upper-middle-class Japanese Brazilian high school students in the city were already getting together among themselves. According to Marisa Eiko Kinoshita (b. 1971), a PUC-educated plastic artist, when she was a high school student at the elite Colégio

Bandeirantes, all Japanese Brazilian students went to Morumbi Shopping Center after school for bowling every day. That was their major gathering place before Shopping Paulista was built. She comments, "As adolescents they form Nikkei groups for their racial identity but that passes." Tyuitiro Hirai (b. 1971), who also attended Bandeirantes and then Poli, describes the situation thus: "In high school there are five Japanese in the class of fifty students but they have never seen each other before, but just after a week they are together, forming a group." Christiane Kimie Maeda (b. 1976) studied at FAU but attended a private high school where "there were many Japanese [Brazilians]," but she "was never part of such a [Japanese Brazilian] group"—all of her friends were "Brazilians." She remained the only Japanese in her group until she was forced to deal with Brazilian racial stereotypes of the Japanese in school at a personal level. After that she "began to walk more with the Nikkei."[29]

In the late 1990s, young Sanseis' and Yonseis' gathering became much more pronounced in São Paulo City. They got together independently from other generations of Japanese Brazilians and their ethnic associations, instead hanging around in the evenings in the public parks of such middle-class residential districts as Jabaquara, Jardim da Saúde, and Vila Mariana, as Kawamura pointed out to me in 1999 with an expression of surprise.[30] They were getting together on Friday afternoons and evenings, as well as on weekends at major shopping centers in the city, such as Shopping Paulista and Shopping Tatuapé, which was described by Brazilian TVs and newspapers as "the Sansei's world."[31] They went to the same "Japanese" beauty salons, since "not everybody knows how to cut flat Japanese hair, and that that is the reason naturally they go to certain places for haircuts."[32] They hosted dance parties (*bailes*) reserved exclusively for Japanese Brazilians on Saturday nights.[33] Olga Futemma (chapter 5) expresses concerns about the "new generation of young middle-class Japanese [descendants]," who are "going back to conservatism." They "form groups at school" and "marry among themselves," she says, despite the "Brazilian norm of miscegenation." Futemma continues, "I don't understand why they are becoming conservative. This is no good. They are Brazilians but want to be Japanese. They see themselves as better than other Brazilian citizens."[34] But is this really just young middle-class Japanese Brazilians' "returning" to the old "conservatism," based on their shared middle-class position? Or are they, as a collective, aiming at something else? Koichi Mori argues that what connects young Nikkeis is their "vague racial consciousness."[35] Akio Koyama also notes that young Sanseis who do not speak Japanese form groups at school, not because of Japanese culture but for the *face*; they "naturally" get together among themselves and therefore feel easy among themselves and trust one another. He refers to this as "an *unconscious* communal consciousness" or "feeling among the Japanese."[36]

Collectively these young self-identified Nikkeis enjoy sharing Japanese food, drinks, and popular culture—singing Japanese songs at karaoke, watching Japanese anime, and reading manga or comic books—and playing sports, such as baseball and volleyball, on all-Japanese teams. They get together among themselves for what they call "Nikkei colony parties." The membership of such an informal group (*turma*) is defined largely by Japanese ancestry, but some descendants of other Asian groups are also included. Even a small number of non-Japanese Brazilians who love Japanese culture join them. Their college-educated Nisei parents, who intermarried among themselves but many of whom chose not to socialize with other Japanese Brazilians for many years, have expressed surprise at some of their Sansei children's strong preference for befriending other Nikkeis. For instance, Yoriko Matsuno (chapter 3) states that her son, who became a medical doctor like his father, "does not like Nikkeis and has always preferred white women," and is married to a white Brazilian woman who is also a medical doctor. However, her daughter, who majored in pharmacy, "found more Nikkeis in college" and "socialized with many of them."[37] Erica M. Yamaoka's son "likes Japanese Brazilians very much," and the majority of his friends are "Asians," whereas her daughter, who studied in the United States, Switzerland, and Australia, has never dated Japanese Brazilians. In college Yamaoka's son was "more Asian than Japanese," and his group included the "Chinese," *mestiços,* and a few *gaijins,* who "liked to drink with Sanseis and Yonseis and who were more Asian than Asians are."[38] Sachiko Tomino's two children, as USP undergraduate students, also belonged to Nikkei *turmas;* whereas her son's group included two Chinese, a man and a woman, who were not dating each other, her daughter was making friends with Japanese descendants only, and her daughter's boyfriend was a *mestiço* born to a Korean father and a Japanese mother.[39] In short, what connects these young Japanese Brazilians and their non-Nikkei friends with one another is their shared sense of strong national belonging to Brazil and fondness for Japanese culture. Therefore, membership is rather loosely defined, except for their shared socioeconomic position.

Iossuke Tanaka, who was a very active member of the Piratininga Club during the late 1950s (chapter 3), had three Sansei sons born in the late 1960s and early 1970s. His oldest and youngest sons never married, and his middle son, a banker, married a Sansei woman. Tanaka commented in June 2008 on Japanese Brazilian youths getting together among themselves:

"They feel comfortable among themselves as they have *a different face.* There are a small number of Nikkeis scattered in any big organization. If they see the same *face* among others, they feel comfortable; their *face* is different from Italian, Spanish, and any other descendants, and it creates feelings of familiarity among them. But we do not know how long it will last; it is diminishing rather quickly."[40] Has this collective Nikkei consciousness really diminished? In June 2010, when I interviewed Akio Ogawa in his office near Avenida Paulista, he advised that I should go to see young Japanese Brazilians getting together in groups on Friday evenings at Shopping Paulista, adding, "Almost all of them have a *face* like mine, but they do not speak Japanese at all."[41] I visited the mall on the evening of June 11, 2010, but did not see any Asian-looking youth in groups at the food court. I moved up to the top floor to see what was going on around the movie theater, where *Toy Story III* was playing. Soon three groups of Asian-descendant teenagers (thirteen in total), looking like high school students, showed up. Then three girls and four boys, all seemingly Asian descendants, entered the theater. Not a single non-Asian descendant was included among them. According to Sansei Hector Nobuo Motoyama, young Japanese Brazilians continue to get together among themselves but have moved on largely from Shopping Paulista to Shopping Santa Cruz, as they "do not stay on at the same place."[42]

These young Japanese Brazilians grew up in middle-class residential districts of São Paulo City, outside Liberdade, among predominantly white middle-class Brazilians. They attended private elementary and junior and high schools where they were the only "Japanese" or one of a few, and had little contact with other Japanese Brazilian youth. Most grew up without learning to speak Japanese or taking any interest in Japanese history and culture. Like other urban upper-middle-class Brazilian youth, they learned English as their second language, attending private English classes as early as first grade, and they identify themselves first and foremost as Brazilians, and then as Westerners. That does not mean that they are not aware of their minority position in the larger society. In fact, what connects these young Japanese Brazilians is the "Japanese face" with "slanted eyes." Like Murakami, who grew up with Brazilians, they all shared the experience of being ridiculed and bullied for the "Japanese face" and "slanted eyes" and called *japonesinho/japonesinha, japa,* and *japinha* (a diminutive form of *japa*). Ana Claudia Ando (b. 1977), for instance, states that she was always yelled at on the street, "*Ah, japonesinha puxado!*" (Hey, little slanted-eyed Japanese girl!). In her youth, Marisa Kinoshita "got her hair permed" and "did everything to erase her Japaneseness." Young Sanseis and Yonseis have been well aware of negative stereotypes of Japanese Brazilians persisting in Brazilian mass media: "Japanese *pasteleiros* (pastry cooks), Japanese *tintureiros* (cleaners), who never speak correct Portuguese, speaking with all kinds of mistakes and being always confused," according to Kinoshita. Douglas Malentaqui points out, "That is the same prejudice as has been against blacks until recently. But there was so much pressure that it changed. Today if you see a black maid in a soap opera, you will protest [against racial stereotyping]. But the Japanese are still half confused [and therefore do not protest]." Tyuichiro Hirai states that negative stereotypes against Japanese Brazilians have been maintained in the Brazilian mind because Japanese descendants never protested to the mass media.[43]

Some of the self-identified Nikkei youth founded and have joined their own ethnic voluntary associations and clubs, such as ABEUNI (Aliança Beneficente Universitária de São Paulo, São Paulo University Students' Beneficial Alliance), Seinen Bunkyo / Comissão de Jovens do Bunkyo (Bunkyo's Youth Commission), ASEBEX (Associação Brasileira de Ex-Bolsistas no Japão, Brazilian Association for Ex-Scholarship-Holders in Japan), and MOVI (Movimento Jovem; the Youth Movement) of Nippon Country Club, none of which is exclusively Nikkei. In order to prevent Japanese culture from disappearing in Brazil, since 2000 Seinen Bunkyo, ABEUNI, ASEBEX, and JCI Brasil-Japão (Junior Chamber International Brazil-Japan) have been hosting annual events together for "Revitalização" (Revitalization). In 2001, around one hundred youth attended the Revitalização meeting held in São Paulo City from twenty-one associations in São Paulo, Paraná, and Rio de Janeiro states.[44]

ABEUNI started in 1984 as an ethnic mutual-aid association involving a small group of Japanese Brazilian college students who volunteered to interpret for elderly Japanese immigrants who did not understand Portuguese. Over the years, ABEUNI came to be known for its large-scale "caravans" bringing medical and public health service to the poor. It is also well known for its successful organization of *festas juninas* (June festivals) and large-scale fundraising *bailes*. ABEUNI's membership is inclusive, but its members have been always predominantly of Japanese ancestry, and only 10 percent are "Brazilians."[45] Christiane Kimie Maeda (b. 1976) met Viviane Caroline Abe (b. 1978) at Cursinho Anglo, a well-known college preparatory school. Abe, who also attended FAU, brought Maeda to ABEUNI. Marcía Ito, a former ABEUNI president, states, "New members are recruited by their friends, who are already members. Nikkeis would like to bring in other Nikkeis with themselves."[46]

Seinen Bunkyo was created in 1997 as Bunkyo's new youth branch during the presidency of Atsushi Yamauchi (chapter 3). As of June 2008, it had approximately two hundred members, predominantly Sansei, aged nineteen to twenty-eight, of whom only 20 percent were women. When I asked him about the gender imbalance, Edwin Hasegawa shared his "personal opinion" with me: Women prefer to participate in *taiko, yosakoi soran,* and sports groups, and do not like administrative work in such an association, where there are discussions and fights over power. Furthermore, according to Hasegawa, parents do not allow their young daughters to go out for meetings at night, on both weekdays and weekends.[47] As in the case of ABEUNI, around one-tenth of Seinen Bunkyo members are not of Japanese descent, and most Japanese Brazilian members are Sanseis. Seinen Bunkyo elected a non-Nikkei male Brazilian member, Luiz Fernando Silva, as its president for 2006.[48] Sansei member Ronaldo Masaki Nakata (b. 1989) maintains, "They like Nikkeis and make friends with us the Nikkei. There is no distinction between Nikkeis and non-Nikkeis. We are the same as long as we are here."[49] On June 28, 2008, I was invited to attend a Seinen Bunkyo orientation session led by Akemi Cumagai for seven new members—either college students or recent graduates, six men and one woman, one Nisei and six Sanseis, including a *mestiço* and a member of MOVI. None of them speaks Japanese. Cumagai was planning to study in Japan at either the University of Tokyo or Tohoku University on a graduate fellowship from Japan's Ministry of Education. I also met one of Seinen Bunkyo's non-Nikkei members, Luciana Palacido Barbosa, a *morena* (light-skinned Afro-Brazilian woman) college student in civil engineering, who grew up with her Japanese Brazilian friends in the district of Butantã and would like very much to marry a Nikkei man.

Some of the urban upper-middle-class Japanese Brazilian youth have been valorizing their Japaneseness collectively by voluntarily separating themselves not only from non–Japanese Brazilians but also largely from less-educated, working-class Japanese Brazilians. Unlike the immigrant and Nisei populations, who tend to dismiss the prevalent Brazilian racism against the "Japanese," young Sanseis and Yonseis have been forced to deal with Brazilian racism individually and directly on a daily basis in primary and junior high schools. They perceive themselves as elite ethnic Brazilians, while positioning themselves above Japanese youths in Japan for "respecting the elderly."

Eric Funabashi (b. 1980), ASEBEX president (2008), told me an interesting story of his self-discovery as a Nikkei. Funabashi was born in São

Paulo City to upper-middle-class Nisei parents, both USP graduates in chemistry, neither of whom speaks Japanese. Funabashi himself began his undergraduate studies at UNICAMP as an agricultural engineering major but graduated as a marking major from ESPM, and was employed by his father as a manager of his tourism company. Funabashi's full-time home-making mother used to be a college professor. His college-educated younger sister, a physical therapist, has dated both Nikkeis and non-Nikkeis and seems to have no preference. As a child, Funabashi "did not like the Japanese and hated to be Japanese"; he was called names, such as "monkey," by other "Japanese" children for being deeply tanned by having grown up in Fortaleza, Ceará state, where his father worked at Shell as a chemist. Funabashi was always the only "Japanese" at school. Outside school, Funabashi became a Boy Scout when he was eight, and at twelve he and a Japanese Brazilian friend "had to change the group because there were many bad *gaijins* [in their group]." His friend chose a "Nikkei group" of Boy Scouts: "In the Nikkei group, we did not have anything Japanese. Things were the same as in the other [non-Nikkei] group. It was like the Japanese colony. I did not know anything Japanese in the Nikkei Boy Scouts group. But at the same time you are more comfortable with other members. When I went there for the first time I felt I could be who I really am; I was no longer a stranger. Everybody was Japanese."[50] Over the years, Funabashi lost touch with his "Brazilian" Boy Scout friends but has stayed in touch with his "Japanese" ones.

Funabashi has two close friends, both Japanese Brazilian men, whom he has known since his high school and college days in Campinas. One of them "really wanted to be Japanese," but the other one, who was born to an Issei father and a Nisei mother, "did not want to be Japanese." Funabashi states, "His father is strongly related to the *colônia.* All of the children hated being Japanese and they did not care about it. He did not want to have anything to do with being Japanese. He did not like the Japanese stereotype as hardworking. He is not really smart and did not care about going to a good university. Things were hard on him."[51] Even though Funabashi "hated Japanese [language] schools and the Japanese language," there was one part of Japanese culture he really liked from childhood: Japanese anime. This does not differentiate him from other young "Brazilian" fans. As a college freshman Funabashi began to buy anime on the Internet, hoping he would not need to read Portuguese subtitles, and that is the reason why he began to study the Japanese language again. Around the same time, a friend suggested he, as a Japanese descendant, should think about applying for scholarships to Japan. Funabashi studied Japanese for two years and won a

Tottori prefectural fellowship as a trainee in tourism marketing. That enabled him to spend a year in Matsue City, where there were no other Brazilians, except two Brazilian women who were married to Japanese men.[52]

Even after spending the year 2006 in Japan, Funabashi did not think he was really a Nikkei except for his "face" until he began to party with other Nikkei youth in 2007. He has since learned that "the Nikkei all share a more similar way of life": "I am not dating now, but throughout my life I have always dated Nikkei women only. When I was in high school, I was always the only Japanese, so I dated non-Nikkeis, and then I realized they did not have the same values I care about as Nikkei women do. I came to understand my grandparents much better after I spent the year in Japan. They are still alive. They came to Brazil when they were very young. They speak Japanese when their friends are around."[53] Funabashi would like very much to marry a Japanese Brazilian woman, but his younger sister does not have the same preference. "When we went to school," he says, "I was the only Japanese boy and she was the only Japanese girl, but she never really cared about it. She is not like me."[54] Edwin Hasegawa is in a similar situation with his younger sister. When he was a child Hasegawa was always ashamed of being "Japanese" but has grown to be very proud of being a Nikkei. By contrast, his sister greatly resents being "Japanese" and has been dating "Brazilian" men only.[55]

Miyuki Shinozuka (b. 1981) is an upper-middle-class Sansei woman with a strong Nikkei identity, unlike Funabashi's and Hasegawa's sisters. Shinozuka, who was born and grew up in São Paulo City, graduated from the Universidade Anhembi Morumbi as a tourism major and works at a large multinational enterprise. She identifies herself as a Brazilian but insists that she, as a Nikkei, "cares about others like the Japanese." As Funabashi did, Shinozuka studied in Japan for a year (2005) on a Tottori prefectural fellowship. In her midtwenties Shinozuka married an elite Sansei man after having dated him for five years, but her seemingly perfect ethnic endogamy did not last, due to the "cultural differences": "Yes, we are Sanseis, but he grew up speaking Japanese all the time, as his father is an Issei. His way of thinking is very Japanese. We have Nikkei culture, but that is not the same as Japanese culture."[56] After her divorce, she began to date a white Brazilian architect at her company, whom she characterizes as "very Brazilian," who sometimes stands her up, saying, "I am busy. I cannot make it." If she protests, he replies, "I just do not feel like going there, so I just don't go." Shinozuka states, "The Japanese are not like that. They'll go if they said they would."[57] Over such "cultural differences" between Brazilians and Nikkeis, Shinozuka broke up with her boyfriend in June 2008, but they soon got back together. It seems that her divorce from her "very Japanese" Sansei husband and troubled relationship with her "very Brazilian" white boyfriend has confirmed her Nikkei identity, which is neither Japanese nor Brazilian but may include both at the same time.

In the Brazilian practice of "whitening," the majority of upper-middle-class Japanese Brazilians should have been "true [white] Brazilians," as their educated parents' money (and therefore social status) has already "whitened" them, and many of their family members have married and/or will marry white Brazilians, as in Kulara Kawamura's family. Ricardo Ninagawa (chapter 5), for instance, strongly denies having any ethnic identity and identifies himself solely as a Brazilian, after having worked as a *dekassegui* in Japan for a total of six years. As of 2005, Ninagawa and his younger brother were still single, but both of his two younger sisters were married to white Brazilians.[58] Eduardo Tamura also admits he was quite tempted to marry a non-Japanese Brazilian woman, but after a serious consideration of his profession as a freelance Portuguese-Japanese translator, he concluded that he would be better off with an educated Japanese Brazilian spouse who would not mind his business in Japanese and/or with the Japanese. His Sansei wife does not read or speak Japanese at all, but she grew up very familiar with Japanese culture.[59] Murakami, as a mixed Sansei, identifies himself as a Nikkei, since he definitely looks "Japanese" to Brazilians. Whether they reject or embrace their Japanese ancestry and/or Nikkei identity, all three men will remain equally "Japanese" in the eyes of Brazilians, given their "Japanese face."

At Seinen Bunkyo, Hasegawa introduced me to Sansei Ronaldo Masaki Nakata (b. 1989) as "a very interesting case." Coincidentally, Nakata is the same age as Murakami, and both of them identify themselves as Nikkei and prefer Nikkei over non-Nikkei women for dating and/or marriage. Both speak Japanese fluently. But otherwise they have nothing in common. Nakata is a *japonês puro* and differs in background and profile not only from Murakami but also from all of the other Seinen Bunkyo members, who are either college students or graduates who work as urban professionals. Nakata comes from a working-class family and has not even completed a middle school education. However, he represents what has been going on among Japanese Brazilians; he is one of the many recent returnee children from Japan.

Nakata was born and grew up in Liberdade as the youngest of three children, all sons, to a Nisei father and a postwar child immigrant mother. As a child, Nakata was called *nihonjin* in Liberdade, but in school he was always called *japa*, not by his name. His father had been a sushi chef, and his family was "always poor," according to Nakata. In 1998, his parents decided to go to Japan as *dekasseguis* to make enough money to start an interior decorating business in São Paulo. Nakata was nine years old, and his other brothers were twenty-one and fifteen. By then, all of his mother's relatives had gone to Japan as *dekasseguis,* and Nakata had many cousins in Japan whom he had never met. The Nakatas settled near Toyota City, Aichi prefecture, but not among Brazilians. In Japan, Nakata's parents and oldest brother worked full-time, and his middle brother worked part-time while attending a Brazilian school. Nakata was enrolled in a local public school, where he was the only foreigner. He had a very hard time in school, particularly with mathematics; his favorite subjects were history—especially medieval Chinese history—and gymnastics. Amazingly, Nakata learned the language quite well, including the Chinese characters. "I did not understand at all in the beginning," he says. "I studied Chinese characters very hard and became able to read within a year." As soon as he became fluent in Japanese, Nakata made friends with many of his classmates, including those who used to bully him. After finishing the seventh grade in a local Japanese school, Nakata was enrolled in a "Brazilian school" for two years. Upon retuning to Brazil with his family in 2005, Nakata attended a public school in São Paulo City to learn Portuguese. "It is as if I had become a *nihonjin* and learned Portuguese as my foreign language. That was difficult." After two years, Nakata quit his Brazilian schooling entirely to help his family with their home furnishing business. Thus, he did not complete a middle school education in either Japan or Brazil.

In June 2008, at the age of nineteen, Nakata was holding two jobs to support himself and his family. His father's business had not made any profit for the first two years but was finally starting to pick up in 2008. He did not want to work for his family business and wanted to do something else; his dream had been to become a professional soccer player in Japan. Meanwhile, Nakata had been facing racism back home: "We are called *japa* wherever we are here in Brazil. We are rarely called by our names. I do not like it. For the last two years, since I came home, I have been called *japa* again. I talk back to them in Japanese, but they make fool of me if I speak Japanese. There are many jokes on the Japanese, and I hate them all. They are ridiculous, such as the Japanese being rich. My family is poor."[60] Nakata had no friends before joining Seinen Bunkyo. He feels very comfortable among the Nikkei: "We have completely different manners. Brazilian Nikkeis have good manners to the elderly, whereas the Japanese youth seem not to care about it. That is the difference. I feel comfortable and relaxed among Nikkeis. We have a different culture and personality. I don't mean

Brazilians are bad. I have black friends, and some Brazilians are good people."[61] Nakata says that his family is "poor," but does not acknowledge any class difference between himself and other Nikkei members of Seinen Bunkyo. Nakata had dated in Japan but did not do so back in Brazil for two years. Recently he had a Japanese Brazilian girlfriend, but he soon broke up with her, saying he "needed to be free." Throughout his narrative, Nakata puts strong emphasis on his Japanese identity, with Japanese as his native language. As such, he positions himself above all of the other Sansei members of Seinen Bunkyo, who are all upper-middle-class Brazilians.

Nakata and I corresponded via e-mail for a while, and he always chose to write in colloquial Japanese to demonstrate his proficient reading and writing skills, something none of the other members can do. Then on September 13, 2009, out of the blue, he asked me to let him stay with me for "a home stay," expecting me to find him a job at my institution. I declined his request, as I didn't have the resources or the moral obligation to support a young adult man whom I barely knew. A postwar Japanese immigrant woman informant remarked that he was "very Brazilian" to ask me for such a thing after having met me only once. I did not think much of it until, when I returned to São Paulo City, he never showed up for an appointment with me, and later sent me a message in Japanese blaming me for not showing up—again, behavior that other young Sanseis told me was "typically" Brazilian. It is ironic that he behaves like a "typical" Brazilian while saying, "I do not like Brazilians because I am Japanese." Nakata's case demonstrates clearly that language acquisition and conscious liking for another culture do not necessarily entail profound acculturation.

Hector Nobuo Motoyama (b. 1984) is another Sansei member of Sainen Bunkyo. Motoyama began to frequent Japanese Brazilian associations such as the Nippon Country Club at the age of eighteen and joined Seinen Bunkyo in March 2008 to play volleyball. A graduate of Mackenzie University in psychology, Motoyama works at a corporate department of human resources. In 2008, Motoyama was taking a Japanese language class in order to go to Japan to work as a psychologist for Brazilian *dekassegui* children, but eventually chose to stay on in Brazil for his professional career. He and his parents traveled to Japan for pleasure in 2009. Motoyama is called Nobu among his Japanese Brazilian friends, but Hector at work. There is another Japanese Brazilian employee at work, and Motoyama says they speak to each other in Japanese, a practice their "Brazilian" co-workers do not like. He has dated ten women, all Japanese Brazilians except for one "Chinese"; he likes Japanese Brazilian women because of "their physical attraction, cute style, and preference of places to have fun, such as Japanese discos."[62] When I contacted him in May 2010 for an interview, Motoyama wrote that he could no longer go to Seinen Bunkyo because of his work schedule and that he was going to a certain church in Liberdade for volleyball instead. Living in the eastern zone of the city, it takes Motoyama one hour to arrive in Liberdade every Saturday morning, starting at eight o'clock coaching a Nikkei women's volleyball team at the gym of Hiroshima Prefectural Association of Brazil. Luciana Barbosa of Seinen Bunkyo is also a member of this Nikkei team. When I arrived at the gym late in the morning of Saturday, June 12, 2010, to meet with Barbosa, there were some twenty young people, both women and men, playing volleyball. They included three non-Nikkeis: a "Korean" woman, a French man, and a Chinese Brazilian man, a college graduate who went to school with Japanese Brazilians and all of whose friends are Japanese Brazilians. Motoyama maintains, "We *look different,* and we *are different.*"[63]

When I met with Motoyama later on the same day at the Liberdade metro station for his prearranged interview, he was with Lucia Mika Yamashita (b. 1979), the team captain. Motoyama and Yamashita invited me to nearby Ichiriki Bakery, a popular Chinese-owned Japanese-style coffee shop in Liberdade, for coffee and cakes, and that is where I interviewed both of them. Yamashita and Motoyama chatted about a disco party in the evening, and they explained to me that every Saturday night the young Nikkei got together for a "Japanese" disco party. Some 90 percent of participants in such parties are Japanese Brazilians. Motoyama estimated that some 75 percent of young Japanese Brazilians prefer to date among themselves.

Motoyama was born to college-educated Nisei parents, both of whom had worked as bankers for years. He has a younger sister (b. 1987). Motoyama attended Mackenzie University for five years, including some postgraduate education, and would like to attend its law school in the future if he finds enough funding. Motoyama's mother was born in the countryside as one of five children and lost her parents when she was in her early teens. She moved to the city with her older brother, who would become a dentist. She worked at a bank during the day and studied at night, majoring in advertising. Motoyama's father lived on a coffee plantation until the age of eighteen, when he moved to the city to work and study. He majored in business administration at Mackenzie University and also worked at the same bank. Motoyama's parents met as a *miai* through his maternal uncle, a dentist, who had gotten to know his father because they played cards together. Motoyama grew up hearing his parents talking about banks all the time. His mother is now retired. In 2005, his father started a gas station in Cotia, São Paulo, with two other people, but their gas station has been robbed a few times. Motoyama states, "My father does not speak Japanese at all. His father spoke it, but he died very young, and his mother spoke Portuguese very well. We always eat Japanese at home." Motoyama had a hard time in his school days: "I studied at Brazilian schools and they did not like Japanese people. I didn't have any friends, either. I was the only Japanese there. I am *different*. It is difficult because it is very clear that we are Japanese, because we have *a different face*. It is difficult to say I am a Brazilian. Psychologically speaking, Japanese Brazilians have no homeland. Here in Brazil, we are the Japanese, but in Japan we are Brazilians. It's difficult."[64] While acknowledging the presence of racism against Japanese descendants in Brazil, Motoyama defines differences between Brazilians and Japanese Brazilians in cultural terms: "For instance, when I go to my parents' house, I always take a present with me because of my culture. That's Japanese culture, and it is not normal for Brazilians to do so. When people offer me candy, it is polite for me to say no the first time, but Brazilians just take it. It is a little thing, but it's strange for me."[65]

In June 2010, Lucia Yamashita was working at Bank of Brazil while waiting for another company to offer her a better job. When I mentioned that I had met many Japanese Brazilian bank employees in São Paulo City, both current and former, Motoyama commented, "In order to work at a bank, we need to pass a test. The Japanese people study a lot. There is a popular saying here: 'If you want to get into public service or get into a better college, kill a Japanese.'"[66] Although Motoyama and Yamashita are both college graduates and urban professionals, they do not agree with each other on the meanings of their being "Japanese" in relation to "Brazilians." Unlike Motoyama, Yamashita is a Nisei born to less-educated postwar immigrants, who met as shipmates in 1958. Her father (b. 1940), who is from Hiroshima prefecture, is now retired, while her mother (b. 1948), who is from Ube City, Yamaguchi prefecture, has been always a full-time homemaker.[67]

Upon immigrating to Brazil, Yamashita's mother and her birth family moved to Bastos, where they settled. She had studied up to the fourth grade in Japan and had no schooling in Brazil; as the oldest child, she had to take care of her younger siblings, all of whom were able to go to school. In 1975, she and her family moved to São Paulo City, where she got reacquainted with the man who was to become Yamashita's father, who was working at the city's municipal market selling vegetables. In 1978, Yamashita's parents got married and soon moved to Espirito Santo state, where her father worked on a golf course until his retirement. Yamashita was born there as the oldest of five children. "We were the only ones in my father's family living outside São Paulo," she says. "Espirito Santo does not have many

Japanese, and we lived in a small town of the countryside. We were the only Japanese family back then. Brazilians were always teasing me by calling me *japonesinha* [little Japanese woman]." When she was eighteen, Yamashita moved to São Paulo City for her college education at FATEC, where she majored in business. Upon graduation, Yamashita went to Japan in 2002 on a Hiroshima prefectural fellowship to work as a trainee in business management for a company in Hiroshima City for eight months. Both of her two younger sisters are college graduates and gainfully employed in Brazil, but neither of her two younger brothers attended college, simply because they did not like studying. One of them went to Japan as a *dekassegui*. "He went for money but is unemployed now. Many Brazilians have returned to Brazil due to the global recession."[68]

Yamashita has always thought of herself as a Brazilian, while refusing to acknowledge the presence of racism against Japanese descendants in Brazil. For Yamashita, being a Japanese descendant is solely cultural. "Everybody thinks I am Japanese," she says, "probably because I am more accustomed to Japanese culture, due to my Japanese parents." She used to date "Brazilians" only, but she came to think it would be "better to date a Nikkei, culturally speaking." Unlike Motoyama, who characterized Brazilians as "rude" and "having no manners," Yamashita thought of Brazilians more positively, as "more open" and "unreserved," and Japanese as "more closed." Motoyama argued, "It's very difficult for the Japanese to throw a can from a car, for example. Brazilians do that."

The time came for Motoyama to join his friends at his church. The three of us left the coffee shop and walked together back to the Liberdade metro station. From there Yamashita drove off to go home, saying, "I am Catholic but do not belong to any particular church." Motoyama invited me to his church, the Igreja Evanjélica Holiness de Liberdade (Evangelical Holiness Church of Liberdade), saying, "I go to Holiness to play volleyball. I don't go there to pray." At his church, I met a dozen young Sanseis and Yonseis, "true" churchgoers, who were preparing for a special dinner party for Lovers' Day (Dia dos Namorados). One of them is a twenty-seven-year-old Sansei, Elise, who had been to the United States on missionary work and is an English teacher who gives private lessons. While Motoyama began to cook in the kitchen, two women and a man were practicing dance, and others were setting up a stage for musical performance. Motoyama introduced me to Yonsei Julia Miki Yagami (b. 1985), who was born to a Sansei father who is a USP professor of marketing and a Nisei mother. Yagami attended FGV, where she finished her undergraduate degree in marketing and a graduate degree in marketing and administration. She works at the

São Paulo office of a major US company.[69] According to Yagami, her Holiness church is small, with three hundred members, of whom only fifty are active, including the elderly Isseis. The church holds a service in Japanese and Portuguese on Sundays. Yagami's paternal Nisei grandfather attended this church, and then her Sansei father began to do so. Both attended it every weekend even though they lived forty minutes away from the city. Now Yagami attends her church every weekend.

Yagami does not speak Japanese at all, and none of her family does so at home. Her maternal grandmother spoke it, but she passed away when Yagami was very young. Most of the young Japanese Brazilians she knows do not speak Japanese either. She "likes being with the Nikkei," although she has never thought about differences between the Nikkei and Brazilians. "It is natural to live with Nikkei," she says. "The Nikkei are a little bit more reserved, more respectful, and better educated. I have many Brazilian friends, but they are less sensitive. The Japanese are more delicate and respectful." Yagami maintains that the young Japanese Brazilians get together among themselves at major shopping centers in the city because "they feel safer if they stay in a group and feel part of the group." Her Sansei boyfriend, whom I also met at the church, is an ITA graduate who works as an engineer. They got to know each other by playing volleyball at a Japanese Brazilian club. He is her first boyfriend, and they have been dating for four years and attending church together for three years. She says they will probably get married. Yagami has never been much interested in the history of Japanese immigration to Brazil, unlike her boyfriend, who talks with his ninety-two-year-old grandmother. According to Yagami, Japanese Brazilians "are moving up, while mixing with Chinese and Koreans." Yagami has always preferred to socialize with Japanese Brazilians, even though the majority of her classmates were always "Brazilians":

> I never liked anyone very much at school. I always liked the Japanese, whom I met at the church and clubs, although I always lived among Brazilians. I have always preferred the Japanese. I don't know why. My parents never told me how to think. They are liberal. My male cousin prefers Brazilian women. I have many [Japanese Brazilian] friends who prefer Brazilians. I have many friends who are *mestiços*. Some of them identify themselves as Japanese, but others do not want to have any contact with Japanese culture.[70]

Yagami's statement presents a clear picture of what has been going on among the Sanseis and Yonseis of her generation from the same class background: even though Yagami and her Japanese Brazilian friends mingle and date among themselves as the Nikkei, many others, including the racially mixed who identify themselves as Brazilians, date and marry white Brazilians either exclusively or inclusively. For example, Sansei Newton Hirata, now a political science professor at the Academia da Força Aérea (Air Force Academy) in Pirassununga, São Paulo, has dated both Japanese Brazilian and "Brazilian" women, and his current girlfriend is a white Brazilian woman. Hirata states, "I think that the current generations of Sanseis and Yonseis are already part of Brazilian culture and had already assimilated into Western values. In this sense, there are no differences between Nikkei and non-Nikkei women."[71] Hirata has never mentioned the "Japanese face" in his discussions on Nikkeiness.

CONCLUSION

The young upper-middle-class Sanseis and Yonseis whom I interviewed grew up among Brazilians but learned that the "face" made them different. Eric Funabashi, for instance, maintains that being a "Japanese" is a "racial thing." "They say Brazil is multiethnic," he says, "but that is not true."[72] They were all called *japones/japonesa* and/or *japa*, and bullied for having a Japanese "face" and "slanted eyes." The bullying stopped when they got into good private senior high schools, where there were many other Japanese descendants. Such experiences certainly fostered racial inferiority complexes regardless of their upper-middle-class positions. In order to negotiate with racial hegemony, some strongly resent being Japanese descendants, identify themselves solely as Brazilians, and date and marry white Brazilians to "whiten" themselves as individuals. Others, who chose to identify themselves as Nikkeis, valorize themselves in cultural terms; Nikkeis are superior to Brazilians culturally. Even though they highly value traditional Japanese culture, especially food, as well as Japan's advanced technology, they also position themselves as culturally superior to the Japanese in Japan. Furthermore, like their Sansei and Yonsei peers who refuse to identify as Nikkeis, they are, for one, Brazilians/Westerners, and thereby position themselves above the Japanese as "Orientals." In this politics of position, race is replaced by culture as a source of self-valorization. Like Yamashita, Akiyoshi, after having dated two "Brazilian" men, is now dating her first Nikkei boyfriend, a college-educated freelance professional photographer who is also a Seinen Bunkyo member. She says she has come to realize that it is "better marrying a Nikkei to preserve and maintain the culture and Nikkei generations."[73] She thinks her Nisei parents would have preferred to see their Sansei daughters date and marry Nikkeis, even though they never told them to do so. Thus, young Nikkeis regard ethnic-class endogamy as a cultural preference, not as a means of resistance against racial hegemony.

These self-identified young Nikkeis do not challenge Brazil's racial hegemony collectively, and some are oblivious to Brazilian racism. For instance, Shinozuka told me in June 2008 that she had always been called *japa* by her classmates and how much she had resented it.[74] Still, a few weeks later, she e-mailed me a photo of a baby boy "singing" a John Lennon song, which she picked up on YouTube, with her own subject line, "*Japa* Lennon." When I e-mailed her back to ask about her usage of *japa*, she replied, "*Japa* is not a racial slur but can be offensive depending on the context. It's just slang to me."[75] Of *japinha*, Eduardo Tamura states, "We [Sanseis like him] do not feel that it is so racist, but some Isseis and Niseis do not like this term."[76] Akiyoshi also maintains, "*Japinha* is more affectionate [than *japa*]. For example, I am not a tall person, so my friends sometimes call me *japinha*." Yet she quickly adds, "Well, it depends on the context. If a stranger calls me *japa* when I am walking on the street, I consider it insulting and offensive. I hate it."[77] In fact, there is a mixed Japanese Brazilian musician who is known as "JD Japinha" and "Japinha Ricardo": Ricardo Di Roberto, a DJ and member of the band CPM 22, who was born to an "Italian" father and a "Japanese" mother in 1973 in São Paulo City. Di Roberto says he is mixed and therefore "a typical *paulistano*," and that everybody can tell he is "Japanese."[78] Not surprisingly, Di Roberto does not seem to mind his pejorative nickname.

Needless to say, not all self-identified Nikkei youth share the same collective identity or take collective action among themselves. For example, Murakami says that language proficiency in Japanese, not Japanese ancestry, is an important component of his Nikkei identity. Murakami has never joined a Japanese Brazilian youth association or club, and separates himself from other self-identified upper-middle-class Nikkei youth who do not speak Japanese. He regards himself as "not a common case." "Most Sanseis are unable to communicate in Japanese," he says, and "it is even more rare for any Sansei with a non-Japanese parent to do so." He maintains, "I feel more comfortable with Japanese descendants who do speak the Japanese language. But this applies not only to Japanese descendants. I feel much more comfortable in the company of Chinese who do speak Japanese better, than of Japanese-descendants who don't speak Japanese at all and behave like non-Japanese."[79] As a *mestiço* Sansei in a bilingual environment, Murakami positions himself above other young Sanseis, especially those who are not racially mixed and therefore, in his opinion, have no excuse for not speaking the language but who nevertheless choose to identify themselves collectively as Nikkeis.

The story of self-identified young Nikkeis makes an interesting parallel to that of urban middle-class Afro-Brazilians, whom Afro-Brazilian scholar Kabengele Munanga calls "conscious blacks."[80] Sharing the same educational background and socioeconomic position, they choose to identify themselves as blacks and marry only among themselves. Such "class exclusivity" has always been the nature of the Movimento Negro (Black Movement) in urban Brazil, as George Reid Andrews argues.[81] Yet, over the years, the individual practice of "whitening" has always been prevalent, even among Afro-Brazilians involved in the Movimento Negro, and the majority of male Afro-Brazilian activists used to marry white Brazilian women.[82] Only recently has racial endogamy become much more pronounced among self-identified middle-class blacks in their thirties and forties who grew up and attended schools and colleges largely with white Brazilians.[83] They do not recognize much cultural difference between themselves and the white middle class except for their race, and therefore value themselves above the majority of the urban Afro-Brazilian population, who are poor. Nevertheless, the formation of a self-identified black middle class does not mean that the individual practice of "whitening" has lost its effect among middle-class Afro-Brazilian youth in urban Brazil. In fact, self-identified black youth often find themselves caught between their political identity and their personal preference. For instance, Christian Moura, a twenty-four-year-old Afro-Brazilian student at the Faculdade Zumbi dos Palmares (Zumbi of Palmares College) whose color is "just a little bit inked," as his Afro-Brazilian activist women friends jokingly say, is dating a woman who is lighter-skinned than he is. He confides to me that he feels guilty; he, as a self-identified black man, is supposed to be with a black woman. But, at the same time, Moura says that his girlfriend also wants to be with a white man for her own "whitening."[84]

Self-identified Nikkei youth continue to perceive themselves as elite ethnic Brazilians and position themselves above the Japanese youth in Japan for their "respecting the elderly." Their self-affirmation as Nikkeis is not any sort of affirmation of a fixed ethnic identity but the creation of a new cultural identity under the same label of Nikkei. As Stuart Hall articulates, cultural identity is "not an essence but a *positioning*," and therefore "there is always a politics of identity, a politics of position, which has no absolute guarantee in an unproblematic, transcendental, 'law of origin.' "[85] The "conscious Nikkei" in São Paulo City continue to challenge and redefine their position in the face of power inequalities embedded in their racially stratified society. But the story is not likely to end here. Individually, many of them will surely continue to struggle to position and reposition themselves within the dominant structures of "whitening" in Brazilian culture, just as Moura and many other young "conscious blacks" are doing in São Paulo City.

In June 2010, when I saw him again in São Paulo City, Murakami was talking about going to Japan as a *dekassegui* for "certain personal reasons." In November 2011, he traveled to Japan for the first time; he got a job as a Portuguese-Japanese translator at a city hall in central Japan. His work contract was up at the end of March 2012, but he wanted to stay on in Japan by working in Osaka City as a translator for a small company until August 2013, or, if possible, August 2014. Unfortunately, things did not work out, and with no money left, he returned to São Paulo and rather reluctantly resumed his undergraduate studies, insisting that he was very eager to go back to Japan for another *dekassegui* as soon as he could. Even though he never learned how to cook, Murakami bought an electric rice cooker in Japan and brought it back to Brazil. Of course, the cooker would not function in Brazil without an appropriate electric adapter. In his e-mail message of July 2012, Murakami said he was on his way to buy one at a store downtown, as if it were an important token/symbol of his individual Nikkei identity, which seems to have been strengthened by his four-month stay in Japan.

Around the time when Murakami returned home from Japan, Akiyoshi, a *dekassegui* returnee and Sansei member of Seinen Bunkyo, traveled not back to Japan but to the United States. In April 2012, she spent her three-week vacation in Los Angeles, where she volunteered at the Japanese American National Museum. In Los Angeles, she was invited to a Japanese American household composed of Nisei and Sansei Americans and was surprised to see them take off their shoes, something she claims Japanese Brazilians seldom do. She also noted how cluttered the big house was and ascribed it to Japanese Americans' Japaneseness, which she judged by her experiences in Japan: "I felt I was in a familiar situation. Japan doesn't have much space, so they need to stack things or they seem to accumulate the stuff. It sounds strange that Americans act like this, but I understand they have Japanese characteristics in their *blood*." At the same time, she was "surprised and disappointed" that elderly Japanese Americans did not speak Japanese and that younger generations did not seem to care about learning the language, stating, "American Nikkeis seem to be more American, whereas Brazilian Nikkeis seem to be more Japanese." Yet, Japanese Brazilians and Japanese Americans share something important in common: "They are persistent and honest, which is characteristically Japanese, and furthermore they are successful people, which is attributable to the value they learned from the experiences of migration."[86] Back in São Paulo City, Akiyoshi began her new job (obviously an upward career move) in May 2012. Her Sansei boyfriend, a freelance photographer, was having a hard time supporting himself, and Akiyoshi, who was determined to marry a Japanese Brazilian man to share cultural values, said they still did "not have enough material conditions for marriage." Several months later she e-mailed and asked me whether I knew any websites listing job openings specifically for foreigners in the United States, but did not explain why she was looking for the information. She seemed disappointed at my negative reply. Unlike Murakami, a mixed Sansei man who has been willing to go back to Japan to affirm his strong cultural identity as a more authentic Japanese, Akiyoshi, as a "pure" Sansei professional woman, might be headed to the United States to explore her transnational Nikkei identity.

Chapter Seven

JAPANESE BRAZILIANS AND THEIR BRAZILIAN IDENTITY IN JAPAN

I feel more comfortable identifying myself as Brazilian. I don't have to say, "*Sou brasileira mas uma descendente japonesa*" [I am Brazilian but a Japanese descendant]. It's in the face. A friend of mine who became a naturalized Japanese citizen kept her Portuguese first name legally, but got rid of her Japanese middle name. She says her Brazilian identity would have disappeared otherwise. Her children do not look like Japanese, and she thinks that they would be discriminated against if they do not have Japanese names. So she dares to call her black-looking children by their Japanese names, even though they do not speak Japanese well. Generally, in order to show that they are indeed Nikkeis, non-Nikkei mothers call their mixed children by their Japanese names.

—*Andrea Yumi Minami, staff member*
of a NGO in Hamamatsu, 2010[1]

O n July 20, 2010, Andrea Yumi Minami was narrating her story to me in her office in Hamamatsu, Shizuoka prefecture. Minami was born in 1962 in Jacaréi, São Paulo state, to a postwar immigrant couple from Kumamoto prefecture, who had arrived in Brazil in 1961 with their son (b. 1958). She became her parents' first Nisei child and was followed by two younger brothers. Minami arrived in Japan in 1990 as a *dekassegui* in Hamamatsu, with her white Brazilian husband and their three-year-old daughter. By then all of the members of her birth family—her Issei parents, her older brother, and her two Nisei younger brothers—had already moved to Hamamatsu as *dekasseguis*. Minami's second daughter was born in 1993, and after her divorce (1995), she raised her daughters as a single mother, with the help of her parents. Minami began to work at her NGO in 2001, after her younger daughter started her primary education. In the following year, she worked as a counselor for Hamamatsu's project to help school-age Brazilian children who had dropped out or never attended school in Japan. In fact, the Japanese government does not require foreign children to complete Japan's nine-year mandatory education. Minami continued, "Among Brazilians who had their children attend Japanese schools, many bought houses rather than renting. They decided to live in Japan permanently, partly for their children's Japanese education. In Hamamatsu, some Brazilian children have graduated from college and have gained full-time employment. There are many young Brazilian part-timers also, working at convenience stores and so on. They are no longer *dekasseguis;* they are immigrants."[2] Thus, as an immigrant, Minami herself had settled in Hamamatsu, where both of her daughters attended local Japanese schools.

Minami's discussion of her Japanese Brazilian identity centers on "the Japanese face": Everybody is supposed to "see" her being "Japanese" "in her face." The expression *kao de wakaru* ("it's in the face") is, in fact, a Japanese translation of a common Brazilian saying on the "Japanese" in Brazil: "Tá [Está] na cara."[3] Minami continued, "My daughters do not want to use their Portuguese first names; they use their Japanese middle names instead. They do not look much like *mestiças*. They know they are Brazilians, not Japanese." Minami has been using only her Japanese middle name, Yumi, without her Portuguese first name, Andrea. When she was in high school, her Brazilian classmates began to call her Yumi, saying, "You do not have the face that looks like Andrea. You are Madama Yumi." It seems that "Madama Yumi" came from Puccini's *Madama Butterfly*. Thus, Minami's "Brazilian" high school classmates nicknamed her for her "Japanese face," which Minami does not seem to have cared about. Many years later, in Japan, Minami is saying that for racially mixed Brazilian children who do not look Japanese, their Japaneseness is *not* "in the face." She perceives some other Brazilians in Japan in the same way she was perceived by her "Brazilian" classmates back in Brazil. In Japan, her "Japanese face" is supposed to allow her to position herself as superior to many other Brazilians in Japan who do not "look Japanese."

In the summer of 2010, I did research and field work with and on Japanese Brazilians in São Paulo and Japan (Tokyo, Yokohama, Hamamatsu, and Kobe). By the time I conducted those interviews, the global recession that began in 2008 had caused mass unemployment among Japanese Brazilian workers in Japan and, with no prospect of employment in the immediate future, some started to return to Brazil, which often resulted in serious readjustment problems. Many of the problems had to do with changes in identity—national, class, race, and gender—through mass transnational migrations. How do Japanese Brazilians perceive themselves in relation or in contrast to the local Japanese who do not treat them as Japanese? What does it mean to be Japanese Brazilian in Japan, after all?

The global recession had a significant effect on the lives of Japanese Brazilian workers and their families in Japan, and many who lost jobs and had no prospect of finding employment in Japan began to return to Brazil, either temporarily or permanently. As a result, the Brazilian population in Japan began to decline in September 2008, and the pace of this decrease escalated in November of the same year. Small-scale regional surveys conducted with Brazilians in Japan show that between December 2008 and July–September 2009 from 40 to 47 percent of them were unemployed.[4] The number of Brazilian workers and their family members returning to Brazil peaked between January 2009 and March 2009, with around nine thousand returnees each month, and began to fall in April 2009, but still with an average of four thousand Brazilians returning from Japan each month afterward. Naoto Higuchi argues that the fact that 25 percent of Brazilians in Japan returned to Brazil within a year and a half after September 2008 indicates that their financial foundation in Japan was quite fragile. He attributes this mass return migration to the fact that the majority of them were temporary workers employed indirectly though temp agencies in the export-oriented auto and electronics industries, which were affected most severely by the global recession. Higuchi points out that the percentage of returnees is highest in the category of *teijūsha* (long-term residents) with one-year or three-year visas, mostly Sanseis and Yonseis who are younger and less fluent in Japanese, and non-Japanese-descendant spouses of Japanese Brazilians. Furthermore, even among those who hold permanent residency in Japan, some 20 percent returned to Brazil.[5]

In São Paulo City, Japanese Brazilians continued to speak highly of Japan for its economic power. An elderly Nisei taxi driver in his late seventies admired how well off Japan was financially, at least in comparison to Brazil, and insisted that *dekasseguis* from Brazil could still make a good living there. Having a successful Sansei daughter practicing law, he said, "You have to rob others if you want to be rich here in Brazil." A prewar child immigrant man in his eighties said to me, "*Only* one-quarter of Brazilians came back to Brazil, and the majority have stayed on in Japan. Of course, there is no longer overtime work, but my daughters are doing just fine in Japan, owing to the strong yen." One of his younger sisters, also a prewar child immigrant, was widowed young and had a hard time making it in Brazil. Holding Japanese nationality, she went back to Japan in 1991 as a *dekassegui* and has settled back in Japan permanently. Her Nisei daughter and son-in-law bought a house in Okazaki City, Aichi prefecture, and she commuted there every weekday to take care of her grandchildren while living alone in public housing in a different city.[6] Throughout the 2000s, I often heard Japanese Brazilians in São Paulo City talking about family members doing very well in Japan, despite Japan's prolonged recession since the mid-1990s. The purchase of a house in Japan was always used as a proof of one's great financial success there: they were no longer *dekassegui* workers as they moved up into the middle classes in Japan and could afford not only cars but houses as well. Interestingly, it was rarely mentioned in Brazil where they worked or what jobs they held in Japan. A very common phrase I heard in São Paulo City was "My son has bought a house in Japan and he and his family are not coming back to Brazil. They are doing very well in Japan." It should be noted that the allegedly successful offspring was usually a son, not a daughter.

Repatriation of Japanese Brazilians was nothing new in São Paulo; Japanese Brazilian newspapers had been reporting from the beginning of the 2000s on the prevalent unemployment of former *dekasseguis* and the various problems that Japanese Brazilian returnee children had been facing back in Brazil. Ronald Nakata (chapter 6) was a relatively successful case as a returnee child. The late Nisei psychiatrist Décio Issamu Nakagawa (1951–2011) and his psychologist wife, Kyoko Yanagida Nakagawa, had cofounded Project Kaeru (*kaeru* meaning "to return") in the late 1990s to treat the psychological problems of Brazilian returnees from Japan.[7]

Over many years, Japanese Brazilians had been moving back and forth between Brazil and Japan as *dekassegui* repeaters. Some families came back permanently after having saved enough money, as in the case of Nakata and his family, who lived and worked in Aichi prefecture (1999–2005), and Sabrina Akiyoshi's mother and older sister, who worked in Mie prefecture (2000–2004) (chapter 6). Among the *dekassegui* repeaters I had met in São Paulo City, Gustavo and Carolina Kobayashi (chapter 5) finally decided to end their decade-long *dekassegui* life in Japan and returned home permanently in April 2010. Back in Brazil, they had a hard time adjusting and could not find any jobs for months to follow. Out of his frustration with the situation back home, Gustavo began to consider going back to Japan, saying that he and his wife could save 350,000 yen a month in Japan by working together at a *bentoya*. He was correct in the sense that Japan's *bento* industry has not produced mass unemployment, as have the electronics and automobile industries, even though one cannot find as much overtime work as before.[8] As discussed in chapter 5, Gustavo and Carolina Kobayashi had always chosen to live among the Japanese in Japan, separate from other

Brazilians. Furthermore, Gustavo is fluent in Japanese and holds double nationality. The couple could easily find employment again in Japan.

In June 2010, the *bairro oriental* of Liberdade was back the way it used to be before the centenary festivities began, with even fewer "Japanese" businesses and many more "Chinese" restaurants and stores. Japanese food culture remained very popular in São Paulo City. Marukai and Casa Bueno, the two major Chinese-owned "Japanese" supermarkets, were more crowded than two years earlier, with "Brazilian" customers busy shopping for Japanese ingredients. In March 2010, Sukiya, Japan's large fast-food *gyudon* ("beef bowl") restaurant chain, had opened its first Brazilian restaurant in the Liberdade district, across the São Joaquim metro station. The *festa oriental* held in front of the Liberdade metro station every weekend was packed with mostly non-Japanese Brazilians, who loved and enjoyed "Japanese" food in a Japan miraculously located in the heart of the city. There I saw Japanese-looking youths working at "Japanese" stores, something I had not previously observed. A postwar immigrant woman who frequents such stores observed, "There are many Nikkei youth working at shops in Liberdade. They speak Japanese fluently but they do not know how to read or write the language. I bet they are new returnees from Japan."[9]

When I visited the Sukiya restaurant for lunch on June 7, 2010, a young Brazilian male server came to my table to take my order. To my surprise, he introduced himself to me in fluent Japanese: "My name is Hideki. I am a *mestiço*, but am really a Nikkei. I am not a *dekassegui* returnee. I am a regular, full-time employee of Sukiya in Japan and have been transferred to this new chain restaurant." He said that he had gone to Japan for *dekassegui* at the age of seventeen and worked there for twenty years, in Hamamatsu and then in Yokohama. Hideki, who did not give me his last name, added that he was the restaurant manager. Thus, Hideki positioned himself above the ordinary recent *dekassegui* returnees, many of whom did not speak Japanese and were jobless in Brazil. In his own view, living in Japan had made him more Nikkei and hence less *mestiço*. In order to hear more details of his life in Japan, I made an appointment with Hideki for an interview, but he stood me up not only once but twice in the following weeks. I visited Sukiya several more times but never saw "Hideki" again. I encountered similar individual politics of position with an Afro-Brazilian man. When I visited Hinodê, a traditional Japanese restaurant that the Sekiguchis own in Liberdade (chapter 4), on June 17, 2010, a young *sushiman* working at the counter said firmly to me, "I am not a *nordestino*. I am a *paulistano*." *Nordestinos* had come to dominate sushi chef work in São Paulo City (chapter 1), and he wanted to position himself above them. While *nordestino* implies darker skin color, *paulistano* suggests possible "whiteness" or at least lighter skin color and thus a higher socioeconomic position.

On June 13, 2010, I visited the Comunidade Evangelica Luterana Congregação Japonesa de São Paulo, a Japanese Brazilian Lutheran church in Liberdade, at the invitation of Pastor Hirotaka Tokuhiro. At lunch after a service in Japanese, I met ten Japanese-speaking parishioners, including two recent *dekassegui* returnees from Japan. One was a middle-aged *mestiça* woman who barely spoke. The other one was a forty-three-year-old Nisei woman who had married a postwar Japanese immigrant in Brazil, moved to Bolivia with him, and, as a divorcée, eventually moved to Japan for *dekassegui* with her daughters, all of whom had settled down in Japan permanently. She met her common-law Japanese Brazilian husband in Japan when both of them worked at the same factory. She was now back in São Paulo City, living in his apartment and taking care of his affairs. He was still working in Japan and sending her money. In return, she had his aging mother stay with her in his apartment for a few months of the year (his siblings took care of her the rest of the time). Longtime church member Kazuyo Yoneda (chapter 2) had been taking care of her second daughter (b. 1950), a recent *dekassegui* returnee, since 2009. Yoneda's daughter and her husband worked in Japan for five years, came back for a year, and went back to Japan again for two years, but the husband died of a heart attack there. Her daughter came back to Brazil but left again for Japan, where she became clinically depressed. She and her own daughter's family eventually returned to Brazil at the beginning of 2009, with debts, even though they had sold their house in Japan, where they became homeless in the end. Yoneda's Sansei granddaughter, married with two young Japanese-born children (ages four and one-and-a-half), left her mother with Yoneda and moved to Goiás state with her family. It was not an easy situation for Yoneda, who, after the passing of her husband in 1982, lived with her second single son, a Bank of Brazil employee, relying on him and some of her other children financially. Yet Yoneda, a devout Lutheran, cheerfully stated that her second daughter's health was improving, "thanks to God."[10] One thing was certain: Yoneda's daughter could not go to Japan ever again.

In Japan, all Japanese Brazilians came to be called Brazilians by the local Japanese, not Nikkeijin or Japanese Brazilians. In order to distinguish themselves from the Nikkei of other nationalities, Japanese Brazilians, some of whom are married to non-Japanese Brazilians and have racially mixed children, have also commonly identified themselves simply as Brazilians. Furthermore, any child born to Brazilian parents in Japan is a Brazilian citizen, and is to be registered as a foreign resident with Japan's Ministry of

Justice. That is because Japan determines nationality by jus sanguinis (right of blood) and does not approve of dual nationality, unlike Brazil and the United States, whose policies are based on jus soli (right of the soil). That means that one needs to have at least one Japanese parent to be born a Japanese citizen. If either parent chooses double nationality for a child at birth, s/he is obligated by the Japanese government to choose one of them before s/he turns twenty-two. Yet even if one then chooses Japanese nationality, under Brazilian law anyone of Brazilian birth never loses his/her Brazilian nationality. Similarly, if a Brazilian becomes a naturalized Japanese citizen, like Minami's friend mentioned above, s/he remains a Brazilian citizen and in reality holds double nationality.

Despite Japan's long history of mass overseas migration, the Japanese government did not establish any official museum on Japanese emigration until October 2002, when the Japanese Overseas Migration Museum (JOMM) came into being in Yokohama under the JICA administration. In July 2010, one of its research staff members stated, "In Japan we do not talk about *dekassegui* any longer. There are already one hundred Brazilian children who have graduated from universities in Japan. Brazilians have been well assimilated into Japanese society."[11] His statement did not correspond to the situation that I had been observing in São Paulo City or to what *Nikkey Shimbun* and *São Paulo Shimbun* had been reporting. Is it his personal opinion or a reflection of the state's official understanding of Japanese Brazilians in Japan?

In Yokohama, where Chinese and Korean nationals have always outnumbered Brazilians, foreign residents have concentrated in Tsurumi Ward, which developed as part of the Keihin Industrial Region.[12] Okinawans, who began to migrate to Yokohama in 1918, also concentrated in Tsurumi Ward, where "Little Okinawa" came into being. Starting in the 1980s, Latin Americans of Okinawan descent moved into Tsurumi Ward as *dekasseguis,* and some have settled there permanently.[13] In fact, in 1983–1984 the first Okinawan *dekassegui* agency in Vila Carrão of São Paulo City established its Japanese branch in Tsurumi Ward.[14] As a result, the majority of the Nikkei in Tsurumi Ward have always been of Okinawan descent, from Bolivia, Brazil, Argentina, and Peru. Outside Tsurumi Ward, the local Japanese in Yokohama have had rare interpersonal contact with Brazilians.

At JOMM, I met several retired JICA agents, all college-educated men, who had worked for Japanese immigrants in Latin America, and who were volunteering there after their retirement. Takeshi Nagase (chapter 4) was one of them. Another former agent, Isao Kaburaki (b. 1932), who had worked several years as an agricultural instructor for postwar Japanese immigrants in the Colônia Guatapará of São Paulo state, as well as in other Japanese immigrant agricultural settlements/communities in Argentina and Bolivia, expressed strong frustration with Japan's "Nikkeijin problem," which the Ministry of Foreign Affairs "cannot touch":

> In March 2009, the Japanese government finally established the Department of Foreign Residents within the Ministry of Justice. There is no such word as "Nikkeijin" used in the Immigration Control and Refugee Recognition Act. In short, the Ministry of Foreign Affairs regards the Nikkeijin as foreigners, not as Japanese. There remains a feeling that the Nikkeijin share the same *Japanese blood,* but the Ministry of Foreign Affairs is afraid that it could be criticized by the Brazilian and Peruvian governments for discriminating against Brazilians and Peruvians of non-Japanese ancestry by favoring Japanese descendants over them.[15]

Kaburaki was aware that the situation would not be resolved easily: "The Japanese in Japan are prejudiced; they brownnose Caucasians but despise Africans. They also look down on the Nikkeijin for coming from a different cultural background, being unable to speak Japanese, and not being culturally Japanese, despite their *Japanese face.*"[16] Thus, Kaburaki uses "Japanese blood" and "Japanese face" interchangeably. In his thinking, the Nikkei's Japanese ancestry is "visible" in their faces, despite their cultural otherness.

Kaburaki's "biological" interpretation of Nikkeiness is shared by young Japanese sociologist Naoko Horikawa, who studied the Nikkeis from South America in Japan and Okinawa (2002) for her PhD dissertation (2012). Claiming "empathy for Nikkeijin," Horikawa states, "A distinction between Nikkeijin in Japan and myself in England is appearance. I look Japanese (although sometimes I am considered Chinese) while Nikkeijin share their *visible features* with local Japanese." Horikawa conducted "in-depth" interviews with thirty-six Nikkeijins (eighteen men and eighteen women; twenty-two from Brazil, six from Argentina, four from Bolivia, and two from Peru) in Oizumi and Ōta of Gunma prefecture, Yokohama's Tsurumi Ward, and Okinawa prefecture.[17] Her sampling of informants is critically limited by her lack of language skills in Spanish and Portuguese, and she sought out only those who spoke Japanese and who had the "Japanese face."

Masayuki Fukasawa (b. 1965) writes that when he and his wife, both Japanese, worked as *dekasseguis* in Ōta City of Gunma prefecture from 1995 to 1999, there were local companies that employed "Japanese-faced" Nikkeis only. At the same time, Fukasawa himself was perceived and treated in Japan as a Nikkei not only by the local Japanese but also by Nikkei *dekasse-gui* coworkers, even though he is a Japanese-born Japanese national with a "Japanese face"; Fukasawa had always lived in Japan until 1992, and had spent only three years in São Paulo City before returning to work in Japan to save enough money to purchase an apartment in São Paulo City.[18] His "Japanese face" surely helped him work as a *dekassegui* Brazilian but not to such a degree that he could be treated as a Japanese in Japan.

Unlike Yokohama, Hamamatsu is Japan's major "Brazil Town," where Christina Oda (chapter 5) has continued to work after she resumed her *dekassegui* life in 2005. It is an industrial city of central Japan known for the production of automobiles and musical instruments by such companies as Suzuki, Yamaha, and Kawai. Hamamatsu has held the largest number of Brazilians in Japan since the beginning of *dekassegui*, and since 1991, Brazilians have constituted the majority of foreign residents in Hamamatsu, reaching 60.28 percent at the end of 2006. At the end of 1998, 9,795 Brazilians resided in Hamamatsu, including 5,701 (58.2 percent) with "long-term resident visas," 3,924 (40.1 percent) with "spouse visas," and 28 with permanent residency.[19]

As mentioned, Minami and her white Brazilian husband, together with their infant daughter, arrived in Hamamatsu in 1990 for their first *dekassegui*. Minami maintains that her choice of a marriage partner was determined not by race but by class: she had chosen to marry a "Brazilian" just because she wanted to marry her "social superior"; if she had chosen to marry a Japanese Brazilian man in the countryside, he would have been inferior to her. She and her husband had never thought about *dekassegui* for themselves before, but the loan on their new house was killing them financially because of Brazil's hyperinflation; they wanted to repay it as soon as possible.[20]

In Hamamatsu, Minami's husband did not understand Japanese at all, which caused him daily stress. He did not allow Japanese to be spoken at home, which created a stressful situation for their young daughter. After another daughter was born in Japan in 1993, Minami and her family returned to Brazil in 1994, but Minami suggested that they should go back to Hamamatsu to achieve their financial goals. Her husband did not want to go back but eventually agreed to do so. In Japan in 1995, their marriage dissolved over the issue of whether to raise their children as Japanese or Brazilians. Minami's husband could not make it in Japan, but some other "Brazilian" spouses survived their crises and have stayed on in Japan permanently. Minami stated, "I have *Japanese blood* and cannot change my plans suddenly as Brazilians do, even though I was educated as a Brazilian in Brazilian schools. Many Brazilians have changed their plans; they go home and then come back. They have been going back and forth between Brazil and Japan. I cannot do such a thing."[21] In the end, her ex-husband went back to Brazil by himself. When she got a divorce, many "Brazilian" men in Hamamatsu offered Minami "contracts" for marriage so that they could stay on in Japan legally as a Nisei woman's spouse. In fact, Hirohisa Inoue's "Brazilian" ex-son-in-law married a Nisei woman in Japan in order to stay on as a *dekassegui,* while his daughter came back to Brazil in 2000 with her Japanese-born daughter and resumed her career as a banker in São Paulo City.[22] Minami never remarried, saying, "[In Brazil] I chose to marry a Brazilian. [In Japan] I was told I would be better off if I remarried a Japanese man, but I am culturally different from the Japanese in Japan. It was easier for me not to remarry when I was busy raising my children." She added, "If I had remained in Brazil, my children would not have had the chance to learn Japanese language and culture. My parents and all of my three brothers were already in Japan, and I had nobody to speak to in Japanese. My children would have become Brazilians if they had grown up with my husband's family only. For this reason I am glad I came to Japan."[23] Thus Minami, a Nisei woman who once decided to marry a white Brazilian man in Brazil as her "social superior," came to affirm and valorize her Nikkeiness and "Japanese face" among Brazilians in Japan.

By the mid-1990s, when Minami and her family returned to Japan for their second *dekassegui,* the Brazilian diaspora in Hamamatsu had come to be stratified by class and gender; some male Nisei *dekassegui* workers in Hamamatsu had transformed themselves from temporary manual workers into ethnic entrepreneurs. Such Brazilian business owners in Japan were much better educated than average Brazilian *dekassegui* factory workers there, and 43 percent of them had owned businesses back in Brazil.[24] Having grown up as the Niseis in Brazil speaking Japanese in their families, they already knew how to communicate in Japanese. Having arrived in the late 1980s and at the beginning of the 1990s before Japanese companies began setting up all-Brazilian work units, they worked on assembly lines with the local Japanese workers at factories and were forced to interact with local Japanese men for their daily survival. Not surprisingly, Brazilian business owners in Hamamatsu are all men, who arrived for their first stay in their late twenties and early thirties. Yet their upward mobility in Japan was conditioned inevitably by their Brazilianness. Such "Brazilian businesses" had developed extensively in Hamamatsu over the years, emphasizing a critical problem stemming from their limited market; in many cases their customers were predominantly Brazilians, and did not include many local Japanese.[25]

Among these pioneers the best-known Brazilian is João Toshiei Masuko (b. 1950), owner of SERVITU (meaning "easement"), a famous Brazilian supermarket/restaurant/bakery. Masuko commented, "Brazilians have a strong tendency to want to be independent business owners. Unlike the Japanese, they would like to become entrepreneurs rather than working at big-name corporations."[26] Masuko was born in São Paulo state as the second oldest of seven children to prewar immigrants from Fukushima prefecture. He grew up in the old "Japan Town" of the Pinheiros district, where he once worked at the Brazilian branch of Yaohan and later owned his own business. Masaku's father "had a very hard time in Brazil because of the language barrier and the different food and customs but could not return to Japan because of the war." He was passionate about the education of his Nisei children and taught them "all wonderful things about Japan, such as the Emperor, Japanese spirit, and work ethics." Masuko did not take his father's words seriously until 1988, when he arrived in Japan, at which time, he says, "I realized how right my father had been when Japan became number one in the world."[27]

Masuko began his *dekassegui* career at a factory of Sagara Plastics in Fukuroi City, Shizuoka prefecture. He arrived with a forty-five-day tourist visa and switched to a work visa after three months. He was the only foreigner working there, and the Japanese "did not know how to use foreign workers." He stayed in Japan for less than two years on his first *dekassegui* and went back to Brazil with his savings. He soon came back to Japan and began to work as a manager for a Brazilian restaurant, São Paulo, in Hamamatsu. In 1991, Masuko obtained permanent residency in Japan. He had originally planned on going back to Brazil to start a business there, but a great number of Brazilians started to arrive in Hamamatsu as *dekasseguis*: "They did not speak Japanese and everybody came to ask me for help. The local police relied on me [as an interpreter] in the name of international cooperation. I could not go home." While staying on in Hamamatsu, Masuko "came to like Japan better." When he was managing the Brazilian restaurant, he met a retired local Japanese man at Hamamatsu's International Center and became his student in Japanese in order to learn how to read the language. In 1993, with his own savings of three million yen, he started his own business in an apartment in Hamamatsu's Daiku District: SERVITU, a grocery store with imported Brazilian goods. Masuko's business thrived on the rapidly increasing number of Brazilian customers, not only from within Hamamatsu but from its suburbs and nearby cities and towns of Shizuoka. Soon Masuko moved his store to Hamamatsu's Sunayama district, where he at first rented only one apartment but ended up renting the whole building, with a Brazilian restaurant on its fifth floor. Also, in response to his Brazilian customers' request, Masuko opened a Brazilian bread factory. As a result, in the late 1990s, Masuko became known as the most successful Brazilian in the region. As he commented in 2010, "Back then, anything and everything could sell very well."[28]

Marcelo Shuji Yoshimura (chapter 5), a former bank auditor who arrived in Hamamatsu in January 1990, started his first business with a Japanese Brazilian friend in 1994. They opened a Brazilian restaurant next to the first Japanese branch of the Bank of Brazil, established in Hamamatsu in July 1993. Their restaurant was packed with Brazilians who came to the bank to send money to Brazil—until the remittance system changed and Brazilians became able to use registered mail. Then Yoshimura started an international "call-back" telephone business with an acquaintance, but they split up in the end. In 2004, Yoshimura started his third business on his own, Business Solutions Management Inc., across from the city hall, in the same building where the Consulate of Brazil is located. As its CEO, Yoshimura did business until 2010 with Brazil's Caixa Econômico Federal (Federal Savings Bank) by providing logistical services to its Brazilian employees in Hamamatsu.[29]

Other Nisei men had also become successful business owners in Hamamatsu. Etsuo Ishikawa (b. 1961), a Nisei and a graduate of the Universidade de Moji das Cruzes Law School, arrived in Japan in 1989 to work as a *dekassegui* for three years, opened a law office in Hamamatsu, and eventually, in 2003, became the second Brazilian lawyer authorized by the Ministry of Justice to practice law in Japan. In 2003, Ishikawa also founded an NGO, Associação Brasileira da Hamamatsu (Brazilian Association of Hamamatsu), with Yoshimura as vice president. Tetsuyoshi Kodama (b. 1965) arrived in Japan in 1990 with his Sansei wife and two young children, ages five years, and six months. He passed an exam to become a taxi driver in 1991 and worked as one for four years, became a temp agent and a part-time interpreter, and eventually established himself as a karate master and owner of Kodama Dōjō (Kodama Gym) for karate and kickboxing, with nearly eighty students, more than half of whom are local Japanese children. Nelson Omachi (b. 1964) arrived in Japan as a *dekassegui* in 1991, opened his first business in 1994, and has been the co-owner of Omachi Oriental Refresh since 2004. Kenzo Yamada (b. 1955), together with a few friends, started

Intercall Japan Ltd. in 1997. Edson M. Tamada, a high school dropout from São Paulo, built a multimillion-dollar food company, I. B. Fox, with seventy binational staff members and revenue of $16 million as of 2001.[30]

The formation of ethnic Brazilian businesses in Hamamatsu enabled newly arrived Japanese Brazilians to live comfortably there without learning the Japanese language, with Brazilian supermarkets, restaurants, beauty salons, karaoke, moving companies, and various agencies for travel, insurance, and so on. Furthermore, some three hundred *dekassegui* temp agencies operated in Hamamatsu alone, owned and staffed by former *dekassegui* workers, including Oda's brother-in-law. Those numerous ethnic enterprises and services sold ethnic Brazilian newspapers and paid the newspapers to publish their advertisements. The first one was *International Press* (*IP*), founded in 1991 by postwar immigrant businessman Yoshio Muranaga, who arrived in Japan from Manaus in 1989. The second was *Tudo Bem* (*TB*), begun by postwar immigrant businessman Masakazu Shoji (b. 1942), who immigrated to Brazil in 1960 upon graduating from Kobe High School. The third, *Folha Mundial* (World Newspaper; *FM*), was started by *mestiço* Nisei Eduardo Shibayama, who arrived in Japan in 1991 as a *dekassegui* at the age of twenty-three. In addition, João Masuko in Hamamatsu cofounded *Nova Visão* (New Vision), a weekly (and monthly as of 2001) magazine in Portuguese for Brazilians in Japan.[31]

IP and *TB* also expanded their businesses in publishing and mass media. Shoji and *TB* launched *Made in Japan,* the first monthly magazine in Portuguese for Brazilians in Japan. *IP* established IPC Television Network Company (IPCTV) in 1996 and began twenty-four-hour broadcasting in Portuguese and Spanish via satellite relay.[32] Ethnic Brazilian media connected Brazilians in Japan with their homeland and even developed a strong sense of national belonging to Brazil. Japanese anthropologist Shigehiko Shiramizu writes, "With the further development of convenient ethnic businesses and media, Brazilians in Japan can live as if they were still in Brazil. . . . In terms of entertainment, they seem to have very little interaction with 'the Japanese' "[33]—just as Japanese immigrants and their descendants in São Paulo began watching NHK continually and living in a virtual Japan (chapter 4).

Many Japanese Brazilians who arrived in Japan after Japan's revision of the Immigration Control and Refugee Recognition Act in June 1990 were different from an earlier wave of *dekassegui* Brazilian workers: "There were many who did not understand the Japanese language at all. They are Nikkeis but never heard of *miso* [soy bean paste], soy sauce, or *mochi* [Japanese rice cake]. They are from the countryside of Brazil. Even though they say they learned the language at the factories where they had worked, that was not good enough."[34] In the mid-1990s, Amelia Yagihara (chapter 5), as a tour guide, had to escort thirty-six Japanese Brazilians from São Paulo to Tokyo. All of the seats that her company had purchased sold out very quickly. Most of Yagihara's customers were Niseis, all from rural Brazil, and they did not speak Japanese at all. This was also their first trip by air. Her company took care of their tickets only, while *dekassegui* temp agencies in São Paulo City found them jobs in Japan. Yagihara's customers were "not educated and [were] poorly informed of Japan and even of Brazil." They understood Japan as "just an island" but took pride in being "Japanese." Most of them did not understand what birth certificates are.[35]

The majority of the "newcomers" were temporary workers indirectly employed through temp agencies in Japan. In reality, there was no need for them to learn the language; they were assigned to work at factories only among Brazilians, were assisted by agents and interpreters who spoke Portuguese and Japanese, and never had to read a work manual. If they got sick, an agent also escorted them to a doctor's office. This means that they could easily be alienated from the local Japanese, although the two groups came into daily contact in various areas outside the workplace. Accordingly, local xenophobia of Brazilians grew strongly, and Brazilians were often suspected of crimes. This is the situation that Christina Oda described in her interview (chapter 5).

Renato Takada Yamano (b. 1979), a Sansei from São Paulo City, narrates his story as a former "typical *dekassegui* worker" in Japan. Yamano was born in Liberdade and grew up in the Ipiranga district, where his father bought a house and he attended public schools and made friends only with "poor black children": "There are many rich Nikkeis, who live in [the district of] Paraiso and around Paulista Shopping Center. I grew up without having any ethnic Nikkei identity." Yamano attended the Universidade de São Judas in Mocca but dropped out in his second year; he was busy with a samba team and often skipped classes, and furthermore wanted to buy a car with the money he was earning by working at an insurance company. Yamano had a good time for a year or so but began to regret his decision, thinking that there would be nothing for him in Brazil as he had not finished college. That was when a friend of his called from Japan and suggested he become a *dekassegui*. Thus Yamano arrived in Japan in April 2000 and started out working on an assembly line at a car seat factory in Saitama prefecture. For the next eight years, he moved to various Japanese cities to work for better pay, while going home three times. He had intended to save money in Japan for a year or two to go home to start a business in São Paulo

City but ended up paying half of the expenses for his younger sister's college education in physical therapy until 2005. Yamano held ten different jobs as an unskilled *dekassegui* worker for eight years, often moving for better wages, thinking "there would be other and even better jobs available if/ when [he] got fired."[36]

In the mid-1990s, general *dekassegui* Brazilian workers in Japan, especially in Hamamatsu and the other "Brazil Towns," were enjoying convenient lives, as "they could get anything Brazilian," including underwear made in Brazil.[37] In the late 1990s, in the middle of Japan's recession, more and more Japanese Brazilians and their families began to settle down in Japan, as the *New York Times* reported in 2001. With 254,000 Brazilians living in Japan, the amount of money sent home had dropped 60 percent since 1997, falling to $294 million in 2000, according to Brazil's Central Bank. The *Times* attributed this drastic decline to Brazilians' spending their salaries in Japan by "tapping into a network of Portuguese-speaking real estate agents and car salesmen."[38] That was, of course, made possible by the development of the Brazilian ethnic businesses and media. In Hamamatsu, according to Toyoie Kitagawa, in 1992 those who had stayed in Japan for less than two years constituted 73 percent, but the proportion shrank to 33.7 percent in 1996, when those who had stayed in Japan for more than four years constituted 35.2 percent. Those who had no intention of returning home constituted 70.6 percent (1992) and 67.3 percent (1996).[39] According to a 2000 Hamamatsu survey of foreign residents, Brazilians who had lived in Japan for more than seven years constituted 45.5 percent of all Brazilian respondents.[40] Anthropologist Shigehiro Ikegami attributes Japanese Brazilians' prolongation of their stays to three factors. First, because of Japan's prolonged recession, they could not save as much money as they had hoped. Second, public security back in Brazil had been deteriorating further so that *dekassegui* returnees were often robbed. Third, many *dekassegui* returnees had been unsuccessful in the new businesses they started with their *dekassegui* savings.[41]

According to Yoshimura, it was around 2004 that it became popular and common for Brazilians in Hamamatsu to buy not only cars but also houses.[42] Yamano stated,

> Brazilians living in Hamamatsu in particular had bought cars and houses and they were working to pay loans. In the case of houses, they were paying 50,000 or 60,000 yen, the same amount for a rent. That is the way Brazilians were thinking. They never thought about the recession. There were many jobs available for them to choose. It was fine to buy new cars and houses. They

could earn 350,000 yen a month if they did sufficient overtime work. They did not have to learn Japanese; there were interpreters helping them at work. They could shop at Brazilian stores in Hamamatsu.[43]

With more Japanese Brazilians and their families prolonging their stays in Japan, the number of Brazilian youth had increased during the 1990s. In the case of Hamamatsu, Brazilians under the age of nineteen constituted only 10.9 percent of the Brazilian population as of March 31, 1992, but over the next nine years, the percentage doubled (20.1 percent). Accordingly, the number of school-age children increased rapidly. In 1989, there were only four Brazilian students enrolled in local elementary and junior high schools in Hamamatsu, but their number grew quickly to 137 (1991) and to 537 (1998). "Brazilian schools" were founded in Hamamatsu in the late 1990s and at the beginning of the 2000s, including Colegio Anglo Americano (1995–1998), Escola Brasileira de Hamamatsu (1998), Colegio Pitagolas Hamamatsu (2002), and Escola Alegria de Saber (2001).[44] Minami's nephew and Oda's son once attended such Brazilian schools in Hamamatsu, albeit not for long. Having a child attend a Brazilian school was a big financial burden for his/her parents, who had to pay the monthly tuition of 40,000 to 50,000 yen. According to Eunice Akemi Ishikawa, during the early 2000s, parents usually chose to have their children attend Brazilian schools in Hamamatsu only when both parents worked and they could afford to spend the mother's earnings on their children's education. Such parents stated that they did not mind spending much money on their children's Brazilian education. Eunice Ishikawa maintains that Brazilian children enrolled in Brazilian schools would surely have an easier time in adjusting back in Brazil, mainly because of their language abilities in Portuguese, but they would still face difficulties in the Brazilian educational curriculum, which the Brazilian schools in Japan did not always follow. Furthermore, many of the Brazilian children were not likely to go back to Brazil in the end, and those who did not attend Japanese schools or learn the Japanese language would have a very limited chance to advance in the Japanese labor market; they were likely to become unskilled manual workers, as their parents were.[45] This explains why Christina Oda sent her only child alone to her parents in São Paulo City for his education, while staying on with her husband to earn money for his future.

Brazilian children's schooling in Japan has often been neglected by their parents. As of 2001, there were 35,000 school-age Brazilians in Japan, and only 7,000 of them attended public schools.[46] In 2006, there were 2,600 school-age children in Hamamatsu; 1,400 were attending public schools,

700 were enrolled in Brazilian schools, and the rest were not schooled at all.[47] Yoshimura attributes this neglect to Brazilians' thinking of their life in Japan as "only temporary"; Brazilian-born children often did not come to Japan with their parents; they came several years later and had a hard time attending local schools. Yoshimura himself had his two Japanese-born Sansei children—a senior in high school and a seventh-grader as of 2010—attend local public schools. He and his wife have not been able to help them with their schoolwork, since they could not teach Japanese, and the Japanese way of doing mathematics was different from that in Brazil. Yoshimura's older child was to graduate from high school in March 2011 and planned on attending a vocational junior college.[48] Minami had her two "mixed" daughters attend Japanese public schools, and her older daughter married a local Japanese man when both of them were barely twenty. According to Minami, Brazilian children who have had Japanese schooling with Japanese children have a strong tendency to marry the Japanese.[49] In many cases, the cultural gap between parents and children seems to have widened with the passage of time.

The Brazilian population in Hamamatsu peaked in 2008 at 19,461; then the global recession hit the Japanese economy very hard. Minami spoke of "the worst time," which was from October to December 2008, when "some 80 percent of Brazilians were fired." "We had a terribly great number of Brazilians coming into my NGO to ask for help, waiting at the door at 7:00 A.M.," she said. "They were all hired by temp agencies, which did everything for them. They themselves knew nothing. After losing their jobs, they wanted to know what to do. They needed the information. They became desperate to learn the Japanese language for the very first time."[50] The number of Brazilian citizens in Hamamatsu declined to 18,247 (2009), 14,959 (2010), 12,488 (2011), and 12,341 (March 2012), thus it shrank by 63.41 percent over three years and three months.[51] In a survey conducted with 2,773 Brazilians in Hamamatsu in January and February 2009, those already unemployed and others who had been informed that they would be fired constituted 47.35 percent and 13.85 percent, respectively. Among the unemployed, 21.4 percent had been jobless for four weeks, 14.24 percent for eight weeks, and 3.20 percent for more than twenty-five weeks.[52] A consultant from Hello Work in Hamamatsu (the Japanese government's employment service center) commented, "They've stayed on as long as they were able to receive unemployment insurance and social welfare for living costs or housing only if they did not own real estate or cars [otherwise they would not have been eligible]. Those who are still in Japan are staying on for their children's Japanese education."[53] The same Hamamatsu survey demonstrates the clear correlation between language skills and chance of employment; the better one speaks Japanese, the better chance one has to be employed.[54] Minami stated that employment depended on language skills in Japanese, and if one mastered the language there would be a job, and that is the reason why her NGO offers Japanese language classes for foreigners. Yet, according to my Japanese Brazilian informants in Hamamatsu, most Brazilians were not willing to learn Japanese even in a financial crisis.

After the beginning of the global recession, some of the Japanese Brazilians in Hamamatsu moved to other prefectures or cities of Japan for jobs, and some others returned to Brazil. But that did not mean there were no more Brazilians coming in; as of July 2010 there were still Japanese Brazilians arriving from Brazil. Yoshimura explains their situation, in relation to the "face":

> Those who worked in Japan have a hard time in getting used to Brazilian ways when they return. They move from a stable and safe country to a Brazil with many robberies. Being scared, they come back to Japan. Once returning to Brazil, one begins to compare between Brazil and Japan and he/she comes back to Japan. One of my customers this morning told me that he got robbed as soon as he got back to Brazil. He got scared and came back to Japan, deciding to stay here permanently. Having *the Japanese face* in Brazil means you have money. That creates danger for your life.[55]

One may wonder if Japanese Brazilians still residing in Hamamatsu after the global recession would likely stay on in Japan permanently. Having already settled in Hamamatsu a decade earlier, Minami became a grandmother of a Japanese child in 2008; her older daughter (b. 1987) married a young Japanese man (b. 1988) in 2007 and gave birth to a baby boy in the following year. By contrast, her older Issei brother, after two rounds of *dekassegui*, was settled back in Brazil permanently with his Japanese Brazilian wife and their only child. On their first *dekassegui*, "both my older brother and his wife worked until 10 P.M. every weekday and Saturdays for overtime and took only Sundays off. They did no shopping on Sundays. Naturally they saved lots of money." A few years after a son was born in Brazil, the couple decided to go back to Hamamatsu, but even though they enrolled him in a Brazilian school, he was bullied by other Brazilian children and called *gordo* ("fat"). It was stressful for Minami's nephew to live in Japan with his parents working at factories all the time. In the end, Minami's older brother and his wife returned to Brazil for the sake of their child. Minami's postwar immigrants parents, who were in their seventies, planned on returning to Brazil upon retirement. Minami still owned her house in Brazil, which her older brother took care of and rented out. She said to me, "I'll go home one day, but I just do not know when."[56]

João Masuko decided to stay in Japan permanently already in 1993, when he opened SERVITU, but his wife has never come to Japan, refusing to move, and their four children arrived later, around the mid-1990s, each when they were fourteen or fifteen years old. All of them married Japanese Brazilians, but Masuko said he did not understand why they had not married Japanese in Japan instead. His three daughters were living in Japan, but his son had been going back and forth between Brazil and Japan and in July 2010 went back to Brazil again. All six of Masuko's siblings except one were also living in Japan; his prewar immigrant parents had returned to Japan to be with him and eventually passed away in Hamamatsu. Masuko had been preparing to become a naturalized Japanese citizen but, as of July 2010, was reconsidering this move as his friends told him Brazilian nationality would be more beneficial for his business. He has gone back to Brazil only once, in 1998. Masuko said of himself, "I think I am Japanese, and the Japanese think I am Japanese."[57]

The global recession had hit Masuko's business very hard, with the rapidly declining number of his Brazilian customers. "This recession happens only once in a century," he said. "We are the victims, and we have to protect what we have now." He was confident in the future of Brazil. "Brazil is in a rapid process of economic development. The value of the *real* [Brazilian currency] will definitely go up, as much money will be invested in Brazil from all over the world for the World Cup and Olympics. A great amount of money will be spent in Brazil." Yet he did not intend to go back to Brazil permanently. "It is easy to live in Japan," he said. "It's stable. I cannot sleep well back in Brazil; I would wake up on hearing a big noise at night."[58]

Yoshimura maintained that not all Brazilians with permanent residency were really determined to stay on in Japan permanently; many had opted for permanent residency just to avoid the nuisance of renewing their visas, at the strong suggestion of the Immigration Bureau of Japan. Yoshimura said that he would have to stay on at least until his younger child graduates from high school. But, at the same time, he said he was sure to feel the same way his grandparents felt when they moved back to Japan in 1971, during prewar Japanese immigrants' "going-home" boom (chapter 2): "They had no friends or family but an older brother. They were used to food culture in Brazil with bread. But here in Japan breakfast was rice and miso soup. In six months, they went back to Brazil and died there. They had always wanted to go back to Japan, and traveled to Japan and Hawaii before, but vacationing in Japan was different from going home permanently."[59] This might well be Yoshimura's way of saying that he would be staying on in Japan permanently. That does not mean that Yoshimura, as a Japanese descendant, could feel comfortable enough living in Japan, or that, as a Brazilian, he would not perceive Japan or the Japanese negatively. For instance, Yoshimura commented positively on his Brazilian identity in comparison with the Japanese:

> Brazilians do not think of the future. They have no long-term goals nor save money. Brazilians are happy to live today only. Brazil is free, but life is hard in Japan. Japan is very well organized, but the Japanese kill themselves if they cannot succeed. There are so many suicides, thirty-five thousand a year. The Japanese think themselves as members of groups and do not act as individuals. They do not change their rules. When I was working at a factory, I told my [Japanese] boss that there would be an easier way to do the same work, but I was told that we should continue to do the work in the way it had been done for years, without changing it.[60]

Others expressed their willingness to return to Brazil, for example, Hiromi Ono (b. 1954), a postwar child immigrant from Yamanashi prefecture (chapter 4), who had been living in Hamamatsu since 2000 and had become a copublisher of a local "free paper" in Portuguese. Her common-law husband of ten years, a Nisei of Okinawan descent who used to be a professional musician back in São Paulo, was working at a factory in Fukuroi City. They planned on "going home together one day." Having already completed some formal training at Nelson Ohmachi's salon, Ono intended to make a living as a massage therapist back in São Paulo City.

Nisei Kayoko Hamada (b. 1950) also said she would go home. As a junior high school graduate with proficiency in Japanese, Hamada used to own a luncheonette (lunch counter) and then a restaurant in São Paulo City. Having wanted to visit Japan for a long time, Hamada sold her apartment and arrived in Japan in 2000. First, she worked on an assembly line at Nippon Hum (Nippon Meat Packers) in Ibaraki prefecture for two years and returned to Brazil for six months. With nothing to do back home, she began her second *dekassegui* round by working at a *bentoya* in Saitama prefecture for a year. According to Hamada, her Japanese coworkers at the *bentoya*, who all thought of her as Japanese, were surprised when she told them she is Brazilian. In 2003, she moved to Hamamatsu to work as a cook at a Brazilian restaurant. She stated, "I love Japan. It is very safe. Japan is not bad at all. I got my home broken into three times in Brazil. The Japanese are nice and kind. I am very happy I came to Japan." One of her friends, who had gone back to Brazil after working in Japan for seventeen years, would really like to come back to Japan to work again, because she got accustomed to life in Japan, and there was "no work in Brazil for those who are above thirty years old." "I feel like I should go home soon," Hamada said, laughing, without specifying when she would.[61]

Renato Yamano, a Sansei from São Paulo City, was planning on returning to Brazil "in time" for the Olympics in Rio de Janeiro (2016), believing that the Brazilian national economy should have improved by then. As discussed above, he arrived in Japan in 2000 as a typical *dekassegui* worker but had learned the Japanese language, mostly on his own, over the years, and moved up in 2008 as an interpreter and translator for workers at a factory. In 2009, an NGO hired him to facilitate the education of school-age Brazilian children in Hamamatsu. In Hamamatsu, he met and married a *mestiça* from São José dos Campos, São Paulo state in 2007 but got a divorce after a year because he was "too busy with his work, studies, and hobbies, such as samba practice, to have enough time to spend with her." His ex-wife had already gone back to Brazil, but they remained in touch. With stable, full-time employment at an NGO in Hamamatsu, Yamano was studying Japanese to pass the national language exam to be qualified for its top level and had also begun to study English to prepare for his return to Brazil.[62]

Emiko Arakaki (b. 1954) said she "would definitely go home," but added that her home was "not Brazil but Okinawa," where her aging father and her other kin lived and her late mother's grave was located. Her older Nisei daughter (b. 1979), an aspiring businesswoman, planned on returning to Brazil, with her husband, also an Okinawan Brazilian, and their child, whom she was raising in Portuguese. However, her younger daughter (b. 1981), also married to an Okinawan Brazilian, would not go back to Brazil because of her traumatic experiences during a robbery with gunshots back in São Paulo City. None of Arakaki's siblings still lived in Brazil, except for her youngest sister, who continued to live in Vila Carrão and took care of Arakaki's house, which was registered under her daughters' names. Arakaki's other younger sister had met and married a young Okinawan man in São Paulo and moved with him to Argentina. Her oldest brother had left Okinawa in 1978 for Hamamatsu, where he and his children were working as agents of a *dekassegui* temp agency. Arakaki's younger brother by seven years, who used to co-own the business with her in São Paulo City, had also moved to Japan around the same time as Arakaki and her daughters. Arakaki's daughters still resented her for removing from a comfortable life in São Paulo City, where they had grown up with maids, and for having made them into factory workers in Japan.[63]

Needless to say, not all Brazilians have lived in Hamamatsu and the major "Brazil Towns." In fact, Brazilians in Japan dispersed geographically in their search for better-paying jobs or, more recently, for any jobs at all. Life has been different for Brazilians in Japan without concentrations of Japanese Brazilian workers. The Kansai region, the south-central part of mainland Japan, has such major cities as Kobe, Osaka, and Kyoto, but it is on the periphery of the "map" of Brazilians in Japan.

A most shocking crime involving a Brazilian family took place in the Kansai region around 2:50 A.M. on Friday, July 9, 2010, as Japan's *Asahi Shimbun* reported on its front page under the headline "A 9th Grader Suspected of Arson."[64] In Takarazuka City of Hyogo prefecture, a fifteen-year-old junior high school female student, a Brazilian citizen, and her fourteen-year-old Japanese classmate stared a fire in the former's two-story family home. They were about to do the same to the Japanese classmate's home when the police arrested them. The Brazilian girl's thirty-one-year-old mother of Japanese descent died in the fire, and her mother's thirty-nine-year-old common-law "Brazilian" husband (the girl's stepfather) and their nine-year-old daughter were severely injured. In the following days, Japan's mass media emphasized the Brazilian family's otherness: domestic violence, intergenerational cultural and language gaps, and the girl's having been bullied by her Japanese classmates for being a Brazilian/foreigner. The Brazilian girl arrived in Japan at the age of four and attended local Japanese schools only. She spoke Japanese fluently but had not acquired language skills sufficient for her Japanese schooling.[65]

In nearby Kobe, only 633 Brazilians were registered at the end of 2009 among a total of 44,219 foreign residents, including 13,105 Chinese, 21,861 Koreans, 974 Philippines, 210 Peruvians, and 1,316 Americans.[66] This is where Brazilians came to form their mutual-aid association after the Great Earthquake of Kobe in 1995, which developed into an NGO in 2001: Comunidade Brasileira de Kansai (Brazilian Community of Kansai, CBK). Most of the prewar immigrants departed from the port of Kobe, where the Japanese government built the Asylum of Emigrants in 1928 (chapter 1) and where in 2001 Kobe City opened the Kobe Port Emigrant Memorial (chapter 2), which was inspired by and/or modeled after the Japanese Immigrants Monument in Santos inaugurated in June 1998 (conclusion).[67]

The Asylum of Emigrants reopened as the Kobe Emigration Center in 1952 but eventually closed in 1971. Located in Kobe's high-end residential district, it was once deserted and came to be nicknamed "the ghost house."[68]

In 2007, with support from Hyogo prefecture and the Japanese government, Kobe City finally decided to turn the former Emigration Center into the Kobe Center for Overseas Migration and Cultural Interaction, including the Emigration Museum. The new center was inaugurated in 2009 and has been administered by the Nippaku Kyokai / Associação Nipo-Brasileira (Japanese Brazilian Association), a NGO established in Kobe in 1926.[69] From the Japan Rail train station of Motomachi of Kobe, I walked up the hilly streets to reach the center as emigrants used to do in groups upon arriving at the same train station. Admission was free for the Emigration Museum, but except for me there were no visitors, even though it was a late Saturday morning during summer vacation, and the nearby port of Kobe and Kobe's Chinatown, as famous tourist sites, were packed with tourists and families with small children.

CBK's headquarters are located on the third floor of the former Emigration Center. CBK's founder and president is Nisei Marina Matsubara (b. 1954) from São Paulo City, who arrived in Japan in 1988 with her family not as *dekasseguis* but because her Nisei husband, Nelson Matsubara (b. 1951), had been hired as a professional soccer coach in Japan. The Matsubaras eventually moved to Kobe in 1995, where Nelson became a coach for Vissel Kobe, Kobe's professional soccer team. As the mother of three daughters, Marina Matsubara founded CBK for the education of Brazilian children.[70] All three of her daughters attended college in Japan, two at Keio University, an elite private university in Tokyo. Every Saturday Matsubara offered a Portuguese class to young Brazilian children. In July 2010, twenty-five Japanese Brazilian children, including two in junior high schools, were attending CBK's weekly Portuguese class.

At CBK, I met two former postwar immigrants who had returned from Brazil much earlier than *dekassegui* began. CBK's vice president, Hachiro Torenji (b. 1944), had immigrated to Brazil in 1966 as an industrial immigrant with state sponsorship at the age of twenty-two. He grew up in Kobe, seeing emigrants departing the port for Brazil and dreaming of moving overseas. In Brazil, he married a Japanese "bride immigrant," and they had two sons. The Torenjis returned to Japan in 1976 because the younger son needed heart surgery. Torenji intended to return to Brazil after his son's operation, but his parents stopped him from doing so, and his wife wanted to stay on in Japan. Back in Kobe, Torenji opened a small luncheonette/bar across from the former Emigration Center to support his family. His parents and his wife had told him repeatedly not to tell anybody he had once immigrated to Brazil, because it would "shame" them all.[71] The other early "returnee" whom I met at CBK is a middle-aged postwar child immigrant;

she immigrated to Brazil with her family when she was seven years old. Like the Torenjis, her parents decided to move back to Japan some years later, and she has lived her life back in Japan since then, where she married a Japanese man and had a family.

While the Brazilian children were attending the Portuguese class taught by Matsubara, five women were waiting together outside the classroom and chatting among themselves, three Japanese Brazilian women who identified themselves by their first names only—Kiyoko, Carmen, and Marta—and two Japanese women. Kiyoko, a Nisei grandmother in her early sixties, kept quiet. Nisei/Sansei Marta and her Nisei/Sansei husband, both from Osasco, São Paulo, arrived in Japan in 2005 as *dekasseguis*. Marta spoke Portuguese only and was busy texting in Portuguese, whereas her thirteen-year-old daughter was talking to others only in Japanese.

The two Japanese women, both born in 1967, are married to Japanese Brazilian welders whose incomes dropped by half over a year because of the global recession. These two women met only after they began to bring their children to CBK for Portuguese classes on Saturdays. Both said their husbands would very much like to go back to Brazil if there were jobs available for them. Neither of them has been to Brazil, despite many years of marriage, saying that it would cost them too much to travel to Brazil, and it seems quite unlikely that they and their families would move to Brazil in the future.

Taeko Nozaki, who was born in Iwate prefecture and grew up in Tokyo, met her Brazilian husband (b. 1976) in Niigata prefecture, where both of them were employed as temporary workers, and they married in 1998. Her father approved of their marriage on the ground that her husband would become a full-time worker employed directly by the company. He is a Sansei who was born to a Nisei man and a Brazilian mother in Bauru, São Paulo but grew up in Campinas, São Paulo, where his father worked as a salesman. Her husband arrived in Japan in 1990 at the age of sixteen with his parents. Nozaki said, "My father-in-law worked very hard in Japan for twenty years and has bought three houses back in Campinas. He would buy a weekly issue of *IP* every week, saying he really wanted to go back to Brazil." Nozaki and her family lived in Kyoto City, where she worked as a local postal office clerk and her husband as a welder, supporting two young two daughters with Western names: Evelyn (b. 1999) and Katherine (b. 2003), both holding dual nationality. Looking like a typical Brazilian *morena*, Evelyn was called *gaijin* at her local school and bullied by her classmates. Nozaki said her husband was even darker-skinned, as his seventy-five-year-old "Spanish" Brazilian mother was "mixed with blacks." A local Japanese child in her neighborhood told Nozaki's husband to wash his hands because of "the white lines standing out in his dark-skinned hands." Referring to her husband as a Brazilian, Nozaki said, "Unlike the Japanese, Brazilians do not make any budget for the future."[72]

Kasumi Hanashiro's case is very different. Hanashiro, a college graduate as an English major, was born and grew up in Amagasaki City, Hyogo, where she met her husband through mutual friends. Her husband (b. 1961), a self-employed welder, was born in Santo André, São Paulo, to Okinawan immigrants and grew up as a Nisei among Okinawan descendants, speaking Portuguese. In 1974, at the age of thirteen, he and half of his family moved from Brazil to Japan as *rainichisha* (those who came to Japan; Okinawan descendants who migrated from South America to Japan in the 1970s) and settled down among the Okinawan/Uchinanchu in Amagasaki. Since the 1920s, Okinawans had migrated to the industrial areas of the Kansai Area, where they came to form their own ethnic communities. The *rainichisha* socialized among themselves, established their own Japanese-style mutual-aid rotating credit associations (*tanomoshikō*), and formed an amateur soccer team and named it Santo André FC, as the majority of them came from Santo André, the hometown of Hanashiro's husband.[73] Hisatoshi Tajima, who himself was once a young *rainichisha*, maintains that the youth, who behaved differently and lacked proficiency in Japanese, used to introduce themselves to the local Japanese as being from Brazil; it usually took ten years or so for them to start to behave like Japanese by the local Japanese standard and to stop mentioning their Brazilian origin, after having attended night school for their middle and high school education.[74] Hanashiro's husband must have continued to identify himself as a Brazilian, rather than Okinawan or Japanese.

The Hanashiros' three children—one daughter (b. 1997) and two sons (b. 1999 and b. 2003)—are all Japanese nationals with Japanese names; Hanashiro and her husband did not choose dual nationality for their children for fear that their sons might be called in by the Brazilian government for military service. Hanashiro was learning from Kiyoko how to cook Brazilian cuisine for her "Brazilian" family. But it was not just things Brazilian she was dealing with; she and her family were also living in the global Okinawan kinship network: "A relative of my husband's died in Brazil at the age of ninety-four. We need to attend her memorial service in Amagasaki next weekend, even though there is no grave for her in Japan."[75] Unlike Nozaki's, Hanashiro's three "unmixed" and Okinawan-descendant children looked Japanese. Even though both of their husbands were Brazilian-born Japanese Brazilians who immigrated to Japan in their teens, race surely differentiated their Japanese-born children's experiences in Japan. Although Okinawans are commonly known for their stereotypical "clean-cut facial features," according to Tajima,[76] Hanashiro's children's "Japanese face," in combination with their Japanese demeanor, can easily confirm their Japaneseness in the eyes of the local Japanese, though they may have developed or may develop stronger Okinawan identity among the Okinawans in Amagasaki. By contrast, Nozaki's "mixed" daughters, especially Evelyn, cannot escape from ostensible otherness. Even though she is a three-quarters Japanese descendant who was born in Japan and grew up as a Japanese child attending local Japanese schools, her Japaneseness is not "in the face," and therefore the [non-Japanese] face does not help.

CONCLUSION

In Japan, Japanese Brazilians have positioned themselves in relation to the local Japanese, as well as among themselves. In São Paulo, the (Japanese) "face" signified their otherness. After all, "it's in the face." In Japan, Japanese Brazilians have continued to refer to their (Japanese) "face" and treated it interchangeably with their "Japanese blood." Unmixed or "pure" Japanese Brazilians with the "Japanese face," such as Minami, positioned themselves above "mixed" Japanese Brazilians and non-Nikkei Brazilians, whom they called simply "Brazilians" among themselves. In São Paulo City, I often heard throughout the 2000s from Japanese Brazilian *dekassegui* returnees that "mixed" Japanese Brazilian children had a much harder time in Japan than "racially pure" children of Japanese descent, even though the situation had never been that simple. In their common discourse on Nikkeiness, they always emphasized their racial/ethnic advantage in Japan, due to their "purity of blood."

But basing one's ethnic identity on the "Japanese face" has been repeatedly challenged in Japan, where "the face" could be misleading, as the local Japanese also have the "Japanese face" and it is also difficult to distinguish the Japanese and Japanese descendants from other East Asian nationals and their descendants, especially those who were born and grew up in Japan, such as Korean residents in Japan. Especially in Hamamatsu and other middle-sized industrial cities of central Japan, where many *dekassegui* Japanese Brazilians and their families had settled down, the local Japanese could "see" the cultural otherness beyond the supposed shared ancestry. Some Japanese Brazilians did not expect discrimination in Japan and therefore were surprised and offended to be treated simply as foreigners (chapter 5).

Some Japanese Brazilians in Japan use "pure Japanese" to refer to the Japanese in Japan. For instance, Nisei Emerson Masaaki Tokunaga (b. 1967) started his interview in Hamamatsu by asking me rather suspiciously whether I was a "pure Japanese." I asked him what he meant by the phrase, and he rephrased his question: "Were you born and raised in Japan?" I said yes, and he stated that I was surely a "pure Japanese" then, no matter how many years I had lived outside Japan, in the same way he, having spent half his life in Japan, would be forever a Brazilian.[77] In São Paulo, he and I would have been in the same category: we would have been perceived together just as *japoneses* by "Brazilians" for the "Japanese face," and as *japoneses puros* ("pure Japanese") by Japanese Brazilians for our "unmixed" Japanese ancestry. During his interview, Tokunaga, as a proud Brazilian with an engineering degree, treated me as a "pure Japanese" who knew nothing about Brazil.

Japanese Brazilians in Hamamatsu, who "became" Brazilians in relation to the local Japanese only by moving to Japan, are aware that they could not be perceived as "true" Brazilians because of the "face," and they apply their self-perception to the Nikkei in general. For instance, Ono and Arakaki presented an intriguing argument relating to a mutual Brazilian woman friend born to a postwar immigrant father and a Nisei mother in São Paulo. Ono said, "Do you know she is married to an American? Well, her husband is not a real American. He is a Nikkei." Then Ono mentioned that Arakaki had been interviewed by the *New York Times* on Brazilians in Hamamatsu. Arakaki proudly followed her up, "I was interviewed, not only once but twice. The first reporter was not a real American. He is Nikkei. But the second one is a real one—a white American." In their discourse, no Nikkei can possibly be a "true" Brazilian or American: the Japanese "face" determines Japaneseness, wherever s/he is from or is now.

Another interesting Japanese Brazilian discourse is on self-perceived "whitening" in Japan. For instance, Hisahiro Inoue, a Nisei man in São Paulo, maintained that he had become "very white" during his six years as a *dekassegui* in Japan during the 1990s (chapter 3). In Hamamatsu, Marcelo Yoshimura also claimed that he had become "very white" after having lived in Japan for some twenty years. Clearly, such Brazilian notion of "whitening" has nothing to do with skin color, even though when I interviewed Inoue in 2010, it was during the winter and he was not tanned at all, so he looked rather pale; back in São Paulo City, Inoue was no longer an unskilled *dekassegui* factory worker as he had been in Japan, but occupied a top administrative position at the Sindicato dos Permissionários em Centrais de Abastecimento de Alimentos do Estado de São Paulo (Union of Permit

Holders in State Food Supply Centers of São Paulo). By contrast, Yoshimura was a college-educated white-collar worker in Brazil and by coming to Japan became a *dekassegui* factory worker, even though he eventually built his own businesses. It was midsummer in Japan when I met with Yoshimura in his office, and all of the local Japanese I saw on the streets were tanned. If, as the Brazilians say, "money whitens," then just being able to live and work in a First World country and be paid in yen could be regarded as a huge step up for Brazilians; they became "whiter" than Brazilians in Brazil.

In Hamamatsu, I met a young *mestiço* Brazilian who stopped by Hiromi Ono's office and handed her a *kairanban* (circular). He spoke Japanese fluently and was wearing a commercial apron with the name of an *izakaya* (Japanese pub). He cheerfully posed for a few photos and made a brief self-introduction: "My name is Lucío Saigo. I'm a *mestiço*. I'm twenty-three years old now. I came to Japan ten years ago when I was thirteen." After he went back to work at the bar, Ono remarked that she had never seen him before. Lucío Saigo's case makes a striking contrast to that of "Hideki" of Sukiya restaurant in the Liberdade district of São Paulo City, another young *mestiço*, who emphasized his Nikkeiness as well as his legitimate membership in Japanese society as a full-time regular employee of a Japanese company. Unlike Hideki, who gave me his Japanese middle name only, without his last name or his Portuguese first name, Lucío Saigo volunteered both his first and last names, even though the Japanese usually introduce themselves by their last names only, and also identified himself as *mestiço*. According to Minami, many years ago life was hard in Japan for racially mixed Japanese Brazilians, "even for those who were just slightly darker skinned," but things changed by 2010; many TV celebrities in Japan are now racially mixed (with Caucasians), and racially mixed (more Caucasian-looking) young Japanese Brazilian women were married to older and wealthier Japanese business owners.[78] In this context, Lucío Saigo is able to position himself above not only "pure" Japanese Brazilians but also the local Japanese by emphasizing his Brazilianness/whiteness. As Stuart Hall enunciates, "We all write and speak from a particular place and time, from a history and a culture which is specific. What we say is always 'in context,' *positioned*."[79] Therefore, cultural identity is "a matter of 'becoming,' as well as 'being.'"[80]

Minami's day-to-day politics of position is embodied in her double-sided business card, with which she "becomes" a Brazilian to the Japanese whom she meets for her work at an NGO for foreign residents, especially Brazilians, in Hamamatsu. One side of her card is in Japanese, and the other in alphabets (English and Portuguese). Both sides are the same in content, except for her first name or lack of it. While her name in alphabets is simply Yumi Minami, her full name, Minami Andrea Yumi, is printed on the other side, in the Japanese order. Thus her Portuguese first name, Andrea shows up only on the Japanese side, although she has not used it since her high school days in Brazil, as discussed. Her "Japaneseness" is eternally "in her face" for Brazilians both in São Paulo and in Hamamatsu, but her "Brazilianness" is "invisible," so that it has to be in print for the Japanese to "see." In the end, it's all about one's positionality.

CONCLUSION

On June 8, 2010, Yasumi Nakayama and I traveled from São Paulo City to Santos. We met at the Jabaquara bus station and took a long-distance bus together. Santos is where Nakayama, as a cooperative immigrant, landed on April 5, 1938, with thirteen members of his extended family, all from Kagoshima prefecture. On our way to Santos, Nakayama recalled his experiences as a ten-year-old boy on the *Montevideo Maru*, departing Kobe on February 21, 1938, until his family's eventual landing at the port of Santos. Once a small farming community on the fringe of the national economy, Santos had become Brazil's biggest port city during the "Golden Age" of coffee in western São Paulo; it had replaced Rio de Janeiro by 1894 as the most important coffee export center—and an importer of immigrant labor.[1]

From Santos' bus terminal, Nakayama and I took a taxi to the Roberto Mario Santini Municipal Park, where the so-called Japanese Immigrants Monument stands, with the inscription by Japan's then prime minister, Ryutaro Hashimoto, which reads, *Nihon Imin Burajiru Jōriku Kinen* (In Memory of the Landing of Japanese Immigrants in Brazil). Nakayama told me that the monument had originally been placed on Ponta da Praia Beach but was moved to the current location in 2009. The monument, titled *Kono Daichi ni Yume o / À Esta Terra* (Dreams to This Land / To This Land), represents a young adult man, his wife, and their son. Standing at the port upon arrival, the adult man extends his right arm toward the continent, and his wife and their young son gaze in that direction; they are about to embark on their new life in São Paulo under the patriarch's strong leadership.

Nakayama had visited the monument only once before. Back in 2004, when he was still the MHIJB vice director, Nakayama was invited by Fumio

Oura to accompany him to Santos in a car driven by Yoshimune Watanabe. Oura, also a prewar child immigrant, had some business to do in Santos as the director of Kyusaikai / Assistência Social Dom José Gaspar (Salvation Society/Dom José Gaspar Social Assistance), a Japanese Brazilian Catholic charitable association in São Paulo City.[2] The three Japanese immigrant men spent an hour in front of the monument, discussing what was going on with Japanese Brazilians. The immigrants' statue was looking toward a bright future in Brazil, but in reality, Japanese Brazilians had been migrating "back" to Japan on a large scale. By 2004, the number of Brazilians in Japan had reached 270,000 or 280,000, already outnumbering the total of Japanese immigrants to Brazil. According to Nakayama, the three men concluded, albeit rather jokingly, that the "contradiction" would be resolved if the statue were turned around to point in the opposite direction: from Brazil to Japan.[3]

The Japanese Immigrants Monument in Santos had originally been proposed in the late 1980s by Kami Arata (b. 1922), a prewar child immigrant from Okayama (1933), and president of the Japanese Association of Santos, for the celebration of the eightieth anniversary of Japanese immigration to Brazil, albeit without success. Eventually, to celebrate the ninetieth anniversary, Kenren established its Planning Committee for the Immigrants Monument, chaired by Iossuke Tanaka (chapter 3), then president of the Hiroshima Prefectural Association. Kenren invited the public to enter the prize contest for the best design and chose the one by Gunki Motonaga (1931–2010), a college-educated postwar immigrant man (1953), who worked at Bunkyo as Kiyoshi Yamamoto's right arm and later became executive director of Tunibra Turismo, a major Japanese Brazilian tourism company in São Paulo City. Motonaga's original pencil-drawn image consisted of an adult immigrant man only. It was Iossuke Tanaka who added an adult immigrant woman and a young boy in order to reflect the reality of prewar *colono* immigration. Eventually Kenren commissioned Claudia Fernandes, a Brazilian sculptor, to create the statue of the immigrants.[4] The Japanese Immigrants Monument was finally inaugurated on June 21, 1998, after ten years of many collective and individual fundraising efforts among Japanese Brazilians. The inauguration ceremony was held in Santos under the leadership of Yataro Amino, Kenren's postwar immigrant president, with the presence of many high-ranking Japanese and Brazilian bureaucrats and politicians, together with Tomi Nakagawa, the only surviving *Kasato Maru* immigrant.[5] Since then Santos' Japanese Immigrants Monument has been visited by Japan's imperial family members and other important official guests from Japan for every important state event.

Yasumi Nakayama standing in front of the Japanese Immigrants Monument in Santos, São Paulo, June 7, 2010. Photo by author.

After visiting the monument, Nakayama and I had a sushi lunch at the Japanese restaurant of the famous Estrela de Ouro Club (Golden Star Club), founded and managed by the Japanese Association of Santos. The restaurant's walls were all decorated with enlarged old photos of Japanese descendants in Santos, who were very active in fishing and many recreational activities among themselves until 1942, when the Brazilian government evacuated Japanese descendants from Santos as enemy aliens. As a result, the Japanese Association of Santos was not reestablished until 1952. After lunch, Nakayama and I walked toward the port of Santos, where all Japanese immigrants had arrived at its Fourteenth Wharf until 1973. Unfortunately, we were not able to see the wharf itself, as a big paper storage house had been built over it in the late 1990s. The historical site has been sealed forever from public eyes.

On the long-distance bus back to São Paulo City, Nakayama continued to narrate his immigrant life to me. He had already spent nearly seventy-three years in Brazil and had formed his family: his Nisei wife, Michiko; their three Nisei/Sansei college-educated adult children; and a grandchild—all Brazilian citizens of "pure" Japanese ancestry. That made him the only Japanese in his own family. In rural São Paulo, with only one year of formal Brazilian schooling, Nakayama had never attained much fluency in Portuguese, but he perfected his Japanese on his own and never failed to keep his journal in Japanese. He looked and sounded very sad when he talked about his younger brother, who had been left behind in Japan at the age of five; he was diagnosed with trachoma at the Asylum of Emigrants in Kobe at the time of emigration and was sent back alone to Kagoshima prefecture, where he was raised by one of his paternal uncles. Nakayama's parents intended to bring their younger son to Brazil in a few years but could never afford to send the money for his passage. The Nakayamas were not reunited until 1972, when Nakayama's younger brother traveled to Brazil for the first time, with one of his older female cousins. Unfortunately, Nakayama's mother had been long gone. Nakayama's father lived with Nakayama and his family until his passing in 1985 at the age of eighty-five. It took Nakayama fifty-five long years to finally return to his homeland, for which he had always longed; in 1993, he and Michiko participated in a Japanese Brazilian package tour to Japan, during which they visited not only his younger brother in Miyazaki prefecture but also Michiko's parents' hometown, Shimonoseki City, Yamaguchi prefecture, where one of her cousins had become a successful business owner. Nakayama and Michiko traveled to Japan for the second time in December 2007 and called on his younger brother, who had been on dialysis for kidney failure.[6] As fate had it, the two brothers, both Japanese nationals, lived very different lives in the two different countries.

In February 2008, when Japanese Brazilians' participation in the São Paulo Carnival made headlines in Brazilian mass media, Nakayama was busy volunteering at the MHIJB for the special events in commemoration of the centenary of Japanese immigration to Brazil. Nakayama wrote of his trip to Japan in a letter to me: "In thinking back, I had this hidden desire to experience a winter in Japan for my trip. At the end of last year, I was so happy to see snow falling. I got so excited that I went out to take photos of the snow. In Japan, I suffered not from a cold temperature but too much heat all over Japan. Everything was overheated. I thought Japan had better save its money for heating."[7] Like many other prewar child immigrants, Nakayama was always proud of being a Japanese national with a Japanese passport, but his Japanese identity in Brazil had been inevitably challenged historically in the changing national, international, and global context, as many other stories in this book demonstrate. My day trip to Santos with Nakayama was coming to an end. As our bus was approaching the Jabaquara bus station, Nakayama stated, "The Brazilian Nikkei today do not really accept things Japanese. That is the reflection of Brazil's national orientation. Brazil transforms all foreign cultures into a Brazilian one." Nakayama does not seem to identify himself as a Brazilian Nikkei; he has remained Japanese in his self-perception.

What does it mean to be "Japanese" in São Paulo? What is Japanese Brazilian identity, after all? I answer these questions by summarizing my arguments on gender, race, and national identity in a rather chronological fashion.

GENDER AND GENDER RELATIONS

Japan's overseas migration, which had begun soon after the Meiji Restoration (1868), was always imagined and constructed predominantly in a single male form; many men returned home with savings, while others, who chose to settle down in Hawai'i and on the West Coast of the mainland United States, were later followed by their wives and children, or young women as so-called picture brides.[8] This gendered migration pattern changed when the Japanese began to migrate to Brazil in 1908.

Under Brazilian regulations, all prewar Japanese *colono* immigrants had to arrive in a family, which had to be headed by a married patriarch and include at least three "economically active" members between the ages of twelve and forty-five. As a result, women constituted around 40 percent of the prewar Japanese immigrant population, a proportion that enabled the Japanese to intermarry among themselves and preserve their language, customs, and traditions. Needless to say, a relative gender balance in numbers did not create any kind of gender equality. Adult immigrant women were expected to perform not only mandatory plantation labor but also all daily domestic work, including childbearing and rearing. Even though it was essential for the immigrant family's survival, women's work was perceived as merely supportive of their men for the family's public honor. Therefore, women were not rewarded for their labor, and women's work itself was not considered as valuable as men's. In some ways, women's work was not even regarded as work; "real" work was supposed to be performed by men only.

In rural São Paulo, ethnic endogamy was arranged and practiced widely among the Japanese for their family honor in combination with their mediated national identity. Every young "Japanese" woman's sexual conduct was always under the watchful eyes of her family members for their public honor but also under the eyes of many other adult men in the same "colony" for their national honor as the Japanese in Brazil. Such ethnic endogamy continued to be practiced widely in São Paulo City, where young Niseis formed and participated in their own exclusively Nisei clubs, which were sharply divided by class. As members of the same clubs, they dated among themselves and conducted ethnic-class endogamy. While their male counterparts quickly moved up the social ladder, educated Nisei women became full-time homemakers either upon marriage or after the birth of their first children. As elite Nisei couples, they identified themselves as Brazilians/Westerners and refused to socialize with less-educated Japanese Brazilians, many of whom were active in various ethnic Japanese associations.

By the beginning of the 1970s, intermarriage had become more common for the educated Niseis in the city, but there was clearly a double standard by gender. Prewar immigrant parents tolerated their Nisei sons' marriages to white Brazilian women, but they continued to disapprove of their daughters' marriages to white Brazilian boyfriends. This attitude reflected the parents' perception of their sons as successful Brazilian men and of their daughters as "more Japanese" and therefore more responsible for the family's Japanese ethnicity. Thus, as in the case of the indigenous population in Peru, gender subordination was understood and expressed in ethnic terms.[9] Higher education did not enable Japanese Brazilian women to escape from their gendered patriarchal obligations in the diaspora. As a result, educated Nisei and Sansei women often found themselves caught between Japanese ethnicity and Brazilian womanhood and forced to choose the former over the latter. By contrast, intermarried Japanese Brazilian men were able to keep Japanese ethnicity and Brazilian manhood, without losing either.

Within the next few decades, Japanese Brazilians of both sexes conducted intermarriage on a large scale, with seemingly equal frequency.

While educated Japanese Brazilian men married Brazilian women of diverse races, colors, and classes, educated Japanese Brazilian women largely conducted class endogamy interracially with educated white Brazilian men, rather than choosing to marry less-educated Japanese Brazilian men. This accords with the general rule that women usually marry up. At the same time, it may also suggest that educated Japanese Brazilian women elevated their positions well enough to resist ethnic patriarchal rule in the diaspora, to cross racial boundaries to conduct class endogamy, and, furthermore, to take advantage of the social capital of whiteness under racial hegemony. Thus, Japanese Brazilian women began "whitening" themselves though interracial marriage. By the end of the twentieth century, educated Japanese Brazilians' practice of intermarriage took another turn; Japanese Brazilian women intermarried *more* frequently than their male counterparts. Japanese Brazilians attributed this to the stereotypical Brazilian perception of Japanese Brazilian women as "exotic and mysterious" but "good wives who obey and serve their husbands well, unlike Brazilian women." That is, patriarchy and racism were mutually reinforcing.

In the late 1980s and early 1990s, Japan's emergence as the world's economic power enhanced the self-perception of upper-middle-class Sanseis and Yonseis. During the 1990s, as high school and college students, some of them began to hang out in racially defined groups and formed voluntary associations, identifying themselves collectively as the Nikkei. They continued to socialize and date among themselves and conduct ethnic-class endogamy, often for the sake of "preserving Nikkei culture." But, unlike those in previous generations, upper-middle-class Sansei and Yonsei women did not plan on giving up their careers upon marriage and/or the birth of their first child, and educated and therefore "whitened" Japanese Brazilian parents did not expect their successful daughters to sacrifice themselves as "free" caretakers.

Meanwhile, gender subordination came to be reproduced and even strengthened in the formation of the Brazilian diaspora in Japan. *Dekassegui* started in the predominantly single male form with unskilled foreign guest workers, but later changed into (originally temporary) settlement in the host society in family units. Even though both men and women were hired as assembly line workers at the same factories, male labor was valued more highly than female labor, and men were paid much better than women: college-educated Japanese Brazilian women were paid much less than younger, much-less-educated Japanese Brazilian men. At the same time, better-educated men were able to use their educational and professional backgrounds back in Brazil to attract women in the Brazilian diaspora and network with local Japanese men, while highly educated women could rarely take advantage of their backgrounds in Brazil and often ended up marrying less-educated and/or younger men in the diaspora. Some men, especially Nisei men with proficiency in Japanese who arrived in Japan in the early stage of *dekassegui,* were able to move up the social ladder as successful business owners within the diaspora. *Dekassegui* also provided single Japanese Brazilian women with better employment opportunities to support themselves and their children, without depending on men.

RACE AND RACIAL IDENTITY

Prewar Japanese immigrants arrived in Brazil after European immigrants stopped coming to Brazil. All of the subsidized prewar immigrants arrived in Brazil as *colonos* and worked as contract laborers on coffee plantations in rural São Paulo. In reality, Brazilian elites never perceived the Japanese as whites.

With the intention of returning home in the near future, prewar immigrants distinguished themselves from the non-Japanese populations, whom they pejoratively called *gaijin.* Working almost exclusively among the Japanese in the countryside, Japanese immigrants remained rather oblivious to Brazilian perceptions of race and Brazilian racism until the mid-1930s, when the Brazilian government began to severely limit the entry of Japanese immigrants, who had come to be known as forming "racial cysts." In fact, by the early 1930s, successful Japanese immigrant men had become landowners, posing a threat to elite Brazilians. Brazilian anti-Japanese sentiment focusing on stereotypical Japanese phenotypes, most prominently "slanted eyes," began to dominate Brazilian public discourse on the Japanese. Discriminatory treatment of Japanese immigrants and racism against the Japanese escalated during World War II, when the Japanese, together with Germans and Italians, were watched by the Brazilian authorities and imprisoned for various reasons.

After the turn of the 1940s, Japanese immigrants and their children began to move to São Paulo City, and their migration escalated after the war and peaked in the 1950s and early 1960s. In terms of class, they underwent a downward shift from rural landowners to urban working classes. Japanese immigrants and the Niseis understood white middle-class Brazilians' overt prejudice as a reflection of their class position as poor immigrants, not as racism. In the city, with no or little capital investment, Japanese immigrant families could manage to open small family businesses, most prominently in the cleaning service, with the use of free labor by the young Niseis, whereas many Niseis were able to receive higher education as Brazilian citizens. Thus some Niseis' process of individual "whitening" began through the power of elite Brazilian college education in certain fields, which provided them with highly paid trades such as law, medicine, dentistry, pharmacy, and engineering. The educated Niseis, by identifying themselves as Brazilians/Westerners first and foremost, separated themselves from their uneducated counterparts, as well as the immigrant population. They married among themselves exclusively, yet did not necessarily oppose interracial marriages in the way their Issei parents had. The elite Niseis maintained at least in public that there was "no racism in Brazil" and often stated that they, as the Niseis, were not ready to marry white middle-class Brazilians but that their Sansei children, as "true" Brazilians, would surely do so. After the turn of the 1970s, intermarriage became increasingly common for educated Japanese Brazilian men. Many successful Nisei men married white Brazilian women, either of equal social standing or of lower classes, "whitening" themselves and their offspring. As Carl Degler maintains, "Men more often marry lighter than women. As one informant put it, 'The woman does not marry whom she wants, but with him who wants her.' "[10] Yet, interestingly, other educated Japanese Brazilian men married much-less-educated women of African descent. By contrast, educated Japanese Brazilian women either married educated Japanese Brazilian men or stayed single and often ended up serving as caretakers until their parents' passing. This may suggest that educated Japanese Brazilian women had less chance of "whitening" because of their gender. But by the end of the twentieth century, the situation began to change for women; it has been widely said, at least among Japanese Brazilians, that Japanese Brazilian women are more suitable for intermarriage than their male counterparts.

Unlike the older generations of Japanese descendants, who refused to understand their position in terms of race, the younger generation of upper-middle-class Sanseis and Yonseis grew up with "Brazilian" children in the city. Every day in school they dealt with Brazilian racism against their "Japanese faces" with "slanted eyes," despite their successful Nisei parents' "whitening" through college education and respected positions as urban professionals. For the urban upper-middle-class Japanese Brazilian youth, being "Japanese" is racial, not ethnic. While many continue to "whiten" themselves by opting to marry white upper-middle-class Brazilians and often refuse to identify themselves as Japanese descendants, some others, who identify themselves as Nikkei Brazilians, prefer to socialize with, date, and marry other young Japanese Brazilians of the same socioeconomic standing. Among them there is no clear consensus on what it means to be

Nikkei in Brazil. Even among self-identified Nikkei youth, who all position themselves above Japanese youth in Japan, their individual definitions of Nikkeiness may differ substantially.

TRANSFORMATION OF NATIONAL IDENTITY

Until the end of World War II, the majority of Japanese immigrants identified themselves as overseas Japanese and took strong national pride in the military expansion of the Japanese Empire as loyal subjects of the emperor. In rural São Paulo, Japanese immigrants made every effort to raise their children, both Japanese-born and Brazilian-born, as good Japanese nationals. Their mediated Japanese identity came to be challenged at the end of World War II. With no direct communication with their homeland during the war, the majority of Japanese descendants in Brazil refused to believe in Japan's defeat, and the resulting bloody *kachi-make* conflicts in the late 1940s intensified Brazilian racism against the Japanese. Only after the defeat of Japan did prewar immigrants reluctantly decide to settle down in Brazil with their Brazilian-born children. Whereas prewar immigrant parents retained strong Japanese identity, as many of their Nisei children began to move up the social ladder they identified themselves as Brazilians/Westerners and positioned themselves as better than the Japanese, while conducting ethnic-class endogamy exclusively among themselves.

Prewar immigrants' mediated national identity as Japanese was challenged severely and even crushed by the influx of new immigrants from postwar Japan starting in 1953. Postwar immigrants, many of whom came as young single adult men with high school diplomas or college degrees, were much more individualistic and were eager to make it in Brazilian society, rather than working forever for prewar immigrant employers. Positioning postwar immigrants below them as the "newly arrived," many prewar immigrant parents, who perceived themselves as more "authentically" Japanese, did not wish their Nisei daughters to marry postwar immigrant men; instead, Nisei women were expected to marry successful college-educated Nisei men—yet these men identified themselves as Brazilians/Westerners. Over the years, prewar and postwar immigrants did not find a way to create a unified Japanese identity because of their generational differences.

Japan's emergence as a global economic power in the early 1980s changed Brazilian perceptions of Japan and the Japanese quickly and drastically. It boosted new ethnic pride among educated Japanese Brazilians, especially the younger generation, in São Paulo, who began to position themselves as Japanese descendants above other educated Brazilians. As Brazilians in general began to migrate to the First World in the 1980s because of Brazil's hyperinflation, Japanese Brazilians' "return" labor migration to Japan began with postwar immigrant men and soon extended to prewar child immigrants and the Niseis, who held dual nationality and were often fluent in Japanese. After the Japanese government's amendment of immigration law in June 1990, *dekassegui* quickly drew in younger generations of Japanese Brazilians, including the racially mixed, who had little or no proficiency in Japanese. Many Japanese Brazilians "became" Brazilians only by moving to Japan as foreign guest workers. In the Brazilian diaspora in Japan, some Nisei men emerged as successful ethnic business owners for the increasing numbers of Japanese Brazilian workers and their family members. Over the years, more and more Japanese Brazilians decided to settle in Japan permanently with their Japanese-born children, even though the children are Brazilian nationals according to Japanese law. Many of them positioned themselves above other Brazilians of the same/similar socioeconomic standing in Brazil inasmuch as they were privileged to be living in a First World country. In other words, they "whitened" themselves by living in Japan.

In the year of the centenary of Japanese immigration to Brazil (2008), the global recession hit the already sluggish Japanese economy, left many Brazilian workers unemployed, and put "Japan Town" ethnic Brazilian businesses in serious financial trouble. As a result, one-quarter of Brazilian residents in Japan, including the Japanese-born, returned to Brazil by April 2010. In relation to—or in reaction against—the local Japanese, many of whom would not accept them, Japanese Brazilians remaining in Japan became increasingly nationalistic, referring to the bright future of the Brazilian economy with the World Cup (2014) and the Summer Olympics (2016), and idealizing and romanticizing Brazil as their homeland, to which many of them would never return permanently. But they did not form any homogenized collective identity as Brazilians in Japan. With or without the "Japanese face," Japanese Brazilians in Japan all play their "cards of identity," individually or collectively, not only among themselves but also with the local Japanese, in terms of gender, class, and race, as well as in terms of being Brazilians/Westerners and/or being Japanese descendants, and having language proficiency in Portuguese, Japanese, and even English.

What does the Japanese Immigrants Monument in Santos mean to Japanese Brazilians in São Paulo, especially prewar immigrants? It was clear to me that Yasumi Nakayama did not have any emotional attachment to the monument when he and I visited there in June 2010, even though he seemed to enjoy the trip to Santos and was very cheerful and talkative the whole time. Nor would he have visited it back in 2004, if Oura had not insisted. Not surprisingly, Nakayama's own complex history of prewar immigration to Brazil does not accord with the monument's representation. A married couple and their young son under the age of twelve would not have qualified for state-sponsored immigration to Brazil. The statue of the young immigrant family is an imagined, romanticized, and extremely simplified form of overseas labor migration.

Nakayama states in his essay that after his first visit to the monument in Santos he came to understand the political importance of such monuments for the state of Japan, not for Nakayama or any other individual who lived through the history.[11] In other words, with its public use of certain representations, the state creates and/or changes the narrative of Japanese immigration to Brazil, from the transnational transfer of labor as a commodity to the glorious transplant of family, kinship, community, and eventually the nation, through and under the protection of the state's patriarchal rule. In principle, any monument may easily be manipulated as a spectacle for those who are in power or who seek for power. Tourists and other visitors see the statue in Santos and may get an easy feeling that they understand what immigrating to Brazil was like for the Japanese. In short, any statue is simplification with a purpose: like the Brazilian stereotype of "slanted eyes," the statue of the immigrant family reduces the complexity of human experience into support for the state's hegemonic rule. Certainly Nakayama could not see himself in the Japanese Immigrants Monument in Santos.

Japanese Brazilians in São Paulo continue to struggle to position themselves within the broader construction of racial hegemony, while the structure of that hegemony simultaneously positions them in ways that undermine their efforts. For that reason their efforts have backfired, as did the *kachi-make* conflicts. As all of the stories in this book demonstrate, Japanese Brazilians' strategies for negotiating Brazil's racial and class formation are in constant flux, both across and within generations of immigrants, as well as both across and within class and gender. For that reason the identity of Japanese Brazilians can never be simply fixed. Brazilians of Japanese descent can be so marked in the larger society by focusing on arbitrary facial features, such as "slanted eyes," but how the people so marked and positioned respond to that positioning can never be simultaneously reduced to a fixed, timeless understanding of what it means to be "Japanese" in Brazil.

The Japanese Immigrants Monument remains an important tourist site in and for the city of Santos. In 2008, the image of the statue almost made it "back home" for Japan's national celebration of "The Year of Interchange between Japan and Brazil." On April 17, 2007, Japan's Ministry of Finance announced that it would issue a commemorative 500-yen coin on the centenary, bearing the image of Santos' statue with the official consent of Kenren, which built the monument. Then, on April 30, 2008, the ministry made a surprise announcement that the commemorative coin would be redesigned entirely, replacing the image of the statue with the *Kasato Maru* on one side and cherry blossoms and coffee beans on the other, owing to a disagreement with the sculptor over her copyright of the image. It was also decided that the new coin would be available for sale on June 18, 2008, exactly one hundred years after the arrival of the *Kasato Maru* in Santos.[12] The date was apparently changed under pressure from Japan's Ministry of Foreign Affairs. It was soon reported in Japan's mass media that the Japan mint had already minted 4,800,000 coins with the original design and that remaking them all was to cost the Japanese government 7–8 million yen (US$0.7–0.8 million). According to *Nikkey Shimbun*, Claudia Fernandes, the sculptor, allegedly demanded that Kenren pay three or four million US dollars for her copyright of the image. Each side hired a lawyer to negotiate the deal, but no agreement was made in the end. When *Nikkey Shimbun*'s reporter directly contacted Fernandes in person, she maintained that she had never asked Kenren for any payment for her copyright, adding, "It would be an honor for my design to be used for the coin."[13] Of course, for the Japanese government, it cost much less to remake the coin than to make the payment, through Kenren, to the Brazilian sculptor, if she had truly made such a demand. But why the dispute? Why had the Japanese government chosen this image in the first place? The monument in Santos was planned and constructed by Japanese Brazilians in São Paulo. Therefore choosing its image for the commemorative coin might have constituted friendly diplomacy with Brazil, some 310,000 of whose citizens were living in Japan. If the Japanese government had not adopted this image for the commemorative coin, the sculptor might never have thought about her copyright.

In such a situation, reminiscent of Akira Kurosawa's *Rashomon* (1950), it is impossible to know who is telling the whole truth; probably everybody involved is telling his or her own subjective truth, based on some objective facts, in order to defend him/herself. However, one thing is crystal clear: the image of Japanese immigrants became a commodity that other people own. Japanese immigrants and their descendants have no ownership of their own image, which is divorced from reality. This is another illustration that Japanese Brazilians are not completely in control of how their identity is constructed or represented under hegemonic power. They are positioned for their "slanted eyes." And that is why they constantly struggle to position themselves in their own terms. In his/her daily politics of position, every Japanese Brazilian in São Paulo continues to be forced to define and redefine what it means to be "Japanese" in Brazil.

Notes

Introduction

1. Bunkyo Yonjūnenshi Hensan Iinkai, ed., *Bunkyo Yonjūnenshi* [Bunkyo's History of Forty Years] (São Paulo: Burajiru Nihon Bunka Kyokai, 1998), 123–143.

2. Thomas H. Holloway, *Immigrants on the Land: Coffee and Society in São Paulo, 1886–1934* (Chapel Hill: University of North Carolina Press, 1980), 70–71.

3. Colônia Geinōshi Hensan Iinkai, ed., *Colônia Geinōshi* [Colônia's History of Entertainment] (São Paulo: Colônia Geinōshi Hensan Iinkai, 1986), 283–284.

4. Shuhei Hosokawa, *Shinemaya Brajiru o Yuku: Nikkei Imin no Kyoshu to Aidentitii* [Cinema-Men Wonder in Brazil: Japanese Immigrants' Homesickness and Identity] (Tokyo: Shinchō Shinsho, 1999), 194.

5. Ibid., 194–195.

6. Saefugi Mifugi, "Tizuka to Yurika: 'Gaijin' ni miru Simai no Kento" [Tizuka and Yurika: The Sisters' Achievements Seen in 'Gaijin'], in Colônia Geinōshi, *Colônia Geinōshi*, 280–281; Tania Nomura, ed., *Universo em segredo: A mulher nikkei no Brasil* (São Paulo: Diário Nippak, 1990), 42.

7. Colônia Geinōshi, *Colônia Geinōshi*, 284.

8. Ibid.

9. Ibid.

10. Stuart Hall, "Old and New Identities, Old and New Ethnicities," in *Culture, Globalization, and the World-System: Contemporary Conditions for the Representation of Identity*, ed. Anthony D. King (Minneapolis: University of Minnesota Press, 1997), 49.

11. Colônia Geinōshi, *Colônia Geinōshi*, 284.

12. Mifugi, "Tizuka to Yurika," 281.

13. Ibid., 281–282; Hosokawa, *Shinemaya*, 198.

14. Katsuzo Yamamoto, *Burajiru to Gojūnen* [Fifty Years with Brazil] (São Paulo: Jitsugyo no Burajirusha, 1982), 123–124.

15. Author interview (hereafter AI), Shizu Saito (1922–2009), July 1, 2002.

16. Hosokawa, *Shinemaya*, 195–197.

17. Ibid., 198.

18. Ibid., 198–200.

19. Ibid., 198.

20. Ibid.

21. Lisa Lowe, *Immigrant Acts: On Asian American Cultural Politics* (Durham, NC: Duke University Press, 1996), 76.

22. Sidney W. Mintz, *Workers in Cane: Puerto Rican Life History* (New York: W. W. Norton, 1974); Daphne Patai, *Brazilian Women Speak: Contemporary Life Histories* (New Brunswick, NJ: Rutgers University Press, 1988); Daniel James, *Doña María's Story: Life, History, Memory, and Political Identity* (Durham, NC: Duke University Press, 2000); and Matthew C. Gutmann and Catherine Lutz, *Breaking Ranks: Iraq Veterans Speak Out against the War* (Berkeley: University of California Press, 2010).

23. Steve J. Stern, *Remembering Pinochet's Chile: On the Eve of London 1998* (Durham, NC: Duke University Press, 2004), 227.

24. Heidi Tinsman, *Partners in Conflict: The Politics of Gender, Sexuality, and Labor in the Chilean Agrarian Reform, 1950–1973* (Durham, NC: Duke University Press, 2002), 17.

25. Patai, *Brazilian Women Speak*, 6.

26. AI, Sachiko Tomino, July 5, 2002.

27. Michael George Hanchard, "Racism, Eroticism, and the Paradox of a U.S. Black Researcher in Brazil," in *Racing Research, Researching Race: Methodological Dilemmas in Critical Race Studies*, ed. France Winddance Twine and Jonathan W. Warren (New York: New York University Press, 2000), 166.

28. Ibid., 166–167.

29. Esperança Fujinkai, ed., *Esperança Sōritsu Yonjūgoshūnen Kinengō* [Esperança: A Special Issue in Commemoration of Its 45th Anniversary], no. 40 (December 1994).

30. AI, Hirofumi Ikesaki, June 26, 2008.

31. AI, Haruko Fujitani, December 31, 1997.

32. AI, Masae Okada, December 31, 1997.

33. Max Weber, *From Max Weber: Essays in Sociology*, trans. and ed. H. H. Gerth and C. Wright Mills (New York: Oxford University Press, 1958), 159–195.

34. Jeffrey Lesser, *A Discontented Diaspora: Japanese-Brazilians and the Meanings of Ethnic Militancy* (Durham, NC: Duke University Press, 2007).

CHAPTER ONE: IMMIGRATION AND DIASPORA

1. Japan, Ministry of Foreign Affairs, "Burajiru Renbō Kyowakoku Kiso Deita" [Basic Data on the Federative Republic of Brazil], www.mofa.go.jp/mofaj/area/brazil /data.html, accessed January 6, 2015; Centro de Estudos Nipo-Brasileiros, ed., *Burajiru ni Okeru Nikkei Jinko Chōsa Hōkokusho, 1987–1988* [A Survey on the Nikkei Population in Brazil, 1987–1988] (São Paulo: Centro de Estudos Nipo-Brasileiros, n.d.), 14, 15, 17 (table 2-3).

2. Melissa Nobles, *Race and Censuses in Modern Politics* (Stanford, CA: Stanford University Press, 2000), 104 (table 3), and 105 (table 4).

3. Author interview (hereafter AI), Suely Harumi Satow, July 16, 2001; and AI, Edna Roland, June 22, 2001.

4. Jeffrey Lesser, *A Discontented Diaspora: Japanese-Brazilians and the Meanings*

of Ethnic Militancy (Durham, NC: Duke University Press, 2007), xxiii, figures 3, 4, and 5, and 152.

5. Tiago Mata Machado, "Mizoguchi e Ozu são destaques da mostra" [Mizoguchi and Ozu Are Prominent in the Showing], *Folha de São Paulo*, July 1, 2001; and Luciana Pareja, "Cinema Japão traça um panorama de produção nipônica e de seus diretores, com sessões gratuitas no MAM e na PUC" [MAM's Cinema Japan Brings a Panorama of Japanese Production and Its Directors, with Free Admissions at the MAM and PUC], *Folha de São Paulo*, July 1, 2001.

6. Personal communication (hereafter PC), Katsunori Wakisaka (b. 1923), a prewar child immigrant from Hiroshima prefecture (1928), July 5, 2001.

7. Takeyuki Tsuda, *The Benefits of Being Minority: The Ethnic Status of the Japanese-Brazilians in Brazil*, Working Paper 21, Center for Comparative Immigration Studies, University of California, San Diego, May 2000, 5.

8. Jeffrey Lesser, *Negotiating National Identity: Immigrants, Minorities, and the Struggle for Ethnicity in Brazil* (Durham, NC: Duke University Press, 1999), 16.

9. Holloway, *Immigrants on the Land*, 35–39, 42.

10. Ibid., 42–43; Chiyoko Mita, *"Dekasegi" Kara "Dekassegui" Ye: Burajiru Imin 100-nen ni Miru Hito to Bunka no Dainamizumu* [From "Dekasegi" to "Dekassegui": The Dynamism in Humans and Cultures Observed over the One Hundred Years after the Beginning of Immigration to Brazil] (Tokyo: Fuji Shuppan, 2009), 33–34.

11. Seiichi Izumi, "Burajiru no Nikkei Colônia" [The Nikkei Colony in Brazil], in *Imin: Burajiru Imin no Jittai Chōsa* [The Immigrant: A Survey on Japanese Immigrants in Brazil], ed. Seiichi Izumi (Tokyo: Kokin Shoten, 1957), 18; Hiroshi Saito, *Burajiru no Nihonjin* [The Japanese in Brazil] (Tokyo: Maruzen Kabushiki Kaisha, 1960), 82–83.

12. Rokurō Kōyama, *Imin Yonjūnenshi* [Forty-Year History of (Japanese) Immigration (to Brazil)] (São Paulo: Rokurō Kōyama, 1949), 7–19; Alan Takeo Moriyama, *Imingaisha: Japanese Emigration Companies and Hawaii, 1894–1908* (Honolulu: University of Hawai'i Press, 1985), 49–59.

13. Michio Yamada, *Fune ni Miru Nihonjin Iminshi: Kasato Maru kara Kuruzu Kyakusen Ye* [A History of Emigration through Ships: From the *Kasato Maru* to Cruise Ships] (Tokyo: Chūōkōronsha, 1998), 13.

14. Kōyama, *Imin Yonjūnenshi*, 23–24.

15. Arquivo Público do Estado de São Paulo (Public Archives of the State of São Paulo, hereafter APESP), Seção de Manuscritos [Manuscript Section], CO9826 (Movimento Migratório [Migratory Movement], 1915–1919), "Movimento de entrada de imigrantes, por nacionalidades pelo porto de Santos nos anos de 1912 à 1916" [Movement of Immigrants Entering, by Nationality, through the Port of Santos in the Years from 1912 to 1916].

16. Kōyama, *Imin Yonjūnenshi*, 89–91; and Yamada, *Fune ni Miru*, 65, 68.

17. Yamada, *Fune ni Miru*, 69; and Izumi, "Burajiru no Nikkei Colônia," 22, table 2.

18. Eiichiro Azuma, *Between Two Empires: Race, History, and Transnationalism in Japanese America* (Oxford: Oxford University Press, 2005), 81; Shigeshi Nagata, *Nanbei Ichijun* [A Tour to South America] (1921; repr., Tokyo: Nihon Tosho Sentā, 1998).

19. Hisashi Nagata, "Burajiru Rikkokai Hachijūnen no Rekishi no Nakakara" [From the 80-Year History of the Brazilian Association of Rikkokai], in *Burajiru Rikkyokai Sōritsu Hachijūshunen Kinenshi* [A Commemorative Issue on the 80th Anniversary of the Brazilian Association of Rikkokai], ed. Burajiru Rikkyokai (São Paulo: Burajiru Rikkokai, 2007), 84–94; and Gen Oura, *Yuba Isamu no Shōgai* [The Life of Isamu Yuba] (São Paulo: San Pauro Seinen Toshokan, 2013), 57–58 and 68–69.

20. Teiichi Suzuki, ed., *The Japanese Immigrant in Brazil: Narrative Part* (Tokyo: University of Tokyo Press, 1969), 195.

21. Ikutaro Aoyagi, *Burajiru ni Okeru Nihonjin Hatsutenshi* [The History of Japanese Development in Brazil], vol. 2 (Tokyo: Burajiru ni Okeru Nihonjin Hatsutenshi Kankō Iinkai, 1942), chapters 1–3; and Saito, *Burajiru no Nihonjin*, 216–218.

22. Zaihaku Nihonjin Bunka Kyokai, ed., *Hakukoku Shin Kenpo Shingikai ni Okeru Nihon Imin Kaiseki no Mondai* [The Problem of the Exclusion of the Japanese in the Council on Brazil's New Constitution] (São Paulo: Zaihaku Nihonjin Bunka Kyokai, 1934).

23. Izumi, "Burajiru no Nikkei Colônia," 22, table 2; Yasuo Wakatsuki and Jōji Suzuki, *Kaigai Ijū Seiseku Shiron* [A Historical Discussion of Japan's Overseas Migration Policies] (Tokyo: Fukumura Shuppan, 1974), 67–71.

24. Teiichi Suzuki, *Japanese Immigrant in Brazil*, 194–195.

25. Izumi, "Burajiru no Nikkei Colônia," 29.

26. Takashi Maeyama, "Ethnicity, Secret Societies, and Associations: The Japanese in Brazil," *Comparative Studies in Society and History* 21, no. 4 (1979): 591.

27. Takashi Maeyama, *Ibunka Sesshoku to Aidentiti: Brajiru Shakai to Nikkeijin* [Cultural Contact and Identity: Brazilian Society and Japanese Brazilians] (Tokyo: Ochanomizu Shobo, 2001), 220.

28. Izumi, "Burajiru no Nikkei Colônia," 18, 21.

29. Takashi Maeyama, *Imin no Nihon Kaiki Undo* [Japanese Immigrants' Repatriation Movement to Japan] (Tokyo: NHK, 1982), 36.

30. Izumi, "Burajiru no Nikkei Colônia," 34–36.

31. Tomoo Handa, *Imin no Seikatsu no Rekishi: Brajiru Nikkei Imin no Ayunda Michi* [A History of the Immigrant Life: The Path Japanese Brazilians Walked] (São Paulo: Centro de Estudos Nipo-Brasileiros, 1970), chapters 18–52.

32. Kenren Sanjū-shunen Kinenshi Hensan Iinkai, ed., *Burajiru Kenren Dai-Yongo: Kenren 30 Anos, 1966–1996* [The Fourth Volume of Brazilian Kenren: Kenren 30 Years, 1966–1999] (São Paulo: Burajiru Todōfukenjinkai Rengōkai, 1997), 90, 50, 20.

33. Maeyama, *Imin no Nihon Kaiki Undo*, 94.

34. Emílio Willems, *Aspectos da aculturação dos Japoneses no estado de São Paulo* [Aspects of the Acculturation of the Japanese in the State of São Paulo] (São Paulo: Universidade de São Paulo, Faculdade de Filosofia, Ciencias e Letras, 1948), 109–110.

35. Hiroshi Saito, *Gaikokujin ni Natta Nihonjin: Burajiru Imin no Ikikata to Kawarikata* [The Japanese Who Became Foreigners: How Japanese Immigrants Lived and Changed in Brazil] (Tokyo: Simul Press, 1978), 7–8.

36. Maeyama, *Imin no Nihon Kaiki Undo*, 139–141.

37. Imin 70-nenshi Hensan Iinkai, ed., *Burajiru Nihon Imin 70-nenshi, 1908–1978* [The 70-Year History of Japanese Immigration to Brazil] (São Paulo: Burajiru Nihon Bunka Kyokai, 1980), 308.

38. Burajirujihōsha, ed., *Burajiru Nenkan* [A Yearbook of Brazil] (São Paulo: Burajirujihōsha, 1933), 108.

39. Takashi Maeyama, *Esunishitii to Burajiru Nikkeijin* [Ethnicity and Japanese Brazilians] (Tokyo: Ochanomizu Shobo, 1996), 317.

40. Handa, *Imin no Seikatsu*, 476.

41. Seiichiro Nakajima, "Saikin Burajiru Imin no Jisseikatsu" [The Real Life of Recent Japanese Immigrants in Brazil], in *Ishokumin Kōshūkai Kōenshū* [Collection of Lectures on Immigration and Colonization], ed. Takumukyoku Takumusho (1932; repr., Tokyo: Nihon Tosho Sentā, 1999), 304–305.

42. Bunkyo Yonjūnenshi Hensan Iinkai, ed., *Bunkyo Yonjūnenshi* [Bunkyo's History of Forty Years] (São Paulo: Burajiru Nihon Bunka Kyokai, 1998), 18.

43. Shungoro Wako, *Bauru Kannai no Hōjin* [The Japanese within the Jurisdiction of Bauru] (1939; repr., Tokyo: Nihon Tosho Sentā, 1999), 1–2.

44. APESP, Seção de Manuscritos, CO9831 (Movimento Migratório, 1936–1939) and CO9832 (Movimento Migratório, 1940–1941).

45. Centro de Estudos Nipo-Brasileiros, ed., *Burajiru Nihon Imin Nikkei Shakaishi Nenphō: Handa Tomoo Hen-cho Kaitei Zōho Ban* [Chronological Table of Japanese Immigration to Brazil and Japanese Brazilian Social History: A Revised an Expanded Version of the Original by Tomoo Handa] (São Paulo: Centro de Estudos Nipo-Brasileiros, 1996), 96–97.

46. Imin Hachijūnnenshi Hensan Iinkai, ed. *Burajiru Nihon Imin Hachijūnenshi* [The 80-Year History of Japanese Immigration to Brazil] (São Paulo: Imin Hachijūnnensai Iinkai and Burajiru Nihon Bunka Kyokai, 1991), 146–150.

47. Nihon Maikuro Shashin, ed., "Burajiru Nihon Imin Shiryokan Shozo Bunsho Shiryo" [Documents Housed at the Museum of Japanese Immigration to Brazil], 35 mm microfilm rolls, 73 vols. (Tokyo: Nihon Maikuro Shashin, 1985), vols. 35, 36, and 37.

48. AI, Yasumi Nakayama, June 13, 2008.

49. Imin Hachijūnnenshi, *Burajiru Nihon Imin*, 168–173.

50. Rogério Dezem, *Inventário Deops: Módulo III, Japoneses: Shindô-Renmei: Terrorismo e Represessão* (São Paulo: Arquivo do Estado, Impresa Oficial, 2000), 64–81.

51. *Yomiuri Shimbun*, "Kachigumi Kanashii Hanseiki: Burajiru no San Kazoku Kikoku" [A Sad Half a Century for *Kachigumi:* Three Families Return from Brazil], November 18, 1973, morning edition, 23.

52. Teiichi Suzuki, *Japanese Immigrant in Brazil*, 36, table 2.

53. Paulista Shimbunsha, ed., *Colônia Sangyō Chizu* [The Map of the Colônia's Industry], (São Paulo: Paulista Shimbunsha, 1962), 55–69; Shigetoshi Ogyū, "Burajiru Nikkei Imin Gojūnen no Hensen Katei" [Japanese Brazilians: Their Residential and Occupational Changes in the Last Fifty Years], *Kaigai Jijō* 11, no. 12 (December 1963): 32.

54. Maeyama, *Ibunka Sesshoku*, 24–28.

55. Kaigai Ijū Jigyodan, ed., *Kaigai Ijū Jigyodan Jūnenshi* [Ten-Year History of Japan Emigration Service] (Tokyo: Kaigai Ijū Jigyodan, 1973), 19–21.

56. Sengo Ijū 50-shunen Kinesai Jikko Iinkai, ed., *Burajiru Imin Sengo Ijū no 50-nen* [Fifty Years of Postwar Japanese Immigration to Brazil] (São Paulo: Burajiru-Nippon Ijūsha Kyokai, 2004), 32.

57. Kaikyoren merged into Kaigai Ijū Jigyodan / Japan Emigration Service (JEMIS) in 1963, and was eventually replaced by Kokusai Kyoryoku Kikō / Japan International Cooperation Agency (JICA) in 1974.

58. Diplomatic Archives of the Ministry of Foreign Affairs of Japan, J'-1-1-0-1, *Honpō Ijū Hōki Narabini Seisaku Kankei Zattuken* [Materials on State Laws and Policies Concerning Overseas Migration], vol. 3 (1957).

59. Kaigai Ijū Jigyodan, *Kaigai Ijū Jigyodan Jūnenshi*, 30–37.

60. Seishi Yonhyakunen Saiten Nihonjin Kyoryokuka, ed., *São Paulo Yonhyaku-nensai, 1554–1954* [The Celebrations on the 400th Year of São Paulo City, 1554–1954] (São Paulo: Seishi Yonhyakunen Saiten Nihonjin Kyoryokukai, 1957), 67–71.

61. Bunkyo Yonjūnenshi, *Bunkyo Yonjūnenshi*, 218–220.

62. Masatake Suzuki, *Suzuki Teiichi: Burajiru Nikkei Shakai ni Ikita Kisai no Shogai* [Teiichi Suzuki: The Life of a Genius Who Lived in the Brazilian Nikkei Society] (São Paulo: Centro de Estudos Nipo-Brasileiros, 2007), chapter 7.

63. Bunkyo Yonjūnenshi, *Bunkyo Yonjūnenshi*, chapter 4.

64. Kiyoshi Yamamoto, "Zaihaku Nikkeijin Jinko Suikei" [Inductive Statistics of the Nikkei Population in Brazil], *Jidai*, no. 8 (March 1949): 32 (table 4).

65. Paulista Shimbunsha, ed., *Paulista Nenkan 1963-nenban* [Paulista Yearbook of 1963] (São Paulo: Paulista Shimbunsha, 1963), 21.

66. Bunkyo Yonjūnenshi, *Bunkyo Yonjūnenshi*, 264, 266.

67. Maeyama, *Esuniciti to Burajiru Nikkeijin*, 238.

68. Takashi Maeyama, "Nisei no Naka no Nihon" [Japan within the Nisei], in *Raten-teki Nihonjin: Burajiru Nisei no Hatsugen* [The Latin Japanese: Opinions Expressed by the Nisei of Brazil], ed. Morio Ōno (Tokyo: NHK, 1969), 143; Maeyama, *Ibuka Sesshoku to Aidentiti*, 25, 27.

69. Imin Hachijūnnenshi, *Burajiru Nihon Imin*, 264–267; Handa, *Imin no Seikatsu*, chapter 22; Hiroshi Saito, *Gaikokujin*, 105–118.

70. Lesser, *Discontented Diaspora*, chapters 3–5.

71. PC, Masao Daigo (b. 1935), a postwar immigrant (1960), April 28, 2012.

72. Centro de Estudos Nipo-Brasileiros, *Burajiru ni Okeru*, 37 (table 2.20), 120 (table 4.24).

73. Mita, *"Dekasegi" Kara*, 153.

74. Masato Ninomiya, "Japanese Brazilian Historical Overview," in *Encyclopedia of Japanese Descendants in the Americas: An Illustrated History of the Nikkei*, ed. Akemi Kikumura-Yano (Walnut Creek, CA: Alta Mira Press, 2002), 118.

75. Yoko Sellek, "Nikkeijin: The Phenomenon of Return Migration," in *Japan's Minorities: The Illusion of Homogeneity*, ed. Michael Weiner (London: Routledge, 1997),

190–191; and Keiko Yamanaka, "Return Migration of Japanese-Brazilians to Japan: The Nikkeijin as Ethnic Minority and Political Construct," *Diaspora* 5, no. 1 (1996): 80.

76. Kiyoto Tanno, "Gaikokujin Rōdōsha Mondai no Kongen wa Doko ni Arunoka" [Where Are the Roots of the Issues of Foreign Workers?], *Nihon Rōdō Kenkyu Zasshi*, no. 587 (June 2009): 30; Betsy Brody, *Opening the Doors: Immigration, Ethnicity, and Globalization in Japan* (New York: Routledge, 2001), chapter 5; data compiled by the Centro de Informação e Apoio ao Trabalhador no Exterior (Center of Information and Help for Emigrant Workers, or CIATE), June 1999.

77. Japan, Ministry of Foreign Affairs, "Zainich Burajirujin ni Kansuru Deita" [Data on Brazilians Residing in Japan], June 2005, www.mofa.go.jp/mofaj/area/latin america/kaigi/brazil/data.html, accessed March 21, 2012.

78. Naoto Higuchi and Kiyoto Tanno, "What's Driving Brazil-Japan Migration? The Making and Remaking of Brazilian Niche in Japan," *International Journal of Japanese Sociology*, no. 12 (2003): 33–38.

79. Kazuaki Tezuka, Hiroshi Komai, Goro Oda, and Taka-aki Ogata, eds., *Gaikokujin Rōdōsha no Shūrō Jittai: Sōgōteki Jittai Hokokushū* [Employment of Foreign Guest Workers in Japan: A Thorough Report on the Reality] (Tokyo: Akashi Shoten, 1992), 252.

80. Sellek, "Nikkeijin," 193.

81. Nyukan Kyokai / Japan Immigration Association, ed., *Zairyu Gaikokujin Tōkei Heisei 21-nenban / Statistics on the Foreigners Registered in Japan 2009* (Tokyo: Nyukan Kyokai / Japan Immigration Association, 2010), 76–77, table 4.

82. Cláudia Emi and Andréia Ferreira, "Japão ou Brasil," *Made in Japan*, no. 9 (June 1998): 30–39, 34.

83. Jōmō Shimbunsha, ed., *Samba no Machi Kara: Gaikokujin to Tomo ni ikiru Gunma Ōizumi* [From a Town of Samba: Living with Foreigners in Oizumi of Gunma] (Maebashi-shi, Japan: Jōmō Shimbunsha, 1997), 108–110, 114–116.

84. Masayuki Fukasawa, *Parareru Wārudo* [Parallel World] (Tokyo: Ushio Shuppan, 1999), 186–188.

85. Angelo Ishi, "Searching Home, Wealth, Pride, and 'Class': Japanese Brazilians in the 'Land of Yen,'" in *In Search for Home Abroad: Japanese Brazilians and the Transnational Moment*, ed. Jeffery Lesser (Durham, NC: Duke University Press, 2003), 92.

86. Andréia Ferreira and Nelson Watanabe, "Hora de Voltar," *Made in Japan*, no. 26 (June 1999): 26–29; CIATE, ed., *Resultado de Questionários sobre Dekasseguis* [Results of Questionnaires on Dekasseguis] (São Paulo: CITAE, 1999), 12.

87. Andréia Ferreira, "Os novos imigrantes," *Made in Japan*, no. 21 (June 1998): 20.

88. Daniel Touro Linger, *No One Home: Brazilian Selves Made in Japan* (Stanford, CA: Stanford University Press, 2001).

89. Fukasawa, *Parareru Wārudo*, 35.

90. *Veja*, "O povo da diáspora," 24, no. 32 (August 7, 1991): 37.

91. Koichi Mori, "Burajiru kara no Nikkeijin Dekassegui no Tokucho to Suii" [Characteristics and Changes among the *Dekassegui* Workers from Brazil], in *Kyodo Kenkyu Dekassegui Nikkei Brajirujin*, ed. Masako Watanebe, vol. 1, *Ronbun-hen: Shūrō*

to Seikatu [Articles: Employment and Life], 2 vols. (Tokyo: Akashi Shoten, 1995), 505–515; Kiyoto Tanno, "Sōgō Dekaseguigyo no Tanjō: Nikkei Ryokosha no Henyo to Burajiru Nikkei Komuniti no Shihon Chikuseki" [The Birth of General *Dekassegui* Business: Transformation of Nikkei Travel Agencies and the Japanese Brazilian Community's Capital Accumulation," Ōhara Shakai Mondai Kenkyoso Zasshi, no. 573 (August 2006): 57–58.

92. AI, Tadao Ebihara (b. 1949), June 13, 2013.

93. AI, Tsuruyo Sugimoto, June 16, 2010.

94. AI, Hideto Miyazaki (b. 1950), June 13, 2013; Kiyoto Tanno, "Sōgō Dekasseguigyo no Tanjo: Nikkei Ryokōsha no Henyo to Burajiru Nikkei Komuniti no Shihon Chikuseki" [The Birth of General *Dekassegui* Business: Transformation of Nikkei Travel Agencies and Japanese Brazilian Community's Capital Accumulation"], *Ōhara Shakai Mondai Kenkyusho Zasshi*, no. 573 (August 2006): 53–54.

95. Higuchi and Tanno, "What's Driving Brazil-Japan Migration?," 42.

96. PC, Shōzō Otokawa, superintendent of CIATE, June 14, 1999.

97. Teiichi Suzuki, *Japanese Immigrant in Brazil*, 169–191.

98. AI, Wagner M. Horiuchi, June 10, 2002.

99. Takamich Kajita, Kiyoto Tanno, and Naoto Higuchi, *Kao no Mienai Teijūka: Nikkei Burajirujin to Kokka Shijō Imin Nettowāku / Invisible Residents: Japanese Brazilians vis-à-vis the State, the Market, and the Immigrant Network* (Nagoya-shi, Japan: Nagoya Daigaku Shuppankai, 2005), 266–267.

100. Masayuki Fukasawa, "Iminka-suru Dekasegui-tachi, Ne o Haru Zainichi Hakujin Shakai, Rensai Dai 1-kai: Jitsu wa 33 man-nin ga Nihon Zaijū" [*Dekasseguis* Becoming Immigrants, Brazilian Society Rooting in Japan, Series No. 1: In Reality 330,000 Are Living in Japan], *Nikkey Shimbun*, August 24, 2007, www.nikkeyshimbun .com.br/070824-71colonia.html, accessed April 23, 2008.

101. *Nikkey Shimbun*, "Zainichi Hakujin 31-mannin ni: Izen Tsuzuku Teijū no Nami" [More than 310,000 Brazilians Living in Japan: Their Wave of Settlement Continues], May 24, 2007, www.nikkeyshimbun.com.br/07054-73colonia.html, accessed June 10, 2007.

102. Cíntia Yamashiro, "Miss Centenário Brasil-Japão é de Mogi das Cruzes: Katarina Eiko Nakahara, de 26 anos, foi eleita a nikkei mais bonita no fim de maio," *Revista Mundo OK*, no. 7 (June 2008): 40; *Nikkey Shimbun,* "Misu Hyakushunen, Mottomo Utsukushi Nikkei Josei Kettei!" [Miss Centenrary, the Most Beautiful Nikkei Woman Chosen!], May 21, 2008, www.nikkeyshimbun.com.br/080521-71colonia.html, accessed March 19, 2012; and *Nikkey Shimbun*, "Oh Mimi Ko Mimi" [Big Ears, Small Ears], March 26, 2010, http://200.218.30.171/nikkey/html/show/100326-74colonia.html, accessed March 19, 2012.

103. Kenren Sanjū-shunen, *Burajiru Kenren Dai-Yongo*, 248–249; Japan, Ministry of Foreign Affairs, "Zaigai Senkyo" [Absentee-Balloting System for Japanese Citizens Overseas], www.mofa.go.jp/mofaj/toko/senkyo/vote1.html, accessed on October 15, 2011.

104. *Nikkey Shimbun*, "65-nen Mae no Onshu o Koete: Tojisha Hidaka ga Kataru Anohi (9) Tsukimono ga Ochita Syunkan: Hyakunensai de Kōtaishi Omukae" [Beyond

the Grievance He Had 65 Years Ago: The Very Day Hidaka, the Person Concerned, Talked about, no. 9: The Moment His Obsession Disappeared by Welcoming the Crown Prince], February 18, 2011, http://200.218.30.171/nikkey/html/show/110218-72colonia .html, accessed February 2, 2012.

105. AI, Iossuke Tanaka, June 25, 2008.

106. *Veja*, "Ao gusto brasileiro: Comida japonesa se torna popular como o churrasco nas principais capitais do Brasil" [To the Brazilian Taste: Japanese Food Becomes Popular Like the Barbecue in the Main Capitals of Brazil], 36, no. 28 (June 16, 2003): 83.

107. Leo Nishihata, "Shushi oxente" [Amazing Sushi of the Northeast], in *100 anos da imigração japonesa: As surpreendentes histórias do povo que ajudou a mudar o Brasil*, ed. Editora Abril (São Paulo: Editora Abril, 2008), 86–91.

108. Japan, Ministry of Justice, "Zairyu Gaikokujin Tōkei Tōkeihyo" [Stastitical Tables of Foreign Residents in Japan], www.moj.go.jp/housei/toukei/toukei_ichiran _touroku.html, accessed May 24, 2015; Coco Masters, "Japan to Immigrants: Thanks, but You Can Go Home Now," *Time*, April 20, 2009, www.time.com/time/world/article /0,8599,1892469,00.html, accessed April 20, 2009; *Nikkey Shimbun*, "Kikoku Shienkin, Shinseishasu Zentai de 2 mannin, Burajiru ga 9 wari Shimeru" [Government-Sponsored Repatriation: 20,000 Applied and Brazilians Constitute 90 percent], April 20, 2010, http://200.218.30.171/nikkey/html/show/100420-61colonia.html, accessed March 30, 2012; *Nikkey Shimbun*, "Shinsaigo Kihakusha Hakujin Sōsū wa Yaku 3-zennin: Zaikaku 22-mannin" [The Number of Brazilians Who Have Gone Back to Brazil after the (Great Tohoku) Earthquake Is Approximately 3,000; Total of Brazilians in Japan Is Around 220,000], October 5, 2011, www.nikkeyshimbun.com.br/nikkey/html/show /111005-71colonia.html, accessed October 17, 2011.

CHAPTER TWO: PREWAR CHILD IMMIGRANTS
AND THEIR JAPANESE IDENTITY

1. Author interview (hereafter AI), Sumiko Mizumoto (1920–2011), June 19, 2001.

2. Tomoo Handa, *Imin no Seikatsu: Brajiru Nikkei Imin no Ayunda Michi* [A History of the Immigrant Life: The Path Japanese Brazilians Walked] (São Paulo: Centro de Estudos Nipo-Brasileiros, 1970), 490–491; Shungoro Wako, *Bauru Kannai no Hōjin* [The Japanese within the Jurisdiction of Bauru] (1939; repr., Tokyo: Nihon Tosho Sentā, 1999), 17.

3. Katsuo Uchiyama, *Sōbō no 92-nen: Burajiru Imin no Kiroku* [The Nation's 92 Years: A Record of Japanese Immigration to Brazil] (Tokyo: Tokyo Shimbun Shuppankyoku, 2001), 130–143.

4. Torahiko Tamiya, *Burajiru no Nihonjin* [The Japanese in Brazil] (Tokyo: Asahi Shimbunsha, 1975), 129–141.

5. Gunki Motonaga, "Horonagaku Soshite Tanoshikatta Ano Jidai no Koto: Bunkyo Uramenshi no Ichibu" [On Those Old Days with Bittersweet Memories: Part of the Hidden History of Bunkyo], in *Bunkyo Yonjūnenshi*, ed. Bunkyo Yonjūnenshi Hensan Iinkai (São Paulo: Burajiru Nihon Bunka Kyokai, 1998), 238.

6. Kinenshi Henshū Iinkai, ed., *Burajiru Nikkei Rōjin Kurabu Rengōkai 30-nen no Ayumi: Rōkuren Setsuritsu 30-shūnen Kinen* [The Course of 30 Years for the Association of the Brazilian Nikkei Clubs for the Elderly: Commemoration of Rōkuren's 30th Anniversary] (São Paulo: Burajiru Nikkei Rōjin Kurabu Rengōkai, 2008).

7. AI, Yoshie Miyano, June 13, 1999; AI, Tsuruyo Sugimoto, June 16, 2010.

8. On Brazil's "racial democracy," see, for instance, Edward E. Telles, *Race in Another America: The Significance of Skin Color in Brazil* (Princeton, NJ: Princeton University Press, 2004), 33–38.

9. Takashi Maeyama, *Esuniciti to Burajiru Nikkeijin* [Ethnicity and Japanese Brazilians] (Tokyo: Ochanomizu Shobo, 1996), 209–229.

10. Seiichi Izumi, "Burajiru no Nikkei Colônia" [The Nikkei Colony in Brazil], in *Imin: Burajiru Imin no Jittai Chōsa* [The Immigrant: A Survey on Japanese Immigrants in Brazil], ed. Seiichi Izumi (Tokyo: Kokin Shoten, 1957), 29–32.

11. AI, Sumiko Mizumoto, June 19, 2001.

12. AI, Shizu Saito, July 1, 2001.

13. AI, Yasumi Nakayama, June 8, 2010; Iossuke Tanaka, *Senzen Imin Kōkai Monogatari* [Prewar Immigrants' Stories of Voyage] (São Paulo: Centro de Estudos Nipo-Brasileiros, 2010), 16.

14. AI, Shizu Saito, July 1, 2002.

15. AI, Tsuruyo Sugimoto, June 16, 2010.

16. Takashi Maeyama, *Imin no Nihon Kaiki Undo* [Japanese Immigrants' Repatriation Movement to Japan] (Tokyo: NHK, 1982), 63–70.

17. AI, Masashi Sugimoto, June 14, 2010.

18. AI, Tsutomu Akahoshi, July 3, 2002.

19. AI, Iossuke Tanaka, June 24, 2008.

20. Shigeichi Sakai, *Burajiru Nikki* [A Diary in Brazil] (Tokyo: Kawadeshobō Shinsha, 1957), 16–21.

21. AI, Sumiko Mizumoto, June 19, 2001.

22. AI, Shizu Saito, July 1, 2002.

23. Izumi, "Burajiru no Nikkei Colônia," 38–41.

24. Teiichi Suzuki, ed., *The Japanese Immigrant in Brazil: Narrative Part* (Tokyo: University of Tokyo Press, 1969), 215–216.

25. Hiroshi Saito, *Burajiru no Nihonjin* [The Japanese in Brazil] (Tokyo: Maruzen Kabushiki Kaisha, 1960), 265.

26. AI, Shizu Saito, July 1, 2002.

27. AI, Kazuyo Yoneda, June 13, 2010.

28. AI, Tsuruko Kikuchi, June 6, 2002.

29. Ibid.

30. Handa, *Imin no Seikatsu,* 314–315.

31. Izumi, "Burajiru no Nikkei Colônina," 63–64.

32. Kiyoshi Shima, "Chihō Shōtoshi no Nikkei Colônia: Sorocaba-sen Álvares Machado no Jirei" [The Nikkei Colônia in a Small Provincial City: The Case of

Álvares Machado on the Sorocaba Line," in *Imin: Burajiru Imin no Jittai Chōsa* [The Immigrant: A Survey on Japanese Immigrants in Brazil], ed. Seiichi Izumi (Tokyo: Kokin Shoten, 1957), 447.

33. AI, Yoshie Miyano, June 13, 1999.

34. AI, Kazuyo Yoneda, June 13, 2010.

35. Tomoo Handa, *Burajiru Imin no Seikatsu: Handa Tomoo Gabunshū* [The Life of Japanese Immigrants in Brazil: Collection of Paintings and Essays by Tomoo Handa] (Akita: Mumyōsha Shuppan, 1986), 85.

36. AI, Tsuruyo Sugimoto, June 16, 2010.

37. AI, Yasuto Shigeoka, June 24, 2008.

38. Sonya Lipsett-Rivera, "A Slap in the Face of Honor: Social Transgression and Women in Late Colonial Mexico," in *The Faces of Honor: Sex, Shame, and Violence in Colonial Latin America,* ed. Lyman L. Johnson and Sonya Lipsett-Rivera (Albuquerque: University of New Mexico Press, 1998), 179.

39. Sakai, *Burajiru Nikki,* 71–75.

40. Hiroshi Saito, "Seishu Imin no Dōka to Zatkkon: Willems-shi no Kenkyu o Yonde" [Japanese Immigrants' Assimilation and Mixed Marriage in São Paulo: Based on a Reading of Mr. Willems's Study," *Jidai,* no. 8 (March 1949): 9.

41. AI, Sumiko Mizumoto, June 19, 2001.

42. Ibid.

43. Izumi, "Burajiru no Nikkei Colônia," 45.

44. AI, Yoshiro Fujita, June 14, 2008; AI, Masuji Kiyotani and Tumoru Kiyotani, June 14, 2002.

45. AI, Yasumi Nakayama, June 13, 2008.

46. AI, Hirofumi Ikesaki, June 26, 2008.

47. Rokurō Kōyama, *Imin Yonjūnenshi* [Forty-Year History of (Japanese) Immigration (to Brazil)] (São Paulo: Rokurō Kōyama, 1949), 285; Masao Daigo, *Minami Hankyū no za Japanīzu: Burajiru ni Okeru Nihonjin no Tekiō* [The Japanese in the Southern Hemisphere: The Japanese's Adaptation in Brazil] (Tokyo: Bungeishunjūsha, 1981), 197–198.

48. AI, Sumu Arata, June 11, 2010; AI, Masayuki Mizuno, June 15, 2013.

49. AI, Yasuto Shigeoka, June 20, 2008, and July 1, 2008.

50. AI, Yoshiaki Umezaki, June 16, 2010; AI, Yasumi Nakayama, June 8, 2010.

51. AI, Shizu Saito, July 1, 2002.

52. AI, Toshi Yamane, June 21, 2002.

53. AI, Tsuruko Kikuchi, June 6, 2002.

54. AI, Haruko Fujitani, January 10, 1998.

55. AI, Sumiko Mizumoto, June 19, 2001.

56. Laís de Barros Monteiro Guimarães, *Liberdade* (São Paulo: Prefeitura do Municipio de São Paulo, Secretaria Municipal de Cultura, 1979), 91–93.

57. AI, Masuji Kiyotani, June 14, 2002.

58. Sumiko Mizumoto, *Rodeira, Ashita Mata: Burajiru 47-nen no Kiroku* [Small

Wheel, See You Again Tomorrow: A Record of My 47 Years in Brazil] (Tokyo: Seibunsha, 1979), 116.

59. Ibid., 115–116.

60. Saito, *Burajiru to Nihonjin*, 9, 12.

61. Masuji Kiyotani, *Tōi Hibi no Koto* [On Those Old Days] (São Paulo: Masuji Kiyotani, 1985), 121–128.

62. Burajiru Okinawa Kenjinkai Nihongo Henshu Iinkai, ed., *Burajiru Okinawa-kenjin Iminshi: Kasato Maru kara 90-nen* [The History of Okinawan Immigration: 90 Years since the *Kasato Maru*] (São Paulo: Associação Okinawa Kenjin do Brasil, 2000), 422, 429–430.

63. *Colônia*, "Jun-Nisei Zadankai: 'Umoreta Sedai' wa Kataru" [A Roundtable Discussion by Quasi-Niseis: "A Buried Generation" Speaks], no. 86 (1970): 24–32.

64. Ibid., 26.

65. Ibid., 27–29.

66. Ibid., 30–31.

67. Atsushi Imoto, "Jun-Nisei Zadankai ni Shusseki Shite: Nanika o Gisei ni Shinakerebararararai Jidai ga Atta" [Having Attended the Roundtable Discussion on the Quasi-Nisei: There Was a Time When Something Had to Be Sacrificed], *Colônia*, no. 86 (1970): 23.

68. Takashi Maeyama, "Kagaisha Fumei no Higaisha: Colônia Bungakuron Oboegaki" [Victims without Victimizers: A Note on the Discussions on *Colônia*'s Literature], *Colônia Bungaku*, no. 26 (March 1975): 72–74.

69. *Colônia*, "Rōgo no Sekkei" [Retirement Plans], no. 29 (July 1961): 20–21; *Colônia*, "Colônia no Shiwa" [Colônia's Wrinkles], no. 47 (February 1965): 2–31.

70. Chiyoko Mita, *"Dekasegi" Kara "Dekassegui" Ye: Burajiru Imin 100-nen ni miru Hito to Bunka no Dainamizumu* [From "Dekasegi" to "Dekassegui": The Dynamism in Humans and Cultures Observed over the One Hundred Years after the Beginning of Immigration to Brazil]. Tokyo: Fuji Shuppan, 2009), 132.

71. Masao Suzuki, "Kieta Sora no Kakehashi: JAL Kaisōroku (3): VARIG ga Hito-ashi Hayaku Chokkobin o Shūshū" [The Disappeared Sky Bridge: Recollections of Japan Air Lines, No. 3: VARIG Started Its Direct Flight Earlier], *São Paulo Shimbun*, September 29, 2011, www.saopauloshimbun.com/index.php/conteudo/show/id/6024/cat/105, accessed January 29, 2012; Masao Suzuki, "Kieta Sora no Kakehashi: JAL Kaisōroku (4): Osato Gaeri to Banpaku ga Ōkina Tenki" [The Disappeared Sky Bridge: Recollections of Japan Air Lines, No. 4: Visiting Homeland and Expo Became the Big Turning Point], *São Paulo Shimbun*, September 30, 2011, www.saopauloshimbun.com/index.php/conteudo/show/id/6044/cat/105, accessed January 29, 2012.

72. Mita, *"Dekasegi" Kara*, 133.

73. Chikako Hironaka, *Inochi Ori-Ori* [Moments of Life] (São Paulo: Nippaku Mainichi Shimbunsha, 1994), 3–4, 16, 23–24, 32.

74. AI, Sumiko Mizumoto, June 19, 2001.

75. Ibid.

76. Esperança Fujinkai, ed., *Relação de Associadas (1998)* [Register of Association Members (1998)] (São Paulo: Esperança Fujinkai, 1998).

77. Hironaka, *Inochi Ori-Ori,* 140.

78. Gen Oura, *Kodomo Imin Oura Fumio: Noson ni Ikiru Jun-Nisei no Kisei* [Child Immigrant Fumio Oura: The Course of a Quasi-Nisei Living in an Agricultural Village] (São Paulo: Fumio Oura, 2012).

CHAPTER THREE: NISEIS AND THEIR BRAZILIAN IDENTITY

1. Author interview (hereafter AI), Iossuke Tanaka, June 25, 2008.

2. Jeffrey Lesser, *A Discontened Diaspora: Japanese-Brazilians and the Meanings of Ethnic Militancy* (Durham, NC: Duke University Press, 2007), 141.

3. Masayoshi Norichika, "'Garantido' Shōkō" [Small Thoughts on "Guaranteed"], *São Paulo Shimbun* 1 (May 8, 2008); 2 (May 15, 2008); and 3 (May 22, 2008).

4. AI, Iossuke Tanaka, June 25, 2008.

5. Hiroshi Saito, *Burajiru to Nihonjin: Ibunka ni Ikite 50-nen* [Brazil and the Japanese: Living 50 Years as a Bridge] (Tokyo: Simul Press, 1984), 7–8.

6. Shungoro Wako, *Bauru Kannai no Hōjin* [The Japanese within the Jurisdiction of Bauru] (1939; repr., Tokyo: Nihon Tosho Sentā, 1999), 18; Takashi Maeyama, *Esunisiti to Burajuru Nikkeijin* [Ethnicity and Japanese Brazilians] (Tokyo: Ochanomizu Shobo, 1996), 338–339.

7. Maeyama, *Esuniciti to Burajiru Nikkeijin,* 356.

8. Sho Kawahara, "Dai Nisei no Shichō" [The *Dai*-Nisei's Current Trend of Thought], *Gakuyu,* no. 4 (August 1936): 21.

9. Maeyama, *Esunisiti to Burajiru Nikkeijin,* 344–345.

10. Kawahara, "Dai Nisei no Shichō," 18 and 21. There is no breakdown by sex.

11. Maeyama, *Esunisiti to Burajiru Nikkeijin,* 346, table 2-1.

12. José Yamashiro, "Burajiru to Nihon" [Brazil and Japan], in *Ratenteki Nihonjin: Burajiru Nisei no Hatsugen* [The Latin Japanese: Opinions Expressed by the Nisei of Brazil], ed. Morio Ōno (Tokyo: NHK, 1969), 98–102; and Ryukiti Yamashiro, "Watakushi no Kiroku" [A Record of Myself], unpublished manuscript dated September 1959, 156–161, 169, housed at the MHIJB.

13. Kenro Shimamoto, "Wareware no Shinjo" [Our Feelings], *Gakuyu,* no. 4 (August 1936): 17.

14. Maeyama, *Esunisiti to Burajiru Nikkeijin,* 357.

15. *Gakuyu,* "Seishi Hojin Kishukusha Tanboki" [Reports on Japanese Dormitories in São Paulo City], no. 8 (September 1938): 70–88.

16. "Dai-Nisei Shokun to Nihon Bunka o Kataru" [A Talk on Japanese Culture with *Dai*-Nisei Men], *Bunka* 11, no. 1 (November 1938): 30, 26.

17. Maeyama, *Esunisiti to Burajiru Nikkeijin,* 344.

18. Katsuo Uchiyama, *Sōbō no 92-nen: Burajiru Imin no Kiroku* [The Nation's 92 Years: A Record of Japanese Immigration to Brazil] (Tokyo: Tokyo Shimbun Shuppankyoku, 2001), 98–115.

19. Paulista Shimbunsha, ed., *Colônia Sangyō Chizu* [The Map of the Colônia's Industry] (São Paulo: Paulista Shimbunsha, 1962), 6.

20. AI, Iossuke Tanaka, June 24, 2008.

21. AI, Atsushi Yamauchi, June 17, 2010.

22. AI, Tiyoko Oba, June 28, 2005; AI, Yukie Yano, January 8, 1998; AI, Eiko Kanazawa, June 25, 2001.

23. Imin 70-nenshi Hensan Iinkai, ed., *Burajiru Nihon Imin 70-nenshi, 1908–1978* [The 70-Year History of Japanese Immigration to Brazil] (São Paulo: Burajiru Nihon Bunka Kyokai, 1980), 310; and Bunkyo Yonjūnenshi Hensan Iinkai, ed., *Bunkyo Yonjūnenshi* [Bunkyo's History of Forty Years] (São Paulo: Burajiru Nihon Bunka Kyokai, 1998), 223.

24. AI, Iossuke Tanaka, June 24, 2008; and AI, Atsushi Yamauchi, June 17, 2010.

25. Personal communication (hereafter PC), Bernardo Y. Shinohara (b. 1944), June 6, 2010.

26. Paulista Shimbunsha, ed., *Paulista Nenkan 1950-nenban* [Paulista Yearbook of 1950] (São Paulo: Paulista Shinbunsha, 1950), 131, 135, 132.

27. Tomoo Handa, *Imin no Seikatsu no Rekishi: Brajiru Nikkei Imin no Ayunda Michi* [A History of the Immigrant Life: The Path Japanese Brazilians Walked] (São Paulo: Centro de Estudos Nipo-Brasileiros, 1970), 506.

28. Seiichi Izumi, "Burajiru no Nikkei Colônia" [The Nikkei Colony in Brazil], in *Imin: Burajiru Imin no Jittai Chōsa* [The Immigrant: A Survey on Japanese Immigrants in Brazil], ed. Seiichi Izumi (Tokyo: Kokin Shoten, 1957), 107.

29. Ibid., 65–66.

30. AI, Iossuke Tanaka, June 25, 2008.

31. AI, Iossuke Tanaka, June 24 and 25, 2008.

32. São Paulo Gakuseikai, ed. *Nijūnen no Ayumi* [The Course of Twenty Years] (São Paulo: São Paulo Gakuseikai, 1974), 11 and 13.

33. AI, Atsushi Yamauchi, June 17, 2010.

34. AI, Iossuke Tanaka, June 25, 2008. As of 1950, it took six years to finish USP Law School.

35. Paulista Shimbunsha, *Paulista Nenkan 1950-nenban,* 132–133.

36. AI, Nobue Miyazaki, June 26, 2002.

37. Tomie Higuchi, "Shinshin Gakushi no Haha wa Kataru (1): Kankyo no Motsu Chikara" [Mothers of Emerging University Graduates Talk, No. 1: The Power of an Environment], *Kaihō,* no. 5 (March–April 1957): 34–36.

38. AI, Midory Kimura Figuchi, January 22 and 23, 1998.

39. AI, Shizue Higaki Arai, June 9, 2008.

40. AI, Senichi Adachi, July 5, 2002.

41. AI, Atsushi Yamauchi, June 17, 2010.

42. Takashi Maeyama, "Nisei no Naka no Nihon" [Japan within the Nisei], in *Ratenteki Nihonjin: Burajiru Nisei no Hatsugen* [The Latin Japanese: Opinions Expressed by the Nisei of Brazil], ed. Morio Ōno (Tokyo: NHK, 1969), 145–146.

43. AI, Iossuke Tanaka, June 25, 2008.

44. Senichi Adachi, "Nihon Bunka Sentā no Dekiru Made: Keika Hokoku ni Kaete" [Until the Center of Japanese Culture Was Completed: In Place of a Report on Its Process], in *Colônia Bekkan: Nihon Bunka Sentā Rakusei Kinengo* [*Colônia* Special Issue in Commemoration of the Inauguration of the Center of Japanese Culture] (São Paulo: São Paulo Nihon Bunka Kyokai, 1964), 64–65.

45. AI, Iossuke Tanaka, June 25, 2008.

46. AI, Atsushi Yamauchi, June 17, 2010.

47. Toshio Sonehara, "Nisei wa Nani o Dō Suruka: Dokutoku no Bakku Bōnn Keisei no Tameni" [What and How Do the Nisei Do It: For the Purpose of Creating Their Own Backbone], *Kaihō*, no. 19 (July–August 1959): 11–12.

48. AI, Iossuke Tanaka, June 25, 2008.

49. *Colônia*, "Zadankai: Seinen no Ikigai o Saguru" [Roundtable Discussion: Seeking Purposes of Life for Young Men], no. 30 (September 1961): 16–19.

50. *Asahi Shimbun*, "Nanbei no Nikkeijin: Nihon no Shimbunkisha wa Kō Mita" [The Nikkeis in South America: This Is the Way a Japanese Newspaper Reporter Perceived Them] (1965), reprinted in *Nippak Mainichi Shimbun Shin-nen Tokubetsugo 1966* [Nippak Mainichi Shimbun New Year Special Issue 1966] (São Paulo: Nippak Mainichi Shimbunsha, 1966), n.p.

51. Burajiru Rikkokai, ed. *Burajiru Rikkokai Yonjūnenshi* [Forty-Year History of the Brazilian Association of Rikkokai] (São Paulo: Burajiru Rikkokai, 1966), 156, 297; AI, Iossuke Tanaka, June 25, 2008; AI, Atsushi Yamauchi, June 17, 2010.

52. AI, Atsushi Yamauchi, June 17, 2010.

53. AI, Senichi Adachi, July 5, 2002.

54. PC, Bernardo Y. Shinohara, February 12, 2012.

55. Teiichi Suzuki, ed., *The Japanese Immigrant in Brazil: Narrative Part* (Tokyo: University of Tokyo Press, 1969), 159, table 156.

56. Hiroshi Nagai, "Dōka to Yūryhoji" [Assimilation and Excellent Offspring], *Colônia*, no. 60 (August–September 1966): 18–20; and Kōnosuke Ozeki, "Fuetekita Konketsukon: Taikyokutekina Tachibakara Kangaeyō" [The Increase of Interracial Marriages: Let's Take a Broad View of the Situation], *Colônia*, no. 53 (August 1965): 3.

57. Centro de Estudos Nipo-Brasileiros, ed., *Burajiru Nihon Imin Nikkei Shakaishi Nenphō: Handa Tomoo Hen-cho Kaitei Zōho Ban* [Chronological Table of Japanese Immigration to Brazil and Japanese Brazilian Social History: A Revised an Expanded Version of the Original by Tomoo Handa], (São Paulo: Centro de Estudos Nipo-Brasileiros, 1996), 152.

58. *Colônia*, "Zadankai: Shokuba no Mikon Nisei Danjo no Renai to Kekkon-kan" [Roundtable Discussion: Single, Professional Nisei Men and Women's Perception of Dating and Marriage], no. 53 (August 1965): 7.

59. Burajiru Rikkokai, *Burajiru Rikkokai Yonjūnenshi*, 292–307.

60. *Colônia*, "Colônia no Kekkon Mondai: Sōdan o Ukeru Mono no Tachiba kara" [Marriage Problems in the Colônia: From the Position of Marriage Consultants], no. 43 (October 1964): 6.

61. *Colônia*, "Zadankai: Shokuba no Mikon Nisei-Danjo," 7–8.

62. *Colônia*, "Konohito o Tazunete: Nōgaku Hakushi Ikuta Hiroshi-shi" [Interview of Hiroshi Ikuta, Doctor of Agriculture], no. 51 (June 1965): 19.

63. Tsuyako Hirai, "Seishinteki Seikatu eno Kyoryoku o" [For the Sake of Our Cooperation in Spiritual Life], *Kaihō*, no. 8 (September–October 1957): 17; *Colônia*, "Zadankai: Hahaoya no Me kara Mita Nisei no Shomondai" [Roundtable Discussion: Various Problems the Nisei Are Facing from the Perspectives of their Mothers], no. 57 (February–March 1966): 5; Susumu Miyao, "Nihon Imin no Ayumi to Nisei" [The Path of Japanese Immigrants and the Nisei], in *Ratenteki Nihonin: Burajiru Nisei no Hatsugen* [The Latin Japanese: Opinions Expressed by the Nisei of Brazil], ed. Morio Ōno (Tokyo: NHK, 1969), 91.

64. AI, Sandra Akahoshi, July 3, 2002.

65. AI, Shizu Saito, July 1, 2002; AI, Masami Takiyama, July 4, 2002; AI, Emi Ito, January 9, 1998 and June 25, 2008.

66. Miyao, "Nihon Imin no Ayumi to Nisei," 92.

67. *Asahi Shimbun*, "Nanbei no Nihon," n.p.

68. *Semanário Nikkei*, "Colônia no Teiryu: Nihongo Kyoiku" [*Colônia*'s Undercurrent: Japanese Language Education], no. 151 (October 15, 1966): 29.

69. Paulista Shimbunsha, ed., *Paulista Nenkan 1966-nenban* [Paulista Yearbook of 1966] (São Paulo: Paulista Shimbunsha, 1966), 49.

70. AI, Nobue Miyazaki, June 26, 2002.

71. *Colônia*, "Zadankai: Seinen no Ikigai o Saguru," 16–17.

72. AI, Atsushi Yamauchi, June 17, 2010.

73. Toshio Tomimatsu, "Nandemo Mite Yaro" [I'll See Anything and Everything], *Colônia*, no. 34 (June 1962): 29.

74. *Colônia*, "Nihon Mitamama: Nisei Ryugakusei no Me ni Utsutta Gendai Nihon no Sugada" [Japan as It Is: How Modern Japan Has Been Perceived by Nisei Students Who Studied There], no. 52 (July 1965): 9, 12.

75. *Colônia Bungaku*, "Zadankai: 'Nihon' wa Nani o Dou Kangen Suruka. Nisei Shakaijin no Seikatsu to Iken" [Roundtable Discussion: What and How Does "Japan" Contribute Back to Us? Nisei Professionals' Lives and Opinions], no. 23 (March 1974): 28–36, 31, 33, 35–36.

76. AI, Yukie Yano, January 8, 1998.

77. AI, Mariana Kazumi Fujitani and Yuko Hanada, December 31, 1997.

78. AI, Hirohisa Inoue, June 5, 2010.

79. AI, Hisahiro Inoue, June 7, 2010.

80. Ibid.

81. AI, Hisahiro Inoue, June 5, 2010.

82. AI, Midory Kimura Figuchi, January 22, 1998.

83. Ibid.

84. AI, Delma Arashiro, June 14, 1999.

85. AI, Yuriko Matsuno, June 27, 2001.

86. Ibid.

87. AI, Eria M. Yamaoka, June 27, 2001.

88. Ibid.

89. AI, Hiroko Nakama , June 26, 2001.

90. AI, Senichi Adachi, July 5, 2002.

91. AI, Sandra Akahoshi, July 3, 2002.

92. AI, Akio Ogawa, June 9, 2010.

93. Osamu Toyama, *Burajiru Nikkei Shakai Hyakunen no Suiryu* [The Nikkei Society of Brazil and Its Stream over One Hundred Years] (São Paulo: Osamu Toyama, 2006), chapters 16–24.

94. Takeshi Horie, "Nikkijin to wa Nanika: Adachi Senichi, Watanbe Kazuo, Hanseiki no Kōsaku (4): Nihon Bunka o Kokoro ni Yadosu Mono Kore Subete 'Nikkeijin'?" [What Is the Nikkeijin: The Crossroads between Senichi Adachi and Kazuo Watanabe over Half a Century, No. 4: Is Everybody Who Has Japanese Culture in His/Her Heart a New "Nikkeijin"?], *Nikkey Shimbun,* October 7, 2003, www.nikkeyshimbun.com.br/2003/031007-72colonia.html, accessed December 31, 2011.

95. PC, Atsushi Yamauchi, February 14 and 15, 2012.

96. PC, Bernardo Y. Shinohara, February 12, 2012.

97. *Nikkey Shimbun,* "Kotoshi wa Bunkyo Kaicho Kaisenki" [Another Election for Bunkyo Presidency to Take Place This Year], January 1, 2005, www.nikkeyshimbun.com.br/050101-10especial.html, accessed December 31, 2011.

98. Horie, "Nikkijin to wa Nanika."

99. Mizuaki Wakahara, "Direction's Eye: Nikkei Brazileiros, Vol. 10: Kazuo Watanabe," www.direction-dcord.com/2011/06/16071613.html, accessed December 12, 2011.

100. Katsuhiro Yago, "Burajiru Nikkeijin 7: Kogoto Shimbei Nagare Nya Sakarayenu [Brazilian Nikkeis, No. 7: Mr. Complaining Cannot Resist the Stream], *Yomiuri Shimbun,* June 12, 1978, evening edition, 10.

101. Jorge J. Okubaro, *O Súdito (Banzai, Massateru!)* [The Subject (Long Live Massateru!)] (São Paulo: Editora Terceiro Nome, 2006).

102. Jorge J. Okubaro, "A colônia nipo-brasileira vista através dos olhos de um jornalista nissei" [The Nikkei *Colônia* Seen through the Eyes of a Nisei Journalist], unpublished paper presented at a seminar at the Centro de Estudos Nipo-Brasileiros, June 20, 2011, www.100nen.com.br/ja/jinmonken/, accessed February 27, 2012.

103. Kiyoshi Harada, ed., *O Nikkei no Brasil* (São Paulo: Editora Atlas, 2008).

104. *Nikkey Shimbun,* " 'Nisei wa Gensai no Hihonjin yori Nihonjinpoi,' Seishi de Gaimusho Kenshusei OB kai-Harada-san" ["Niseis Are More Japanese Than Today's Japanese Are," Said Mr. Harada at a Meeting for the Former Trainees at Japan's Ministry of Foreign Affairs in São Paulo City], June 14, 2008, www.nikkeyshimbun.com.br/080614-61colonia.html, accessed September 29, 2011.

105. Wakahara, "Direction's Eye."

106. Ibid.; italics mine.

107. AI, Iossuke Tanaka, June 24, 2008.

108. Iossuke Tanaka, letter to author dated May 12, 2009.

CHAPTER FOUR: POSTWAR IMMIGRANTS
AND THEIR NEW JAPANESE IDENTITY

1. Author interview (hereafter AI), Sachiko Tomino (b. 1952), June 25, 1999.

2. Masatake Suzuki, "Sengo Imin Shiron: Sono Sekaiku to Yakuwari" [An Essay on Postwar Immigrants: Their Character and Roles], in *Burajiru Imin Sengo Ijū*, ed. Sengo Ijū (São Paulo: Burajiru-Nippon Ijūsha Kyokai, 2004), 287 and 293–294.

3. Centro de Estudos Nipo-Brasileiros, ed., *Burajiru Nihon Imin Nikkei Shakaishi Nenphō: Handa Tomoo Hen-cho Kaitei Zōho Ban* [Chronological Table of Japanese Immigration to Brazil and Japanese Brazilian Social History: A Revised an Expanded Version of the Original by Tomoo Handa] (São Paulo: Centro de Estudos Nipo-Brasileiros, 1996), 116, 119, 266.

4. Burajiru Okinawa Kenjinkai Nihongo Henshu Iinkai, ed., *Burajiru Okinawa-kenjin Iminshi: Kasato Maru kara 90-nen* [The History of Okinawan Immigration: 90 Years since the *Kasato Maru*] (São Paulo: Associação Okinawa Kenjin do Brasil, 2000), 175.

5. Tsutomu Nakamura, "Sengo Burajiru Imin to Nihon no Taihaku Toshi" [Postwar Japanese Immigration to Brazil and Japan's Capital Investment in Brazil], in *Burajiru Imin Sengo Ijū*, 146; and Centro de Estudos, *Burajiru Nihon Imin*, 117.

6. Sengo Ijū 50-shunen Kinesai Jikko Iinkai, ed., *Burajiru Imin Sengo Ijū no 50-nen* [Fifty Years of Postwar Japanese Immigration to Brazil] (São Paulo: Burajiru-Nippon Ijūsha Kyokai, 2004), 205–206.

7. Ibid., 36, 50.

8. Yukio Akimoto, "Ginko no Madoguchi de" [At a Bank Counter], *Colônia*, no. 31 (December 1961): 8–9.

9. Kaigai Ijū Jigyodan, ed., *Kaigai Ijū Jigyodan Jūnenshi* [Ten-Year History of Japan Emigration Service] (Tokyo: Kaigai Ijū Jigyodan, 1973), 118–119.

10. Akemi Kikumura-Yano, ed., *Encyclopedia of Japanese Descendants in the Americas: An Illustrated History of the Nikkei* (Walnut Creek, CA: Altamira Press, 2002), 145, table 4.1.

11. AI, Hiroshi Komori, June 19, 2010; and AI, Yasuo Shiobara, June 15, 2010.

12. Teiichi Suzuki, ed., *The Japanese Immigrant in Brazil: Narrative Part* (Tokyo: University of Tokyo Press, 1969), 182–183.

13. Kiyoshi Shima, "Ijūsen no Chōsa" [A Survey on an Immigrant Ship], in *Imin: Burajiru Imin no Jitsutai Chōsa* [The Immigrant: A Survey on Japanese Immigrants in Brazil], ed. Seiichi Izumi (Tokyo: Kokin Shoten, 1957), 541.

14. Teiichi Suzuki, *Japanese Immigrant in Brazil*, 182–183.

15. *Nikkey Shimbun*, "Sengo Imin no Yakuwari towa Nanika: Tokubetsu Zadankai [What Are the Roles of Postwar Immigrants? A Special Roundtable Discussion], June 30, 2011, www.nikkeyshimbun.com.br/nikkey/html/show/110630-b1colonia.html, accessed November 17, 2011.

16. Sengo Ijū, *Burajiru Nihon Imin*, 266.

17. Tomoo Handa, *Imin no Seikatsu no Rekishi: Brajiru Nikkei Imin no Ayunda Michi* [A History of the Immigrant Life: The Path Japanese Brazilians Walked] (São Paulo: Centro de Estudos Nipo-Brasileiros, 1970), chapter 68.

18. Soichi Ōya, *Sekai no Uragawa o Yuku: Nanboku Amerika Hen* [Traveling on the Other Side of the Globe: The Americas] (Tokyo: Bungeishunjūsha, 1956), 87–88.

19. Hitotsubashi Daigau Nanbei Enseitai, "Hitotsubashi Daigau Nanbei Ensesitai Hokousho: Imin Seikatsu o Tazunete" [A Report by the Expeditionary Team to South America of Hitotsubashi University: Visiting with Japanese Immigrants in Brazil], *Colônia*, no. 24 (August 1960): 56–57.

20. AI, Senichi Adachi, July 5, 2002.

21. AI, Hiroshi Komori, June 19, 2010.

22. *Yomiuri Shimbun*, "Burajiru Seinen Imin ga Satsujin: Sengohyaku-nin Ukeire Chushi, Cotia Sangyo Kumiai 'Jinsen ga Zusan to Kōgi'" [A Young Immigrant Man Commits a Murder: Cotia Agricultural Cooperative Will Not Accept 1,500 Immigrants, Protesting against Japan's Sloppy Selection Process], December 17, 1957, morning edition, 7.

23. Sengo Ijū, *Burajiru Nihon Imin*, 263.

24. AI, Senichi Adachi, July 5, 2002.

25. Personal communication (hereafter PC), Goro Tamura, March 8, 2012.

26. AI, Senichi Adachi, July 5, 2002.

27. Takuji Fujii, "Mohoya Hakikirenu Genjo" [The Current Situation One Cannot Handle], *Kaihō*, no. 19 (July–August 1959): 34–35.

28. Paulista Shimbunsha, ed., *Paulita Nenkan 1963-nenban* [Paulista Yearbook of 1963] (São Paulo: Paulista Shinbunsha, 1963), 14, 16.

29. Katsuzo Yamamoto, "Colônia Jōka Undō to Imin Kihonhō" [Movement for the Purification of the *Colônia* and Basic Laws on Immigration], *Colônia*, no. 36 (November 1962): 15.

30. AI, Senichi Adachi, July 5, 2002.

31. AI, Hiroshi Komori, June 19, 2010; PC, Goro Tamura, March 8, 2012; AI, Sakiko Ozawa, June 9, 1999; PC, Masaru Takanashi, July 4, 2002.

32. AI, Senichi Adachi, July 5, 2002.

33. *Semanário Nikkei*, "Hanayome Maru ha Doko Ye" [Where Did the Bride-Ship Go], no. 148 (August 26, 1966): 5–6.

34. Noriko Shimada, "Sengo no Burajiru 'Hanayome Imin': Sono Rekishiteki Haikei to Joseizō" [Postwar "Bride Immigrants" to Brazil: Its Historical Background and the Image of Women], in *Shashin Hanayome, Sensō Hanayome no Tadotta Michi: Josei Iminshi no Hakkutsu / Crossing Ocean: A New Look at the History of Japanese Picture Brides and War Brides*, ed. Noriko Shimada (Tokyo: Akashi Shoten, 2009), 122–123.

35. Ibid.

36. AI, Takeshi Nagase, July 15, 2010.

37. Sengo Ijū, *Burajiru Nihon Imin*, 272 and 278.

38. Shimada, "Sengo no Burajiru 'Hanayome Imin,'" 132.

39. Sengo Ijū, *Burajiru Nihon Imin,* 206.

40. AI, Reiko Uehara, June 27, 2001.

41. Ibid.

42. Yutaka Aida, *Kōseki: Ijū Sanjūichinenme no Jōsensha Meibo* [Trail of a Voyage: Those Who Were on the Passenger List Thirty-One Years Ago] (Tokyo: NHK, 2003), 397–497.

43. Miyoko Konami, *Kaigai ni Tobitatsu Hanayometachi* [Brides Flying Away Overseas] (Tokyo: Kōdansha, 1986), 272 and 41.

44. Taeko Sase, "Burajiru Rikkokai Sōritsu 90 Shūnen ni Yosete" [An Essay in Commemoration of the 90th Anniversary of Rikkokai], in *Rikko no Kizuna: Burazil Rikkokai Sōritsu Kyujūshunen Kinen* [The Bond of Rikko in Commemoration of the 90th Anniversary of the Brazilian Association of Rikkokai], ed. Burajiru Rikkokai (São Paulo: Brajiru Rikkokai, 2007), 66–69.

45. Burajiru Rikkokai, ed., *Rikko no Kizuna: Burajiru Rikkokai Sōritsu Kyujū-shunen Kinen* [The Bond of Rikko in Commemoration of the 90th Anniversary of Brazilian Association of Rikkokai] (São Paulo: Burajiru Rikkokai, 2007), 11, 27.

46. Sengo Ijū, *Burajiru Nihon Imin,* 281.

47. Konami, *Kaigai ni Tobitatsu Hanayometachi,* no page number assigned, after the end of the text and 164, 148.

48. Burajiru Rikkokai, *Rikko no Kizuna,* 14.

49. AI, Senichi Adachi, July 5, 2002.

50. Shima, "Ijūsen no Chōsa," 560.

51. AI, Katsuko Sumida, June 17, 2010.

52. AI, Teruko Moriyama (b. 1936), June 26, 2008; *Yomiuri Shimbun,* "Burajiru Imin 90 Kazoku Shuppatsu" [Ninety Immigrant Families Departing for Brazil], December 4, 1956, morning edition, 7.

53. AI, Emiko Arakaki, July 20, 2010.

54. AI, Kazuya Matsuhira, June 12, 2010.

55. AI, Kazuko Ezawa, January 22, 1998, and June 30, 2001.

56. AI, Kiyoe Sekiguchi, June 23, 2008.

57. AI, Teiko Saeki, January 4, 1998; PC, June 20, 2008.

58. Burajiru Rikkokai, *Rikko no Kizuna,* 11.

59. AI, Hiromi Ono, July 22, 2010.

60. AI, Kazuya Matsuhira, June 12, 2010.

61. AI, Toshio Hata, June 5, 2010.

62. AI, Yasuo Shiobara, June 15, 2010.

63. AI, Kazuko Ezawa, January 22, 1998, and June 30, 2001; AI, Hiroko Nakama, June 26, 2001.

64. *Yomiuri Shimbun,* "Shimedasareru Brazil Imin" [Japanese Immigrants Being Pushed Out in Brazil], August 3, 1980, morning edition, 5.

65. AI, Yasuo Shiobara, June 15, 2010.

66. Akio Koyama, "Interview of Akio Koyama," *Quem e Quem,* October 2000, www.100nen.com.br/ja/qq/000014/20030411000047.cfm, accessed May 14, 2012.

67. PC, Goro Tamura, March 8, 2012.

68. AI, Andrea Yumi Minami, July 20, 2010.

69. Burajiru Rikkokai, *Rikko no Kizuna*, 11; Tomonobu Omiya, *Dekassegui: Gyakuryu-suru Nikkei Burajirujin* [*Dekassegui*: Japanese Brazilians Repatriating to Japan] (Tokyo: Shoshisha, 1997), 44.

70. AI, Natsue Sakagami, June 13, 1999; AI, Hanae Yukimura, June 15 and 22, 2008; and Omiya, *Dekassegui*, 185.

71. AI, Sachiko Tomino, June 25, 1999.

72. AI, Hanae Yukimura, June 22, 2008.

73. AI, Natsue Sakagami, June 13, 1999.

74. PC, December 1997–January 1998.

75. AI, Yaeko Hashida (b. 1947), June 12, 2001.

76. PC, June 15, 2010.

77. AI, Kiyoe Sekiguchi, June 23, 2008.

78. AI, Hiromi Ono, July 22, 2010.

79. AI, Emiko Arakaki, July 20, 2010.

80. AI, Sachiko Tomino, July 5, 2002.

81. AI, Reiko Uehara, June 27, 2001, and July 2, 2001.

82. AI, Hiroko Nakama, June 26 and 28, 2001; and July 6, 2001.

83. AI, Kiyoe Sekiguchi, June 23, 2008.

84. AI, Yoko Yoshida, June 10, 2001.

85. AI, Mari Tozuka, June 13, 2001.

86. AI, Mikiko Nagashima, June 12, 2008.

87. AI, Lina Mitsuko Nishimoto, January 21, 1998.

88. Masatake Suzuki, "Sengo Imin Shiron," 282, 290–291, 294.

89. Masatake Suzuki, *Suzuki Teiichi*, 17.

90. AI, Hisashi Nagata, June 10, 2010.

91. Masayuki Fukasawa, "Hyakunen no Chie, Imin to 'Nihon Seishin,' Enkakuchi Nashonarisumu 13-kai: NHK Shichosha wa Nisei Chūsin [One Hundred Years of Wisdom—Immigrants and "Japanese Spirit"—Remote Nationalism, No. 13: Nisseis Constitute the Majority of NHK Viewers], *Nikkey Shimbun,* August 7, 2008, www .nikkeyshimbun.com.br/080807-62colonia.html, accessed August 21, 2008.

92. AI, Senichi Adachi, July 5, 2002.

CHAPTER FIVE: NISEIS, SANSEIS,
AND THEIR CLASS-GENDER IDENTITY

1. Author interview (hereafter AI), Christina Sakura Oda (b. 1964), June 20, 2001.

2. AI, Edna Roland, June 22, 2001.

3. AI, Christina Sakura Oda, June 20, 2001.

4. Paulista Shimbunsha, ed., *Paulista Nenkan 1950-nenban* [Paulista Yearbook of 1950] (São Paulo: Paulista Shimbunsha, 1950), 189.

5. AI, Senichi Adachi, July 5, 2002.

6. AI, Olga Toshiko Futemma, June 20, 2002.

7. Takashi Maeyama, "Nisei no Naka no Nihon" [Japan within the Nisei], in *Ratenteki Nihonjin: Burajiru Nisei no Hatsugen* [The Latin Japanese: Opinions Expressed by the Nisei of Brazil], ed. Morio Ōno (Tokyo: NHK, 1969), 127, 150–152.

8. Maeyama, *Imin no Nihon Kaiki Undo* [Japanese Immigrants' Repatriation Movement to Japan] (Tokyo: NHK, 1982), 95.

9. AI, Yoshiro Fujita, June 14, 2008.

10. Katsunori Yago, "Burajiru Nikkeijin 9: Gōryu—Usureyuku 'Nisei Ishiki'" [Brazilian Nikkeis, No. 9: Merging—The "Nisei Consciousness" Disappearing], *Yomiuri Shimbun*, June 16, 1978, evening edition, 10.

11. AI, Olga Toshiko Futemma, June 20, 2002.

12. Leo Nishihata, "Amores possíveis" [Possible Loves], in *100 anos da imigração japonesa: As surpreendentes histórias do povo que ajudou a mudar o Brasil* [100 Years of Japanese Immigration: The Surprising Stories of the People Who Helped Change Brazil], ed. Editora Abril, 80.

13. AI, Olga Toshiko Futemma, June 20, 2002.

14. Ibid.

15. AI, Suely Harumi Satow, July 16, 2001.

16. Ibid.

17. AI, Eneida Almeida Reis (b. 1957), July 10, 2001.

18. AI, Christina Sakura Oda, June 20, 2001.

19. AI, Atsushi Yamauchi, June 17, 2010.

20. Centro de Estudos Nipo-Brasileiros, ed., *Burajiru ni Okeru Nikkei Shakaishi Nenphō: Handa Tomoo hen-cho Kaitei Zōho Ban* [Chronological Table of Japanese Immigration to Brazil and Japanese Brazilian Social History: A Revised an Expanded Version of the Original by Tomoo Handa] (São Paulo: Centro de Estudos Nipo-Brasileiros, 1996), 105, table 4.12.

21. Edward E. Telles, *Race in Another America: The Significance of Skin Color in Brazil* (Princeton, NJ: Princeton University Press, 2004), 176 (table 7.2), 178.

22. AI, Koichi Mori, June 4, 2002.

23. AI, Sachiko Tomino, July 5, 2002.

24. AI, Tamiko Hosokawa, June 13, 2002.

25. Personal communication (hereafter PC), July 14, 2001.

26. Sueann Caulfield, *In Defense of Honor: Sexual Morality, Modernity, and Nation in Early Twentieth-Century Brazil* (Durham, NC: Duke University Press, 2000), 164.

27. Carl N. Degler, *Neither Black nor White: Slavery and Race Relations in Brazil and the United States* (1971; repr., Madison: University of Wisconsin Press, 1986), 188, 191.

28. AI, Sachiko Tomino, July 5, 2002.

29. Sengo Ijū 50-shunen Kinesai Jikko Iinkai, ed., *Burajiru Imin Sengo Ijū no 50-nen* [Fifty Years of Postwar Japanese Immigration to Brazil] (São Paulo: Burajiru-Nippon Ijūsha Kyokai, 2004), 281.

30. AI, Tamiko Hosokawa, June 13, 2002.

31. AI, Amelia Yagihara, June 14, 2010.

32. PC, Reiko Uehara, June 14, 2010.

33. AI, Amelia Yagihara, June 14, 2010.

34. AI, Masami Takiyama, July 4, 2002.

35. AI, Rosa Aiko Utimura, June 7, 1999.

36. PC, Mariana Fujitani, January 10, 1998.

37. AI, Christina Sakura Oda, June 20, 2001.

38. Masayuki Fukasawa, *Parareru Wārudo* [Parallel World] (Tokyo: Ushio Shuppan, 1999), 33; Tomonobu Omiya, *Dekassegui Gyakuryu-suru Nikkei Burajirujin* [*Dekassegui*: Japanese Brazilians Repatriating to Japan] (Tokyo: Shoshisha, 1997), 163.

39. AI, Mikiko Nagashima, June 12, 2008; AI, Masako Sakamoto, June 8, 2001.

40. AI, Christina Sakura Oda, June 20, 2001.

41. AI, Marcelo Shuji Yoshimura, July 21, 2010.

42. Keiko Yamanaka, "Return Migration of Japanese-Brazilians to Japan: The Nikkeijin as Ethnic Minority and Political Construct," *Diaspora* 5, no. 1 (1996): 85.

43. *Made in Japan*, no. 46 (July 2001), advertisement section with no page numbers; *Made in Japan*, no. 93 (June 2005): 64 and 72.

44. I have not been able to find statistical data to support these claims.

45. PC, July 20, 2010.

46. Japan, Ministry of Health, Labor, and Welfare, "Konin Dai-2-hyo: Fufu no Kokuseki-betsu ni Mita Konin Kensu no Nenji Suii" [Marriages, Table -2: Changes over the Years in Marriages by the Nationality of a Spouse], www.mhlw.go.jp/toukei/saikin/hw/jinkou/suii09/marr2.html, accessed August 15, 2012.

47. PC, Reiko Uehara, June 14, 2010.

48. AI, Amelia Yagihara, June 10 and 14, 2010.

49. AI, Christina Sakura Oda, June 20, 2001.

50. AI, Amelia Yagihara, June 14, 2010.

51. PC, Shigeru Kojima, July 13, 2010.

52. AI, Masashi Sugimoto and Tsuruyo Sugimoto, June 16, 2010.

53. AI, Kiyoe Sekiguchi, June 23, 2008.

54. AI, Isabel Natsumi Yonamine, June 12, 2002.

55. AI, Gustavo Akitoshi Kobayashi, June 19, 2008.

56. Ibid.

57. AI, Ricardo Takeshi Ninagawa, June 24, 2005.

58. Ibid.

59. AI, Masashi Sugimoto, June 16, 2010.

60. PC, Tsuyuro Sugimoto, April 10, 2012.

61. Ishi, "Searching Home," 88, 80, 93.

62. Ibid., 85, 93.

63. AI, Christina Sakura Oda, June 20, 2001.

64. Ibid.

65. AI, Andrea Yumi Minami, July 20, 2010.

66. AI, Christina Sakura Oda, June 20, 2001.

67. Ibid.

68. AI, Hiromi Ono, July 22, 2010; italics mine.

69. AI, Andrea Yumi Minami, July 20, 2010.

70. Jhony Arai and Andréia Ferreira, "90 anos depois, quem são os descendentes de japoneses," *Made in Japan*, no. 9 (June 1998): 54.

71. AI, Gustavo Akitoshi Kobayashi, June 19, 2008.

72. Ibid.

73. AI, Ricardo Ninagawa, June 24, 2005.

74. AI, Isabel Natsumi Yonamine, June 12, 2002.

75. Ibid.

CHAPTER SIX: SANSEIS, YONSEIS, AND THEIR RACIAL IDENTITY

1. Author interview (hereafter AI), Hugo Shinji Murakami, June 26, 2008.

2. Ibid.

3. *Japão Aquí*, "Japonês ou brasileiro: Como se sente o jovem nikkei?" [Japanese or Brazilian: How Does the Nikkei Youth Feel?] 1, no. 3 (July 1997): 38–44, especially 43.

4. AI, Eduardo Seiji Tamura, June 28, 2005.

5. Ibid.

6. AI, Yaeko Hashida, June 12, 2001.

7. AI, Natsue Sakagami, June 6, 2001.

8. Seinen Bunkyo, "Christina Agari Entrevista" [Christina Agari Interview], December 2002, www.bunkyo.org.br/seinen/menu/not_entrevistacris.asp, accessed March 24, 2007.

9. Bunkyo 50-nenshi Hensan Iikai, ed., *Bunkyo 50-nenshi* [Bunkyo's History of 50 Years] (São Paulo: Burajiru Nihon Bunka Fukushi Kyokai, 2007), 284.

10. AI, Edwin Hideki Hasegawa, June 28, 2008.

11. Personal communication (hereafter PC), Sabrina Mayumi Akiyoshi, March 20, 2012.

12. AI, Newton Hirata, June 25, 2002; PC, Newton Hirata, May 15, 2012.

13. PC, Eduardo Seiji Tamura, January 17, 2006.

14. Angelo Ishi, "Searching Home, Wealth, Pride, and 'Class': Japanese Brazilians in the 'Land of Yen,'" in *In Search for Home Abroad: Japanese Brazilians and the Transnational Moment*, ed. Jeffery Lesser (Durham, NC: Duke University Press, 2003), 73–102.

15. PC, Eduardo Seiji Tamura, January 17, 2006.

16. *Japão Aquí*, "Japonês ou brasileiro," 39, 41–42.

17. AI, Keiko Nakahara Alvarenga, June 11, 2010; italics mine.

18. AI, Eduardo Seiji Tamura, June 25, 2005.

19. AI, Wagner M. Horiuchi, June 10, 2002.

20. AI, Eduardo Seiji Tamura, June 25, 2005.

21. Ibid.

22. AI, Kulara Kawamura, June 22, 1999.

23. AI, Alice Minemura, June 8, 1999.

24. *Japão Aquí*, "Japonês ou brasileiro," 43.

25. AI, Akio Ogawa, June 9, 2010.

26. AI, Tamiko Hosokawa, June 13, 2002.

27. Ibid.; italics mine.

28. AI, Eduardo Seiji Tamura, June 25, 2005; italics mine.

29. *Japão Aqui*, "Japonês ou brasileiro," 42.

30. AI, Kulara Kawamura, June 22, 1999.

31. *Bumba*, " 'Nikkeijin': Korega Watashitachi no Seikatsu Desu" ["Nikkeijin": This Is Our Lifestyle], no. 12 (2001): 16–21.

32. *Japão Aqui*, "Japonês ou brasileiro," 42.

33. *Bumba*, "Nikkeijin," 16.

34. AI, Olga Toshiko Futemma, June 20, 2002.

35. PC, Koichi Mori, June 4, 2002.

36. Bunkyo 50-nenshi, *Bunkyo 50-nenshi*, 274; italics mine.

37. AI, Yoriko Matsuno, June 27, 2001.

38. AI, Erica M. Yamaoka, June 27, 2001.

39. AI, Sachiko Tomino, July 5, 2002.

40. AI, Iossuke Tanaka, June 25, 2008; italics mine.

41. AI, Akio Ogawa, June 9, 2010; italics mine.

42. AI, Hector Nobuo Motoyama, June 12, 2010.

43. *Japão Aqui*, "Japonês ou brasileiro," 39, 42–43.

44. Jhony Arai, "Mãos à obra: Associações de jovens nikkeis do brasil buscam soluções para não desaparecer," *Made in Japan*, no. 46 (June 2001): 64–65.

45. Cely Carmo, "Mutirão da Solidaridade" [Effort of Solidarity], *Japão Aqui* 1, no. 4 (August 1997): 32–34; *Bumba*, "Nikkeijin," 17.

46. *Japão Aqui*, "Japonês ou brasileiro," 42; *Bumba*, "Nikkeijin," 18.

47. PC, Edwin Hideki Hasegawa, October 8, 2008.

48. Seinen Bunkyo, "Quem Somos, História" [Who Are We, History], www.bunkyonet.org.br/comissaodejovens/quem-somos/historia, accessed May 19, 2012.

49. AI, Ronaldo Masaki Nakata, June 28, 2008.

50. AI, Eric Funabashi, June 27, 2008.

51. Ibid.

52. Ibid.

53. Ibid.

54. Ibid.

55. AI, Edwin Hideki Hasegawa, June 28, 2008.

56. AI, Miyuki Shinozuka, June 27, 2008.

57. Ibid.

58. AI, Ricardo Ninagawa, June 24, 2005.

59. AI, Eduardo Seiji Tamura, June 29, 2005.

60. AI, Ronaldo Masaki Nakata, June 28, 2008.

61. Ibid.

62. PC, Hector Nobuo Motoyama, November 14, 2008.

63. AI, Hector Nobuo Motoyama, June 12, 2010; italics mine.

64. Ibid.; italics mine.

65. Ibid.

66. Ibid.

67. AI, Lucia Mika Yamashita, June 12, 2010.

68. Ibid.

69. AI, Julia Miki Yagami, June 12, 2010.

70. Ibid.

71. PC, Newton Hirata, May 15, 2012.

72. AI, Eric Funabashi, June 27, 2008.

73. PC, Sabrina Mayumi Akiyoshi, May 15, 2012.

74. AI, Miyuki Shinozuka, June 27, 2008.

75. Ibid.

76. PC, Eduardo Seiji Tamura, July 21, 2012.

77. PC, Sabrina Mayumi Akiyoshi, July 23, 2012.

78. Nike Stadiums. *PLAYMAKERS Tokyo*, directed by Santiago Stelly (Tokyo: Niki Stadiums, 2010), part 2 of 3, https://www.youtube.com/watch?v=tx6dcx6dtPY, accessed July 21, 2012.

79. PC, Hugo Shinji Murakami, October 15, 2008.

80. AI, Kabengele Munanga, June 24, 2002.

81. George Reid Andrews, *Blacks and Whites in São Paulo, Brazil, 1888–1988* (Madison: University of Wisconsin Press, 1991), chapters 6–7.

82. AI, Kabengele Munanga, June 24, 2002; AI, João Carlos B. Martins, June 15, 2005.

83. AI, Alexandre Mello, June 15, 2005; AI, José Vicente, June 27, 2005; AI, Liliani Santos, June 17, 2005.

84. AI, Christian Moura, June 23, 2005.

85. Stuart Hall, "Cultural Identity and Diaspora," in *Identity: Community, Culture, Difference,* ed. Jonathan Rutherford (London: Lawrence and Wishart, 1990), 226; italics in source.

86. PC, Sabrina Mayumi Akiyoshi, May 20, 2012; italics mine.

CHAPTER SEVEN: JAPANESE BRAZILIANS
AND THEIR BRAZILIAN IDENTITY IN JAPAN

1. Author interview (hereafter AI), Andrea Yumi Minami, July 20, 2010.

2. Ibid.

3. Takashi Maeyama, "Chikyu no Uragawa kara Nihonjin o Miru: Burajiru, Amerika, Nihon" [Looking at the Japanese from the Other Side of the Globe: Brazil, the United States, and Japan], *Chūōkōron* 95, no. 4 (April 1980): 126–127.

4. Naoto Higuchi, "Keizai Kiki to Zainichi Burajirujin: Nani ga Tairyo Shitsugyo Kikoku o Motarashitanoka" [Economic Crises and Brazilians in Japan: What Brought Them Mass Unemployment and Made Them Return to Brazil], *Ōhara Shakai Mondai Kenkyusho,* no. 622 (August 2010): 53 (table 3).

5. Higuchi, "Keizai Kiki," 54–55, 59.

6. Personal communication (hereafter PC), June 19, 2010; June 6, 2010 (italics in source); and June 7, 2010 (italics mine).

7. Masato Ninomiya, ed., *Dekassgeui 10 Anos de História e Suas Perspectivas Futuras / Dekassegui sono 10-nen no Rekishi to Shōraizō* [Dekassegui Ten Years of History and Its Future Perspectives] (São Paulo: CIATE and Centro de Estabilização de Emprego nas Indústrias, 1998), 41–42, 96–97.

8. Higuchi, "Keizai Kiki," 59–60.

9. PC, Misako Fukushima, June 15, 2010.

10. AI, Kazuyo Yoneda, June 13, 2010.

11. PC, Shigeru Kojima, July 13, 2010.

12. In 1996, 3,943 Brazilians lived in Yokohama, including 1,414 registered in Tsurumi Ward. Minoru Numata, *Tabunka Kyosei o Mezasu Chiiki Zukuri: Yokohama, Tsurumi Ushio kara no Hōkoku* [Area Planning Aiming at Multiculturalism: A Report from Tsurumi and Ushio of Yokohama] (Tokyo: Akashi Shoten, 1996), 11.

13. Naoko Horikawa, "New Lives in the Ancestral Homeland: Return Migration from South America to Mainland Japan and Okinawa" (PhD diss., University of Hull, 2012), chapter 5.

14. Kiyoto Tanno, "Sōgō Dekaseguigyo no Tanjo: Nikkei Ryokōsha no Henyo to Burajiru Nikkei Komuniti no Shihon Chikuseki" [The Birth of General *Dekassegui* Business: Transformation of Nikkei Travel Agencies and Japanese Brazilian Community's Capital Accumulation], *Ōhara Shakai Mondai Kenkyusho Zasshi*, no. 573 (August 2006): 47–48.

15. AI, Isao Kaburaki, July 17, 2010; italics mine.

16. Ibid.; italics mine.

17. Horikawa, "New Lives," 17, 298–300; italics mine.

18. Masayuki Fukasawa, *Parareru Wārudo* [Parallel World] (Tokyo: Ushio Shuppan, 1999), 54–56, 59.

19. Shigehiro Ikegami, "Burajirujin Zōka no Yōin to Zōka no Yōsō" [Factors Contributing to the Increase of Japanese Brazilians and Their Condition," in *Burajirujin to Kokusaikasuru Chiiki Shakai: Kyojū Kyoiku Iryō* [Brazilians and the Local Community in the Process of Internationalization: Residence, Education, and Medical Care], ed. Shigehiro Ikegami (Tokyo: Akashi Shoten, 2001), 22–24, 26–27 (table 1-3); Hamamatsu Foundation for International Communication and Exchange (hereafter HICE), "Hamamatsu-shi ni Tsuite no Deita Tōkei: Hamamatsu-shi no Gaikokuji Tōrokushasū" [Data and Statisics on Hamamatsu City: Numbers of Foreign Residents in Hamamatsu City], www.hi-hice.jp/index.php, accessed April 10, 2012; HICE, "Hamamatsu-shi no Gaikokujin Tōrokushasū " [Numbers of Foreign Residents Registered in Hamamatsu City], www.hi-hice.jp/aboutus/statistics.html, accessed April 10, 2012.

20. AI, Andrea Yumi Minami, July 20, 2010.

21. Ibid.; italics mine.

22. AI, Hisahiro Inoue, June 7, 2010.

23. AI, Andrea Yumi Minami, July 20, 2010.

24. Takamichi Kajita, Kiyoto Tanno, and Naoto Higuchi, *Kao no Mienai Teijūka: Nikkei Burajirujin to Kokka Shijō Imin Nettowāku / Invisible Residents: Japanese Brazilians vis-à-vis the State, the Market, and the Immigrant Network* (Nagoya-shi, Japan: Nagoya Daigaku Shuppankai, 2005), 213.

25. *Chunichi Shimbun,* "Rōdō Kigyo Jibun no Chikara de Idomitai" [Labor, Entrepreneurship, Business, I Would Like to Try on My Own], December 27, 2007, www.chunichi.co.jp/shizuoka/hold/emigrant/CK2007122402074712.html, accessed March 18, 2012.

26. *Chunichi Shimbun,* "Nippon de Ikiru: Burajiru Imin 100 Nen: Dai 3 bu—Rōdō, Kigyo, Jibun no Chikara de Idomitai" [Living in Japan: 100 Years of Immigration to Brazil—Part 3: Work, Starting Business, They Want to Challenge on Their Own], December 24, 2007, www.chunichi.co.jp/shizuoka/hold/emigrant/CK2007122402074712. html, accessed April 6, 2012.

27. AI, João Toshiei Masuko, July 20, 2010.

28. Ibid.

29. AI, Marcelo Shuji Yoshimura, July 21, 2010.

30. *Nikkey Shimbun,* "Burajiru Kokusei no Gaikokujin Bengoshi, Nihon demo Wazuka Sannin" [A Foreign Lawyer Who Is a Brazilian Citizen, One of the Only Three in Japan], August 21, 2004, www.nikkeyshimbun.com.br/2004/040821-71colonia.html, accessed May 21, 2012; Mami Maruko, "Helping Brazilian Kids Master Local Life: Japanese-Brazilian Tetsuyoshi Kodama Proudly Serves as a Bridge between Communities," *Japan Times,* August 23, 2011, www.japantimes.co.jp/text/fl20110823ww.html# .T_y5D45TcVs, accessed August 6, 2012; AI, Nelson Omachi, July 22, 2010; James Brooke, "Hamamatsu Journal: Sons and Daughters of Japan, Back from Brazil," *New York Times,* November 27, 2001, A4.

31. Angelo Ishi, "Dekassegui Keikensha no Manga kara Hanshin Daishinsai Hōdō made: Porutogaru Media no Kaishingeki" [Comics by a Former Dekassegui until the Rreports on the Great Hanshin Earthquake: The Great Advancement of Mass Media in the Portuguese Language], in *Esunikku Media: Tabunka Shakai Nihon o Mezashite/ Ethnic Media: Toward the Multicultural Japan,* ed. Shigehiro Shiramizu (Tokyo: Akashi Shoten, 1996), 98–99, 104–128, 146.

32. Ibid., 146.

33. Shigehiko Shiramizu, *Esunikku Media Kenkyu: Ekkyō Tabunka Aidentiti* [Ethnic Media Studies: Border Crossing, Multiculturalism, and Identity] (Tokyo: Akashi Shoten, 2004), 167.

34. AI, Andrea Yumi Minami, July 20, 2010.

35. AI, Amelia Yagihara, June 14, 2010.

36. AI, Renato Takada Yamano, July 21, 2010.

37. Ishi, "Dekassegi Keikensha," 98.

38. Brooke, "Hamamatsu Journal," A4.

39. Toyoie Kitagawa, "Hamamatsu-shi ni Okeru Nikkei Burajirujin no Seikatsu Kankyo to Ishiki—Nichi-haku Ryokoku *Chōsa* o Fumaete" [Japanese Brazilians' Living Environment and Consciousness, Based on a Research Conducted both in Japan and

in Brazil], *Toyo Daigaku Shakaigakubu Kiyō* 34, no. 1 (July 1996): 138–139, cited in Ikegami, "Burajirujin Zōka," 27.

40. Eunice Akami Ishikawa, "Kazoku wa Kodomo no Kyoiku ni Dō Kakawaruka: Dekasseegui-gata Raifu Sutairu to Oya no Nayami" [How Should Parents Engage Themselves in the Education of Their Children: *Dekassegui* Lifestyle and Parents' Worries], in *Gaikokujin no Kodomo to Nihon no Kyōiku: Fushūgaku Mondai to Tabunka Kyōsei no Kadai* [Foreign Children and Japanese Education: Problems of No Schooling and Multiculturalism as a Goal], ed. Takashi Miyajima and Haruo Ōta (Tokyo: Tokyo Daigaku Shuppankai, 2005), 79.

41. Ikegami, "Burajirujin Zōka," 27–28.

42. AI, Marcelo Shuji Yoshimura, July 21, 2010.

43. AI, Renato Takada Yamano, July 21, 2010.

44. Ikegami, "Burajirujin Zōka," 28–30, 33.

45. Ishikawa, "Kazoku wa Kodomo no Kyoiku," 92.

46. Brooke, "Hamamatsu Journal."

47. *Chunichi Shimbun*, "Nippon de Ikiru Brazil Imin 100-nen—Dai 1-bu Sugao 'Gakko' Nihongo o Hanashitai" [Living in Japan: 100 Years of Immigration to Brazil—Part 1: Unpainted Face, "School," and Desire to Speak Japanese], June 19, 2007, www.chunichi.co.jp/shizuoka/hold/emigrant/CK2007061902027684.html, accessed April 6, 2012.

48. AI, Marcelo Shuji Yoshimura, July 21, 2010.

49. AI, Andrea Yumi Minami, July 20, 2010.

50. Ibid.

51. HICE, "Hamamatsu-shi ni Tsuite no Deita Tōkei"; HICE, "Hamamatsu-shi no Gaikokujin Tōrokushasū."

52. Grupo Gambarê! Brasileiros, "Resultado da pesquisa da cidade de Hamamatsu Avaliação sobre a situação dos brasileiros diante da crise econômica," March 12, 2009, 10–11, www.hi-hice.jp/doc/aboutus/report/Pesquisa_Gambare.pdf, accessed April 10, 2012.

53. PC, Mr. Suzuki, July 22, 2010.

54. Grupo Gambarê!, "Resultado da pesquisa," 22–23.

55. AI, Marcelo Shuji Yoshimura, July 21, 2010; italics mine.

56. AI, Andrea Yumi Minami, July 20, 2010.

57. AI, João Toshiei Masuko, July 20, 2010.

58. Ibid.

59. AI, Marcelo Shuji Yoshimura, July 21, 2010.

60. Ibid.

61. AI, Kayoko Hamada, July 20, 2010.

62. AI, Renato Takada Yamano, July 21, 2010.

63. AI, Emiko Arakaki, July 20, 2010.

64. *Asahi Shimbun*, "Chu 3 Jitaku Hoka Yōgui" [A Nineth Grader Charged of Home Arson], July 9, 2010, 1.

65. *Japan Times*, "Two Teenage Girls Held over Fatal Hyogo Home Arson

Targeting Kin," July 10, 2010, www.japantimes.co.jp/text/nn20100710a2.html, accessed July 12, 2010.

66. Nyukan Kyokai / Japan Immigration Association, *Zairyu Gaikokujin Tōkei Heisei 21 nen-ban / Statistics on the Foreigners Registered in Japan 2009* (Tokyo: Nyukan Kyokai / Japan Immigration Association, 2010), 115.

67. Yataro Amino, "Higan no Jōriku Kinenhi Konryu Made" [Until the Inauguration of the Japanese Immigrants Monument, Which Was Our Ardent Wish], in *Burajiru Kenren No. 5: Sōritsu 40-shūnen Kenrenshi, 1966–2006* [The Fifth Volume of Brazilian Kenren in Commemoration of Kenren's 40th Anniversary, 1966–2006], ed. Kenren 40-shūnen Kinenshi Hensan Iinkai (São Paulo: Burajiru Todōfukenjinkai Rengōkai, 2008), 230.

68. AI, Hachiro Torenji, July 24, 2010.

69. Kobe Center for Overseas Migration and Cultural Interaction, "Tatemono no Rekishi" [History of the Buidling], http://www.kobe-center.jp/history.html, accessed March 18, 2012; Nippaku Kyokai / Associação Nipo-Brasileira, "Kyokai ni Tsuite/About Associação Nipo-Brasileira," http://www.nippaku-k.or.jp/about/index.html, accessed January 28, 2017.

70. *Nikkey Shimbun*, "Zainichi Burajirujin o Shien, CBK ni Matsubara-san" [Supporting Brazilians in Japan, Mrs. Matsubara of CBK], February 3, 2004, http//www.nikkeyshimbun.com.br/2004/040203-72colonia.html, accessed July 30, 2010.

71. AI, Hachiro Torenji, July 24, 2010.

72. AI, Taeko Nozaki, July 24, 2010.

73. Hisatoshi Tajima, "Okinawakeijin ni Okeru Tasōteki Sutandâdo Keisei o Meguru Mondai: Rainichi Rakichū Uchinanchu Burajirujin Diaspora no Hikakukenkyu / The Construction of a Cultural Multi-Standard of Okinawan-Brazilians: A Comparative Study Based on the Cases in Mainland Japan and Okinawa," *Gengo to Kenkyu/ Language and Culture* (Bunkyo University, Japan) 23 (March 2011): 138, 143, 145.

74. Ibid., 150.

75. AI, Kasumi Hanashiro, July 24, 2010.

76. Tajima, "Okinawakeijin," 150.

77. AI, Emerson Masaaki Tokunaga, July 20, 2010.

78. AI, Andrea Yumi Minami, July 20, 2010.

79. Stuart Hall, "Cultural Identity and Diaspora," in *Identity: Community, Culture, Difference*, ed. Jonathan Rutherford (London: Lawrence and Wishart, 1990), 222; italics in source.

80. Ibid., 225.

Conclusion

1. Ian Read, *The Hierarchies of Slavery in Santos, Brazil, 1822–1888* (Stanford, CA: Stanford University Press, 2012), chapter 1; Thomas H. Holloway, *Immigrants on the Land: Coffee and Society in São Paulo, 1886–1934* (Chapel Hill: University of North Carolina Press, 1980), 9.

2. Takashi Maeyama, *Dona Margarita Watanabe: Imin-Rojin Fukushi no 53-Nen*

[Dona Margarita Watanabe: The 53 Years Spent for the Welfare of Elderly Immigrants] (Tokyo: Ochanomizu Shobo, 1996), chapters 7–8; and Gen Oura, *Kodomo Imin Oura Fumio: Noson ni Ikiru Jun-Nisei no Kisei* [Child Immigrant Fumio Oura: The Course of a Quasi-Nisei Living in an Agricultural Village] (São Paulo: Fumio Oura, 2012), 154–172.

3. Yasumi Nakayama, "Nihon Imin Burajiru Jyoriku Kinenhi to Kami-san" [Monument for the Landing of Japanese Immigrants and Mr. Kami], *Kokkyo Chitai,* no. 22 (October 2009): 12–16, 14.

4. Fumio Oura, "Atogaki ni Kaete Watashi to Yuba-mura (Matawa Isamu)" [Postscript: Yuba Village (or Isamu) and Me], in Gen Oura, *Yuba Isamu no Shōgai,* 322–323.

5. Yataro Amino, "Higan no Jōriku Kinenhi Konryu Made" [Until the Inauguration of the Japanese Immigrants Monument, Which Was Our Ardent Wish], in *Burajiru Kenren No. 5: Sōritsu 40-shūnen Kenrenshi, 1966–2006* [The Fifth Volume of Brazilian Kenren in Commemoration of Kenren's 40th Anniversary, 1966–2006], ed. Kenren 40-shūnen Kinenshi Hensan Iinkai (São Paulo: Burajiru Todōfukenjinkai Rengōkai, 2008), 229–230.

6. Author interview, Yasumi Nakayama, June 13, 2008, and June 8, 2010.

7. Yasumi Nakayama, letter to author, dated February 21, 2008.

8. Hiroshi Saito, *Burajiru no Nihonjin* [The Japanese in Brazil] (Tokyo: Maruzen Kabushiki Kaisha, 1960), 17–19, 61–63.

9. Marisol de la Cadena, " 'Women Are More Indian': Ethnicity and Gender in a Community near Cuzco," in *Ethnicity, Markets, and Migration in the Andes: At the Crossroads of History and Anthropology,* ed. Brooke Larson, Olivia Harris, and Enrique Tandeter (Durham, NC: Duke University Press, 1995), 336–342.

10. Carl N. Degler, *Neither Black nor White: Slavery and Race Relations in Brazil and the United States* (1971; repr. Madison: University of Wisconsin Press, 1986), 191.

11. Nakayama, "Nihon Imin," 15.

12. National Diet Library, "Hōdō Happyo, Heisei 20 Nen 4 Gatsu 20 Nichi, Zaimusho" [Public Accouncemet from the Ministry of Finance dated April 20, 2008], warp .ndl.go.jp/info:ndljp/pid/1022127/www.mof.go.jp/jouhou/sonota/kokko/kk200430.htm, accessed June 7, 2013.

13. *Nikkey Shimbun,* "Zendai Mimon no Kinen Kōka Tsukuri Naoshi" [We've Never Heard of Remaking a Commemorative Coin Before], May 1, 2008, www.nikkey shimbun.com.br/080501-71colonia.html, accessed June 6, 2013.

Glossary

bahiana	migrant woman from the state of Bahia; often used pejoratively to refer to uneducated dark-skinned Afro-Brazilian women from the northeast of Brazil
bentoya	shop selling takeout lunches
caboclo	uneducated rural person of native Brazilian ancestry
camarada	wage worker on a farm or plantation
colônia	colony
colono	contract coffee plantation worker
cursinho	specialized private school that trains students to pass college entrance examinations
dekassegui	Japanese Brazilian "return" labor migration to Japan or a Japanese Brazilian foreign guest worker in Japan
escola normal	normal school; teacher's college
fazenda	coffee plantation
fazendeiro	coffee plantation owner
feira	open-air market
feirante	merchant who retails his/her wares in large open-air markets for consumers
fujinkai	women's association
gaijin	foreigner
Gosei	fifth-generation Japanese descendant
grupo escolar	Brazil's four-year primary school
Issei	first-generation Japanese descendent / immigrant
kachigumi	victory group
kenjinkai	association for those from the same prefecture of Japan
kihaku Nisei	Nisei who, as children, moved to Japan before 1942 for Japanese education and eventually came back to Brazil after the end of World War II
makegumi	defeat group
mestiço/a	racially mixed person
morena	light-skinned Afro-Brazilian woman

nihonjinkai	association for the Japanese
Nikkei	Japanese descendant
Nikkeijin	person of Japanese descent
Nisei	second-generation Japanese descendant
quitanda	fruit and vegetable stand
Sansei	third-generation Japanese descendent
seinenkai	Japanese young male adults' voluntary association; an umbrella term for the youth branches of various Japanese Brazilian associations
shinrai seinen	"newly arrived young men"; a pejorative expression used by prewar immigrants to refer to young postwar immigrant men
shokuminchi	independent Japanese farmers' collective (agricultural) settlement
taiko	traditional Japanese drum
tintureira	person who is engaged in cleaning and dyeing service
viajante	salesman who travels to the countryside for business
yobiyose	immigration sponsored by relatives who are citizens or permanent residents of the host country; some *yobiyose* immigrants paid for their passages, and others had their passages subsidized by the state
Yonsei	fourth-generation Japanese descendent

Bibliography

Archives

Arquivo Municipal de São Paulo, São Paulo, Brazil
Arquivo Público do Estado de São Paulo (APESP), São Paulo, Brazil
Diplomatic Archives of the Ministry of Foreign Affairs of Japan, Tokyo, Japan
Japanese Overseas Migration Museum, Yokohama, Japan
Museu da Imigração do Estado de São Paulo, São Paulo, Brazil
Museu Histórico da Imigração Japonesa no Brasil, São Paulo, Brazil
National Diet Library, Tokyo, Japan
Nippon Rikkokai Foundatin, Tokyo, Japan

Author Interviews (AI)

Adachi, Senichi, July 5, 2002
Akahoshi, Sandra, July 3, 2002
Akahoshi, Tsutomu, July 3, 2002
Alvarenga, Keiko Nakahara, June 11, 2010
Arai, Shizue Higaki, June 9, 2008
Arakaki, Emiko, July 20, 2010
Arashiro, Delma, June 14, 1999
Arata, Sumu, June 11, 2010
Ebihara, Tadao, June 13, 2013
Ezawa, Kazuko, January 22, 1998, and June 30, 2001
Figuchi, Midory Kimura, January 22 and 23, 1998
Fujita, Yoshiro, June 14, 2008
Fujitani, Haruko, December 31, 1997, and January 10, 1998
Fujitani, Mariana Kazumi, December 31, 1997
Fukunaga, Juliana, June 13, 2008

Funabashi, Eric, June 27, 2008
Futemma, Olga Toshiko, June 20, 2002
Hamada, Kayoko, July 20, 2010
Hanada, Yuko, December 31, 1997
Hanashiro, Kasumi, July 24, 2010
Hasegawa, Edwin Hideki, June 28, 2008
Hashida, Yaeko, June 12, 2001
Hata, Toshio, June 14, 2008, and June 5, 2010
Hirata, Newton, June 25, 2002
Horiuchi, Wagner M., June 10, 2002
Hosokawa, Tamiko, June 13, 2002
Ikesaki, Hirofumi, June 26, 2008
Inoue, Hisahiro, June 5 and 7, 2010
Ishihara, Chizuko, June 27, 2001
Ito, Emi, January 9, 1998, and June 25, 2008
Kaburaki, Isao, July 17, 2010
Kanazawa, Eiko, June 25, June 26, and July 18, 2001

Kase, Masayo, June 15, 2010
Kawamura, Kulara, June 22, 1999
Kikuchi, Tsuruko, June 6, 2002
Kiyotani, Masugi, June 14, 2002
Kiyotani, Tsumoru, June 14, 2002
Kobayashi, Gustavo Akitoshi, June 19, 2008
Komori, Hiroshi, June 19, 2010
Martins, João Carlos B., June 15, 2005
Masuko, João Toshiei, July 20, 2010
Matsuhira, Kazuya, June 12, 2010
Matsuno, Yoriko, June 27, 2001
Mello, Alexandre, June 15, 2005
Minami, Andrea Yumi, July 20, 2010
Minemura, Alice, June 8, 1999
Miyagi, Eliane, June 16, 1999
Miyano, Yoshie, June 13, 1999
Miyazaki, Hideto, June 13, 2013
Miyazaki, Nobue, June 26, 2002
Mizumoto, Sumiko, June 19, 2001
Mizuno, Masayuki, June 15, 2013
Mori, Koichi, June 4, 2002
Moriyama, Teruko, June 26, 2008
Morohashi, Shigeki, July 11, 2010
Motoyama, Hector Nobuo, June 12, 2010
Moura, Christan, June 23, 2005
Munanga, Kabengele, June 24, 2002
Murakami, Hugo Shinji, June 26, 2008
Nagase, Takeshi, July 15, 2010
Nagashima, Mikiko, June 12, 2008
Nagata, Hisashi, June 10, 2010
Nakama, Hiroko, June 26 and 28, 2001; July 6, 2001; and June 5, 2002
Nakamura, Akihito, June 11, 2002
Nakata, Ronaldo Masaki, June 28, 2008
Nakayama, Yasumi, June 13, 2008, and June 8, 2010
Ninagawa, Ricardo, June 24, 2005
Nishimoto, Lina Mitsuko, January 21, 1998
Nozaki, Taeko, July 24, 2010
Oba, Tiyoko, June 28, 2005
Oda, Christina Sakura, June 20, 2001

Ogawa, Akio, June 9, 2010
Okada, Masae, December 31, 1997, and January 10, 1998
Okamoto, Yumiko, June 14, 2008
Omachi, Nelson, July 22, 2010
Ono, Hiromi, July 22, 2010
Ozawa, Sakiko, June 9, 1999
Reis, Eneida Almeida, July 10, 2001
Roland, Edna, June 22, 2001
Saeki, Teiko, January 4, 1998
Saito, Shizu, July 1, 2002.
Sakagami, Natsue, June 13, 1999, and June 6, 2001
Sakamoto, Masako, June 8 and 13, 2001
Santos, Liliani, June 17, 2005
Satow, Suely Harumi, July 16, 2001
Sekiguchi, Kiyoe, June 23, 2008
Shigeoka, Yasuto, June 20, 2008; June 24, 2008; and July 1, 2008
Shinozuka, Miyuki, June 27, 2008
Shiobara, Yasuo, June 15, 2010
Sugimoto, Masashi, June 14 and 16, 2010
Sugimoto, Tsuruyo, June 16, 2010
Sumida, Katsuko, June 17, 2010
Takiyama, Masami, July 4, 2002
Tamura, Eduardo Seiji, June 29, 2005
Tamura, Fukuhachi, June 10, 2010
Tanaka, Iossuke, June 24 and 25, 2008
Tokuhiro, Hirotaka, June 6, 2010
Tokunaga, Emerson Masaaki, July 20, 2010
Tomino, Sachiko, June 25, 1999, and July 5, 2002
Torenji, Hachiro, July 24, 2010
Tozuka, Mari, June 13, 2001
Uehara, Reiko, June 27, 2001, and July 2, 2001
Umezaki, Chizuko, June 16, 2010
Umezaki, Yoshiaki, June 16, 2010
Utimura, Rosa Aiko, June 7, 1999
Utiyama, Helena, July 11, 2001
Vicente, José, June 27, 2005
Wakisaka, Geny Akiko, July 5, 2001

Yagami, Julia Miki, June 12, 2010
Yagihara, Amelia, June 10 and 14, 2010
Yamane, Toshi, June 21, 2002
Yamano, Renato Takada, July 21, 2010
Yamaoka, Erica M., June 27, 2001
Yamashita, Lucia Mika, June 12, 2010
Yamauchi, Atsushi, June 17, 2010
Yano, Yukie, January 8, 1998

Yonamine, Isabel Natsumi, June 12, 2002
Yoneda, Kazuyo, June 13, 2010
Yoshida, Yoko, June 10, 2001
Yoshimura, Marcelo Shuji, July 21, 2010
Yukimura, Hanae, June 15 and 22, 2008

Sources

Adachi, Senichi. "Nihon Bunka Sentā no Dekiru Made: Keika Hokoku ni Kaete" [Until the Center of Japanese Culture Was Completed: In Place of a Report on Its Process]. In *Colônia Bekkan: Nihon Bunka Sentā Rakusei Kinengo* [Colônia Special Issue in Commemoration of the Inauguration of the Center of Japanese Culture], 52–83. São Paulo: São Paulo Nihon Bunka Kyokai, 1964.

Aida, Yutaka. *Kōseki: Ijū Sanjūichinenme no Jōsensha Meibo* [Trail of a Voyage: Those Who Were on the Passenger List Thirty-One Years Ago]. Tokyo: NHK, 2003.

Akimmoto, Yukio. "Ginko no Madoguchi de" [At a Bank Counter]. *Colônia*, no. 31 (December 1961): 8–9.

Amino, Yataro. "Higan no Jōriku Kinenhi Konryu Made" [Until the Inauguration of the Japanese Immigrants Monument, Which Was Our Ardent Wish], in *Burajiru Kenren No. 5: Sōritsu 40-shūnen Kenrenshi, 1966–2006* [The Fifth Volume of Brazilian Kenren in Commemoration of Kenren's 40th Anniversary, 1966–2006], edited by Kenren 40-shūnen Kinenshi Hensan Iinkai, 229–232. São Paulo: Burajiru Todōfukenjinkai Rengōkai, 2008.

Andrews, George Reid. *Blacks and Whites in São Paulo, Brazil, 1888–1988.* Madison: University of Wisconsin Press, 1991.

Aoyagi, Ikutaro. *Burajiru ni Okeru Nihonjin Hatsutenshi* [The History of Japanese Development in Brazil]. 2 vols. Tokyo: Burajiru ni Okeru Nihonjin Hatsutenshi Kankō Iinkai, 1942.

Arai, Jhony. "Mãos à obra: Associações de jovens nikkeis do brasil buscam soluções para não desaparecer" [Hands On: Young Brazilian Nikkeis' Associations Seek Solutions Not to Disappear]. *Made in Japan,* no. 46 (June 2001): 64–65.

Arai, Jhony, and Andréia Ferreira. "90 anos depois, quem são os descendentes de japoneses" [After 90 Years, Who Are Japanese Descendants]. *Made in Japan,* no. 9 (June 1998): 50–55.

Asahi Shimbun. "Chu 3 Jitaku Hoka Yōgui" [A Nineth Grader Charged of Home Arson]. July 9, 2010, 1.

——. "Nanbei no Nikkeijin: Nihon no Shimbunkisha wa Kō Mita" [The Nikkeis in South America: This Is the Way a Japanese Newspaper Reporter Perceived Them] (1965). Reprinted in *Nippak Mainichi Shimbun Shin-nen Tokubetsugo 1966* [Nippak Mainichi Shimbun New Year Special Issue 1966]. São Paulo: Nippak Mainichi Shimbunsha, 1966.

Azuma, Eiichiro. *Between Two Empires: Race, History, and Transnationalism in Japanese America*. Oxford: Oxford University Press, 2005.

Brody, Betsy. *Opening the Doors: Immigration, Ethnicity, and Globalization in Japan*. New York: Routledge, 2001.

Brooke, James. "Sons and Daughters of Japan, Back from Brazil." *New York Times*, November 27, 2001, A4.

Bumba. " 'Nikkeijin': Korega Watashitachi no Seikatsu Desu" ["Nikkeijin": This Is Our Lifestyle]. 2, no. 12 (2001): 16–21.

Bunka. "Dai-Nisei Shokun to Nihon Bunka o Kataru" [A Talk on Japanese Culture with *Dai*-Nisei Men]. 11, no. 1 (November 1938): 26–31.

Bunkyo 50-nenshi Hensan Iinkai, ed. *Bunkyo 50-nenshi* [Bunkyo's History of 50 Years]. São Paulo: Burajiru Nihon Bunka Fukushi Kyokai, 2007.

Bunkyo Yonjūnenshi Hensan Iinkai, ed. *Bunkyo Yonjūnenshi* [Bunkyo's History of Forty Years]. São Paulo: Burajiru Nihon Bunka Kyokai, 1998.

Burajirujihōsha, ed. *Burajiru Nenkan* [A Yearbook of Brazil]. São Paulo: Burajirujihōsha, 1933.

Burajiru Okinawa Kenjinkai Nihongo Henshu Iinkai, ed. *Burajiru Okinawa-kenjin Iminshi: Kasato Maru kara 90-nen* [The History of Okinawan Immigration: 90 Years since the *Kasato Maru*]. São Paulo: Associação Okinawa Kenjin do Brasil, 2000.

Burajiru Rikkokai, ed. *Burajiru Rikkokai Yonjūnenshi* [Forty-Year History of the Brazilian Association of Rikkokai]. São Paulo: Burajiru Rikkokai, 1966.

———, ed. *Burajiru Rikkokai Sōritsu Hachijūshunen Kinenshi* [A Commemorative Issue on the 80th Anniversary of Brazilian Association of Rikkokai]. São Paulo: Burajiru Rikkokai, 2007.

———, ed. *Rikko no Kizuna: Burajiru Rikkokai Sōritsu Kyujushunen Kinen* [The Bond of Rikko in Commemoration of the 90th Anniversary of Brazilian Association of Rikkokai]. São Paulo: Burajiru Rikkokai, 2007.

Carmo, Cely. "Mutirão da Solidaridade" [Effort of Solidarity]. *Japão Aqui* 1, no. 4 (August 1997): 32–34.

Caulfield, Sueann. *In Defense of Honor: Sexual Morality, Modernity, and Nation in Early Twentieth-Century Brazil*. Durham, NC: Duke University Press, 2000.

Centro de Estudos Nipo-Brasileiros, ed. *Burajiru Nihon Imin Nikkei Shakaishi Nenphō: Handa Tomoo Hen-cho Kaitei* Zōho Ban [Chronological Table of Japanese Immigration to Brazil and Japanese Brazilian Social History: A Revised an Expanded Version of the Original by Tomoo Handa]. São Paulo: Centro de Estudos Nipo-Brasileiros, 1996.

———, ed. *Burajiru ni Okeru Nikkei Jinko Chōsa Hōkokusho, 1987–1988* [A Survey on the Nikkei Population in Brazil, 1987–1988]. São Paulo: Centro de Estudos Nipo-Brasileiros, n.d.

Centro de Informação e Apoio ao Trabalhador no Exterior (CIATE), ed. *Resultado de Questionários sobre Dekasseguis* [Results of Questionnaires on Dekasseguis]. São Paulo: CITAE, 1999.

Chunichi Shimbun. "Nippon de Ikiru Brazil: Imin 100-nen—Dai 1-bu Sugao 'Gakko' Nihongo o Hanashitai" [Living in Japan: 100 Years of Immigration to Brazil—Part 1: Unpainted Face, "School," and Desire to Speak Japanese]. June 19, 2007. www.chunichi.co.jp/shizuoka/hold/emigrant/CK2007061902027684.html. Accessed April 6, 2012.

———. "Nippon de Ikiru: Burajiru Imin 100 Nen: Dai 3 bu—Rōdō, Kigyo, Jibun no Chikara de Idomitai" [Living in Japan: 100 Years of Immigration to Brazil—Part 3: Work, Starting a Business, They Want to Face Challenges on Their Own]. December 24, 2007. www.chunichi.co.jp/shizuoka/hold/emigrant/CK20071224 02074712.html. Accessed April 6, 2012.

———. "Rōdō Kigyo Jibun no Chikara de Idomitai" [Labor, Entrepreneurship, Business, I Would Like to Try on My Own]. December 27, 2007. www.chunichi .co.jp/shizuoka/hold/emigrant/CK2007122402074712.html. Accessed March 18, 2012.

Clifford, James. *Routes: Travels and Translation in the Late Twentieth Century.* Cambridge, MA: Harvard University Press, 1997.

Colônia. "Colônia no Kekkon Mondai: Sōdan o Ukeru Mono no Tachiba Kara" [Marriage Problems in the Colônia: From the Position of Marriage Consultants]. No. 43 (October 1964): 2–12.

———. "Colônia no Shiwa" [Colônia's Wrinkles]. No. 47 (February 1965): 2–31.

———. "Jun-Nisei Zadankai: 'Umoreta Sedai' wa Kataru" [A Roundtable Discussion by Quasi-Niseis: "A Buried Generation" Speaks]. No. 86 (1970): 24–32.

———. "Kohohito o Tazunete: Nōgaku Hakushi Ikuta Hiroshi-shi" [Interview of Hiroshi Ikuta, Doctor of Agriculture]. No. 51 (June 1965): 18–19.

———. "Nihon Mitamama: Nisei Ryugakusei no Me ni Utsutta Gendai Nihon no Sugada" [Japan as It Is: How Modern Japan Has Been Perceived by Nisei Students Who Studied There]. No. 52 (July 1965): 8–12.

———. "Rōgo no Sekkei" [Retirement Plans]. No. 29 (July 1961): 20–21.

———. "Zadankai: Hahaoya no Me kara Mita Nisei no Shomondai" [Roundtable Discussion: Various Problems the Nisei Are Facing from the Perspectives of their Mothers]. No. 57 (February–March 1966): 2–8.

———. "Zadankai: Seinen no Ikigai o Saguru" [Roundtable Discussion: Seeking Purposes of Life for Young Men]. No. 30 (September 1961): 16–19.

———. "Zadankai: Shokuba no Mikon Nisei Danjo no Renai to Kekkon-kan" [Roundtable Discussion: Single, Professional Nisei Men and Women's Perception of Dating and Marriage]. No. 53 (August 1965): 4–8.

Colônia Bungaku. "Zadankai: 'Nihon' wa Nani o Dou Kangen Suruka. Nisei Shakaijin no Seikatsu to Iken" [Roundtable Discussion: What and How Does "Japan" Contribute Back to Us? Nisei Professionals' Lives and Opinions]. No. 23 (March 1974): 28–36.

Colônia Geinōshi Hensan Iinkai, ed. *Colônia Geinōshi* [Colônia's History of Entertainment]. São Paulo: Colônia Geinōshi Hensan Iinkai, 1986.

Daigo, Masao. *Minami Hankyū no za Japanīzu: Burajiru ni Okeru Nihonjin no Tekiō*

[The Japanese in the Southern Hemisphere: The Japanese's Adaptation in Brazil]. Tokyo: Bungeishunjūsha, 1981.

Degler, Carl N. *Neither Black nor White: Slavery and Race Relations in Brazil and the United States. 1971*. Madison: University of Wisconsin Press, 1986.

De la Cadena, Marisol. "'Women Are More Indian': Ethnicity and Gender in a Community near Cuzco." In *Ethnicity, Markets, and Migration in the Andes: At the Crossroads of History and Anthropology*, edited by Brooke Larson, Olivia Harris, and Enrique Tandeter, 329–348. Durham, NC: Duke University Press, 1995.

Dezem, Rogério. *Inventário Depos: Módulo III, Japoneses: Shindô-Renmei: Terrorismo e Represessão* [São Paulo State Department of Political and Social Order Inventory, Module III, The Japanese: Shindō Renmei: Terrorism and Repression]. São Paulo: Arquivo do Estado, Impresa Oficial, 2000.

Emi, Cláudia, and Andréia Ferreira. "Japão ou Brasil" [Japan or Brazil]. *Made in Japan*, no. 9 (June 1998): 30–39.

Esperança Fujinkai, ed. *Esperança Sōritsu Yonjūgoshūnen Kinengō* [Esperança: A Special Issue in Commemoration of Its 45th Anniversary], no. 40 (December 1994).

———, ed. *Relação de Associadas (1998)* [Register of Association Members (1998)]. São Paulo: Esperança Fujinkai, 1998.

Ferreira, Andréia. "Os novos imigrantes" [The New Immigrants]. *Made in Japan*, no. 21 (June 1998): 18–27.

Ferreira, Andréia, and Nelson Watanabe. "Hora de Voltar" [The Hour of Return]. *Made in Japan*, no. 26 (June 1999): 26–29.

Fujii, Takuji. "Mohoya Hakikirenu Genjo" [The Current Situation One Cannot Handle]. *Kaihō*, no. 19 (July–August 1959): 34–36.

Fukasawa, Masayuki. "Hyakunen no Chie, Imin to 'Nihon Seishin,' Enkakuchi Nashonarisumu 13-kai: NHK Shichosha wa Nisei Chūsin" [One Hundred Years of Wisdom—Immigrants and "Japanese Spirit"—Remote Nationalism, No. 13: Niseis Constitute the Majority of NHK Viewers]. *Nikkey Shimbun*, August 7, 2008. www.nikkeyshimbun.com.br/080807-62colonia.html. Accessed August 21, 2008.

———. "Iminka-suru Dekassegui-tachi, Ne o Haru Zainichi Hakujin Shakai, Rensai Dai 1-kai: Jitsu wa 33 man-nin ga Nihon Zaijū" [*Dekasseguis* Becoming Immigrants, Brazilian Society Rooting in Japan, Series No. 1: In Reality 330,000 Are Living in Japan]. *Nikkey Shimbun*, August 24, 2007. www.nikkeyshimbun.com .br/070824-71colonia.html. Accessed April 23, 2008.

———. *Parareru Wārudo* [Parallel World]. Tokyo: Ushio Shuppan, 1999.

Gaijin: Os caminhos da liberdade [Gaijin: The Pathways to Liberty]. Directed by Tizuka Yamasaki. Produced by Carlos Alberto Diniz. São Paulo, 1980.

Gakuyu. "Seishi Hojin Kishukusha Tanboki" [Reports on Japanese Dormitories in São Paulo City]. No. 8 (September 1938): 70–88.

Grupo Gambarê! Brasileiros. "Resultado da pesquisa da cidade de Hamamatsu Avaliação sobre a situação dos brasileiros diante da crise econômica" [Results of Hamamatsu City's Survey to Evaluate the Situation of Brazilians during the

Economic Crisis]. March 12, 2009. www.hi-hice.jp/doc/aboutus/report/Pesquisa _Gambare.pdf. Accessed April 10, 2012.

Guimarães, Laís de Barros Monteiro. *Liberdade*. São Paulo: Prefeitura do Municipio de São Paulo, Secretaria Municipal de Cultura, 1979.

Gutmann, Matthew C., and Catherine Lutz. *Breaking Ranks: Iraq Veterans Speak Out against the War*. Berkeley: University of California Press, 2010.

Hall, Stuart. "Cultural Identity and Diaspora." In *Identity: Community, Culture, Difference*, edited by Jonathan Rutherford, 222–237. London: Lawrence and Wishart, 1990.

———. "The Local and the Global: Globalization and Ethnicity." In *Culture, Globalization, and the World-System: Contemporary Conditions for the Representation of Identity*, edited by Anthony D. King, 19–39. Minneapolis: University of Minnesota, 1997.

———. "Old and New Identities, Old and New Ethnicities." In *Culture, Globalization, and the World-System: Contemporary Conditions for the Representation of Identity*, edited by Anthony D. King, 41–68. Minneapolis: University of Minnesota Press, 1997.

Hamamatsu Foundation for International Communication and Exchange (HICE). "Hamamatsu-shi ni Tsuite no Deita Tōkei: Hamamatsu-shi no Gaikokuji Tōrokushasū" [Data and Statisics on Hamamatsu City: Numbers of Foreign Residents in Hamamatsu City]. www.hi-hice.jp/index.php. Accessed April 10, 2012.

———. "Hamamatsu-shi no Gaikokujin Tōrokushasū " [Numbers of Foreign Residents Registered in Hamamatsu City]. www.hi-hice.jp/aboutus/statistics.html. Accessed April 10, 2012.

Hanchard, Michael George. "Racism, Eroticism, and the Paradox of a U.S. Black Researcher in Brazil." In *Racing Research, Researching Race: Methodological Dilemmas in Critical Race Studies*, edited by France Winddance Twine and Jonathan W. Warren, 165–185. New York: New York University Press, 2000.

Handa, Tomoo. *Burajiru Imin no Seikatsu: Handa Tomoo Gabunshū* [The Life of Japanese Immigrants in Brazil: Collection of Paintings and Essays by Tomoo Handa]. Akita, Japan: Mumyōsha Shuppan, 1986.

———. *Imin no Seikatsu no Rekishi: Brajiru Nikkei Imin no Ayunda Michi* [A History of the Immigrant Life: The Path Japanese Brazilians Walked]. São Paulo: Centro de Estudos Nipo-Brasileiros, 1970.

Harada, Kiyoshi, ed. *O Nikkei no Brasil* [The Nikkei in Brazil]. São Paulo: Editora Atlas, 2008.

Higuchi, Naoto. "Keizai Kiki to Zainichi Burajirujin: Nani ga Tairyo Shitsugyo Kikoku o Motarashitanoka" [Economic Crises and Brazilians in Japan: What Brought Them Mass Unemployment and Made Them Return to Brazil]. *Ōhara Shakai Mondai Kenkyusho*, no. 622 (August 2010): 50–66.

Higuchi, Naoto, and Kiyoto Tanno. "What's Driving Brazil-Japan Migration? The Making and Remaking of Brazilian Niche in Japan." *International Journal of Japanese Sociology*, no. 12 (2003): 33–47.

Higuchi, Tomie. "Shinshin Gakushi no Haha wa Kataru (1): Kankyo no Motsu Chikara" [Mothers of Emerging University Graduates Talk, No. 1: The Power of an Environment]. *Kaihō*, no. 5 (March–April 1957): 34–36.

Hirabayashi, Lane Ryo, Akemi Kikumura-Yano, and James A. Hirabayashi, eds. *New Worlds, New Lives: Globalization and People of Japanese Descent in the Americas and from Latin America in Japan*. Stanford, CA: Stanford University Press, 2002.

Hirai, Tsuyako. "Seishinteki Seikatu eno Kyoryoku o" [For the Sake of Our Cooperation in Spiritual Life]. *Kaihō*, no. 8 (September–October 1957): 16–17.

Hironaka, Chikako. *Inochi Ori-Ori* [Moments of Life]. São Paulo: Nippak Mainichi Shimbunsha, 1994.

Hitotsubashi Daigau Nanbei Enseitai. "Hitotsubashi Daigau Nanbei Ensesitai Hokousho: Imin Seikatsu o Tazunete" [A Report by the Expeditionary Team to South America of Hitotsubashi University: Visiting with Japanese Immigrants in Brazil]. *Colônia*, no. 24 (August 1960): 56–57.

Holloway, Thomas H. *Immigrants on the Land: Coffee and Society in São Paulo, 1886–1934*. Chapel Hill: University of North Carolina Press, 1980.

Horie, Takeshi. "Nikkijin to wa Nanika: Adachi Senichi, Watanbe Kazuo, Hanseiki no Kōsaku (4): Nihon Bunka o Kokoro ni Yadosu Mono Kore Subete 'Nikkeijin'?" [What Is the Nikkeijin? The Crossroads between Senichi Adachi and Kazuo Watanabe over Half a Century, No. 4: Is Everybody Who Has Japanese Culture in His/Her Heart a New "Nikkeijin"?]. *Nikkey Shimbun*, October 7, 2003. www.nikkey shimbun.com.br/2003/031007-72colonia.html. Accessed December 31, 2011.

Horikawa, Naoko. "New Lives in the Ancestral Homeland: Return Migration from South America to Mainland Japan and Okinawa." PhD diss., University of Hull, 2012.

Hosokawa, Shuhei. *Shinemaya Burajiru o Yuku: Nikkei Imin no Kyoshu to Aidentitii* [Chinema-Men Wonder in Brazil: Japanese Immigrants' Homesickness and Identity]. Tokyo: Shinchō Shinsho, 1999.

Ikegami, Shigehiro. "Burajirujin Zōka no Yōin to Zōka no Yōsō" [Factors Contributing to the Increase of Japanese Brazilians and Their Condition]. In *Burajirujin to Kokusaikasuru Chiiki Shakai: Kyojū Kyōiku Iryō* [Brazilians and the Local Community in the Process of Internationalization: Residence, Education, and Medical Care], edited by Shigehiro Ikegami, 18–37. Tokyo: Akashi Shoten, 2001.

Imin 70-nenshi Hensan Iinkai, ed. *Burajiru Nihon Imin 70-nenshi, 1908–1978* [The 70-Year History of Japanese Immigration to Brazil]. São Paulo: Burajiru Nihon Bunka Kyokai, 1980.

Imin Hachijūnenshi Hensan Iinkai, ed. *Burajiru Nihon Imin Hachijūnenshi* [The Eighty-Year History of Japanese Immigration to Brazil]. São Paulo: Imin Hachijūnensai Iinkai and Burajiru Nihon Bunka Kyokai, 1991.

Imoto, Atsushi. "Jun-Nisei Zadankai ni Shusseki Shite: Nanika o Gisei ni Shinakerebarararai Jidai ga Atta" [Having Attended the Roundtable Discussion on the Quasi-Nisei: There Was a Time When Something Had to Be Sacrificed]. *Colônia*, no. 86 (1970): 22–23.

Ishi, Angelo. "Between Privilege and Prejudice: Japanese-Brazilian Migrants in 'The Land of Yen and the Ancestors.'" In *Transcultural Japan: At the Borderlands of Race, Gender, and Identity*, edited by David Blake Willis and Stephen Murphy-Shigematsu, 113–136. London: Routledge, 2008.

———. "Dekassegui Keikensha no Manga kara Hanshin Daishinsai Hōdō made: Porutogaru Media no Kaishingeki" [Comics by a Former Dakassegui until the Reports on the Great Hanshin Earthquake: The Great Advancement of Mass Media in the Portuguese Language]. In *Esunikku Media: Tabunka Shakai Nihon o Mezashite / Ethnic Media: Toward the Multicultural Japan*, edited by Shigehiro Shiramizu, 95–147. Tokyo: Akashi Shoten, 1996.

———. "Searching Home, Wealth, Pride, and 'Class': Japanese Brazilians in the 'Land of Yen.'" In *In Search for Home Abroad: Japanese Brazilians and the Transnational Moment*, edited by Jeffery Lesser, 73–102. Durham, NC: Duke University Press, 2003.

Ishikawa, Eunice Akemi. "Kazoku wa Kodomo no Kyoiku ni Dō Kakawaruka: Dekassegui-gata Raifu Sutairu to Oya no Nayami" [How Should Parents Engage Themselves in the Education of Their Children: *Dekassegui* Lifestyle and Parents' Worries]. In *Gaikokujin no Kodomo to Nihon no Kyoiku: Fushūgaku Mondai to Tabunka Kyosei no Kadai* [Foreign Children and Japanese Education: Problems of No Schooling and Multiculturalism as a Goal], edited by Takashi Miyajima and Haruo Ōta, 77–96. Tokyo: Tokyo Daigaku Shuppankai, 2005.

Izumi, Seiichi. "Burajiru no Nikkei Colônia" [The Nikkei Colony in Brazil]. In *Imin: Burajiru Imin no Jittai Chōsa* [The Immigrant: A Survey on Japanese Immigrants in Brazil], edited by Seiichi Izumi, 9–127. Tokyo: Kokin Shoten, 1957.

James, Daniel. *Doña María's Story: Life, History, Memory, and Political Identity*. Durham, NC: Duke University Press, 2000.

Japan, Ministry of Foreign Affairs. "Burajiru Renbō Kyowakoku Kiso Deita" [Basic Data on the Federative Republic of Brazil]. www.mofa.go.jp/mofaj/area/brazil/data.html. Accessed January 6, 2015.

———. "Zaigai Senkyo" [Absentee-Balloting System for Japanese Citizens Overseas]. www.mofa.go.jp/mofaj/toko/senkyo/vote1.html. Accessed on October 15, 2011.

———. "Zainich Burajirujin ni Kansuru Deita" [Data on Brazilians Residing in Japan]. June 2005. www.mofa.go.jp/mofaj/area/latinamerica/kaigi/brazil/data.html. Accessed March 21, 2012.

Japan, Ministry of Health, Labor, and Welfare. "Konin Dai-2-hyo: Fufu no Kokusekibetsu ni Mita Konin Kensu no Nenji Suii" [Marriages, Table 2: Changes over the Years in Marriages by the Nationality of a Spouse]. www.mhlw.go.jp/toukei/saikin/hw/jinkou/suii09/marr2.html. Accessed August 15, 2012.

Japan, Ministry of Justice. "Zairyu Gaikokujin Tōkei Tōkeihyo" [Stastitical Tables of Foreign Residents in Japan]. www.moj.go.jp/housei/toukei/toukei_ichiran_tou roku.html. Accessed May 24, 2015.

Japan Times. "Two Teenage Girls Held over Fatal Hyogo Home Arson Targeting Kin." July 10, 2010. www.japantimes.co.jp/text/nn20100710a2.html. Accessed July 12, 2010.

Japão Aquí. "Japonês ou brasileiro: Como se sente o jovem nikkei?" [Japanese or Brazilian: How Does the Nikkei Youth Feel?]. Vol. 1, no. 3 (July 1997): 38–44.

Jōmō Shimbunsha, ed. *Samba no Machi Kara: Gaikokujin to Tomo ni Ikiru Gunma Ōizumi* [From a Town of Samba: Living with Foreigners in Oizumi of Gunma]. Maebashi-shi, Japan: Jōmō Shimbunsha, 1997.

Jornal Nippo-Brasil, ed. *Guida de Eventos em Comemoração ao Centenário da Imigração Japonesa no Brasil* [Guide of Events in Commemoraion of the Centenary of Japanese Immigration in Brazil]. São Paulo: Jornal Nippo-Brasil, 2008.

Kaigai Ijū Jigyodan, ed. *Kaigai Ijū Jigyodan Jūnenshi* [Ten-Year History of Japan Emigration Service]. Tokyo: Kaigai Ijū Jigyodan, 1973.

Kaigai Ijū Shiryōkan, ed. *Tenji Annai: Warera Shinsekai ni Sankasu* [Guide to the Exhibit: We Participate in the New World]. Tokyo: JICA, 2004.

Kaihō. "Nikkei Daigakusei ga Ryo-Kyoju ni Kiku Kai: Kagaku to Kankyo" [A Meeting for Nikkei College Students to Ask Questions to Both of the Professors: Science and Environment]. No. 17 (March–April 1959): 38–45.

Kajita, Takamichi, Kiyoto Tanno, and Naoto Higuchi. *Kao no Mienai Teijūka: Nikkei Burajirujin to Kokka Shijō Imin Nettowāku / Invisible Residents: Japanese Brazilians vis-à-vis the State, the Market, and the Immigrant Network.* Nagoya-shi, Japan: Nagoya Daigaku Shuppankai, 2005.

Kawahara, Sho. "Dai Nisei no Shichō" [The *Dai*-Nisei's Current Trend of Thought]. *Gakuyu*, no. 4 (August 1936): 18–21.

Kenren 40-shunen Kinenshi Hensan Iinkai, ed. *Burajiru Kenren No. 5: Sōritsu 40-shūnen Kenrenshi, 1966–2006* [The Fifth Volume of Brazilian Kenren in Commemoration of Kenren's 40th Anniversary, 1966–2006]. São Paulo: Burajiru Todōfukenjinkai Rengōkai, 2008.

Kenren Sanjū-shunen Kinenshi Hensan Iinkai, ed. *Burajiru Kenren Dai-Yongo: Kenren 30 Anos, 1966–1996* [The Fourth Volume of Brazilian Kenren: Kenren 30 Years, 1966–1999]. São Paulo: Burajiru Todōfukenjinkai Rengōkai, 1997.

Kikumura-Yano, Akemi, ed. *Encyclopedia of Japanese Descendants in the Americas: An Illustrated History of the Nikkei.* Walnut Creek, CA: Altamira Press, 2002.

Kinenshi Henshū Iinkai, ed. *Burajiru Nikkei Rōjin Kurabu Rengōkai 30-nen no Ayumi: Rōkuren Setsuritsu 30-shūnen Kinen* [The Course of 30 Years for the Association of the Brazilian Nikkei Clubs for the Elderly: Commemoration of Rōkuren's 30th Anniversary]. São Paulo: Burajiru Nikkei Rōjin Kurabu Rengōkai, 2008.

Kishimoto, Koichi. *Nanbei no Senya ni Koritsushite* [Isolated in the Battlefield of South America]. São Paulo: Aranosha, 1947.

Kiyotani, Masuji. *Tōi Hibi no Koto* [On Those Remote Days]. São Paulo: Masuji Kioyotani, 1985.

Kobe Center for Overseas Migration and Cultural Interaction. "Tatemono no Rekishi" [History of the Buidling]. http://www.kobe-center.jp/history.html. Accessed March 18, 2012.

Konami, Miyoko. *Kaigai ni Tobitatsu Hanayometachi* [Brides Flying Away Overseas]. Tokyo: Kōdansha, 1986.

Koyama, Akio. "Interview of Akio Koyama." *Quem e Quem,* October 2000. www
.100nen.com.br/ja/qq/000014/20030411000047.cfm. Accessed May 14, 2012.

Kōyama, Rokurō. *Imin Yonjūnenshi* [Forty-Year History of (Japanese) Immigration (to Brazil)]. São Paulo: Rokurō Kōyama, 1949.

Leão Neto, Valdemar Carneiro. *A crise da imigração japonesa no Brasil, 1930–1934: Contornos diplomáticos* [The Crisis of Japanese Immigration to Brazil, 1930–1934: Diplomatic Outlines]. Brasília: Fundação Alexandre de Gusmão, Instituto de Pesquisa de Relações Internacionais, 1990.

Lesser, Jeffrey. *A Discontented Diaspora: Japanese-Brazilians and the Meanings of Ethnic Militancy.* Durham, NC: Duke University Press, 2007.

———. *Negotiating National Identity: Immigrants, Minorities, and the Struggle for Ethnicity in Brazil.* Durham, NC: Duke University Press, 1999.

Linger, Daniel Touro. *No One Home: Brazilian Selves Made in Japan.* Stanford, CA: Stanford University Press, 2001.

Lipsett-Rivera, Sonya. "A Slap in the Face of Honor: Social Transgression and Women in Late Colonial Mexico." In *The Faces of Honor: Sex, Shame, and Violence in Colonial Latin America,* edited by Lyman L. Johnson and Sonya Lipsett-Rivera, 179–200. Albuquerque: University of New Mexico Press, 1998.

Lowe, Lisa. *Immigrant Acts: On Asian American Cultural Politics.* Durham, NC: Duke University Press, 1996.

Luz, Sérgio Ruiz. "Gaijin pelo avesso" [Gaijin Inside Out]. *Japão Aqui,* 1, no. 1 (April 1997): 85–87.

Machado, Tiago Mata. "Mizoguchi e Ozu são destaques da mostra" [Mizoguchi and Ozu Are Prominent in the Showing]. *Folha de São Paulo,* July 1, 2001.

Maeyama, Takashi. "Chikyu no Uragawa kara Nihonjin o Miru: Burajiru, Amerika, Nihon" [Looking at the Japanese from the Other Side of the Globe: Brazil, the United States, and Japan]. *Chūōkōron* 95, no. 4 (April 1980): 118–128.

———. *Dona Margarita Watanabe: Imin-Rojin Fukushi no 53-Nen* [Dona Margarita Watanabe: The 53 Years Spent for the Welfare of Elderly Immigrants]. Tokyo: Ochanomizu Shobo, 1996.

———. *Esunishitii to Burajiru Nikkeijin* [Ethnicity and Japanese Brazilians]. Tokyo: Ochanomizu Shobo, 1996.

———. "Ethnicity, Secret Societies, and Associations: The Japanese in Brazil." *Comparative Studies in Society and History,* 21, no. 4 (1979): 589–619.

———. *Ibunka Sesshoku to Aidentiti: Brajiru Shakai to Nikkeijin* [Cultural Contact and Identity: Brazilian Society and Japanese Brazilians]. Tokyo: Ochanomizu Shobo, 2001.

———. *Imin no Nihon Kaiki Undo* [Japanese Immigrants' Repatriation Movement to Japan]. Tokyo: NHK, 1982.

———. "Kagaisha Fumei no Higaisha: Colônia Bungakuron Oboegaki" [Victims without Victimizers: A Note on the Discussions on *Colônia*'s Literature]. *Colônia Bungaku,* no. 26 (March 1975): 72–78.

———. "Nisei no Naka no Nihon" [Japan within the Nisei]. In *Ratenteki Nihonjin:*

Burajiru Nisei no Hatsugen [The Latin Japanese: Opinions Expressed by the Nisei of Brazil], edited by Morio Ōno, 121–153. Tokyo: NHK, 1969.

Maruko, Mami. "Helping Brazilian Kids Master Local Life: Japanese-Brazilian Tetsuyoshi Kodama Proudly Serves as a Bridge between Communities." *Japan Times*, August 23, 2011. www.japantimes.co.jp/text/fl20110823ww.html#.T_y5D45TcVs. Accessed August 6, 2012.

Masters, Coco. "Japan to Immigrants: Thanks, but You Can Go Home Now." *Time*, April 20, 2009. www.time.com/time/world/article/0,8599,1892469,00.html. Accessed April 20, 2009.

Masterson, Daniel M., with Sayaka Funada-Classen. *The Japanese in Latin America*. Urbana: University of Illinois Press, 2004.

Mifugi, Saefugi. "Tizuka to Yurika: 'Gaijin' ni miru Simai no Kento" [Tizuka and Yurika: The Sisters' Achievements Seen in *Gaijin*]. In *Colônia Geinōshi*, edited by Colôina Geinōshi Hensan Iinkai, 280–283. São Paulo: Colônia Geinōshi Hensan Iinkai, 1986.

Mintz, Sidney W. *Workers in Cane: Puerto Rican Life History*. New York: W. W. Norton, 1974.

Mita, Chiyoko. *"Dekasegi" Kara "Dekassegui" Ye: Burajiru Imin 100-nen ni miru Hito to Bunka no Dainamizumu* [From "Dekasegi" to "Dekassegui": The Dynamism in Humans and Cultures Observed over the One Hundred Years after the Beginning of Immigration to Brazil]. Tokyo: Fuji Shuppan, 2009.

Miyao, Susumu. "Nihon Imin no Ayumi to Nisei" [The Path of Japanese Immigrants and the Nisei]. In *Ratenteki Nihonin: Burajiru Nisei no Hatsugen* [The Latin Japanese: Opinions Expressed by the Nisei of Brazil], edited by Morio Ōno, 63–93. Tokyo: NHK, 1969.

Mizumoto, Sumiko. *Rodeira, Ashita Mata: Burajiru 47-nen no Kiroku* [Small Wheel, See You Again Tomorrow: A Record of My 47 Years in Brazil]. Tokyo: Seibunsha, 1979.

Mori, Koichi. "Burajiru kara no Nikkeijin Dekassegui no Tokucho to Suii" [Characteristics and Changes among the *Dekassegui* Workers from Brazil]. In *Kyodo Kenkyu Dekassegui Nikkei Brajirujin*, edited by Masako Watanebe, 491–546. Vol. 1, *Ronbunhen: Shūrō to Seikatsu* [Articles: Employment and Life]. 2 vols. Tokyo: Akashi Shoten, 1995.

Moriyama, Alan Takeo. *Imingaisha: Japanese Emigration Companies and Hawaii, 1894–1908*. Honolulu: University of Hawai'i Press, 1985.

Motonaga, Gunki. "Horonagaku Soshite Tanoshikatta Ano Jidai no Koto: Bunkyo Uramenshi no Ichibu" [On Those Old Days with Bittersweet Memories: Part of the Hidden History of Bunkyo]. In *Bunkyo Yonjūnenshi* [Bunkyo's History of Forty Years], edited by Bunkyo Yonjūnenshi Hensan Iinkai, 236–241. São Paulo: Burajiru Nihon Bunka Kyokai, 1998.

Nagai, Hiroshi. "Dōka to Yūryhoji" [Assimilation and Excellent Offspring]. *Colônia*, no. 60 (August–September 1966): 18–20.

Nagata, Hisashi. "Burajiru Rikkokai Hachijūnen no Rekishi no Nakakara" [From the 80-Year History of the Brazilian Association of Rikkokai]. In *Burajiru Rikkokai*

Sōritsu Hachijūshunen Kinenshi [A Commemorative Issue on the 80th Anniversary of the Brazilian Association of Rikkokai], edited by Burajiru Rikkokai, 82–121. São Paulo: Burajiru Rikkokai, 2007.

Nagata, Shigeshi. *Nanbei Ichijun* [A Tour to South America]. 1921. Tokyo: Nihon Tosho Sentā, 1998.

Nakajima, Seiichiro. "Saikin Burajiru Imin no Jisseikatsu" [The Real Life of Recent Japanese Immigrants in Brazil]. In *Ishokumin Kōshūkai Kōenshū* [Collection of Lectures on Immigration and Colonization], edited by Takumusho Takumu-kyoku, 304–333. 1932. Tokyo: Nihon Tosho Sentā, 1999.

Nakamura, Tsutomu. "Sengo Burajiru Imin to Nihon no Taihaku Toshi" [Postwar Japanese Immigration to Brazil and Japan's Capital Investment in Brazil]. In *Burajiru Imin Sengo Ijū no 50-nen* [Fifty Years of Postwar Japanese Immigration to Brazil], edited by Sengo Ijū 50-shunen Kinesai Jikko Iinkai, 146–150. São Paulo: Burajiru-Nippon Ijūsha Kyokai, 2004.

Nakayama, Yasumi. "Nihon Imin Burajiru Jyoriku Kinenhi to Kami-san" [Monument for the Landing of Japanese Immigrants and Mr. Kami]. *Kokkyo Chitai*, no. 22 (October 2009): 12–15.

National Diet Library. "Hodo Happyo, Heisei 20 Nen 4 Gatsu 20 Nichi, Zaimusho" [Public Accouncemet from the Ministry of Finance dated April 20, 2008]. http://warp.ndl.go.jp/info:ndljp/pid/1022127/www.mof.go.jp/jouhou/sonota/kokko/kk200430.htm. Accessed June 7, 2013.

Nihon Maikuro Shashin, ed. "Burajiru Nihon Imin Shiryōkan Shozo Bunsho Shiryo" [Documents Housed at the Museum of Japanese Immigration to Brazil]. 35 mm microfilm rolls. 73 vols. Tokyo: Nihon Maikuro Shashin, 1985.

Nikkey Shimbun. "65-nen Mae no Onshu o Koete: Tojisha Hidaka ga Kataru Anohi (9) Tsukimono ga Ochita Syunkan: Hyakunensai de Kōtaishi Omukae" [Beyond the Grievance He Had 65 Years Ago: The Very Day Hidaka, the Person Concerned, Talked about, no. 9: The Moment His Obsession Disappeared by Welcoming the Crown Prince]. February 18, 2011. http://200.218.30.171/nikkey/html/show/110218-72colonia.html. Accessed February 2, 2012.

———. "Burajiru Kokusei no Gaikokujin Bengoshi, Nihon demo Wazuka Sannin" [A Foreign Lawyer Who Is a Brazilian Citizen, One of the Only Three in Japan]. August 21, 2004. www.nikkeyshimbun.com.br/2004/040821-71colonia.html. Accessed May 21, 2012.

———. "Kikoku Shienkin, Shinseishasu Zentai de 2 mannin: Burajiru ga 9 wari Shimeru" [Government-Sponsored Repatriation: 20,000 Applied and Brazilians Constitute 90 percent]. April 20, 2010. http://200.218.30.171/nikkey/html/show/100420-61colonia.html. Accessed March 30, 2012.

———. "Koramu Jukai" [Column: Sea of Trees]. October 22, 2008. www.nikkeyshimbun.com.br/081022-Column.html. Accessed October 21, 2011.

———. "Kotoshi wa Bunkyo Kaicho Kaiseki" [Another Election for Bunkyo Presidency to Take Place This Year]. January 1, 2005. www.nikkeyshimbun.com.br/050101-10especial.html. Accessed December 31, 2011.

———. "Misu Hyakushunen, Mottomo Utsukushi Nikkei Josei Kettei!" [Miss Cente-nary, the Most Beautiful Nikkei Woman Chosen!]. May 21, 2008. www.nikkey shimbun.com.br/080521-71colonia.html. Accessed March 19, 2012.

———. "'Nisei wa Gensai no Hihonjin yori Nihonjinpoi,' Seishi de Gaimusho Ken-shusei OB kai-Harada-san" ["Niseis Are More Japanese Than Today's Japanese Are." Said Mr. Harada at a Meeting for the Former Trainees at Japan's Ministry of Foreign Affairs in São Paulo City]. June 14, 2008. www.nikkeyshimbun.com .br/080614-61colonia.html. Accessed September 29, 2011.

———. "Oh Mimi Ko Mimi" [Big Ears, Small Ears]. March 26, 2010. http://200.218.30.171 /nikkey/html/show/100326-74colonia.html. Accessed on March 19, 2012.

———. "Sengo Imin no Yakuwari towa Nanika: Tokubetsu Zadankai" [What Are the Roles of Postwar Immigrants? A Special Roundtable Discussion]. June 30, 2011. www.nikkeyshimbun.com.br/nikkey/html/show/110630-b1colonia.html. Ac-cessed November 17, 2011.

———. "Shinsaigo Kihakusha Hakujin Sōsū wa Yaku 3-zennin: Zaikaku 22-mannin" [The Number of Brazilians Who Retuned to Brazil after the (Great Tohoku) Earthquake Is Approximately 3,000; Total of Brazilians in Japan Is around 220,000]. October 5, 2011. www.nikkeyshimbun.com.br/nikkey/html/show /111005-71colonia.html. Accessed October 17, 2011.

———. "Zainichi Burajirujin o Shien, CBK ni Matsubara-san" [Supporting Brazilians in Japan, Mrs. Matsubara of CBK]. February 3, 2004. http//www.nikkeyshimbun .com.br/2004/040203-72colonia.html. Accessed July 30, 2010.

———. "Zainichi Hakujin 31-mannin ni: Izen Tsuzuku Teijū no Nami" [More than 310,000 Brazilians Living in Japan: Their Wave of Settlements Continues]. May 24, 2007. www.nikkeyshimbun.com.br/07054-73colonia.html. Accessed June 10, 2007.

———. "Zendai Mimon no Kinen Kōka Tsukuri Naoshi" [We've Never Heard of Re-making a Commemorative Coin Before]. May 1, 2008. www.nikkeyshimbun.com .br/080501-71colonia.html. Accessed June 6, 2013.

Ninomiya, Masato, ed. *Dekassgeui 10 Anos de História e Suas Perspectivas Futuras / Dekassegui sono 10-nen no Rekishi to Shōraizō* [Dekassegui Ten Years of History and Its Future Perspectives]. São Paulo: CIATE and Centro de Estabilização de Emprego nas Indústrias, 1998.

———. "Japanese Brazilian Historical Overview." In *Encyclopedia of Japanese Descen-dants in the Americas: An Illustrated History of the Nikkei,* edited by Akemi Kikumura-Yano, 116–126. Walnut Creek, CA: AltaMira Press, 2002.

Nippaku Kyokai / Associação Nipo-Brasileira. "Kyokai ni Tsuite/About Associação Nipo-Brasileira." http://www.nippaku-k.or.jp/about/index.html. Accessed Janu-ary 28, 2017.

Nishida, Mieko. *Japanese Brazilian Women and Their Ambiguous Identities: Gender, Eth-nicity, and Class in São Paulo.* Latin American Studies Working Paper Series, No. 5, Latin American Studies Center, University of Maryland at College Park, 2000.

———. *Slavery and Identity: Ethnicity, Gender, and Race in Salvador, Brazil, 1808–1888.* Bloomington: Indiana University Press, 2003.

————. "'Why Does a Nikkei Want to Talk to Other Nikkeis?': Japanese Brazilians and Their Identities in São Paulo." *Critique of Anthropology* 29, no. 4 (December 2009): 423–445.

Nishihata, Leo. "Amores possíveis" [Possible Loves]. In *100 anos da imigração japonesa: As surpreendentes histórias do povo que ajudou a mudar o Brasil* [100 Years of Japanese Immigration: The Surprising Stories of the People Who Helped Change Brazil], edited by Editora Abril, 78–85. São Paulo: Editora Abril, 2008.

————. "Shushi oxente" [Amazing Sushi of the Northeast]. In *100 anos da imigração japonesa: As surpreendentes histórias do povo que ajudou a mudar o Brasil*, edited by Editora Abril, 86–91. São Paulo: Editora Abril, 2008.

Nobles, Melissa. *Race and Censuses in Modern Politics*. Stanford, CA: Stanford University Press, 2000.

Nomura, Tania, ed. *Universo em secgredo: A mulher nikkei no Brasil* [A Secret World: The Nikkei Women in Brazil]. São Paulo: Diário Nippak, 1990.

Norichika, Masayoshi. "'Garantido' Shōkō" [Small Thoughts on "Guaranteed"]. *São Paulo Shimbun* 1 (May 8, 2008); 2 (May 15, 2008); and 3 (May 22, 2008).

Numata, Minoru. *Tabunka Kyosei o Mezasu Chiiki Zukuri: Yokohama, Tsurumi Ushio kara no Hōkoku* [Area Plannig Aiming at Multiculturalism: A Report from Tsurumi and Ushio of Yokohama]. Tokyo: Akashi Shoten, 1996.

Nyukan Kyokai / Japan Immigration Association. *Zairyu Gaikokujin Tōkei Heisei 21-nenban / Statistics on the Foreigners Registered in Japan 2009*. Tokyo: Nyukan Kyokai / Japan Immigration Association, 2010.

Ogyū, Shigetoshi. "Burajiru Nikkei Imin Gojūnen no Hensen Katei" [Japanese Brazilians: Their Residential and Occupational Changes in the Last Fifty Years]. *Kaigai Jijo* 11, no. 12 (December 1963): 25–33.

Okubaro, Jorge J. "A colônia nipo-brasileira vista através dos olhos de um jornalista nissei" [The Nikkei *Colônia* Seen through the Eyes of a Nisei Journalist]. Unpublished paper presented at a seminar at the Centro de Estudos Nipo-Brasileiros, June 20, 2011. www.100nen.com.br/ja/jinmonken/. Accessed February 27, 2012.

————. *O Súdito (Banzai, Massateru!)* [The Subject (Long Live, Massateru!)]. São Paulo: Editora Terceiro Nome, 2006.

Omiya, Tomonobu. *Dekassegui: Gyakuryu-suru Nikkei Burajirujin* [*Dekassegui*: Japanese Brazilians Repatriating to Japan]. Tokyo: Shoshisha, 1997.

Ōta, Tsuneo. *Nihon wa Kōfuku Shiteinai: Burajiru Nikkeijin Shakai o Yurugaseta Jūnen Kōsō.* [Japan Has Not Surrendered: A Ten-Year Inner Conflict that Shook the Japanese Brazilian Society]. Tokyo: Bungeishunjūsha, 1995.

Oura, Fumio. "Atogaki ni Kaete Watashi to Yuba-mura (Matawa Isamu)" [Postscript: Yuba Village or Isamu and Me]. In *Yuba Isamu no Shōgai* [The Life of Isamu Yuba], by Gen Oura, 315–323. São Paulo: São Paulo Seinen Toshokan, 2013.

Oura, Gen. *Kodomo Imin Oura Fumio: Noson ni Ikiru Jun-Nisei no Kisei* [Child Immigrant Fumio Oura: The Course of a Quasi-Nisei Living in an Agricultural Village]. São Paulo: Fumio Oura, 2012.

———. *Yuba Isamu no Shōgai* [The Life of Isamu Yuba]. São Paulo: São Paulo Seinen Toshokan, 2013.

Ōya, Soichi. *Sekai no Uragawa o Yuku: Nanboku Amerika Hen* [Traveling on the Other Side of the Globe: The Americas]. Tokyo: Bungeishunjūsha, 1956.

Ozeki, Kōnosuke. "Fuetekita Konketsukon: Taikyokutekina Tachibakara Kangaeyō" [The Increase of Interracial Marriages: Let's Take a Broad View of the Situation]. *Colônia*, no. 53 (August 1965): 3.

Pareja, Luciana. "Cinema Japão traça um panorama de produção nipônica e de seus diretores, com sessões gratuitas no MAM e na PUC" [MAM's Cinema Japan Brings a Panorama of Japanese Production and Its Directors, with Free Admissions at the MAM and PUC]. *Folha de São Paulo*, July 1, 2001.

Patai, Daphne. *Brazilian Women Speak: Contemporary Life Histories.* New Brunswick, NJ: Rutgers University Press, 1988.

Paulista Shimbunsha, ed. *Colônia Sangyō Chizu* [The Map of the Colônia's Industry]. São Paulo: Paulista Shimbunsha, 1962.

———, ed. *Paulista Nenkan 1950-nenban* [Paulita Yearbook of 1950]. São Paulo: Paulista Shimbunsha, 1950.

———, ed. *Paulista Nenkan 1964-nenban* [Paulista Yearbook of 1964]. São Paulo: Paulista Shimbunsha, 1963.

———, ed. *Paulista Nenkan 1966-nenban* [Paulista Yearbook of 1966]. São Paulo: Paulista Shimbunsha, 1966.

Playmakers Tokyo. Directed by Santiago Stelly. Tokyo: Niki Stadiums, 2010. Part 2 of 3. https://www.youtube.com/watch?v=tx6dcx6dtPY. Accessed July 21, 2012.

Read, Ian. *The Hierarchies of Slavery in Santos, Brazil, 1822–1888.* Stanford, CA: Stanford University Press, 2012.

Roth, Joshua Hotaka. *Brokered Homeland: Japanese Brazilian Migrants in Japan.* Ithaca, NY: Cornell University Press, 2002.

Saito, Hiroshi. *Burajiru no Nihonjin* [The Japanese in Brazil]. Tokyo: Maruzen Kabushiki Kaisha, 1960.

———. *Burajiru to Nihonjin: Ibunka ni Ikite 50-nen* [Brazil and the Japanese: Living 50 Years as a Bridge]. Tokyo: Simul Press, 1984.

———. *Gaikokujin ni Natta Nihonjin: Burajiru Imin no Ikikata to Kawarikata* [The Japanese Who Became Foreigners: How Japanese Immigrants Lived and Changed in Brazil]. Tokyo: Simul Press, 1978.

———. "Seishu Imin no Dōka to Zatkkon: Willems-shi no Kenkyu o Yonde" [Japanese Immigrants' Assimilation and Mixed Marriage in São Paulo: Based on a Reading of Mr. Willems's Study." *Jidai*, no. 8 (March 1949): 4–9.

Sakai, Shigeichi. *Burajiru Nikki* [A Diary in Brazil]. Tokyo: Kawadeshobō Shinsha, 1957.

São Paulo Gakuseikai, ed. *Nijūnen no Ayumi* [The Course of Twenty Years]. São Paulo: São Paulo Gakuseikai, 1974.

Sase, Taeko. "Burajiru Rikkokai Sōritsu 90 Shūnen ni Yosete" [An Essay in Commemoration of the 90th Anniversary of Brazilian Asocciation of Rikkokai]. In *Rikko no Kizuna: Burajiru Rikkokai Sōritsu Kyujūshunen Kinen* [The Bond of Rikko in

Commemoration of the 90th Anniversary of Brazilian Association of Rikkokai],
edited by Burajiru Rikkokai 66–69. São Paulo: Burajiru Rikkokai, 2007.

Seinen Bunkyo. "Christina Agari Entrevista" [Christina Agari Interview]. December 2002.
www.bunkyo.org.br/seinen/menu/not_entrevistacris.asp. Accessed March 24, 2007.

———. "Quem Somos, História" [Who Are We, History]. www.bunkyonet.org.br
/comissaodejovens/quem-somos/historia. Accessed May 19, 2012.

Seishi Yonhyakunen Saiten Nihonjin Kyoryokukai, ed. *São Paulo Yonhyakunensai,
1554–1954* [The Celebrations on the 400th Year of São Paulo City, 1554–1954]. São
Paulo: Seishi Yonhyakunen Saiten Nihonjin Kyoryokukai, 1957.

Sellek, Yoko. "Nikkeijin: The Phenomenon of Return Migration." In *Japan's Minorities:
The Illusion of Homogeneity*, edited by Michael Weiner, 178–210. London: Routledge, 1997.

Semanário Nikkei. "*Colônia* no Teiryu: Nihongo Kyoiku" [*Colônia*'s Undercurrent:
Japanese Language Education]. No. 151 (October 15, 1966): 26–30.

———. "Hanayome Maru ha Doko Ye" [Where Did the Bride-Ship Go?]. No. 148
(August 26, 1966): 5–6.

Sengo Ijū 50-shunen Kinesai Jikko Iinkai, ed. *Burajiru Imin Sengo Ijū no 50-nen* [Fifty
Years of Postwar Japanese Immigration to Brazil]. São Paulo: Burajiru-Nippon
Ijūsha Kyokai, 2004.

Shima, Kiyoshi. "Chihō Shōtoshi no Nikkei Colônia: Sorocaba-sen Álvares Machado
no Jirei" [The Nikkei Colônia in a Small Provincial City: The Case of Álvares
Machado on the Sorocaba Line]. In *Imin: Burajiru Imin no Jitsutai Chōsa* [The
Immigrant: A Survey on Japanese Immigrants in Brazil], edited by Seiichi Izumi,
399–459. Tokyo: Kokin Shoten, 1957.

———. "Ijūsen no Chōsa" [A Survey on an Immigrant Ship]. In *Imin: Burajiru Imin
no Jittai Chōsa* [The Immigrant: A Survey on Japanese Immigrants in Brazil],
edited by Seiichi Izumi, 535–585. Tokyo: Kokin Shoten, 1957.

Shimada, Noriko. "Sengo no Burajiru 'Hanayome Imin': Sono Rekishiteki Haikei to
Joseizō" [Postwar "Bride Immigrants" to Brazil: Its Historical Background and
the Image of Women]. In *Shashin Hanayome, Sensō Hanayome no Tadotta Michi:
Josei Iminshi no Hakkutsu / Crossing the Ocean: A New Look at the History of Japa-
nese Picture Brides and War Brides*, edited by Noriko Shimada, 113–147. Tokyo:
Akashi Shoten, 2009.

Shimamto, Kenro. "Wareware no Shinjo" [Our Feelings]. *Gakuyu*, no. 4 (August 1936):
16–18.

Shiramizu, Shigehiko. *Esunikku Media Kenkyu: Ekkyō Tabunka Aidentiti* [Ethnic
Media Studies: Border Crossing, Multiculturalism, and Identity]. Tokyo: Akahi
Shoten, 2004.

Sonehara, Toshio. "Nisei wa Nani o Dō Suruka: Dokutoku no Bakku Bōnn Keisei no
Tameni" [What and How Do the Nisei Do It: For the Purpose of Creating Their
Own Backbone]. *Kaihō*, no. 19 (July–August 1959): 11–13.

Stern, Steve J. *Remembering Pinochet's Chile: On the Eve of London 1998*. Durham, NC:
Duke University Press, 2004.

Suzuki, Masao. "Kieta Sora no Kakehashi: JAL Kaisōroku (3): VARIG ga Hitoashi Hayaku Chokkobin o Shūshū" [The Disappeared Sky Bridge: Recollections of Japan Air Lines, No. 3: VARIG Started Its Direct Flight Earlier]. *São Paulo Shimbun*, September 29, 2011. www.saopauloshimbun.com/index.php/conteudo/show /id/6024/cat/105. Accessed January 29, 2012.

———. "Kieta Sora no Kakehashi: JAL Kaisōroku (4): Osato Gaeri to Banpaku ga Ōkina Tenki" [The Disappeared Sky Bridge: Recollections of Japan Air Lines, No. 4: Visiting Homeland and Expo Became the Big Turning Point]. *São Paulo Shimbun*, September 30, 2011. www.saopauloshimbun.com/index.php/conteudo/show/id /6044/cat/105. Accessed January 29, 2012.

Suzuki, Masatake. "Sengo Imin Shiron: Sono Sekaiku to Yakuwari" [An Essay on Postwar Immigrants: Their Character and Roles]. In *Burajiru Imin Sengo Ijū no 50-nen* [Fifty Years of Postwar Japanese Immigration to Brazil], edited by Sengo Ijū 50-shunen Kinesai Jikko Iinkai, 282–297. São Paulo: Burajiru-Nippon Ijūsha Kyokai, 2004.

———. *Suzuki Teiichi: Burajiru Nikkei Shakai ni Ikita Kisai no Shogai* [Teiichi Suzuki: The Life of a Genius Who Lived in the Brazilian Nikkei Society]. São Paulo: Centro de Estudos Nipo-Brasileiros, 2007.

Suzuki, Teiichi, ed. *The Japanese Immigrant in Brazil: Narrative Part*. Tokyo: University of Tokyo Press, 1969.

Tajima, Hisatoshi. "Okinawakeijin ni Okeru Tasōteki Sutandâdo Keisei o Meguru Mondai: Rainichi Rakichū Uchinanchu Burajirujin Diaspora no Hikakukenkyu / The Construction of a Cultural Multistandard of Okinawan-Brazilians: A Comparative Study Based on the Cases in Mainland Japan and Okinawa." *Gengo to Kenkyu / Language and Culture* (Bunkyo University, Japan) 23 (March 2011): 139–159.

Takeuchi, Marcia Yumi. *O perigo amarelo em tempos de guerra (1939–1949)* [The Yellow Terror in Times of War (1939–1949)]. São Paulo: Arquivo do Estado e Imprensa Oficial do Estado, 2002.

Tamiya, Torahiko. *Burajiru no Nihonjin* [The Japanese in Brazil]. Tokyo: Asahi Shimbunsha, 1975.

Tanaka, Iossuke. *Senzen Imin Kōkai Monogatari* [Prewar Immigrants' Stories of Voyage]. São Paulo: Centro de Estudos Nipo-Brasileiros, 2010.

Tanno, Kiyoto. "Gaikokujin Rōdōsha Mondai no Kongen wa Doko ni Arunoka" [Where Are the Roots of the Issues of Foreign Workers?], *Nihon Rōdō Kenkyu Zasshi*, no. 587 (June 2009): 27–35.

———. "Sōgō Dekasseguigyo no Tanjo: Nikkei Ryokōsha no Henyo to Burajiru Nikkei Komuniti no Shihon Chikuseki" [The Birth of General *Dekassegui* Business: Transformation of Nikkei Travel Agencies and Japanese Brazilian Community's Capital Accumulation." *Ōhara Shakai Mondai Kenkyusho Zasshi*, no. 573 (August 2006): 39–60.

Telles, Edward E. *Race in Another America: The Significance of Skin Color in Brazil*. Princeton, NJ: Princeton University Press, 2004.

Tezuka, Kazuaki, Hiroshi Komai, Goro Oda, and Taka-aki Ogata, eds. *Gaikokujin*

Rōdōsha no Shūrō Jittai: Sōgōteki Jittai Hokokushū [Employment of Foreign Guest Workers in Japan: A Thorough Report on the Reality]. Tokyo: Akashi Shoten, 1992.

Tinsman, Heidi. *Partners in Conflict: The Politics of Gender, Sexuality, and Labor in the Chilean Agrarian Reform, 1950–1973*. Durham, NC: Duke University Press, 2002.

Tomimatsu, Toshio. "Nandemo Mite Yaro" [I'll See Anything and Everything]. *Colônia*, no. 34 (June 1962): 26–29.

Toyama, Osamu. *Burajiru Nikkei Shakai Hyakunen no Suiryu* [The Nikkei Society of Brazil and Its Stream over One Hundred Years]. São Paulo: Osamu Toyama, 2006.

Tsuda, Takayuki. *The Benefits of Being Minority: The Ethnic Status of the Japanese-Brazilians in Brazil*. Working Paper 21, Center for Comparative Immigration Studies, University of California, San Diego, May 2000.

———. *Strangers in the Ethnic Homeland: Japanese Brazilian Migration in Translational Perspective*. New York: Columbia University Press, 2003.

Uchiyama, Katsuo. *Sōbō no 92-nen: Burajiru Imin no Kiroku* [The Nation's 92 Years: A Record of Japanese Immigration to Brazil]. Tokyo: Tokyo Shimbun Shuppan-kyoku, 2001.

Veja. "Ao gusto brasileiro: Comida japonesa se torna popular como o churrasco nas principais capitais do Brasil" [To the Brazilian Taste: Japanese Food Becomes Popular Like the Barbecue in the Main Capitals of Brazil]. Vol. 36, no. 28 (June 16, 2003): 83.

———. "O povo da diáspora" [The People of the Diaspora]. Vol. 24, no. 32 (August 7, 1991): 36–43.

Wakahara, Mizuaki. "Direction's Eye: Nikkei Brazileiros, Vol. 10: Kazuo Watanabe." www.direction-dcord.com/2011/06/16071613.html. Accessed December 12, 2011.

Wakatsuki, Yasuo, and Jōji Suzuki. *Kaigai Ijū Seiseku Shiron* [A Historical Discussion of Japan's Overseas Migration Policies]. Tokyo: Fukumura Shuppan, 1974.

Wako, Shungoro. *Bauru Kannai no Hōjin* [The Japanese within the Jurisdiction of Bauru]. 1939. Tokyo: Nihon Tosho Sentā, 1999.

Weber, Max. *From Max Weber: Essays in Sociology*. Translated and edited by H. H. Gerth and C. Wright Mills. New York: Oxford University Press, 1958.

Willems, Emílio. *Aspectos da aculturação dos Japoneses no estado de São Paulo* [Aspects of the Acculturation of the Japanese in the State of São Paulo]. São Paulo: Universidade de São Paulo, Faculdade de Filosofia, Ciencias e Letras, 1948.

Yago, Katsuhiro. "Burajiru Nikkeijin 7: Kogoto Shimbei Nagare Nya Sakarayenu [Brazilian Nikkeis, No. 7: Mr. Complaining Cannot Resist the Stream]. *Yomiuri Shimbun*, June 12, 1978, evening edition, 10.

———. "Burajiru Nikkeijin 9: Gōryu—Usureyuku 'Nisei Ishiki'" [Brazilian Nikkeis, No. 9: Merging—The "Nisei Consciousness" Disappearing]. *Yomiuri Shimbun*, June 16, 1978, evening edition, 10.

Yamada, Michio. *Fune ni Miru Nihonjin Iminshi: Kasato Maru kara Kuruzu Kyakusen Ye* [A History of Emigration through Ships: From the *Kasato Maru* to Cruise Ships]. Tokyo: Chūōkōronsha, 1998.

Yamamoto, Katzuzo. *Burajiru to Gojūnen* [Fifty Years with Brazil]. São Paulo: Jitsugyo no Burajirusha, 1982.

———. "Colônia Jōka Undō to Imin Kihonhō" [Movement for the Purification of the *Colônia* and Basic Laws on Immigration]. *Colônia*, no. 36 (November 1962): 15–16.

Yamamoto, Kiyoshi. "Zaihaku Nikkeijin Jinko Suikei" [Inductive Statistics of the Nikkei Population in Brazil]. *Jidai*, no. 8 (March 1949): 23–33.

Yamanaka, Keiko. *Ana Bortz's Law Suit and Minority Rights in Japan.* JPRI Working Paper No. 88. San Francisco: Center for the Pacific Rim at the University of San Francisco, 2002.

———. " 'I Will Go Home, but When?' Labor Migration and Circular Diaspora Formation by Japanese Brazilians in Japan." In *Japan and Global Migration: Foreign Workers and the Advent of a Multicultural Society,* edited by Mike Douglass and Grenda S. Roberts, 123–152. New York: Routledge, 2000.

———. "Return Migration of Japanese-Brazilians to Japan: The Nikkeijin as Ethnic Minority and Political Construct." *Diaspora* 5, no. 1 (1996): 65–98.

Yamashiro, Cíntia. "Miss Centenário Brasil-Japão é de Mogi das Cruzes: Katarina Eiko Nakahara, de 26 anos, foi eleita a nikkei mais bonita no fim de maio" [Miss Brazil-Japan Centenary Is from Mogi das Cruzes: Katarina Eiko Nakamura, of 26 Years Old, Was Chosen as the Most Beautiful at the End of May]. *Revista Mundo OK,* no. 7 (June 2008): 40.

Yamashiro, José. "Burajiru to Nihon" [Brazil and Japan]. In *Ratenteki Nihonjin: Brajiru Nisei no Hatsugen* [The Latin Japanese: Opinions Expressed by the Nisei of Brazil], edited by Morio Ōno, 95–119. Tokyo: NHK, 1969.

Yamashiro, Ryukiti. "Watakushi no Kiroku" [A Record of Myself]. Unpublished manuscript dated September 1959, housed at the MHIJB.

Yamashita, Karen Tei. *Circle K Cycles.* Minneapolis: Coffee House Press, 2001.

Yomiuri Shimbun. "Burajiru Imin 90 Kazoku Shuppatsu" [Ninety Immigrant Families Departing for Brazil], December 4, 1956, morning edition, 7.

———. "Burajiru Seinen Imin ga Satsujin: Sengohyaku-nin Ukeire Chushi, Cotia Sangyo Kumiai 'Jinsen ga Zusan to Kōgi' " [A Young Immigrant Man Commits a Murder: Cotia Agricultural Cooperative Will Not Accept 1,500 Immigrants, Protesting against Japan's Sloppy Selection Process], December 17, 1957, morning edition, 7.

———. "Kachigumi Kanashii Hanseiki: Burajiru no San Kazoku Kikoku" [A Sad Half a Century for *Kachigumi:* Three Families Return from Brazil], November 18, 1973, morning edition, 23.

———. "Shimedasareru Brazil Imin" [Japanese Immigrants Being Pushed Out in Brazil], August 3, 1980, morning edition, 5.

Zaihaku Nihonjin Bunka Kyokai, ed. *Hakukoku Shin Kenpo Shingikai ni Okeru Nihon Imin Kaiseki no Mondai* [The Problem of the Exclusion of the Japanese in the Council on Brazil's New Constitution]. São Paulo: Zaihaku Nihonjin Bunka Kyokai, 1934.

Index

About the Author

Mieko Nishida is professor of history at Hartwick College. She is the author of *Slavery and Identity: Ethnicity, Gender, and Race in Salvador, Brazil, 1808–1888*.

Printed in the United States
By Bookmasters